INDUSTRIAL TECHNOLOGY TRANSFER

NATO ADVANCED STUDY INSTITUTES SERIES

Proceedings of the Advanced Study Institute Programme, which aims at the dissemination of advanced knowledge and the formation of contacts among scientists from different countries.

The series is published by an international board of publishers in conjunction with NATO Scientific Affairs Division

A	Life Sciences	Plenum Publishing Corporation
B	Physics	London and New York
C	Mathematical and Physical Sciences	D. Reidel Publishing Company Dordrecht and Boston
D	Behavioural and Social Sciences	Sijthoff International Publishing Company Leyden, The Neth. and Reading, Mass., USA
E	Applied Science	Noordhoff International Publishing Leyden, The Neth. and Reading, Mass., USA

Serie E: Applied Science – No. 19

INDUSTRIAL TECHNOLOGY TRANSFER

edited by

MARVIN J. CETRON

President, Forecasting International Ltd.,
Arlington, Virginia, USA

and

HAROLD F. DAVIDSON

Physical Scientist, Department of the Army,
Washington, D.C., USA

NOORDHOFF – LEYDEN – 1977

Proceedings of the NATO Advanced Study Institute
on Industrial Technology Transfer
Les Arcs-Bourg St. Maurice, France
June 22-July 4, 1975

ISBN-13: 978-94-010-1297-3 e-ISBN-13: 978-94-010-1295-9
DOI: 10.1007/978-94-010-1295-9

Softcover reprint of the hardcover 1st edition 1977

PREFACE

Technology transfer has a long history, but only recently has it become the subject of study and action. The rapid rate of scientific and technical advance in both Europe and the United States and the existence of large technology gaps among nations has brought the importance of the process into sharper focus, and has caused technology transfer to have implications for countless aspects of both national and international development.

Technology transfer has been variously defined as: the process of information transfer between science, technology and actual utilization of scientific data and ideas, to wit: production of goods and services; the process by which science and technology are diffused throughout human activity; the transfer of research results into operations; the process by which technical information originating in one setting is adapted for use in another setting. Collectively, these and other definitions share a common theme which characterizes the process as one of bringing technology into widespread use in solving mankind's problems in the shortest practical time.

The first NATO Advanced Study Institute (ASI) on Technology Transfer in July, 1973, brought together many of the individuals dealing with quantitative data, based on empirical research. This conference had both the advantages and disadvantages of a somewhat detached point of view. The ASI also had lectures contributed by representatives from government agencies and corporations (and a few university-based scholars) who had been active as practitioners or consultants in policy-making and organizational design for technology transfer.

The purpose of the second NATO Advanced Study Institute on technology transfer was to pass on the knowledge and experience generated by the first to a wider segment of the international community, with particular emphasis on the industrial and the public sector experiences. Principles concerning the transfer of information on technology are of direct interest to all nations, particularly developing countries. The Institute imparted these principles and attempted to extend them by the interaction of experts and individuals as well as by presenting the latest state-of-the-art experiences.

The ASI also provided a teaching forum for international exchange of technology transfer information. It constituted an exploration of industrial applications of technology transfer in the context of the firm, domestic industry, multi-national firms, government policy and activities in international trade and economic growth of the less developed countries. At the same time, the process was examined in terms of its application to large-scale problems such as energy, transportation, telecommunications, medical technology, agricultural technology, etc. Having the benefit of the conceptual base resulting from the first ASI, the second meeting made many inroads into the complexities of the practical application of technology transfer.

The proceedings which follow are not necessarily arranged in order of presentation, rather they are grouped in a sequence which seems logical as a result of the conference discussions. Part I includes Dr. Cetron's introduction at the conference and Admiral Ekas' keynote speech. Part II brings together all of the papers containing quantitative data based upon empirical research. Most of these papers, as in the first ASI, were presented by university-based researchers who have been able to assemble data from a variety of sources. Their conclusions have both the advantages and disadvantages of a somewhat detached academic point of view. Part III on public sector transfer efforts provides many useful insights into the process, and guidelines for the increasing levels of international and corporate activity.

Part IV brings together the contributions of both public and private sector practitioners active in the transfer of technology between nations. As technology becomes a major vehicle for international competition, trade and national development, the concerns and problems of both corporate and governmental transfer policies and activities will become identical. International technology transfer, embedded within a variety of national foreign policies, is the area with the highest level of complexity, least efficiency and greatest potential for worldwide economic and social development. Industry experiences are collected in the final section.

Part V is somewhat smaller than it should be to represent the level of corporate technology transfer activities; but as with the first ASI the confidential nature of such activities, especially within the large multinational corporation, tends to reduce the number and variety of publicly presented discussions. The importance of the area, however, should not be underestimated. Corporations have a long history of technology transfer. Much like the man who one day discovered that all his life he had been speaking prose, corporations are becoming aware that all along they have been transferring technology. The new awareness of industry's role is very important as it opens up a large backlog of experience and a new arena for research, both of which can be expected to contribute to improved future transfer mechanisms and activities.

The proceedings are completed in Part VI with the very detailed summary and insights of the meeting prepared by Walter Hahn and Susan Doscher of the Library of Congress.

Attention is invited to the fact that not all papers presented at the Advanced Study Institute are printed herein. Unfortunately this could not be done due to publisher imposed limits on the size of the book. However, Part VI does discuss all papers presented.

We are grateful to the U. S. National Science Foundation, NATO, the U. S. Army, and the U. S. Navy for their financial support and help in planning this conference. We also owe a debt of gratitude to the members of the Program Committee: Ms. Susan Doscher of the Library of Congress, Dr. Paul Jervis, Dr. Robert Mason, and Mr. Allen W. Pearson of the Oxford Center for Management Studies, Metrics, Inc., and the University of Manchester, respectively. And last but not least, and certainly most importantly, we are most grateful to the many speakers who have contributed to this volume.

A special tribute must go to Dr. Schiller Thebaud to whom this volume is dedicated. A kind, gentle, dedicated man, Dr. Thebaud was killed in an accident shortly after the ASI. We, in the technology transfer community, as well as many individuals in the lesser developed nations will most assuredly feel the loss.

Additionally, a special note of thanks is due Judy Hourigan, who assisted with this volume. She helped organize the drafts of several authors. Further thanks must go to Colonel (Dr.) John E. Wagner for his encouragement, and to the three superb typists without whose diligent, painstaking effort this volume would not have been possible: Beth Buell, Jan Harrison, and Dorothy Van Dyke.

Washington, D.C.
January 10, 1977

M. J. Cetron
H. J. Davidson

TABLE OF CONTENTS

PART I: INTRODUCTION

The introduction is composed of two papers which are broad discussions of Technology Transfer and hopefully set the stage for the papers to follow during the ten working day duration of the Advanced Study Institute. The chairman's introduction examined various world crises or problems which provided opportunities for technology transfer and which hopefully would be susceptible to solution, at least partially, were technology transfer methods and data applied.

According to Cetron, there is at our disposal a host of new technologies in hybrid plant strains, space monitoring capabilities, weather control potential, substitute materials, pollutant controls and world economic institutions which conceivably might alleviate these immediate and future problems and crises. The problem we confront today, however, is how must we allocate our efforts in solving or ameliorating the situation. In other words, what must the "technology rich" do now and in the long range future to avert the disasters of a nuclear war, massive starvation, environmental deterioration, resources depletion and economic extremes. To answer the question, one must first understand the dimensions of the problems and crises, as they exist now and are projected out into the future decades as well as taking a close look at the needs, possibilities and limitations which exist for particular technology transfers.

The predicted world crises of high probability are discussed in the following pages to present a capsule view of the dimensions of each problem and the technology transfers underway or, as yet, needed in each area. Because of societal forecasting, necessity no longer lurks ahead entirely unknown; now is the opportunity for technology transfer to offset the less desired predictions. People must not plead ignorance or lack of knowledge.

Admiral Ekas' paper, as part of the stage setting effort on the first day of the Institute, covered in an introductory manner many of the areas which would be discussed in depth later on. Such diverse topics as Technology Transfer by U. S. Industry, Technology Transfer by the DOD Laboratory Consortium, Technology Transfer by the U. S. Department of Agriculture and other government agencies, among others, as well as Proposed Changes to Eliminate Barriers to Technology Transfer in the United States were introduced.

Admiral Ekas encouraged the conference to look beyond past and present cooperation in military R&D to more effective use of Free World technology for the solution of common problems and for improvement of the quality of life. Cumulative knowledge must be applied to economic problems to provide gainful employment for all our citizens, he noted. A cooperative effort to utilize technological know-how obtained at a cost of billions of dollars must be used to improve the environment, health, education and welfare of all people.

WORLD CRISES: AN OPPORTUNITY FOR TECHNOLOGY TRANSFER CHAIRMAN'S INTRODUCTION

M. J. Cetron

Forecasting International, Ltd.
Arlington, Virginia

"Necessity is the Mother of Invention."
Benjamin Franklin

Historical perspective of technological changes suggest that innovations in societies' processes often occur despite man's efforts to control his surroundings. The fact is man instinctively seeks to retain that with which he is familiar until overt or internal pressures cause decisive action in response to a crisis situation. Necessity or the "Need-Pull" factor was found to be the motivating element for change in 75% of the 567 cases of successfully implemented innovations studied by Myers and Marquis.[1] Also as Roy Rothwell reaffirmed in his project SAPPHO, man displays resistance to innovate processes and the "Technology Push" element is rarely the impetus for utilization of new ideas.[2]

Another aspect of the psychological barrier inherent in man, to the acceptance of technological changes, is his propensity to identify his sense of security with the job he performs. For example, in the early 1900's the United States Navy refused to accept target practice data on continuous-aim firing or to modify their guns aboard ship until forced to do so by President Roosevelt, who in an effort to maintain political tranquility with influential constituents championed the complaints of the naval lieutenant who had borrowed and tested the innovation aboard several British vessels.[3] As Elting Morison points out, high ranking Admirals who had made their careers when gun firing between rolls of a ship was an individual art, not a mechanical process, were the substantial barrier to the transfer of technology. The implication of course is that the Admirals associated their career-security with the processes which had merely been a means to their notoriety. A similar situation occurred shortly after the Civil War, when the U.S. Navy decided they had little need for a fast moving ship propelled by steam, which after all, did not look like a ship as there was no mast or sail. In this instance, the Navy felt bound by their traditional concept of a ship's function (sailing) and identified their entire organization's purpose with the skills of sailing, made obsolete by the steam engine.

The old adage, you can lead a horse to water but you can't make him drink, would exemplify the British Navy's hesitance to use their new but already installed radar equipment upon the H.M.S. Hood. As the story goes, the German's Bismark was sighted on Hood's radar and gunmen prepared to sink it; however, the Admiral, uncomfortable with these new fangled inventions, instructed the men to wait until visual contact was made with the German ship - at which point the Germans, who did not have radar, proceeded to sight and sink the Hood.

The military, however, is not the only social group responsible for resisting technological changes, for private industry research groups often struggle to convince their presidents to market innovative products. As Pearson and Rickards have said, the major barrier to the successful transfer and utilization of technology is often the difficulty which scientists have in convincing the potential user what the product could do, in operational terms.[4] But even when the potential user does understand the capabilities of the product, if personal positions or organizational structure is threatened, the user will reject the idea. For instance, Gillette razor blades initially controlled the market in terms of sales in razor blades, until smaller companies came out with something new -- like Wilkinson with a stainless steel blade, Personna with a platinum edged blade, and Schick with a chromium edged blade. To regain control of the market, Gillette bought the controlling interest of Wilkinson, began selling similar products and advertised both brands in a compare "us" with the "other" type ad. The ridiculous point to this wild story is that Gillette laboratories never regained the percentage advantage they once had in the market and they had early on developed <u>all</u> of these products before their competitors but were told not to market them, so as not to <u>disturb</u> their number one position in the market. This number one position was regained only after they introduced the Trac II innovation.

Today, technology transfers into the operational sector need not occur only after pressures reach crisis status, for we possess a system of early warning indicators for future events, products or crises, through methodologies in societal forecasting. In fact, had a time schedule relative to known international events been included in the goals of the U.S. satellite program, perhaps the urgency to develop and use space technologies - especially monitoring of worldwide activities - would not have evolved from the embarrassment we felt after the Russians stunned us with their space flight. Now pacing parameters of potential problems may be quantitatively measured and projections of future events dated and given a probability rating. From such data, technological transfers should be instituted during the initial phases of a problem, not after the fact.

Such technology transfers - "the multilateral flow of information and techniques across the boundaries of the sciences, technology and practical world"[5] - may happen through structural organizations, multinational corporations, industrial exhibits and meetings or through the exchanges of people and their literature, patents and products. Essentially, technology is transferred in three ways: "(1) the direct transfer of an idea for the same purpose, (2) the utilization of a technology for new and different purposes, and (3) the application of a technology for an entirely different problem."[6] Studies reflect that the most desirable and effective technology transfers occur through the exchange of people.[7] In fact, this personal interchange and transfer of ideas, in response to individual national needs, will be essential if politically sensitive groups, who must necessarily share both the world's resources and its problems, are to deal satisfactorily with the ensuing global crises.

Recent studies in societal forecasting indicate that the following crises (see Figure 1) have a more than average probability of reaching crisis status in the decades ahead: nuclear war, severe food shortages, deterioration of the biosphere, imbalances in the distribution of wealth, shortages of mineral resources, energy shortages and inflation and monetary instability. Additionally, the severity of impact upon U.S. national goals, for example, has been algebraically calculated and ranked as follows:

SEVERITY OF POTENTIAL CRISES AS MEASURED BY IMPACT UPON NATIONAL GOALS[8]

Crisis	Rank*	Impact Figure
Food Shortage	3	-160.8
Deterioration of Biosphere	5	-122.8
Imbalance in the Distribution of Wealth	6	- 33.6
Mineral Resource Shortage	4	-137.9

CRISIS	CRITERIA					
	Number of People Affected	Severity of the Effect	Probability	Reversibility of the Course of Development of the Crisis	Responsibility	Confidence in Judgment
Nuclear War	Very Large	Very Great	Very Low	Possible	Diffuse	Moderate
Severe Food Shortages	Very Large	Very Great	High	Possible	Diffuse	High
Deterioration of the Biosphere	Very Large	Moderate-Great	Moderate	Difficult	Diffuse	Low
Imbalances in the Distribution of Wealth	Very Large	Great	Very High	Very Difficult	None	Moderate
Shortages of Mineral Resources	Large	Moderate-Great	Very High	Very Difficult	None	High
Energy Shortages	Moderate-Great	Moderate-Great	Very High	Very Difficult	Diffuse	High
Inflation and Monetary Instability	Moderate-Great	Moderate-Great	Very High	Very Difficult	None	Moderate

Source: NASA Outlook for Space Study, Forecasting International, Ltd.

Figure 1. Some Important Crises

Energy Shortages	2	-189.3
Inflation	1	-219.4

* "one" indicates most severe

The second NATO sponsored Technology Transfer Conference emphasized the growing need which the world has for the early detection of future events and the peaceful transfer of advanced technologies. For we exist, at this moment, in a world dramatically split not so much by the ideologies of communism or democracy but by the abject poverty found in over 77 developing countries and by the increasing expectations of the already affluent world. The fact is 400 million people in the developing world are suffering from malnutrition today, and 10,000 people are dying weekly of starvation.[9] The projections for the future decades unfortunately point only to a bleaker scenario, with few readily adaptable alternatives. But let there be no mistake, society is not merely suffering because of the inequalities found between the "poor" and the "rich;" but the affluent nations are confronted with their own problems of rapid inflation, outdated economic models, resource shortages and a public voicing increased demands for social benefits, while suffering high unemployment. Furthermore, there is a third dimension to the global problem -- the awkward interaction between the developing and developed nations of the world.

We have at our disposal a host of new technologies in hybrid plant strains, space monitoring capabilities, weather control potential, substitute materials, pollutant controls and world economic institutions which conceivably might alleviate these immediate and future crises. The problem, however, we confront today is how we must allocate our efforts in solving or ameliorating the situation. In other words, what must the "technology rich" do now and in the long range future to avert the disasters of a nuclear war, massive starvation, environmental deterioration, resource depletion and economic extremes. To answer the question, one must first understand the dimensions of the crises, as they exist now and are projected out into the future decades as well as take a close look at the needs, possibilities and limitations which exist for particular technology transfers.

The predicted world crises of high probability are discussed in the following pages to present a capsule view of the dimensions of each problem and the technology transfers underway or, as yet, needed in each area. Because of societal forecasting necessity no longer lurks ahead unknown; now is the opportunity for technology transfer to offset the less desired predictions. People must not plead ignorance.

CRISIS: Massive Starvation

As indicated earlier, starvation is a problem now as well as a projected future crisis of high probability. The recent World Food Conference was unable to resolve what effective and immediate steps should be taken, and forecasts suggest that future decades will see massive starvation in the underdeveloped world and severe shortages elsewhere. For instance in the United States land, fuel, fertilizer and rail car shortages in the face of increasing demands for food and fibers will result in shortages of food: projected production of food and fiber lags behind 1985 extrapolated consumption patterns by as much as 7% to 12% in the opinion of many experts.[10] Certainly since the end of World War II, developing countries have made enormous gains in increasing their total food production: from 1954 to 1973, food production increased by 75%, as compared with the worldwide increase of 69% for the same period.[11] However, because of increased population growth, this represents only a per capita increase of 3% as shown in Figure 2. In fact, per capita food production in the lesser developed nations has been relatively constant for the last two decades, in comparison to per capita production increases of 30% in the developed world.[12] Furthermore, the food supplies in the nations experiencing significant food shortages already remain below minimum nutritional requirements, averaging about 60-85% of the per capita food supplies of the developed nations (see Figure 3).

Despite current food surpluses, the developed world provides very little food to the developing world: while more than 60% of the wheat produced in the U.S. is exported as is more than 50% of the rice and soybean, the bulk of this is exported to the developed worlds (see Figure 4). The developing countries largely grow their own foodstuffs and necessarily must expand future efforts toward increasing their own agricultural productivity. Unfortunately, the bulk of the arable land is already under cultivation in most of the developing nations. In Asia and the Far East, 84% of the land suitable for crops is under cultivation whereas only 26% of such land is cultivated on a worldwide basis.[13] It has been estimated for instance, that there are large portions of Africa available for cultivation:[14] however, the arable land undoubtably is not located in the most famine stricken and drought prone countries of the continent.

Recent poor weather conditions have also contributed to the food shortage problem by reducing crop production throughout the world several times in the last decade; and studies forecast increased periods of unusual weather that will shorten normal growing seasons. The effects of changing weather patterns will be felt severely in the developing countries along with increases in the price of fertilizers and energy for irrigation.

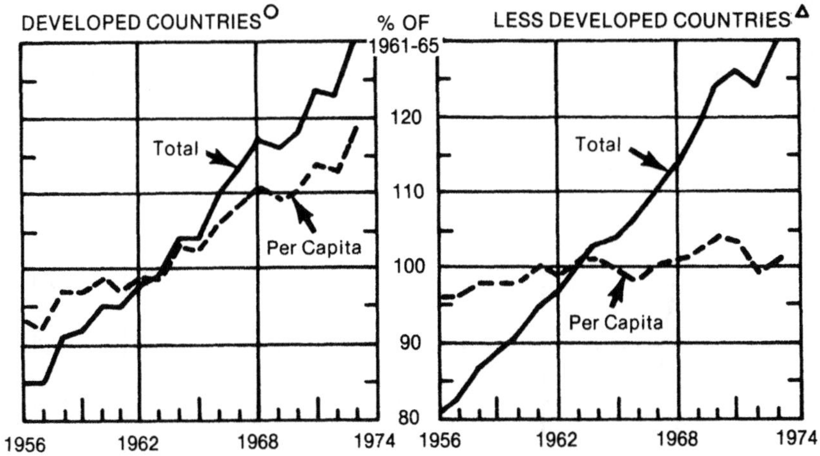

○NORTH AMERICA, EUROPE, U.S.S.R., JAPAN, REPUBLIC OF SOUTH AFRICA, AUSTRALIA, AND NEW ZEALAND

△LATIN AMERICA, ASIA (EXCEPT JAPAN AND COMMUNIST ASIA), AND AFRICA (EXCEPT SOUTH AFRICA)

Source: U.S. Department of Agriculture, 1974 Handbook of Agricultural Charts, No. 477 (Washington, D.C.: Government Printing Office), p. 50.

USDA

Figure 2. World Agricultural Production

FOURTH WORLD COUNTRY	KILOCALORIES /CAPITA PER DAY (1969-71 AVERAGE)	GNP/CAPITA (U.S. DOLLARS) 1972
Bangladesh	1840	70
Central African Republic	2200	160
Chad	2110	80
Ethiopia	2160	80
Gambia	2490	140
India	2070	110
Mali	2060	80
Mauritania	1970	180
Niger	2080	90
Pakistan	2160	130
Senegal	2370	260
Sri Lanka	2170	110
Upper Volta	1710	70
DEVELOPED COUNTRY (10 TOP COUNTRIES IN GNP/CAPITA)		
United States	3330	5590
Sweden	2810	4480
Canada	3180	4440
Switzerland	3190	3940
Denmark	3240	3670
France	3210	3620
West Germany	3220	3390
Norway	2960	3340
Belgium*	3380	3210
Australia	3280	2980

*Belgium-Luxembourg

Source: U.S. Senate, Committee on Agriculture and Forestry, The World Food Conference, pp. 37 and 39; and World Bank Atlas, (Washington, D.C.: The World Bank, 1974), pp. 6-7.

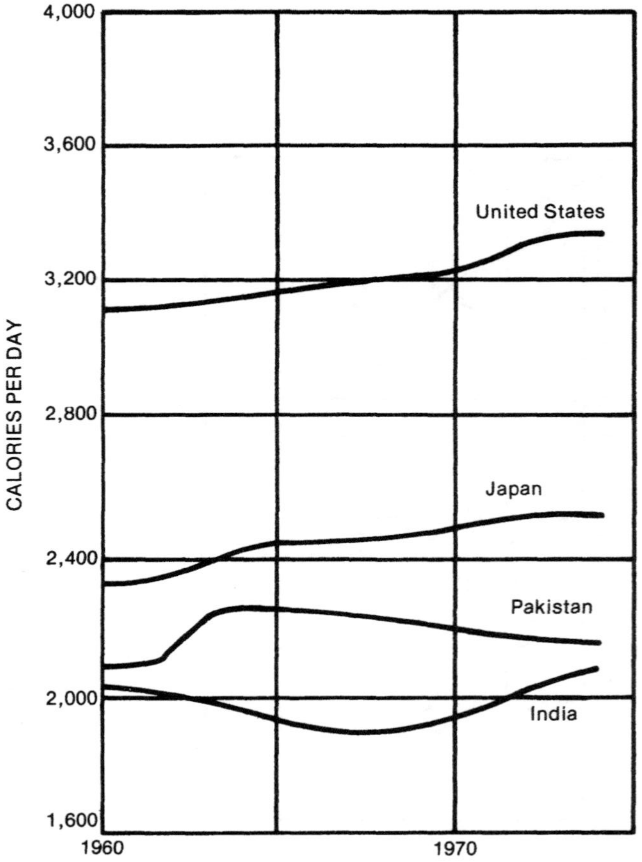

Source: United Nations Statistical Yearbook, 1970; 22nd Issue (New York, 1971), pp. 518-524; and Time, Vol. 104, No. 20 (November 11, 1974), pp. 66-67.

Figure 3. Food Supplies Per Capita

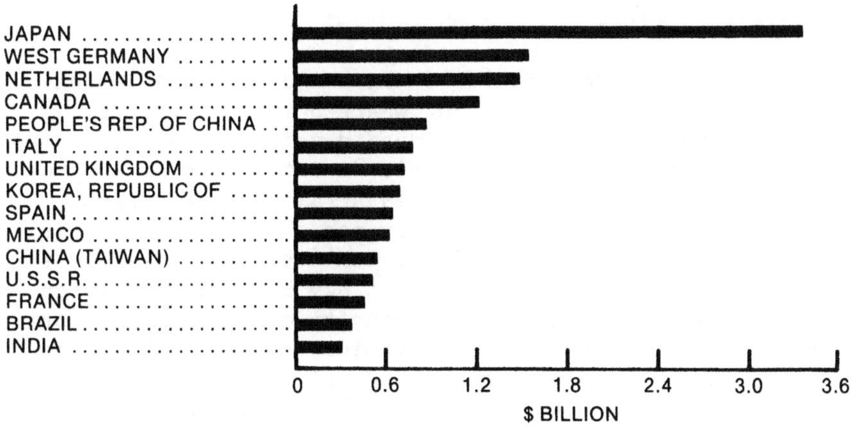

*Year Ending June 30. Data Not Adjusted for Transshipments.

Source: U.S. Department of Agriculture, 1974 Handbook of Agricultural Charts, No. 477 (Washington, D.C.: Government Printing Office), p. 48.

Figure 4. U.S. Agricultural Exports by Country, 1974*

Potential Alternatives

Many writers on the subject of the world food problem have advocated the transfer of existing western technologies to developing countries and the continued development of the "Green Revolution" in affluent areas. Logic dictates that since the "Green Revolution" has refined hybrid strains, fertilizers, pesticides, etc. so that productivity per acre is significantly higher, improved technology will provide even better yields for developed areas and transferred technology will allow developing areas to easily match the productivity of the western world. In short, technology has become a mythical hero. Mythical because while there are advantages to be gained through technology transfers in the agricultural sector, the limitations inherent in the high cost of technology suggest that not enough money will be spent to avert the disaster.

The challenge ahead, therefore, in terms of meeting the developing world's nutritional needs, is an economic one first and second, a technology transfer problem. How will underdeveloped countries afford and manage advanced technologies in agriculture; and what will the "technology rich" do to make balance of payments less of a restriction in the exportation of materials and knowledge? Technology transfer inevitably costs money that lesser developed nations do not have. Typically, an Asian farmer spends $6 per hectare to cultivate his land while he should be spending $20 to $80 per hectare to take full advantage of the technology theoretically available. A further limitation to the direct transfer of western agricultural technologies is the fact that hybrid strains must be developed for individual environments--a further expense; fertilizers are in short supply and highly priced everywhere; and western agriculture requires a sophisticated but small labor market, some machinery, and irrigation and chemical products not readily available to lesser developed countries. Of particular concern are the damaging effects of technology upon the labor force. Western farm automation would create vast unemployment problems. Unneeded farm workers would not have the skills to find other jobs; and in most cases, industrialization is not far enough along to provide numerous opportunities in developing nations.

Some progress has been demonstrated in the benefits of agricultural technology transfer, particularly in Asia. Japan has successfully increased its rice crops and implemented financial loan programs, at low interest rates, to its farmers. From 1965 to 1977, India using new high yield varieties increased its wheat production from 11 million tons to 27 million tons -- an increase unprecedented in history by any other country.[15] However, these same varieties, because they are more genetically uniform then the native strains they replace, are extremely vulnerable to epidemics -- a problem for continued technological research.

Looking to the long range future, a multilateral transfer of developing technologies is necessary in several areas. Many experts look to the ocean as a future source of protein, both from controlled harvesting of fish and substitute food products from the sea. Exchange and cooperation will be necessary in a global sense if these communal resources are to be tapped and environmentally protected. Meager efforts to control weather, especially to produce rain and avert damaging storms, are under way; but the worldwide and long term effects of such changes are, as yet, unknown and require unification of purpose and further study among all nations. Perhaps, we are looking forward to a time when affluent nations will voluntarily reduce their beef consumption (the opposite trend is occurring now), restrict the amount of grain fed cattle, and share improved livestock breeding and health techniques. Additionally, the problem of transportation of food from growing areas to market centers needs further study as well as the control of food loss. It is estimated that currently "one quarter of the world's food disappears between the field and table".[16] Losses often occur from poor harvesting management, rodents, fungus during storage, inefficient handling during transportation and improper distribution. Shared data banks for research, crop conditions and satellite collected information, relative to agriculture, would help provide global dissemination of agricultural technology.

In short, we must encourage worldwide development of hybrid high-yield strains, local fertilizers and the like; but the real break through for the developing countries will come with the growth of economic conditions such that agricultural technology may be afforded and further unemployment or economic decline avoided, as automation is transferred to the agricultural sector.

CRISIS: Energy and Other Non-Renewable Resource Shortages

The United States and other countries, both developed and developing, have assumed a future course of action which includes economic growth at an increasing rate, despite their expanding populations. Figure 5 demonstrates the effects of that increased population on natural resources, without taking into account the fact that per capita consumption is also rising. Only recently have we faced the realities of a finite natural resource supply and the substantial cost of growth, especially in the area of new technologies. Our desire for a rising standard of living and a more equitable level of distribution throughout the world simply

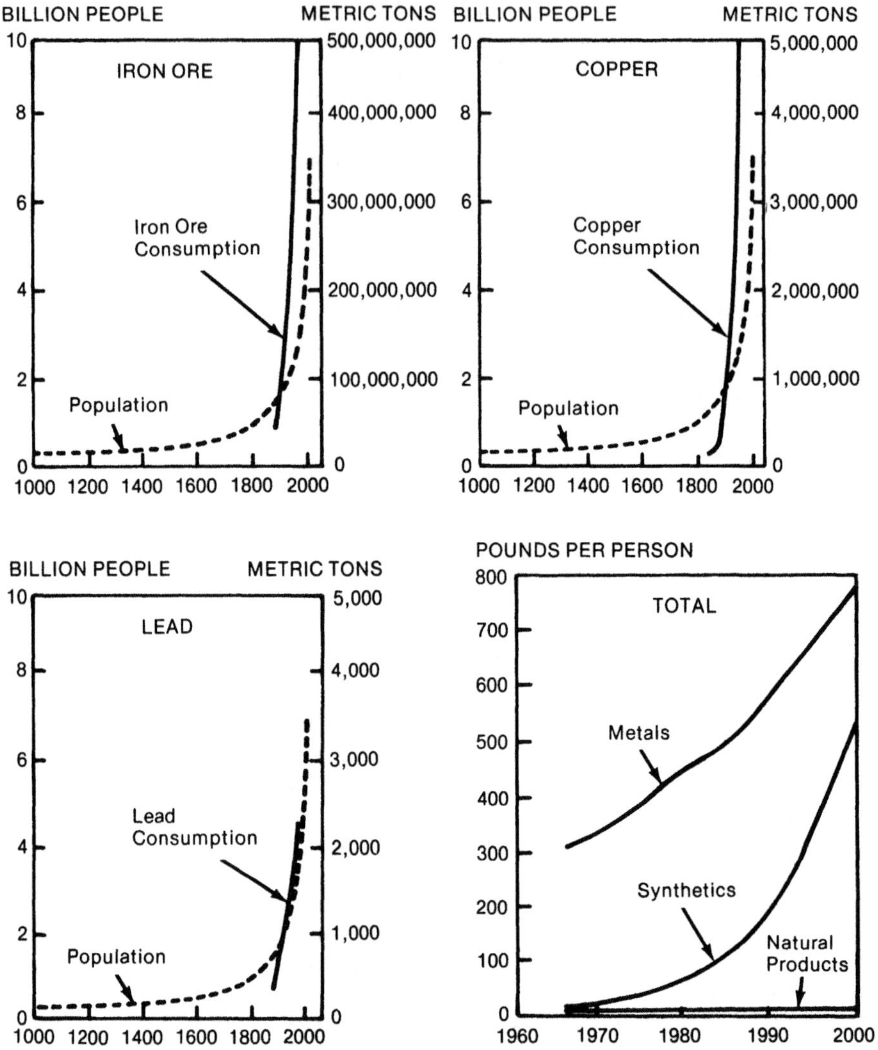

Source: McHale, John, World Facts and Trends (New York: Collier Books, 1972), p. 74, 76.

Figure 5. The Effect of Increased Population on Natural Resources

cannot be satisfied immediately. A totally free market system would leave less developed areas unable to compete in the bidding for scarce resources, now substantially rising in price. Furthermore, existing political allegiances have controlled in the past such resources as oil, phosphate, mercury and bauxite; and we can expect future cartel-like actions to further limit an "ideal" distribution of mineral resources. In short, the problem of natural resource shortages is both one of distribution of existing resources and the need for technology research into new methods and substitute sources.

The fact is future world demands for non-renewable resources, based upon traditional consumption patterns, lead to requirements of materials which significantly exceed anticipated local and worldwide supplies. Figure 6 depicts the energy production and consumption patterns of the European Economic Community, USA, USSR and Japan and reflects that the highly industrialized areas of the world are not energy self-supportive, even among themselves. By the year 2000, it is estimated that the U.S. will import 90% of the chromium, tin, titanium, platinum, beryllium, aluminum and fluorine needed for production. A worldwide projection for the year 2000 forecasts a doubling of the population and an increase in per capita mineral consumption by a factor of 4, thus increasing total mineral consumption by a factor of 8. Given this view, we should find our resources of silver and mercury depleted within the next 10-15 years and copper, lead, tin, zinc, tungsten and barite within 25 years. (See Figure 7 for listing of Proved World Reserves of Selected Minerals.) Decreases in energy sources and other minerals due to scarcity and/or increased prices may mean a percentage reduction in Gross National Product, until more efficient technologies and substitute materials come to pass. Developed and developing countries must pay <u>now</u> for research if future growth is to occur.

<u>Potential Action</u>.

The question is what can we do now, to retain constant supplies of raw materials, in the face of a rising standard of living, while being cognizant of our responsibility to the world environment? In the immediate sense, technology transfer will play a significant role in the education of our public toward conservation and recycling of finite, not just immediately scarce, resources. National and international legislation for controls on resources and tax incentives which preserve virgin resource supplies need development and implementation. Here, the

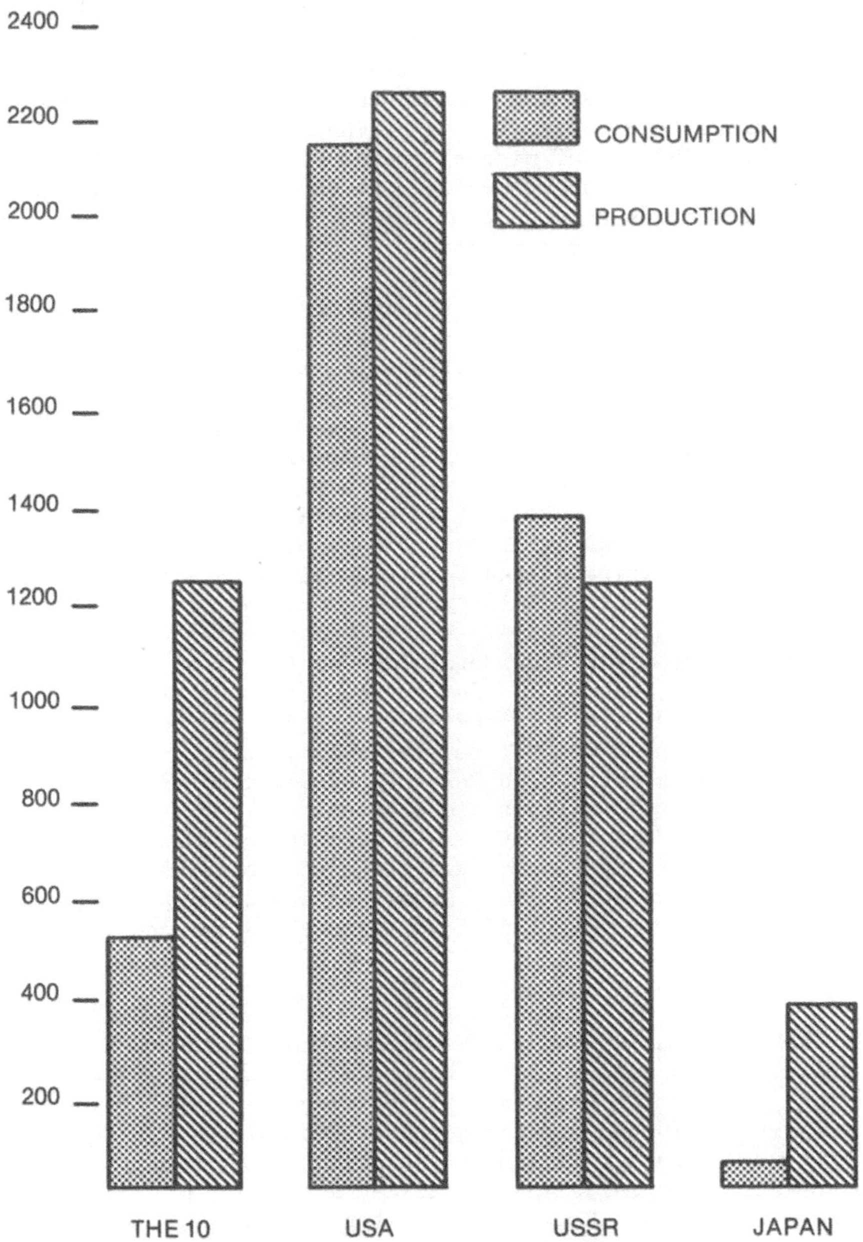

Source: Background Information for the Preparation of "Europe in 30 Years" Forecasting International, November 1973, p. 66.

Figure 6. Energy Production (Million Tons, Coal Equivalent)

More Than 100 Years:	Columbium Potash Phosphorus Magnesium
51-100 Years:	Iron Ore Chromite Nickel Vanadium Cobalt Asbestos Molybdenum
26-50 Years:	Manganese Bauxite Platinum Titanium Antimony Sulfur
15-25 Years:	Copper Lead Tin Zinc Tungsten Barite
10-15 Years:	Mercury Silver

PROVED WORLD RESERVES OF SELECTED MINERALS

Figure 7

Source: Executive Office of the President's Council on International Economic Policy "Critical Imported Materials" December 1974, p. 15.

industrial, research and political sectors must unify their knowledge and priorities to provide beneficial legislation. Additionally, international trade cartels might allow industrial and lesser developed, but resource rich, nations to jointly attain economic growth.

For the long-term changes necessary to deal with the approaching energy and natural resource supply and demand gap, new technologies for development of existing materials are needed and further research for substitute materials, hopefully, will provide for most of our needs. Technology transfer will be essential in this crisis area because development of new sources of energy and raw materials have world environmental implications beyond basic economic leverage.

A major candidate for immediate development will be gasification (or other purification) of coal and conversion of wastes into fuel. The coal-gasification program, coupled with the use of fluidized-bed coal combustors able to remove sulfur oxide, could be a tremendous boom to the energy problem. Negotiation and research is necessary, however, to allay potential destruction of the land by increased strip mining and air pollution.

For the Common Market, especially, recycled plutonium for fission reactors is the nearest hope for alternative energy during the late 1970's, with work toward the introduction of Liquid Metal - Cooled Fast-Breeder Reactor (LMFBR) and eventually thermonuclear fusion.[17] However, the design and dispersal of information on solar energy will be of special interest to developing areas who have the option yet to initially design their buildings for such heat and light sources.[18]

Technology transfer among research and development sectors of government and private industry is helpful for speedier design of these new energy sources; however, in the sensitive area of nuclear power plants, technology transfer is essential. International agreements for production and disposal of nuclear wastes must be drawn up to protect the environment and to reduce the threat of war or blackmail by nations and terrorists groups. Much could be learned from the Dutch in the area of disposal of nuclear wastes. (Robert Rinne of Sandia Laboratories covers very well the current transfers of nuclear technology in his recent paper - "Nuclear Energy Technology Transfer: The Security Barriers."[19]) It should be noted, however, that the United States has already been involved in technology transfer in the energy field with Israel in solar space heating and cooling, with France in Central Solar System, and with Italy in Geothermal energy. However, in the area of fast-breeding systems, the French with their Phoenix and Super-Phoenix Programs are already two years ahead of the U.S. and have no intention of cooperation with us (Super-Phoenix will be operational in 1981 and U.S. similar programs operational in 1983.)[20]

The ocean, as yet, remains a potentially rich source of minerals, oil and gas supplies. This area again is ripe for technology transfer because the science of ocean mining is developmental and the ownership of these resources is under question. Establishment of mining rights and environmental protection laws for the sea, will require international cooperation in the future between the research, private and government sectors. The recent Laws of the Sea Conference recognized the issues of ownership which must be settled, but as each country was eager to protect their own prosperity, no real measures of significance were adopted.[21]

As industry seeks resources from developing nations and transportation between source, developer and user expands worldwide, we can expect an increase in the number of multinational industries and trade unions as well as increased needs for technology transfer. Additionally, current international transfers of space technologies, particularly those of the United States and Russia, will contribute to the reduction of our energy shortage and provide research capabilities useful to development of substitute materials. Satellites not only provide space mirrors to reflect heat energy on designated portions of the earth's surface but also provide monitoring of resources and laboratories for technology research in electromagnetic and particular experiments, high energy physics and various measurements.

CRISIS: Environmental Deterioration

Contamination and misuse of the ecosystem has become a source of concern and international conflict because of the magnitude of pollutants produced by an industrialized society. However, future economic growth will entail increased transportation and development of many more industries upon land and the ocean, causing further pollution. Until recently, most nations had sufficient unused land supplies for waste disposal or industrial development; and they considered the ocean, in particular, a receptacle for unlimited waste disposal. Now individual countries are struggling to implement pollution standards to restore and maintain a safe environment for plants, animals and human beings. At present, there is great need for continued research toward economical and efficient pollution control devices, along with agreements on a unified set of priorities between industry, government, science and the public. Furthermore, individual nations cannot remain isolationists in their solving of these problems as the pollution of oceans, land, air space and outer space has reached worldwide damaging proportions.

Of particular concern, during this period of energy and food shortages and increased shipping of such goods, is the movement toward supertankers. (Figure 8 displays the tremendous increase in the number of such ships under construction between 1966 and 1972). At present, 3 ships per day are lost or broken at sea and estimates foresee as many as 6 per day (2,350 annually) by the year 2000.[21] Over 75% of the collisions occur in the harbors so that most oil spills and ship pollution damages happen in areas already deteriorated by land bound industries near ports.[22] Major tanker accidents currently cause an average daily spill of 384 barrels of oil. Obviously, oil spills, as a result of collision and grounding, will increase in magnitude as both numbers of vessels and the individual size of vessels increase.

Coastal areas reflect horror at each new oil spill because of the death of fish, birds and other animals living in the locality and the damage to recreational areas. But the magnitude of ocean transportation now causes concern for oil spills at any point. Researchers estimate that it takes the dissolved oxygen in 320,000 gallons of air saturated sea water to oxidize one gallon of crude oil completely.[23] Construction impacts of pipelines, transportation, storage and refinery operations for offshore ports, as well as new inland industries, give rise to forecasts of severe pollution problems ahead. Of further concern is the evidence that polycyclic aromatic hydrocarbons are carcinogenic and are known to be present in oil. Also petroleum hydrocarbons become magnified in concentration as they progressively move up the food chain - particularly through fish who act as a sieve while eating.

The growth in supertankers has necessitated dredging of existing or new harbors to create superports. Already dredging spoils reflect 84% of the wastes disposed of in U.S. coastal waters (see Figure 9); and fear exists that destruction of the harbor bottoms will severely damage the fishing industry. Because not all ports are conducive to construction of superports, off-shore ports are seen as the alternative. However, off-shore ports and ocean mining creat substantial disturbances in the ecosystem of the oceans. Dredging and mining cause sludge materials and water from deep and therefore cold regions of the ocean floor to mix suddenly with warmer levels of marine life, resulting in desert ocean areas and long range damages not fully understood.

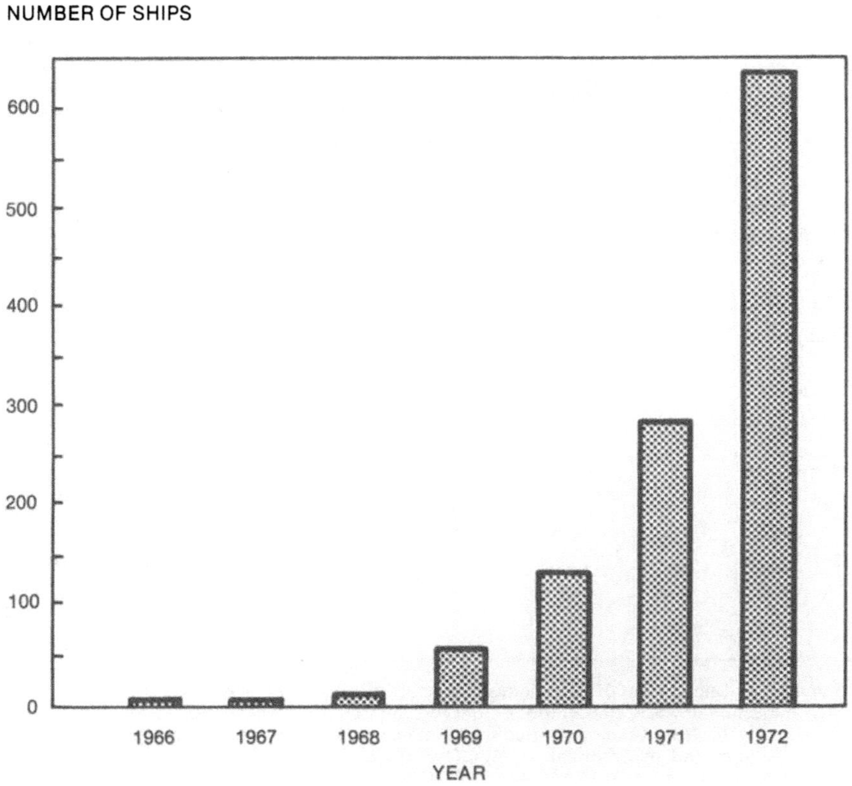

Source: Marcus, Henry S., "The U.S. Superport Controversy," Technology Review.

Figure 8. Growth of Supertankers Number of Ships under Construction or on Order over 200,000 Tons

WASTE TYPE	PACIFIC COAST ANNUAL TONNAGE	ATLANTIC COAST ANNUAL TONNAGE	GULF COAST ANNUAL TONNAGE	TOTAL ANNUAL TONNAGE	PERCENT OF TOTAL ANNUAL TONNAGE
Dredging Spoils	8,320,000	30,880,000	13,000,000	52,200,000	84
Industrial Wastes					
Bulk	981,000	3,011,000	690,000	4,682,000	8
Cont.	300	2,200	6,000	8,500	
Refuse Garbage	26,000			26,000	
Solid Waste				240	
Sewage				5,429,400	
Sludge		4,447,000		4,447,000	7
Miscellaneous	200			200	
Construction				1,161,000	
Debris		574,000		574,000	1
Explosives		15,200		15,200	
Total	9,327,500	38,959,400	13,696,000	61,982,900	100

Source: U.S. Department of Commerce, National Oceanic and Atmospheric Administration, Report to the Congress on Ocean Dumping and Other Man-Induced Changes to Ecosystems, October 1972 through December 1973, (Submitted in Compliance with Title II of the Marine Protection Research and Sanctuaries Act of 1972), March 1974.

Figure 9. Summary of Type and Amount of Wastes Disposed of in U.S. Coastal Waters for the Year 1973

Development and transfer of new technologies for ocean mining, superport systems and pollution controls will be necessary, as the problem of deterioration of the oceans has obviously reached global proportions. Already work is being done in the United States and several European countries to reduce navigation accidents by the use of computerized shipping controls and land and space satellite monitoring of all ships at sea, similar to radar control now present for aircraft.

As yet, it remains unclear whether ocean technology and protection agreements will develop slowly by piecemeal litigation between a few countries or whether the conferences regarding laws of sea will reach agreements on ownership and develop pollution controls sufficient to protect our ecosystem. In either event, technology transfer among industries and governmental research concerns involved in shipping will provide multinational and multilateral forums for future technology transfers of a practical nature.

Though concentration of pollution particles and vehicles in outer space has by no means reached the level present in our oceans, international concern exists now for the long term protection of that air-space. Like ocean laws, agreements on usage and controls of outer space have not been settled. However, the increase in supersonic transportation; the potentially crowding effect of industrialized use and ownership of space satellites; and the increased testing of space objects poses an environmental threat which must again be resolved among the public, governmental, research and industrial sectors and necessarily, by international agreement.

Pollution of the lower air spaces, in contrast to outer space, is already significant. The concern is over particulate emissions from transportation vehicles and industry as these particles cause cancer and create overall temperature changes. (See figures 10 and 11 for sources of pollution). Particles in the atmosphere reflect solar energy back into space and cause temperature reductions when volcanic activity or man-made pollution is high. Counterbalancing this trend is a steady 4% increase since 1910 in the level of CO_2 in the atmosphere, according to the National Academy of Sciences.[24] Carbon dioxide traps heat on the earth because light waves enter the earth's atmosphere as short waves, which easily penetrate the CO_2; however, the light is converted to heat and reradiated from earth as longer, infrared wave lengths, not capable of moving through the CO_2. The "greenhouse effect" of the CO_2 for the moment may offset the destruction of particulate emissions-but neither are beneficial to man's health and both have the power to change world wind and rain patterns. Additionally, there is concern over the eventual destruction of the ozone layer, a protective oxygen

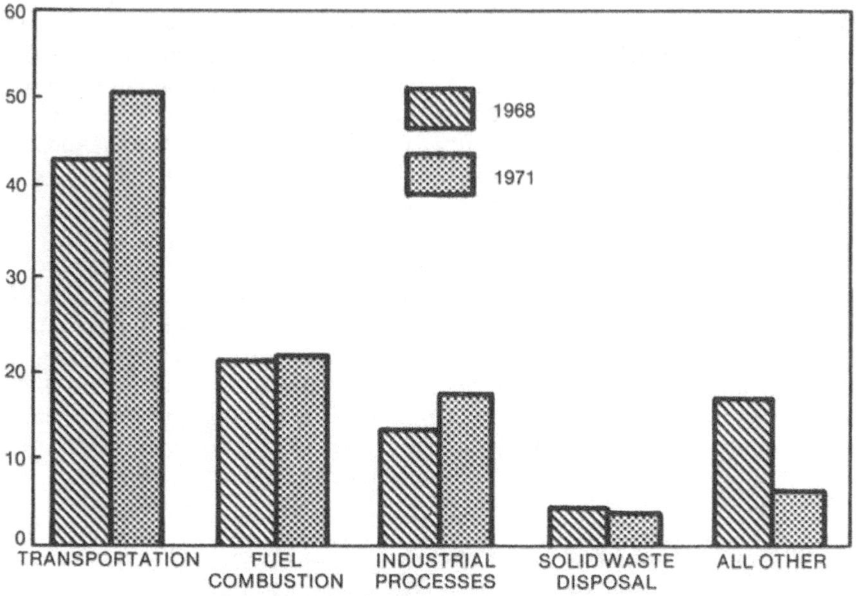

Source: U.S. Environmental Protection Agency.

Figure 10. Air Pollution Emissions by Source

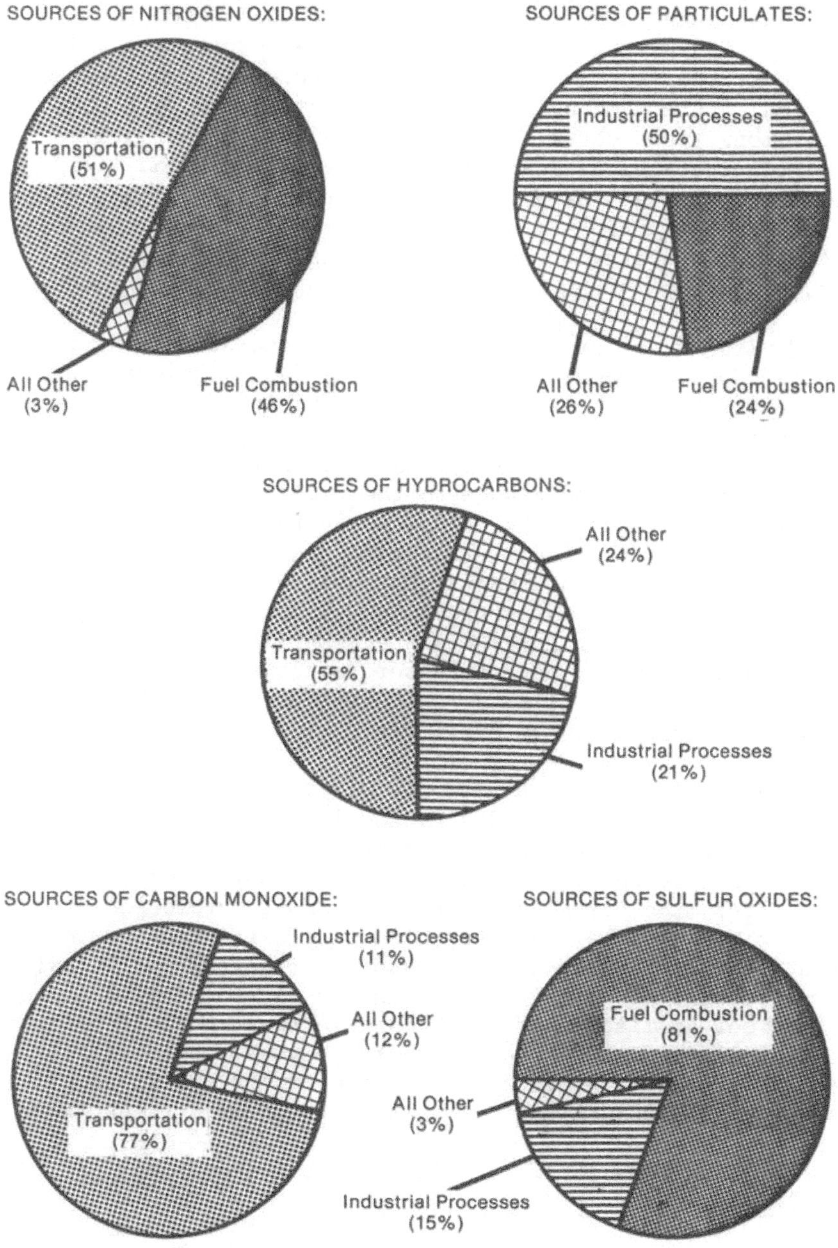

Source: U.S. Environmental Protection Agency.

Figure 11. Sources of Air Pollution Emissions

layer which prohibits cancer causing sun rays from entering the earth's atmosphere. The chlorinated hydrocarbons used in aerosol cans and nitrogen oxides from nuclear explosions and SST's convert the "super oxygen" into ordinary and less protective oxygen; there remains considerable controversy, yet to be resolved among researchers, about the magnitude of pollution required to create significant destruction of the ozone layer. Here again, what began as a localized or national problem of immediate air pollution - a problem requiring interaction between technology and industry primarily - now has international implications, requiring further cooperation among the world powers.

The environmental problems of urbanization, strip mining and fresh water dumping remain largely a local issue; however, the transfer of efficient pollution controls, mining procedures and city planning designs is necessary now because population increases have created pressures on all areas to productively provide for the lives indigenous to the area. Frontier lands are becoming reality of the past. Also, while the rich suffer organizational pollution from urbanization and industrialization, the poor suffer pollution from filth, poverty and the lack of technologies in sewage, water treatment, health care and food supply.[25] Technology transfer will necessarily play a significant role in the development of lesser developed nations, unfortunately within the limits of their economic capability, not the technology theoretically available.

The conflict which exists in most all envisioned technology transfers between science, industry and legislative bodies is one of economics. The catalytic converter for the automobile (transportation is the largest source of air pollution) has been designed after much dragging of the feet among automobile producers; but because the converter places an extra cost on the purchase price of the car and the gasoline required, political bodies are unwilling to effect legislation as progressive as the technology now available. National and international priorities are in need of education toward long range goals which will protect our ecosystem - perhaps education of the public on global issues should be the immediate thrust of technology transfer.

CRISIS: International Conflicts Leading to Conventional or Nuclear War.

Traditional conflicts of "power" will continue to create internal wars, border or independency disputes and ideological conflicts between communism and democracy. However, the threat of conventional or nuclear war has been and will be in future decades enhanced by the struggle of nations to secure economic strength through technology and resources. The realities of starvation, environmental deterioration and a lagging standard of living, in a time when mass communication has brought equality of "desire" but not equality in living standards, will force new coalitions of power among groups previously too small to be a substantial threat to world peace.

Resource blackmail through cartel-like actions is becoming the means to world power, but underlying each of these seemingly harmless economic struggles will be the urgency of a people attempting to literally survive or bitterly attain equality with the exploiting nations.[26] Coupled with the global interdependency we face in dealing with world crisis, each of which engenders a host of new international conflicts, is the availability of conventional, chemical and nuclear weapons. The increase in terrorist activity, often times not representative of local government, adds yet another dimension to the source of future conflicts.

The arms race between the major world powers is very much underway despite conferences to limit such expenditures. It is estimated that the United States will spend $300 billion per year by 1980 - in 1970 dollars - if the arms race continues at its present pace.[27] This expenditure will equal one half the total income of the poorest half of mankind.[28] Furthermore, an enlarging percentage of these military armaments is being sold to small nations unable to develop their own military production lines and to both sides of international conflicts already underway. This type of technology transfer is inevitable but hardly desirable from the standpoint of world peace.

Perhaps most frightening is the spread of chemical or biological warfare technologies and nuclear capabilities. Chemical control of a water system or behavior of a people is an actuality, not a science fiction treat. Policing of laboratories for threatening microbes or chemical stock piles, which when united with others are explosive, is not possible. Tampering with rainfall has already been utilized in the Vietnam conflict. Theft of plutonium or other materials for nuclear weapons would not be difficult, and smuggling such elements through ordinary airports was recently publicized. The technology involved in creating a nuclear weapon is basic to most college science curriculums; and the sale of nuclear power plants to developing countries for potential economic benefits also includes a nuclear capacity: the by-product of a nuclear reactor is a rich plutonium product used in nuclear weapons.

Prevention of war will depend upon our ability to negotiate trade agreements which ease the ensuing political conflicts. Here the spread of available technologies will be of utmost importance in raising the overall standard of living as quickly as possible. Multinational industries and labor unions plus international sharing of data from satellite monitoring or other data banks would aid developing nations and might prevent nuclear accidents. Technology growth and transfer in the peaceful usage, storage and longterm disposal of nuclear products would be advantageous to all. In short, we are in need of technology transfer to promote peaceful usage of the harmful technology capabilities now readily available.

The dilemma confronting our attempts to provide world peace is not so much one of who has the stronger capability to make war, for all groups of nations may pose the threat of even nuclear war, but is one of mounting sources of international conflicts whose solution, in terms of economic equality for all, runs counter to our previous negotiations based on power and selfaggrandizement. Attitudinal changes among the affluent and the poor must come to pass if laws governing shared resources and activities are to be enacted.

CRISIS: Severe Economic Problems for Both the Developed and Developing Nations.

Both the rich and poor, alike, are suffering economic troubles of a significant dimension so as to cause economists and political leaders to reevaluate their fiscal programs. Developed nations are experiencing inflation, shortages, price increases and unemployment while poorer countries have increased poverty, famine and populations. In addition to these problems, there exists the sensitive area of interaction between the industrialized world and the lesser developed areas, which often have untapped resources and certainly a cheap labor force. The struggle over import and export prices, leading to unequal trade balances, and the inability of needier regions to purchase western technology is a source of conflict, potentially causing war but definitely grounds for global concern and action both by industry and economic institutions.

The United States and European Economic Community are in sustained period of inflation combined with unemployment and underemployment. Ordinarily, economic policy would aim toward a trade off between inflation and unemployment; however experiencing both at one time has made the traditional economic models useless. If government attempts strictly a monetary policy where the money supply is not allowed to grow faster than our overall economy, the chances are inflation will not cease and recession will occur also. On the other hand, exponents of fiscal policy - regulation of government spending and tax programs to stimulate or tighten demand - find that tax advantages to increase demand and encourage employment and production have inflationary impacts as well, but to reduce government spending during a period when the public now voices expectations of social benefits would be politically unfavorable and recessionary in impact. Clearly our economic stability depends upon the ability of our political leaders and economic theoreticians to forge innovative policies which include an international capability as well. The steps which the European and OPEC countries have taken toward creation of economic boundaries and institutions of strength exemplify the movement all nations must make: from isolationism to global economic policy.

The economic disparity between the rich and the poor nations of the world is severe. Figures 12 and 13 depict the gap in GNP per capita between the affluent and poor countries and the difference in GNP and population. In the last 25 years, U.S. per capita income has doubled from \$2,500 to \$5,000, while India's per capita income has moved from \$60 to \$100.[29] Population growth trends (see Figure 14) in the lesser developed countries significantly hamper the economic development now occurring. Population control through education and attractive alternative life styles must become a major part of their future economic plans, along with education of the labor force toward management and skills consistent with industrialization. The exact role of future technology transfers between the "technology rich" and needy peoples of the world is unclear because the initial cost of technology itself is a barrier to most solutions for increased economic prosperity.

The global economic problems existing today have no readily acceptable solutions and will certainly increase before they abate. What makes this crises of special concern and particularly open to creative solutions is the fact that the economic conditions of the world are the catalyst for other global problems we foresee as reaching crisis dimensions in future decades. Furthermore, the economic crisis is one of the inhibitors of potential technology transfers which might allow economic growth and abatement of international conflicts, environmental destruction, food shortages and non-renewable resource scarcity.

In Consideration of Technology Transfer

The crises speak for themselves and the need for technology transfer is evident. However, as mentioned before, two significant barriers remain to the transfer of technology: the psychological fear of change itself and the economic limitations of

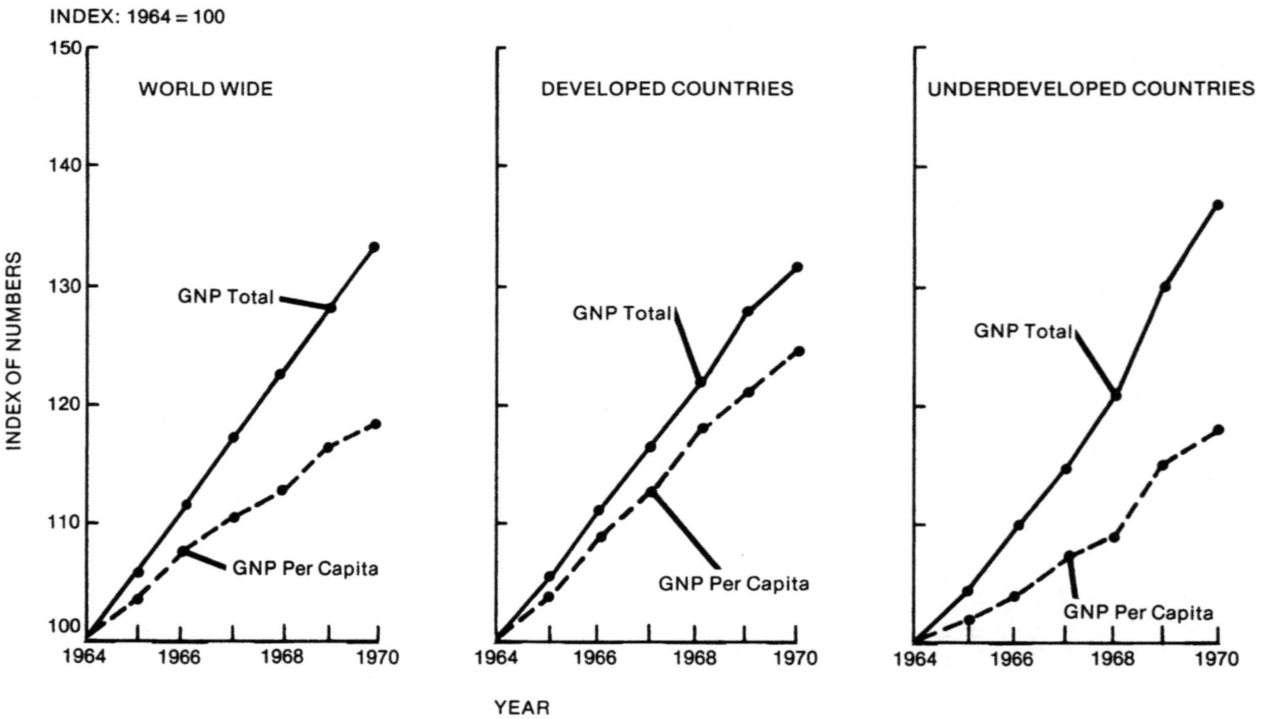

Source: Erhlich, Paul R., and Anne H. Erhlich, Population, Resources Environment: Issues in Human Ecology (San Francisco, Calif.: W. H. Freeman and Co., 1972), p. 433.

Figure 12. GNP and GNP Per Capita

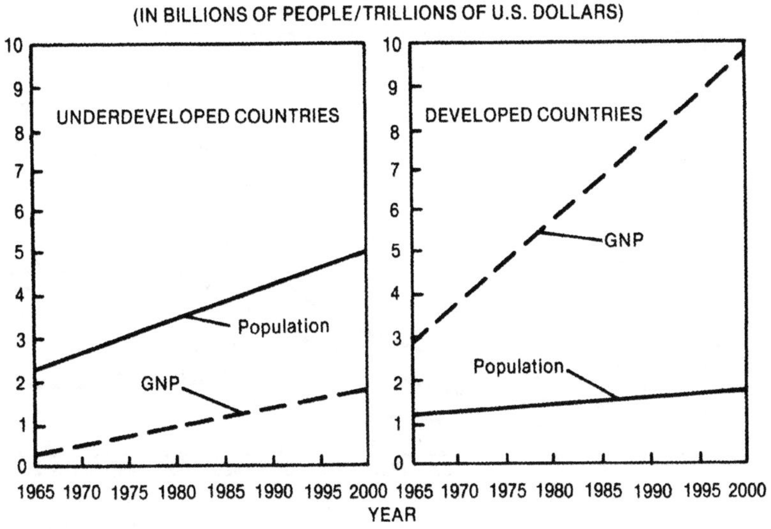

Source: McHale, John, World Facts and Trends (New York: Collier Books, 1972), p. 87.

Figure 13. World Population and Wealth

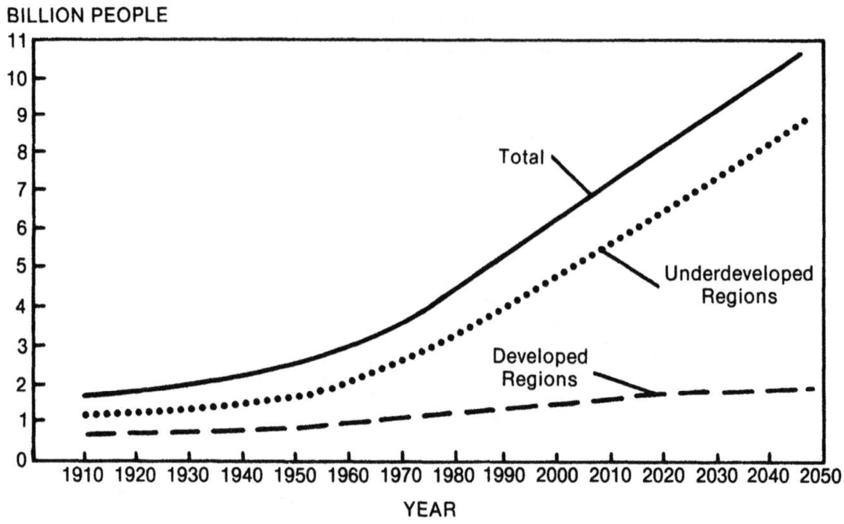

Source: McHale, John, World Facts and Trends (New York: Collier Books, 1972), p. 38.

Figure 14. World Population Growth in Developed and Undeveloped Regions - 1910-2050

particular transfers. Perhaps, continued study of man's motivation is the area for immediate research and application, for underlying the economic barriers is often a traditional predisposition toward self-preservation or the status quo which hinders development of innovative global policies. Additionally, such studies as the Nisenoff and Foster paper, "Development and Implications of a Technique for Quantifying Technology," will ease the economic decision-making process by providing a methodology for determining the economic value of various alternatives ahead in technology transfer.[30]

Besides the instinctual reticence man displays to the acceptance of new ideas, our society must also deal with another problem related to the transfer of technology: the idealization of technology as the means to salvation for earthly crises. This highly unrealistic picture of the role of technology transfer in abating world problems neglects the law of diminishing returns and obscures the intricacies of each situation. The truth is, we are far from a situation where the capability or even the motivation toward answering "humanitarian" needs exists. Costly and often unknown technological changes are ahead; and nationalism, independence and self-preservation are on the rise.

The late Dean Acheson once said that we are a "nation of short-term pragmatists accustomed to dealing with the future only when it becomes the present" and that "we find it hard to regard the future trends as serious realities" or "to treat as real and urgent, problems which appear critical at some future date." However, because of the severity of the crises, themselves, we no longer can affort to delay our actions. If technology is to have the opportunity to ease the world crises now foreseen, it must be through the immediate and increased reliance upon societal forecasting, technology transfer and the art of compromise among international, national and technological leaders. The spirit of cooperation remains new but imperative to our future.

REFERENCES

1. Sumner Myers and Donald G. Marquis, Successful Industrial Innovations, A Study of Factors Underlying Innovation in Selected Firms, National Science Foundation NSF 69-17: Washington, D.C. May 1969

2. Roy Rothwell, "From Invention to the Market Place - Successfully" in Technology Transfer, Davidson, Cetron, and Goldhar (Noordhoff International Publishing, Leiden, The Netherlands, 1974) p. 113

3. Elting E. Morison, Men, Machines, and Modern Times, (Cambridge, Mass.: The M.I.T. Press, 1966), Chapter 1

4. A.W. Pearson and T. Rickards, "Current Problems in Transferring Science to Technology" in Technology Transfer, Davidson, Cetron, and Goldhar. (Noordhoff International Publishing, Leiden, The Netherlands, 1974) p. 67

5. Marvin J. Cetron, "Technology Transfer: Where We Stand Today," Technology Transfer, Davidson, Cetron and Goldhar, (Noordhoff International Publishing, Leiden, The Netherlands, 1974) p. 4

6. Cetron, op cit., p. 4

7. Ibid.

8. M.J. Cetron and Audrey Clayton, "Social Forecasting: A Practical Approach," Technology Forecasting and Social Change, (American Elsevier, August 1975)

9. Present Food Situation and Dimensions and Causes of Hunger and Malnutrition in the World, Preparatory Committee of the World Food Conference, ECOSOC, May 8, 1974, and The New York Times (October 6, 1974), and Time (November 11, 1974) p. 66

10. Norman H. Fisher, "Growing Enough Foods for the Future May Tax U.S. Farm Capacity," The Wall Street Journal (November 19, 1973) p. 1

11. Philip H. Abelson, "The World's Disparate Food Supplies", Science, Vol. 187, No. 4173 (January 24, 1975) p. 217

12. U.S. Department of Agriculture, 1974 Handbook of Agricultural Charts, Agriculture Handbook No. 477 (October 1974) p. 50

13. Paul R. Ehrlich and Anne H. Ehrlich, Population, Resources, Environment, Issues in Human Ecology (San Francisco, W.H. Seeman and Co., 1972), p. 114

14. Ehrlich and Ehrlich, op cit., p. 114

15. Lester R. Brown, In Human Interest (New York: W. W. Norton and Co., Inc. 1974) p. 52

16. "The World Food Crisis," Time, November 11, 1974

17. Background Information for the Preparation of "Europe In 30 Years," Forecasting International, Ltd., Arlington, Virginia, November, 1973, p. 66

18. Op cit.

19. Robert L. Rinne, "Nuclear Energy Technology Transfer: The Security Barriers," Sandia Laboratories, presented at 2nd NATO Technology Transfer Conference, Les Arcs, France, June 1975 (Published in this volume)

20. "Europe in 30 Years," Op cit

21. Arthur Fisher, "The Law At Sea," The New York Times, May 18, 1975

21. United Aircraft Research Laboratories, U.S. Ocean Shipping Technology Forecast and Assessment: Final Report, Vol. IV: State of Society and Industry (prepared under Contract 3-36 204 to U.S. Department of Commerce, Maritime Administration) July 1974, Figure IV, p. 87

22. U.S. Coast Guard, Coast Guard Polluting Incidents In and Around U.S. Water, 1970-1971

23. Council on Environmental Equality, Ocean Dumping: A National Policy (Washington, D.C. October 1970) p. 14

24. W.W. Kellogg and S.H. Schneider, "Climate Stabilization: For Better or for Worse?" Science, (December 27, 1974) p. 1165

25. Alva Myrdal, A Seminar Report-Outlook for Space: 1980-2000 (Hammersmith Farm, Newport, RI, September 30-October 5, 1974), p. 11 & 12

26. Marc-Henry, Outlook For Space: 1980-2000, op cit., pp. 10 and 11

27. Myrdal, Outlook for Space: 1980-2000, op cit., p. 11

28. Ibid.

29. Grant, Outlook for Space, 1980-2000, op cit., p 12

30. Norman Nisenoff and George Foster, "Development and Implications of a Technique for Quantifying Technology," Forecasting International, Ltd. Presented at the 2nd NATO Technology Transfer Conference, Les Arcs, France, June 1975 (Published in this volume)

TECHNOLOGY TRANSFER IN THE UNITED STATES

Rear Admiral C. P. Ekas, Jr., USN

Deputy Chief of Naval Materiel (Development)
Washington, DC

On behalf of the Department of the Navy, let me express our pleasure in joining with NATO, the Department of the Army and the National Science Foundation in cosponsoring this meeting on technology transfer.

Technology transfer is a subject of immense importance to NATO and the Free World. As Dr. Malcolm R. Currie, Director of Defense Research and Engineering, stated to the 94th Congress on 21 April 1975 ". . .Effective international cooperation in R&D can be of vital importance to the security of the United States and the Free World. In an era when all nations of the Free World are under pressure to reduce or limit military spending, the collective resources of the United States and its Allies must be applied in the most efficient manner to provide greater force cost-effectiveness."

"The focus of our efforts in cooperation in R&D is in NATO although our interest is world-wide. It is in NATO that we have our principal treaty commitments and the bulk of the Free World's technological, industrial and military resources."

We are here today to explore effective methods of sharing the unparalleled technological and industrial resources of the NATO partners.

I encourage this conference to look beyond past and present cooperation in military R&D to more effective use of the Free World Technology to solve our common problems and to improve the quality of life of our citizens. Our cumulative knowledge must be applied to economic problems to provide gainful employment for all our citizens. We must work together to use our technological know-how obtained at a cost of billions of dollars to improve the environment, health, education and welfare of all people.

Technology transfer in its relationship to research and development is many things to many people.

In order to communicate better I offer a simple definition of terms - - -

> Technology transfer is the process of matching solutions in the form of existing science, engineering knowledge and hardware to problems in public programs and commerce.

In that context I will describe some of the Technology Transfer Programs in the United States.

TECHNOLOGY TRANSFER BY U.S. INDUSTRY

The significant technology transfer in the United States has taken place when American industry recognized a new, profitable market for high technology products. Aviation, computer and electronics technology developed for the Department of Defense are the most important recent examples of such technology transfer.

American industry has made a profit not only within the United States, but in Europe and elsewhere on the R&D in aviation, computers and electronics that the Department of Defense funded for solely military purposes. For example, the Boeing 707 aircraft can be traced in large measure to Department of Defense supported R&D.

This kind of technology transfer is not new. In 1880, contracts for four large modern warships for the U.S. Navy called for great amounts of steel. The Congress required that the steel be made in the United States. At that time only a small amount of steel was being manufactured in the United States. Thus the four ship contracts became the impetus which started the massive steel industry of the United States.

As you would expect there are technologies which the U.S. Department of Defense has developed which European and Japanese industry have adopted and adapted to better advantage today than has American industry. For example, the U.S. Air Force and Navy sponsored the initial development of numerical-controlled machines including APT. This computer language evolved because of the need for improved quality and throughput of precision parts for military aircraft. Multinational firms have transferred this technology successfully to European and Japanese industry and in many cases they have surpassed the original capability in the United States.

TECHNOLOGY TRANSFER BY THE DOD LABORATORY CONSORTIUM

Until recent years transfer of DOD technology to the civilian market place was on a random chance basis. Industry saw a chance to make money and adapted the DOD technology for the civilian market. This is and probably always will be the primary mechanism.

Technology transfer on a systematic and planned basis began in the late 1960's when several Navy laboratories started experimenting. One experiment involved the use of an in-house transfer agent to help match Navy technology with user needs. The results were encouraging and positive.

Based on this and similar experiences, representatives of eleven DOD laboratories met at the Naval Weapons Center in 1971 and formed the nucleus of an informal consortium. Consortium members cooperated in the transfer of military technology to national problems in the civilian sector. This consortium has grown to 41 member laboratories. Consortium members rely heavily on person-to-person contact with representatives of state and local government and other government laboratories and agencies such as the National Institutes of Health and the Environmental Protection Agency.

DOD has issued strict guidelines within which consortium members operate. In-house effort at any one DOD laboratory is limited to 3% of the professional manyears. The level of effort of the work undertaken must be such that it does not impede the military mission. The work must be compatible with the technological capability of the laboratory. The user must pay for the full costs of the work.

Projects undertaken by the consortium have been primarily in support of federal, state and local government organizations. Having concentrated mainly on national needs and public-sector problems in the past, the Navy is presently shifting more attention to transferring Navy technology to help improve productivity in industry. The disruptive effect on the U.S. economy, as well as in other industrialized nations, arising from the energy shortage is widely recognized, and the Navy is working to do its part in helping to restore the economic vitality of the United States.

The Navy and the Defense Documentation Center have an information exchange program underway for industry and the public sector. All on-going R&D tasks are coded to show whether there is a probable civilian application in addition to the military application. Upon request industry, small business and private agencies can obtain unclassified information in areas of interest by computer searches at the Defense Documentation Center.

TECHNOLOGY TRANSFER BY THE U.S. DEPARTMENT OF AGRICULTURE AND OTHER GOVERNMENT AGENCIES

The civil departments of the federal government also have assigned responsibilities for technology transfer.

The agricultural extension service is the United States' single most effective example of technology transfer as a spur to innovation and productivity. From its beginning in 1862 the Department of Agriculture established a network of agents located in the farming communities to work directly with the farmer. Thirty-two thousand full-time personnel and more than one million volunteers are now involved.

The agents learn the needs and biases of the farmers and help them take advantage of the research conducted by the Agricultural Research Service, state agricultural and forestry schools, universities and business units.

The National Aeronautics and Space Administration (NASA) has had a technology transfer program since June 1962. A major objective of their program is to increase the return on the national investment in aerospace research and development by encouraging additional uses of the knowledge gained in those programs. NASA's technology utilization program, funded at several million dollars a year, has been built around three principal activities. The initial thrust of the program was the wide dissemination of technical information to potential users primarily through publications. Personal interaction between technologist and user was then added to further the transfer process. Finally, as the process progressed, the hardware adaptation activity was included to enable prototype hardware to be demonstrated in the user environment.

The Department of Commerce has launched a patent promotion program. Most recently a highly successful workshop was held on Marine Anti-fouling Paint Systems, co-sponsored by the Navy and Commerce Departments. Nine U.S. companies have already requested licenses and there is foreign interest. Government-owned patents are widely publicized in the Federal Register and the Official Gazette and by the National Technical Information Service which is now pursuing an aggressive program to obtain foreign patent rights and foreign licenses.

The Department of Commerce, through its Experimental Technology Incentives Program (ETIP), is tasked with finding ways "to stimulate desirable technological change for the economic welfare of the nation." ETIP's interests are in civilian research and development and are focused primarily on federally-sponsored applied R&D intended to lead to the development of sponsored applied R&D intended to lead to the development of manufactured goods for sale to non-federal users.

A small but important program at the National Science Foundation is the Intergovernmental Science Program, designed specifically to help states and local governments benefit from the nation's technology. A Department of Defense technologist has been detailed to the National Science Foundation since 1971 to work in the Intergovernmental Science Program. The groundwork laid in helping states and local governments become potential users of technology dates back to the late 1960's. Progress has been such that today the program is on the threshold of marked expansion in the scope of its activities.

TECHNOLOGY TRANSFER BY CENTERS FOR DISTRIBUTION OF TECHNICAL INFORMATION

The U.S. government sponsors a number of centers for distribution of technical information.

The National Technical Information Service (NTIS) of the Department of Commerce provides the most extensive service. NTIS sells government-owned technical reports, computer products and software and other products to U.S. citizens and foreign nationals. They provide weekly abstract newsletters on 23 special interest fields including agriculture and food, building technology, energy, environmental pollution and control, and government inventions for licensing.

The Smithsonian Science Information Exchange (SSIE) provides current information on research in progress. SSIE's data base averages 170,000 summaries of recently funded research in all fields of science. The Defense Department, the National Aeronautics and Space Administration, the Atomic Energy Commission and other federal agencies supply information to SSIE. SSIE search strategies are designed to provide relevant information in specific technical areas.

The Department of Defense operates about 20 Information Analysis Centers on specialized subjects such as plastics, materials, infra-red technology, and shock and vibration. Information on the latest developments in these fields is provided to the customers of these centers frequently before such information is published. These centers are proving to be an effective means of transferring advanced technology.

TECHNOLOGY TRANSFER BY INDUSTRY ASSOCIATIONS AND PROFESSIONAL SOCIETIES

Industry associations and trade associations, in addition to the professional societies such as the American Society of Mechanical Engineers, are involved in technology transfer in the United States.

For example, the National Security Industrial Association (NSIA) which has about 250 corporate members, is establishing a program in technology transfer. NSIA works with the Department of Transportation, the Energy Research and Development Administration and other government agencies as well as the Department of Defense. NSIA held a workshop with the National Science Foundation (NSF) earlier this year where six NSIA member companies described projects in technology transfer. Additional workshops with NSF are planned, and NSIA is eager to assist other government agencies with technology transfer.

The Numerical Control Society, a professional organization which is concerned with the application and technology of numerical control in all industries, has a strong interest in technology transfer. Its May 1975 Annual Conference included major papers on the transfer of technology on numerical control, industry and government interaction in numerical control technology transfer and utilization, and ways to shorten the technological absorption time cycle.

PROPOSED CHANGES TO ELIMINATE BARRIERS TO TECHNOLOGY TRANSFER IN THE UNITED STATES

With the advent of the energy crisis and the economic recession, the President, the Congress and the American public began looking critically at existing laws and practices. There has to be a better way to build the American mouse-trap.

Two bills introduced at the current session of Congress are aimed at improving research and development and technology transfer. S. 32 introduced by Senator Edward M. Kennedy for himself and 27 others is entitled the "National Policy and Priorities for Science and Technology Act of 1975."

This bill would establish a Council of Advisors on Science and Technology in the Executive Office of the President to provide a source of scientific and technological analysis and judgment to the President. Further, the bill would establish an Interagency Federal Coordinating Committee on Science and Technology to coordinate agency research and development efforts and finally, the bill would establish an Intergovernmental Science and Technology Advisory Committee to foster the application of science and technology to State and regional needs.

This bill was also introduced in the House by Rep. T. H. Macdonald as H.R. 5202. H.R. 4461 was introduced by Rep. Olin E. Teague for himself and Rep. Charles A. Mosher and is entitled the "National Science Policy and Organization Act of 1975."

This bill is a comprehensive attempt to realign all of the existing instrumentalities of the Federal government involved in science and technology.

Title III of H.R. 4461 would establish a cabinet level Department of Research and Technology Operations assimilating the National Aeronautics and Space Administration (NASA), the Energy Research and Development Administration (ERDA), the National Bureau of Standards (NBS), the National Science Foundation (NSF), the National Oceanic and Atmospheric Administration (NOAA) and the Science and Technology Information and Utilization Corporation (STIUC). Title IV would establish a Science and Technology Information and Utilization Corporation (STIUC) to make available information to the general public and monitor the utilization of scientific and technological information.

In a related development President Ford pledged to key members of Congress that he would seek to re-establish the Office of Science and Technology. As reported by the New York

Times this Office would be a permanent part of the White House organization.

There is activity to improve the patent and licensing procedures now in use in the United States and the foreign patent program. The Federal Council for Science and Technology approved at its April 16, 1975 meeting a proposed bill "Government Technology Protection and Utilization Act of 1975" for presentation to Congress. The stated prupose of the bill is "to protect and encourage the utilization of government-owned technology and to further the public interests of the United States domestically and abroad." If approved by Congress, a program would be established for obtaining foreign protection of Government-owned inventions and for the commercial utilization of such inventions.

On 11 April 1975, the Deputy Secretary of Defense, Mr. W. P. Clements, Jr., directed a new "initiative" in manufacturing technology. The Army, Navy and Air Force have been asked to identify and "aggressively exploit application of manufacturing technology cost reduction opportunities." If this new initiative is as successful as the DOD initiated numerically controlled tools program of the late 1950's, there should be wide spread benefits for the manufacturing industry.

While there are controversial aspects to many of the preceding proposals, the proposals themselves indicate an effort to change the status quo. I bring them to your attention for what they are: Proposals intended to improve some aspect of technology transfer in the United States.

CLOSING REMARKS

Economic strength and social progress for all NATO countries are essential ingredients of a strong NATO.

We live in an interdependent world and, therefore, must work together to resolve common problems.

I firmly believe that we can effectively use the technological know-how already available in the NATO countries to solve our many economic and social problems.

I urge you to make the most of these two weeks. As Secretary of State Kissinger pointed out in his remarks on 28 May 1975 before the Organization for Economic Cooperation and Development: "International meetings that exhaust themselves in self-indulgent rhetoric or self-righteous propaganda help no one and no cause." I am confident you will agree we have no time for that kind of meeting.

Rather, use this conference to determine how to overcome barriers to technology transfer within our countries and between countries. Identify the best methods for effectively using advanced technology without regard to pride of authorship.

As President Ford told the leaders of the NATO alliance last month:

> ". . .we should rededicate ourselves to the (NATO) alliance as a great joint enterprise, as a commitment to follow common approaches to shared aspirations. We must build on the contribution our Alliance already makes through the Committee on the Challenges of Modern Society in coping with the environmental problems of industrialized societies. We must address the issues of population, food and raw materials. We must find ways to strengthen the world trading and monetary system, and to meet the imperatives of energy development and conservation. With the wealth and technological skills which are the products of our free systems, we can make progress toward a better standard of life in all of our countries if we work together."

We have a unique opportunity to respond to that challenge. Let us now get on with the job.

REFERENCES

1. "The Department of Defense International Cooperative Research and Development," statement by Dr. Malcolm R. Currie, Director of Defense Research and Engineering, before the Research and Development Subcommittee, Armed Services Committee of the United States Senate, 94th Congress, First Session on 21 April 1975.

2. Gee, Sherman, "Military-Civilian Technology Transfer: Progress and Prospects", Defense Management Journal, pp. 46-51, April 1975.

3. NC/CAM - Progress Through Government, Education and Industry Cooperation; Proceedings of the Twelfth Annual Meeting and Technical Conference of the Numerical Control Society, May 18-21, 1975, Washington, DC. Spring Lake, NJ, Numerical Control Society, Inc., 1975.

4. Directory of Federal Technology Transfer. Federal Council on Science and Technology Committee on Domestic Technology Transfer, June 1975.

5. What's Going On In Ongoing Research, a brochure. Smithsonian Science Information Exchange.

6. Defense Documentation Center Referral Data Bank Directory, April 1975. Alexandria, VA, Defense Documentation Center, 1975. (DDC/TR-75/3 AD-A008 200).

7. "Excerpts From Kissinger's Paris Talks", The New York Times, Section C, p. 19, May 29, 1975.

8. "Text of President Ford's Address to the Leaders of the North Atlantic Alliance", The New York Times, Section C, p. 7, May 30, 1975.

PART II: QUANTITATIVE AND QUALITATIVE AREAS

This section begins with the report of the workshop on Empirical Approaches to Understanding Transfer Processes in Technological Change by Fischer and McNicoll. The motivation for holding a workshop on this subject grew out of a number of factors which were informally discussed by several participants during the first week of the Advanced Study Institute. In particular, the lack of empirical studies presented at the Institute, and in the literature on technology transfer, was disturbing. Because of the dearth of empirical work on the subject, the following questions were posed as a basis for workshop discussion:

> Why should empirical approaches to Technology Transfer be considered?
>
> What has been done, to date, in empirical approaches to understanding transfer processes in technological change?
>
> Are the existing approaches satisfactory?
>
> How can the concept of technology transfer be incorporated into other empirical studies?

Are there suggestions on the appropriateness and availability of data for empirically approaching transfer processes in technological change?

The next paper describes work which is directed toward the development of an index to measure the level of technology, or more properly, to give a rank-order of disparate technologies. The object of the paper by Foster and Nisenoff is to enable the practitioner to say something reasonably precise about the facility with which technology is transferred between nations, insofar as it is determined by the nature of the technology being transferred.

Anderson and Johnston discuss Technology Transfer in the British textile industry extracted from information collected for a larger study concerned with the transition of this industry from a craft base to a scientific base.

The development of an industry from a craft towards the adoption of a scientific base involves a number of socio-economic factors as well as technological factors. However, as indicated in this case study, technological developments are of primary importance.

The Critical Role of Communication in Technology Transfer is discussed by George Tressel. Tressel's hypothesis suggests that a basic weakness in the technology transfer process centers about the "communication mismatch". There is a critical difference in language, perspective, and evaluation criteria that separates R&D personnel from industrial management. Unless this communication gulf can be bridged, new technology must diffuse slowly and haltingly between the two communities.

Tressel proposes to explore this hypothesis by developing a system to (1) identify patent technology of potential value to the industrial sector, and (2) develop an initial system to communicate this technology to industrial management in the language and through the channels with which they are familiar.

Feinman's article on Regulatory Barriers to Technology Innovation is must reading for everyone and particularly for individuals who are interested in historical perspectives in Technology Transfer. This paper discusses various technological variations and historical perspectives and regulations from the Roman Empire to today. Many excerpts are taken from the literature and similarities between yesterday and today are very apparent.

EMPIRICAL APPROACHES TO UNDERSTANDING TRANSFER PROCESSES IN TECHNOLOGICAL CHANGE: REPORT ON A WORKSHOP

William A. Fischer

Clarkson College of Technology
Potsdam, N.Y.

Iain McNicoll

University of Stirling
Stirling, Scotland
United Kingdom

The motivation for holding a workshop on "Empirical Approaches to Understanding Transfer Processes in Technological Change" grew out of a number of factors which were informally discussed by several participants during the first week of the Advanced Study Institute. In particular, the lack of empirical studies presented at the Institute, and in the literature on technology transfer, was disturbing for several reasons. In light of the empirical progress currently being made in other applied social science areas it was surprising that relatively little empirical work had been performed in technology transfer. In addition, the lack of progress in empirically examining conceptualizations of the technology transfer process was seen as retarding the ability to distill the common elements from numerous case studies and anecdotal evidence. Such distillation is essential if technology transfer is to move from being an art to a science. On the other hand, there was some skepticism among many participants about the virtues of empirical approaches to a subject as diverse as technology transfer. Because of this skeptism, and because of the dearth of empirical work on the subject, the following questions were posed as a basis for workshop discussion:

1) Why should empirical approaches to technology transfer be considered?

2) What has been done, to date, in empirical approaches to understanding transfer processes in technological change?

3) Are the existing approaches satisfactory?

4) How can the concept of technology transfer be incorporated into other empirical studies?

5) Suggestions on the appropriateness and availability of data for empirically approaching transfer processes in technological change.

The following sections of this report reflect the workshop discussion on each of these questions.

Question #1: Why should empirical approaches to technology transfer be considered?

Three paramount responses to this question resulted from the workshop discussion:

1) There is a need to move away from a preoccupation with anecdotal uniqueness in technology transfer cases towards a recognition of the empirically supportable commonalities which tie these cases together as instances of technology transfer.

2) There is a need to identify the significant descriptive and policy variables in the technology transfer process.

3) We may well have reached a relatively static position in terms of the growth of the state-of-the-art in technology transfer theory. Empirical findings are now needed to generate new hypotheses and to pull the theory to a new level where conceptualization and empirical testing can complement each other.

In addition, the following two caveats were noted during workshop discussion:

a) There was a substantial amount of feeling that unbridled empiricism, particularly predictive and prescriptive model building, is premature in the study of technology transfer, at this point in time.

b) It should be recognized that a tradeoff must be made by the empirical examiner between the need for situation-specific sensitivity versus the need for complexity-reducing general propositions. This is particularly important in those instances where the empirical results are being used in the policymaking process.

Question #2: What has been done, to date, in empirical approaches to understanding transfer processes in technological change?

In an effort to stimulate discussion and in view of the unfamiliarity of many Institute participants with the limited amount of empirical studies on technology transfer performed to date, a simple typology of empirical approaches to understanding transfer processes in technological change was presented at the workshop. This typology was admittedly impromptu and subsequent discussion both in the workshop and at the plenary session resulted in some modifications.

The typology of empirical approaches to transfer processes in technological change is reproduced in figure 1. The definitions evolving out of the Stirling Conference (Bradbury, 1975) were utilized in constructing the typology. Those studies which deal explicitly with horizontal transfer are identified as technology transfer, while those studies primarily concerned with vertical transfer are referred to as "all other transfer processes in technological change"(TPTC). Within these two categories there is a further distinction made as to the focus of the studies. Behavioral studies focus on the motivations for, and the decisions made within, the transfer process. Institutional studies, on the other hand, are primarily concerned with the context within which the transfer process takes place. In addition, two studies which do not satisfy the Stirling definition of transfer processes yet which could have important implications for empirical study on transfer processes were also included. These studies are by Nisenoff and Foster, and OECD, and represent attempts at quantifying technological achievement profiles of nations at particular points in time. By replicating such work for a particular nation over several points in time a quantitative indication of transfer experience can be generated, hence, the rationale for their inclusion in the typology.

Figure 1, then, presents a comprehensive, yet not exhaustive, listing of empirical approaches to understanding transfer processes in technological change performed to date. Although some unpublished work is included, the primary emphasis was on obtainable published sources. The typology is limited to multivariate statistical studies with the exception of the two studies cited above and the input-output studies. The studies identified in figure 1 are fully cited in the reference list at the end of this report.

Figure 1
Empirical Approaches to Understanding Transfer Processes in Technological Change (TPTC)

TPTC

Studies of Technology Transfer: Behavioral	Studies of Technology Transfer: Institutional	Studies of All Other TPTC: Behavioral	Studies of All Other TPTC: Institutional
Horizontal Diffusion Studies (regression analyses)	Regression Analyses of Institutional Factors	Diffusion Studies (regression analyses)	Input-Output Studies
			Carter (U.S. Economy)
Griliches (Hybrid corn)	Spencer & Woroniak (Japan)	Mansfield (twelve innovations)	Rating Systems
			OECD
Hufbauer (synthetic chemicals)	Woroniak (Federal Republic of Germany)	Mohr (adoption of non-traditional programs by health departments)	Nisenoff & Foster
Tilton (semi-conductors)			
Swan (synthetic rubber)		Mansfield et. al. (numerical control in the tool and die industry)	Factor Analysis of Innovation Patterns
Nabseth & Ray (eight innovations)			Walker (88 programs dealt with by state legislations)
Regression Analysis of Technology Transfer Effectiveness		Gray (12 laws adopted by states)	
		Bundgaard-Nielsen & Fiehn (catalytic refining process)	
Thomas (19 Nigerian manufacturing industries)		Mensch	
Factor Analysis of Relationship Between Users & Originators		Lakhani (environment-saving technologies in the U.S. petroleum industry)	
Bar-Zakay (Israeli military-civilian transfer)		Cluster Analysis of Relationship Between Users & Manufacturers	
		Ettlie (numerical control)	
		Sappho Studies (cluster analysis of successful-unsuccessful innovation pairs)	
		Science Policy Research Unit	
		Rothwell et. al.	
		Analysis of Important Factors in Innovation Process	
		Battelle Columbus Laboratories	

Question #3: Are the existing empirical approaches to understanding transfer processes in technological change satisfactory?

The unanimous response of the workshop to this question was: No. However, it was the contention of some participants that at this point in the development of technology transfer as a field of study, and in view of data limitations, it is inappropriate to vigorously pursue empirical study, or to be dismayed by the relative lack of progress in empirical approaches.

Question #4: How can the concept of technology transfer be incorporated into other empirical studies?

The workshop discussion of this question was quite heated and no conclusive response could be reached. The debate focused almost entirely upon the utility, and in fact even the ability, of input-output analysis as a way of empirically approaching technology transfer.

Question #5: Suggestions on the appropriateness and availability of data for empirically approaching transfer processes in technological change.

There was general recognition among the participants at the workshop that data for empirical studies is either unavailable or, when available, extremely poor. One important point raised in the workshop discussion was the difficulty of obtaining data on transfer failures. It was noted that nearly all studies have been concerned with transfer successes. There was also some discussion over the role of anecdotal evidence in understanding transfer process. It was generally agreed that anecdotal evidence and case studies are essential complements to empirical study.

There was little discussion on variable selection and construction. This reflected the feeling among participants that discussion of variables should not be attempted except in reference to specific studies or situations.

Bibliography

Battelle Columbus Laboratories, Interactions of Science and Technology in the Innovative Process: Some Case Studies, Washington D.C., National Science Foundation, 1973, NSF-C667.

Bar-Zakay, Samuel N., Technology Transfer From the Defense to the Civilian Sector in Israel paper presented to the Nato-Advanced Study Institute on Industrial Technology Transfer, June 22-July 4, 1975, Les Arcs-Bourg St. Maurice, France.

Bradbury, Frank R., Review of Technology Transfer Studies, paper presented to the Nato-Advanced Study Institute on Industrial Technology Transfer, June 22-July 4, 1975, Les Arcs-Bourg St. Maurice, France.

Bundgaard-Nielson, M. and Fiehn, Peter, "The Diffusion of New Technology in the U.S. Petroleum Refining Industry," Technological Forecasting and Social Change, Vol. 6, No. 1, 1974, pp. 33-39.

Carter, Anne P., Structural Change in the American Economy, Cambridge, Mass. Harvard University Press, 1970.

Ettlie, John., "Technology transfer-from Innovators to Users," Industrial Engineering, Vol. 5, No. 6, June 1973, pp. 16-23.

Gray, V., "Innovation in the States: A Diffusion Study," American Political Science Review, Vol. 67, December 1973, pp. 1174-1185.

Briliches, Zvi, "Hybrid Corn: An Exploration in the Economics of Technological Change," Econometrica, Vol. 25, No. 4, October 1957, pp. 501-522.

Hufbauer, Gary C., Synthetic Materials and the Theory of International Trade, London, Gerald Duckworth and Co., 1966.

Lakhani, Hyder, "Diffusion of Environment Saving Technological Change-A Petroleum Refining Case Study," Technological Forecasting and Social Change, Vol. 7, No. 1, 1975, pp. 33-55.

Mansfield, E. Industrial Research and Technological Innovation, New York, W.W. Norton, 1968.

Mansfield, E., Rapoport, J., Schness, J., Wagner, S., Hamburger, M., Research and Innovation in the Modern Corporation, New York, W.W. Norton, 1971.

Mensch, Gerhard, "Institutional Barriers to the Science and Technology Interaction," in Davidson, Harold R., Cetron, Marvin C., and Goldhar, Joel D., (editors), Technology Transfer, (Leyden, Netherlands, Noordhoff International Publishing, 1974).

Mohr L., "Determinants of Innovation in Organizations," American Political Science Review, Vol. 63, March 1969, pp. 111-126.

Nabseth, L. and Ray, G.F., The Diffusion of New Industrial Processes, Cambridge, U.K., Cambridge University Press, 1974.

Nisenoff, Norman, An Approach to Quantifying Technology Transfer and its Implications, paper presented to the Nato-Advanced Study Institute on Industrial Technology Transfer, June 22-July 4, 1975, Les Arcs-Bourg St. Maurice, France.

Organization for Economic Cooperation and Development (O.E.C.D.), The Conditions For Success in Technological Innovation, Paris, OECD, 1971, pp. 143-148.

Rothwell, R., Freeman, C., Horlsey, A., Jervis, V.T.P., Robertson, A.B., Townsend, J., Sappho Updated-project Sappho phase II," Research Policy, Vol. 3, No. 3, November 1974, pp. 258-291.

Science Policy Research Unit, University of Sussex, Success and Failure in Industrial Innovation, London, Centre for the Study of Industrial Innovation, 1972.

Spencer, Daniel L. and Woroniak, "The Feasibility of Developing Transfer of Technology Function," Kyklos, Vol. XX, Fasc. 2, 1967.

Swan, Philip L. "The International Diffusion of an Innovation," The Journal of Industrial Economics, Vol. XXII, No. 1, September 1973, pp. 61-69.

Tilton, John E., International Diffusion of Technology: The Case of Semi Conductors, Washington, D.C., The Brookings Institute, 1971.

Thomas, D. Babatunde, Capital Accumulation and Technology Transfer: A Comparative Analysis of Nigerian Manufacturing Industries, New York, Praeger, 1975.

Walker, J., "The Diffusion of Innovations Among the American States," American Political Science Review, Vol. 67, December 1973, pp. 1174-1185.

Woroniak, Alexander, "Technological Transfer in Eastern Europe: Receiving Countries," in Wasowski, Stanislaw (editor), East-West Trade and the Technology Gap, New York, Praeger, 1970.

DEVELOPMENT AND IMPLICATIONS OF A TECHNIQUE FOR QUANTIFYING TECHNOLOGY

George Foster
Norman Nisenoff

Forecasting International, Ltd.
Arlington, Virginia 22201

1. Introduction

This paper describes work currently in progress at Forecasting International, Ltd. (FI), which is directed toward the development of an index to measure the level of technology, or more properly, to give a rank-order of disparate technologies. The object of this endeavor is to be able to say something reasonably precise about the facility with which technology is transferred between nations, insofar as this is determined by the nature of the technology being transferred.* We assume that a nation's absorptive capacity is greatest, i.e., transfer is easiest, for technologies which are at a level similar to those which it already practices. This is an intuitively reasonable assumption, and there is abundant anecdotal evidence which can be interpreted as offering support.[1] In studying technology transfer, one becomes aware that there is no established quantitative index which can be applied to assess the effect or extent

---

*That is, we are dealing only with the technological component of a process which is also dependent on an entire non-technological infrastructure.

[1]See for example, Baranson, Jack, Industrial Technologies for Developing Economies (New York, N.Y.: Frederick A. Praeger, 1969); also Hall, G.R. and R.E. Johnson, "Transfers of U.S. Aerospace Technology to Japan", in Raymond Vernon (ed.) The Technology Factor in International Trade (New York, N.Y.: Columbia University Press, 1970).

of whatever components are involved in the transfer. The problem is, then, to devise an index which ranks both the technology being transferred and that being practiced in the host country. In the absence of such an index, "technology" and "level of technology" are vague concepts hardly more precise than muddled generalities about national character.

We argue that such a measure should consider observable aspects of technology and eschew such quantities as knowledge, which are not directly observable, but must be deduced from observations of technical practices; and others, for example productivity, which are almost impossible to define operationally. We wish also to avoid surrogates such as research expenditures which are frequently employed to compare one industry with another. All such surrogates suffer some deficiencies: research expenditure, for example, is an input to technology, and its correlation with any actual performance tends to be unclear, and at times apparently random. The costs of research differ greatly among countries and industries, which further complicates their use as a measuring function. Many industries consume research results produced by others, and additionally, large areas of technology are not directly fertilized by research.

In the context of the present discussion, we will emphasize actual industrial practice, and restrict our attention to manufactured goods; an activity will be considered technological only if it results in the production and distribution of physical goods. To illustrate what is not included: Vannevar Bush described[2] how he and some friends devised a means of tossing apples at cows using an old gasoline engine. Now this device has many technical elements but seems never to have entered commerce, hence it is not technology by our current definition. Nevertheless, it may be comforting to know that if society ever needs a gasoline-powered-apple-shooter, technology can supply it.

In this discussion, then, a technology is defined as an integrated set of activities involved in the commercial production of physical goods. Our task is to devise a set of rules for selecting technology-related phenomena to be observed; a means of scaling the observations; and an algorithm for combining the results to yield an index number characteristic of that technology. We require that:

1. The index number locates a given technology in a rank-ordering of many technologies;

[2]Bush, Vannevar, Pieces of the Action, (New York, N.Y.: William Morrow and Company, Inc., 1970).

2. The phenomena to be observed should encompass elements in the practice of technology and also of the transfer process;

3. Different observers applying this algorithm should arrive at nearly the same index number for a given technology.

Once such an index is available, it could be used to rank all technologies and would, in fact, serve to define the level of technology operationally.

Since there is no established definition of technological level or any scheme for computing it other than an index such as we propose, we are confronted with a dilemma. In order to validate the measurement system which we derive, it is logically necessary to have some prior ranking of technologies which does not depend on the index. This is resolved by using the intuitive judgment of informed observers.

Psychophysicists have shown that different sets of observers can arrive at comparable rankings for quite complicated perceptions - national power, seriousness of crimes and prestige of professions, for instance.[3] Thus, it is logical to assume that agreement between the rank-ordering of technologies by independent experts, and that provided by the index we shall define, confers some measure of validity upon our methodology and its results.

2. Rationale

Our approach is based upon Professor Vernon's observation[4] that as a product matures, the technical frontier shifts from the characteristics of the product to those of the manufacturing process. In the early stages of development, neither producer nor customer is entirely sure which properties are most useful: designs tend to change rapidly, and the customer is more concerned with performance differences among alternative designs than with cost differences. However, as the product matures, designs are standardized and cost becomes an increasingly important consideration: producers introduce cost-cutting production procedures. Frequently, this involves increasing capital investment and reducing flexibility, but the market is by now fairly well-defined as to size and product requirements, so that the risk is acceptable. Competitors enter the field,

---

[3]Stevens, S.S., Psychophysics, (New York, N.Y.: John Wiley & Sons, 1975)

[4]Vernon, Raymond, Sovereignty at Bay: The Multinational Spread of U.S. Enterprises, (New York, N.Y.: Basic Books, Inc., 1971).

perhaps using different processes, but eventually production methods become standardized also. When all producers make approximately the same product, in basically similar fashion, the technology is stabilized. Vernon's observation suggests that any technology index must consider both product and process characteristics.

Product and production system are somehow related to each other. Our view as to the nature of the relationship between them is derived from a concept developed by Joan Woodward and her associates.[5] They studied the influence of production technology upon management structure, and produced a nine point scale of production measurement, ranging from unit or small batch production at one extreme to continuous processing at the other. It was pointed our that this scale is one of increasing technical complexity.

To a surprising degree, appropriate production method was found to be independent of the specific product. For example, the production of custom-made suits has more in common with other custom production than it has with mass production of clothing. The Woodward group distinguished production of integral products (those sold by the piece), from production of dimensional products which are sold by weight, volume, area or other physical dimension, because the two kinds of production present different management problems. Industries concerned with the manufacture of dimensional products - sometimes called the process industries - are particularly susceptible to the use of highly automated continuous-flow processes.

The Vernon and Woodward insights suggest many possible factors which might be considered as phenomena contributing to the construction of our proposed index. In order to develop from these an index yielding intuitively satisfactory results, we selected a small number of products that were familiar to at least two FI staff members through their having worked in the industry or having studied the product and and production process. Staff were then asked to rank-order these technologies. For each algorithm empirically constructed, employing a sub-set of the candidate influencing factors, the resulting indices were compared with this intuitive ordering. The final selection includes four descriptors of products, and three which apply to the production process. We make the assumption (to be varified later) that these factors indicate activities

---

[5]Woodward, Joan, Industrial Organization: Theory and Practice (Oxford, England: Oxford University Press, 1965).

which must be performed in a new location when the technology is transferred. They are system-specific in the sense in which Hall & Johnson use that term.[6]

3. Index Definition

The factors selected relate to the following phenomena:

Product variables:

Technical difference among products of competing suppliers (S_d)

Technology content of service (T_s)

Extent of suppliers' effort to evolve improved product technology (E_t)

Process variables:

Production system (P_s)

Material form (M_f)

Quality maintenance (Q_m)

The algorithm employed for computing the index, I_t, is then expressed as

$$I_t = (S_d \times T_s \times E_t)\ (P_s \times M_f \times Q_m)$$

Our scaling rules and computational algorithm derive from the findings of Stevens and other students of psychophysics, that perceived intensity of a stimulus increases as some power of the stimulus. If observers are asked to use a descriptive scale such as high, medium or low to rate a stimulus, they tend to treat it as a ratio scale. It has also been found that in combining several perceptions, more appropriate results are produced by using multiplication rather than addition.

Consequently, in applying this and various other algorithms tested, the team members were asked to rate product and process elements on a four point adjectival scale - High, Moderate, Low or Negligible - according to a set of judgmental criteria provided to them as a result of earlier "brain-storming". These ratings were converted to numerical values using a ratio scale (8, 4, 2, 1).

[6] Hall, G.R., and R.E. Johnson, op. cit.

Once the criteria are developed, this approach is very practical since evaluators assign values rapidly without dithering over marginal differences. Efficiency was an important consideration because we calculated index numbers many times trying different sets of elements before settling on the present group. The definitions of the elements finally selected, and criteria which were employed in making the judgment, are detailed in the following paragraphs.

3.1 Product Descriptors

(1) S_d - Technical difference among products of competing suppliers.

This factor was chosen on the assumption that extent of technical difference is related to the state of maturity of the products. If the differences are large, the product technology has not yet "settled down".

Rating	Interpretation	Examples
Negligible - 1 point	Competing products are fungible, differences are matters of taste or style.	Commodity chemicals Most consumer disposables
Low - 2	Differences among competing products are noticeable i.e., product uniformity, but changing supplier does not require user to make significant change in methods.	Specialty plastics
Moderate - 4	Technical differences are large. Changing supplier involves a learning cost to user (reforming catalysts).	Reforming catalysts
High - 8	Unique product from each supplier.	

(2) T_s - Service Technological Content

This factor is intended to measure the technological content of the service which accompanies the product. Service can range from the provision of simple written directions, through training of service maintenance personnel, to assistance from highly trained applications engineers.

Rating	Interpretation	Examples
Negligible - 1 point	Service consists of little more than written direction on package, or occurs only at time of initial contact between supplier and user.	Consumer disposables Basic chemicals
Low - 2	Product service - supplier maintains stock and spare parts, offers repair service, routine trouble shooting.	Automobiles Machine tools
Moderate - 4	Technical service - product service with laboratory or engineering support.	Specialty plastics
High - 8	Product development - supplier continues to interact with user to develop products tailored to his needs.	Custom-designed machinery--special purpose computers, construction equipment

(3) E_t - Technological evolution

This factor is concerned with the producer's efforts to obtain technologically differentiated products. Most industrial product research is of this nature and it is assumed that technological rivalry is most intense when a technology is evolving rapidly, and when the technology is sufficiently rich and complex to offer unexploited opportunities.

Rating	Interpretation	Examples
Negligible - 1 point	Little or no continuing effort.	Basic metals Most consumer goods
Low - 2	Product improvement - periodic reformulation and redesign or continuing effort to obtain marginal quality improvements.	Office machinery Synthetic fibers

Rating	Interpretation	Examples
Moderate - 4	Market development - continuing effort to extend product line or increase application.	Large computers
High - 8	New technology - continuing effort to introduce new technological concepts.	Solid state electronic components

3.2 Process Indicators

(1) P_s - Production system

This element is taken to indicate the technological content of the method of production used.

Rating	Interpretation	Examples
Unit/Small Batch - 1 point	Production of units to customers' requirements. Production of prototypes. Fabrication of large equipment in stages. Production of small batches to customers' orders.	Television transmitters Large electrical generators
Large Batch - 2 points	Production of large batches. Production of large batches on assembly lines. Intermittent production of chemicals in multipurpose plant.	Ready-made clothing Machine parts Paint
Combined - 4	Process production of crystalline substances, subsequently prepared for sale by standardized production methods. Production of components in large batches subsequently processed continuously.	Drugs

Rating	Interpretation	Examples
Mass - 8	Continuous flow production of liquids, gases, and crystalline substances. Mass production.	Petrochemicals, paper, cardboard boxes, nails, screws

(2) M_f - Material form

This factor is included to account for the fact that it is inherently simpler to process materials in bulk form (dimensional products) than it is to process discrete units.

Rating	Interpretation	Examples
Fluid - 1 point	Material is handled predominantly as fluid or free-flowing solid throughout production process.	Petrochemicals
Bulk - 2	Materials are handled largely as dimensional solids, or in bulk form.	Wire or film Nuts and bolts, or resistors
Integral - 4	Material is handled as integral units.	Automobile assembly

(3) Q_m - Quality maintenance

This factor is included on the assumption that expenditures for quality maintenance as a proportion of total product cost, are a measure of the difficulty of the production task. We use the term quality maintenance rather than the more usual quality control because we wish to include such cost items as the provision of dust-free atmosphere, as well as product and material testing.

Rating	Interpretation	Examples
Negligible - 1 point	Observe standardized manufacturing procedures with routine check of machine settings. Visual inspection of product. Good housekeeping procedures to avoid contamination.	Fertilizers Foodstuffs

Rating	Interpretation	Examples
Low - 2	As preceding but coupled with product inspection using go/ no-go gauges on statistical sample.	Machine parts
Moderate - 4	Continuous monitoring and adjustment of process equipment. May be coupled with "on-line" gauging of product.	Chemicals Active electronic components
High - 8	As preceding but coupled with performance testing of all products. Where necessary with careful control of operating environment.	Drugs Computer circuits

Calculation of Technology Index

The following table presents the index numbers calculated for some illustrative products and production processes.

TABLE OF TYPICAL INDICES

	Tech Diff.	Service	Evolution	Product rating	Product system	Mat. Form	Quality Maint.	Process Rating	Tech Index I_t	$\log_2 I_t$
Soft Drink	1	1	1	1	4	1	1	4	4	2
Spec. PVC	2	4	2	16	2	1	4	8	128	7
Ethylene	1	1	2	2	8	1	4	32	64	6
Film grade PVC	1	2	2	4	2	1	4	8	32	5
Vinyl film	1	1	2	2	4	2	4	32	128	7
Household Det.	1	1	2	2	4	1	1	4	8	3
Plywood	1	1	1	1	2	2	2	8	8	3
IC/LSF	8	8	8	512	2	4	8	64	32,768	15
Circuit Board	8	8	4	256	2	4	8	32	16,384	14
Lq. Comp.	8	4	4	128	1	4	8	32	4,096	12
N.C. Lathe	4	4	2	32	1	4	8	32	1,024	10
Auto assembly	2	2	2	8	2	4	2	16	128	7
TV assembly	2	2	2	8	2	4	2	16	128	7

4. Technology Spectrum

Based upon the technology measure or index previously described, we posit that a technological spectrum can be generated to describe the technological capability posssed by a single country. The independent variable will be the technology index while the dependent variable, for the purpose of discussion, could be revenue, value added, number of employees per industry, etc. Further research will be required to establish which dependent variable will be most appropriate. However, given two variables as a minimum, we can generate spectra for various countries.

We interpret the spectrum as describing the state of the nation's technological infrastructure and consequently its ability to accept a given new technology. If the technology lies well within the curve, then the nation has the required variety of skills and supporting industry in place. Transfer from another country may involve little more than transfer of working drawings and manufacturing direction. Transfer of technologies which lie at or near the curve is likely to be conditioned by a limiting resource. There will be a transfer cost associated with overcoming this limitation - supplying the resources or tailoring the technology to local capabilities. Alternatively, the transfer may be incomplete. Technologies which lie outside the spectrum are likely to require considerable subsidy from the transferring institution.

Constructing the national spectrum entails some problems because of variation of product and process mix within industries in a single country and among countries. The automobile industry includes not only the assembly of cars, which involves relatively low technology, but also the manufacture of engines, transmissions, etc., which are at a somewhat more complex level. The level of the automobile industry should clearly be higher in Germany and the United States than in countries which merely assemble imported parts. We do not yet know the appropriate level of aggregation to use. Similarly we are unsure as to whether the technological level of the whole country is an appropriate indicator to measure ease of transfer, or whether we must use a lower level of aggregation. Suppose a country has a high level because of a strong chemical industry; does this mean that it can readily absorb machine-tool technology? In practice this is not a very serious problem, because we must estimate levels by industry to construct the spectrum. What we would like to find is that we can use the technological level of a few key industries to determine a country's absorptive capability.

5. The Course of Future Research

At the present time we are continuing with case studies and data analysis addressed to clarifying the uncertainties raised in the previous section. This research consists primarily of the accumulation and examination of detailed information regarding the circumstances, participants, components, and outcome of individual instances of international technology transfer.

As a result of the earlier work, we are coming to realize that we must extend the Vernon sequence beyond characteristics of product and manufacturing process. Consequently, extending the scope of the investigation toward more nebulous considerations, we intend to formulate a method of incorporating measures of systematic management -- a social technology which we contend is an equally essential dimension of successful technology transfer.

TECHNOLOGY TRANSFER IN THE BRITISH TEXTILE INDUSTRY

Lindsey A. Anderson and Ron Johnston

Liberal Studies in Science
Manchester University

The material for this case study of technology transfer in the British textile industry has been extracted from information collected for a larger study concerned with the transition of this industry from a craft base to a scientific base. The emphasis will therefore be towards establishing the role played by technology transfer in this transition.

The development of an industry from a craft towards the adoption of a scientific base involves a number of socio-economic factors as well as technological factors. However, for the purposes of this case study technological developments are of primary importance.

Outline of the Study

The most striking change observed has been in the structure of the 'textile industry'. In 1900 the range of activities encompassed by this term comprised three major fibre processing industries - spinning, weaving and knitting, the complementary process of textile furnishing and the manufacture of textile processing machinery. Today, however, the 'textile industry' has been extended to include such additional areas as fibre manufacture, non-woven fabric production and warp knitting. Therefore in considering innovations in the textile industry in the last seventy-five years it is useful to distinguish between 'external innovations' which have been developed primarily outside the traditional textile industry and 'internal innovations' which have occurred within the traditional processing areas.

A further important distinction is that between product

innovations and process innovations. Here we are concerned mainly with developments which have occurred in the methods employed in the production of textile materials and are therefore interested primarily in process innovations. However, the plant employed in the processing of textile fibres is a product of the textile machine manufacturing industry and therefore consideration must be given to product innovations in this sector insofar as they have contributed to developments in textile processing.

In this study internal innovations will be further classified as (1) innovations which involve a departure from contemporary practice; (2) innovations which involve an extension of contemporary practice; (3) innovations which involve sophistication of contemporary plant, this class of development being synonymous with incremental product innovations in the manufacture of textile processing machinery.

The Innovations

It is therefore proposed to examine both external and internal innovations which have occurred in the textile industry with a view to assessing the extent to which these have depended upon technology transfer. The definition of technology transfer used here is "the application of a technology to a purpose other than that for which it was designed."

External Innovations

The major external innovations which have occurred can be identified as (a) the development of man-made fibres, this falling into two sectors - the development of regenerated fibres and the development of synthetic fibres; (b) the development of non-woven fabrics; (c) the development of warp knit fabrics. These will be dealt with in turn.

(a) The development of man-made fibres

The major innovations which have occurred in the development of man-made fibres are listed in Table 1. These developments fall into two categories - new fibres and new production techniques.

Table 1. Innovations in the Production of Man-Made Fibres

YEAR	NEW FIBRES	DEVELOPMENTS IN PRODUCTION TECHNIQUES
1885	Nitrocellulose Rayon	
	Cupramonium Rayon	
	Viscose Rayon	
1900		Topham Box
1912		Napper Spinning Bath
1918		Staple Fibre
1926		Delustred Yarn
1938	Nylon	
1939		High Tenacity Rayon
	Vinyon	
	Saran	
1945	Acrylic	Bulked/Textured Yarns
1950		Dope Dyed Fibre
1954	Tricel	
1961	Elastomers	
1964		Split Film Process
1968	Heterofil Nylon	

The first man-made fibres to be produced were regenerated cellulosic fibres which could be used as substitutes for silk.

Three major processes have been developed for the commercial production of artificial silk (rayon) - the nitrocellulose process, the cupramonium process and the viscose process.

Commercial production of rayon using the nitro-cellulose process was first undertaken in France by Count Hilaire Bernigaud de Chardonnet, a professional inventor, and was the result of a conscious effort on his part to produce a substitute for silk, although his research owed nothing to existing textile interests seeking such a substitute. Indeed there is little evidence that the textile industry even recognized the need to find a substitute for silk.

"Chardonnet Silk" made its first major appearance at the Paris Exhibition of 1871 where it attracted a good deal of attention, and from this time on, enterprising textile firms began to take an interest in the use of this material.

It is interesting to note here that the process used by Chardonnet was virtually identical to a process patented some months earlier by J. W. Swann for the extrusion of nitrocellulose through a series of holes or jets to produce filament material for the incandescent lamp. In fact the second process used in the commercial production of rayon, the cuprammonium process, was first used in the production of filaments for the incandescent lamp.

The process was based on the discovery of a Swiss chemist, Schwiezer, that cellulose could be dissolved in a solution of copper oxide and ammonium, and in 1890 a French patent was taken out for the production of artificial silk using Schwiezer's reagent, but with no immediate results. The process was, however, used by a German chemist and an Austrian engineer in the production of electric lamp filaments. Their business prospered and they eventually turned their attention to adapting the process and their production techniques to the manufacture of rayon.

The third and most successful process for the production of rayon, the viscose process, was the result of work done in the paper manufacturing industry by two British chemists, Cross and Bevan on the chemistry of cellulose. Their process for the production of viscose was patented in 1892, viscose being used initially in solid form to produce small moulded articles.

Subsequently, Charles Steam working for the Zurich Incandescent Lamp Co, combined the viscose patent of Cross and Bevan with Swann's process for the extrusion of nitrocellulose to produce filament material for lamps. Realizing the possibilities for producing rayon fibre by this method he collaborated with Cross in setting up the Viscose Spinning Syndicate to develop the technique for spinning viscose fibre.

Having once been successfully developed, the production of rayon increased steadily (see Fig. 1) this sustained growth being attributed mainly to innovations introduced by the fibre manufacturers which modified the product in such a way that it could compete in an ever widening range of existing textile markets. For example, rayon was initially used mainly in the hosiery trade. However, with the introduction of staple fibre the traditional cotton spinning and weaving sectors became potential outlets for the fibre. Similarly the development of high tenacity rayon permitted its use in the production of heavy-duty, industrial fabrics.

Development of the other fibres listed in Table 1 has resulted from interest aroused in the chemical industry in the possibility of producing purely synthetic fibres.

In the early 1920's Staudinger prepared and studied a material, polyoxymethylene, which he found to have many characteristics of natural cellulose. Largely as a result of his work it came to be recognized that the chemical process known as polymerisation could lead to the formation of long chain molecules from which we now know all fibrous materials are composed. During the same period studies of the x-ray diffraction patterns produced by fibrous materials indicated a type of crystalline structure, thus distinguishing them from the resinous substances which were the most usual products of the polymerisation process. This was followed in 1928 by the DuPont Company of America undertaking an extensive programme of fundamental research into the synthesis and characteristics of large molecules which could be used to build up fibre materials. They selected V. H. Carothers to take charge of this research and it was his team that produced the first truly synthetic fibre, nylon.

The success of Carother's work and the practical information which had become available from DuPont's exploitation of nylon triggered off a wave of research activity throughout the world into other possible synthetic materials which resulted in the succeeding years in the production of Vinyan, a copolymer of vinyl chloride and vinyl acelate from the American Viscose Corporation; Saran, a copolymer of vinyl chloride and vinylidene chloride from Dow Chemicals; Polyester from an English chemist

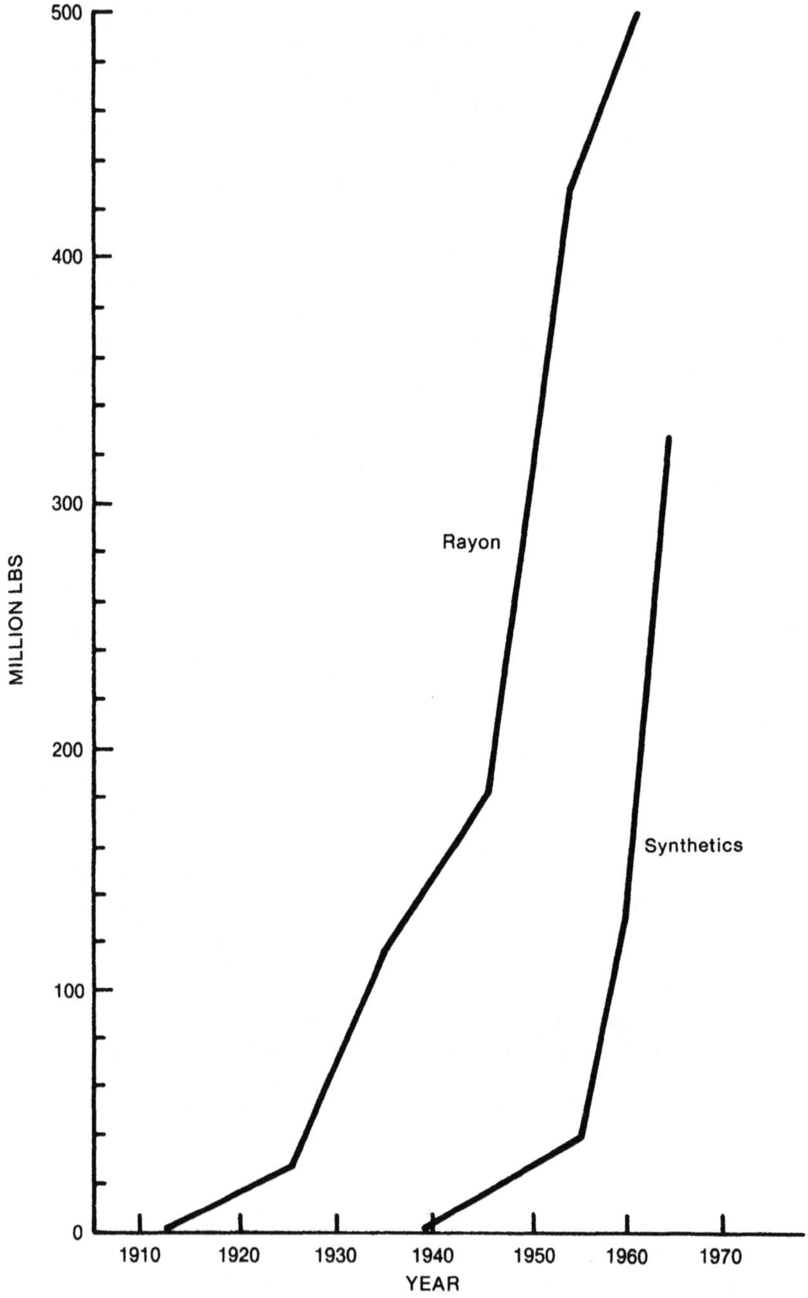

Figure 1. Production of Man-Made Fibres

Whinfield working for Calico Printers Association; and Acrylic fibre - Orlon, a copolymer of acrylonitrile from DuPont.

As was the case with viscose the sustained growth of the synthetic fibres industry resulted from the adaption of the products to existing textile markets.

(b) Non-Woven Fabrics

The term 'non-woven' is used to describe fabrics produced by methods other than the traditional spinning, weaving and knitting processes, the methods employed being centered upon the chemical or mechanical bonding of a fibrous web.

Some types of non-woven fabric have been in existence for as long as the textile industry, these being based on the natural felting properties of wool and hair fibres. The designation of non-woven fabrics as an 'external' innovation is justified by the fact that the growth which has taken place in this sector of the textile industry has been mainly due to chemical, paper and polymer manufacturers entering the field, and applying to the manufacturers of non-woven fabrics their respective technologies.

The oldest method of producing non-woven fabrics is needle punching, this process involving the needling of a fibrous web with hooked or barbed needles in such a way that the web becomes bonded by drawing groups of fibres from one surface of the web to the other, and has been employed since the nineteenth century in the production of padding materials from jute, sisal and hair fibres. However, although some development did take place with regard to this technique it was not until the advent of chemically bonded non-woven fabrics that growth in this sector began.

Chemically bonded non-woven fabrics are produced by bonding a web of fibres with an adhesive bonding agent. The first such fabric was produced in the United States around 1952 and was the partial result of a search for new materials and methods brought about by the shortages of wartime involving the adaption and marriage of both textiles and paper making techniques for the use of waste and shoddy fibres. This first fabric was widely adopted by the clothing industry for use as interlining.

The first such fabric to be produced in the United Kingdom was made by Courtaulds and British Cellophane, cellulose xenthate being used as the bonding agent for staple rayon fibre.

As the potential market for chemically bonded non-woven fabrics came to be realized, interest in their production was stimulated among chemical manufacturers, fibre manufacturers and paper manufacturers. Since then a wide variety of bonding agents have been introduced from the chemical and plastics industries, for example, water based emulsions, thermoplastic fibres and thermoplastic/thermosetting powder. Indeed progress has been largely dependent upon close cooperation between manufacturers, chemical manufacturers and machine builders to obtain the desired results for a specific end use.

(c) Warp-knit Fabric

As was the case with the non-woven fabric industry, the modern warp knitting industry has arisen from a very small and very old sector of the textile industry. The basic principle involved in warp knitting is the use of warp threads, one to each needle, in contrast to weft knitting which in its simplest form makes fabric from a single thread. For many years warp frames were used mainly in the lace making trade; however, lace manufacture as a separate industry with its own machines based on a different principle and warp knitting remained as a very minor branch of the hosiery trade. The modern growth of the industry was stimulated by the application by Sir James Morton of Morton Sundow Fabrics Ltd. of the superiority of the warp knitting principle over that of the loom in high speed fabric production and he, with his colleague Frank Coldroyd, introduced in 1931 the fly needle frame which could attain remarkable speeds of 1000 stitches per minute. However, in order to operate at these speeds it is necessary to employ yarns with a high degree of strength and regularity, both of these properties being exhibited by man-made filament yarns, and the subsequent rapid growth of the warp knitting sector has resulted from the marriage of these two innovations.

The progress of warp knitting since the 1939/45 war is one of the most notable developments in modern textile manufacture. In the 1960's warp knitting was the fastest growing sector of the British hosiery and knitwear trade. Between 1958 and 1963 annual output amounted to nearly 25 million pounds and by 1969 this had risen to 70 million pounds, a high percentage being produced from man-made fibres. This remarkable expansion has gone hand in hand with a high level of innovative activity with regard to the adoption of the basic warp knitting frame to the production of an ever widening range of products. As new markets were sought by the warp knit manufacturers, the needs of the industry were being met by the machine manufacturers.

Internal Innovations

Table 2 lists chronologically and according to the categories previously outlined major technological developments within the textile industry since the turn of the century.

Table 2. Innovations in the Textile Industry - Internal

YEAR	DEPARTURE FROM CONTEMPORARY PRACTICE	EXTENSION OF CONTEMPORARY PRACTICE	SOPHISTICATION OF PLANT
Spinning			
1870		Ring Frame	
1945	Centrifugal Pot Spinning		
1948		High Draft Systems	
1949		Direct Spinning Systems	Nullotey Attachment
		Shirley Autodoffer	Pneumatic Waste Removal
1951		Paper Autoleveler	Large Package Spinning
1958		SRRL Card	
1962		Pneumatic High Production Card	
1965	Unconventional Spinning Systems - 1. Open End Spinning 2. T.N.D. Twistless Yarns 3. Pneumatic Spin Twisting		
Weaving			
1894		Automatic Loom	
1950	Shuttleless Looms	Wira Auto Reaching in Machine	
		Unifil Auto Pirn Winder	Photo Electric Warp Stop Motions
		High Speed Warping Frame	Improved Shuttle Design
Knitting			
1949		Automatic Welting Device	
		Automatic Rib Transfer	Electronic Patterning Control
	Circular Full Fashion Frame		

It should first of all be noted that this table reflects only a handful of examples of 'sophistication' innovations. Certain difficulties are encountered in isolating innovations in this category. For example, although the underlying principles have remained unchanged, the automatic loom of the 1970's differs from that of 1900 with respect to such features as the materials incorporated in its manufacture and its speed of operation. Furthermore, every new model produced by every machine manufacturer incorporates alterations and improvements with respect to such things as the picking and shedding mechanisms or stop motions. However, the diffusion of such innovations is largely dependent on the level of capital investment in the industry, this in turn being related to the economic performance of the industry, capital investment being more likely to result from a good economic performance.

The table indicates that in both spinning and weaving, developments have occurred which fall into the departure category. However, some qualification is necessary here, as although such unconventional spinning methods have been the subject of discussion for many years, it is only since the mid 1960's that such equipment has been available commercially. Moreover, a statistical survey of the type of plant employed in the industry throughout the century (Table 3) gives no indication of their extensive use. This applies also to centrifugal pot spinning. However, it is interesting to note that in this instance, the method of spinning employed involves a transfer of technology from the man-made fibre industry to the traditional sector.

A similar qualification applies to the shuttleless loom, a survey of the plant employed in weaving indicating that only 0.4% of total weaving capacity in 1970 was of this type in the U.K. These 'departure' innovations have therefore made little impact to date.

Turning to the 'extension innovations,' the first point to be noted from the survey of processing equipment in place is the low rate of diffusion in these sectors. Although the ring frame was first introduced in 1970 and the automatic loom in 1894 it has only been within the last fifteen years that these have been widely adopted by the industry. Moreover, four out of the seven innovations listed for spinning - high draft spinning systems, direct spinning systems, the Shirley Autodoffer and the Paper Autoleveler, and one of three listed for weaving - the automatic pirn winder, presuppose the use of the ring spindle and the automatic loom respectively, their rate of diffusion therefore being dependent on the installation of these systems.

As regards the origins of these innovations, with the exception of two, the Shirley Autodoffer and the Wira Automatic

Table 3. Equipment in Use: Spinning and Weaving Sectors

(A) COTTON INDUSTRY

	1913	1927	1937	1949	1957	1970
			(Million Spindles)			
SPINNING PLANT						
Mule	42.5	43.8	28.1	19.1	8.7	0.3
Ring	10.4	13.5	10.7	10.1	9.5	3.3

	1913	1930	1936	1985	1962	1970
			(Thousand Looms)			
WEAVING PLANT						
Non-Auto	786	693	489	294	105	41
Auto	-	-	15	39	50	37
Shuttleless	-	-	-	-	-	3

(B) WOOL TEXTILE INDUSTRY

	1918	1938	1943	1969	1971
		(Million Spindles)			
SPINNING PLANT (WOOLLEN)					
Mule	29	2.2	2.2	1.1	0.8
Ring (Continuous)	0.4	0.5	0.7	1.3	1.3
SPINNING PLANT (WORSTED)					
Mule	0.3	0.3	0.4	1.7	1.4
Ring (Continuous)	3.0	2.9	2.8		
		(Thousand Looms)			
WEAVING PLANT					
Non-Auto	114	77	78	17	12
Auto	-	-	-	11	9

Reaching-in Machine both of which have resulted from the efforts of the Textile Research Associations, the innovations listed have emerged from within the industry largely as a result of cooperation between the manufacturer and the machine builders to fulfil an existing need. For example high draft systems and direct spinning systems replace the traditional six or seven drafting stages with only one or two thereby shortening the spinning process; the autodoffer mechanised the previously manual operation of doffing full packages from spinning frames and the automatic pimwinder eliminates the need for a separate winding department within the weaving shed.

As was the case with the spinning and weaving sectors of the textile industry, the number of major innovations in the hosiery and knitwear sector falling into the 'departure' and 'extension' categories has been limited and have originated within the industry. The one 'departure' innovation, the circular full fashion frame, involves the application of techniques previously employed in the hosiery and weft knit fabric areas to the manufacture of fully fashioned garments, such production having previously been carried out on flat bed machines, while the 'extension' innovations have resulted from the need to automate previously manual operations.

The overall economic picture obtained of this sector of the industry during the twentieth century is one of a growth industry, with both the level of employment and the level of output increasing (Table 4). Under these circumstances, a high level of investment may mean that 'sophistication' innovations assume primary importance.

In this area it appears that there has been a high level of activity with regard to such factors as speed of operation, increased production through the introduction of multiple feeds and increased patterning scope, a development involving the application of electronic controls to patterning.

At this point it is appropriate to comment on the extent to which the development of man-made fibres has affected these traditional processing areas. Figure 2 illustrates the respective levels of fibre consumption, and shows that although these fibres have been adopted to a considerable extent in the cotton and wool textile industries, their major impact has been in the hosiery and knitwear sector where man-made fibres now represent the principle raw material.

Conclusions

It is now possible to draw some general conclusions regarding firstly, the level of innovative activity and secondly, the role

Table 4. Statistics: Hosiery and Knitwear Industry

(A) PRODUCTION

	YEAR			
	1924	1937	1951	1969
Value (£ Million)	43.9	46.1	183.5	424.0
Product				
Stockings/Socks (Thsd. Doz. Prs.)	25.4	35.9	40.7	50.5
Underwear (Thsd. Doz. Prs.)	6.5	12.7	11.5	17.2
Outerwear (Thsd. Doz. Prs.)	4.1	4.9	4.8	9.1
Fabric (Thsd. Lbs.)	-	-	41.5	141.3

(B) EMPLOYMENT

YEAR	AVERAGE NUMBER EMPLOYED (Thousand)
1924	91.6
1933	113.5
1937	119.4
1948	97.8
1954	122.8
1963	124.5
1970	136.6

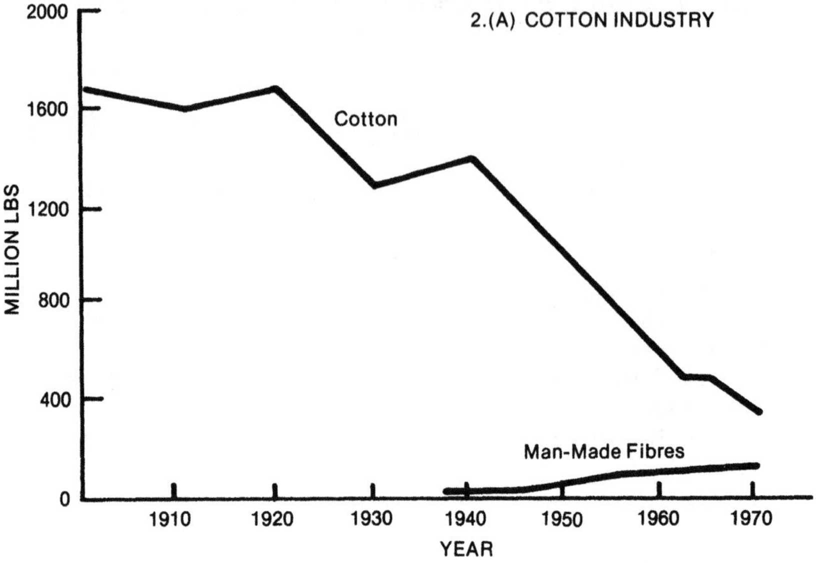
2.(A) COTTON INDUSTRY
Cotton
Man-Made Fibres
MILLION LBS
2000
1600
1200
800
400
0
1910
1920
1930
1940
1950
1960
1970
YEAR

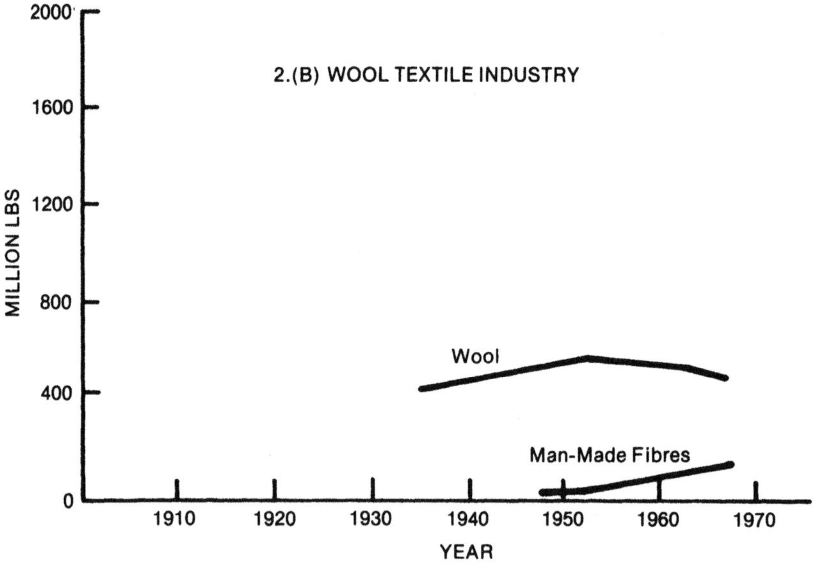
2.(B) WOOL TEXTILE INDUSTRY
Wool
Man-Made Fibres
MILLION LBS
2000
1600
1200
800
400
0
1910
1920
1930
1940
1950
1960
1970
YEAR

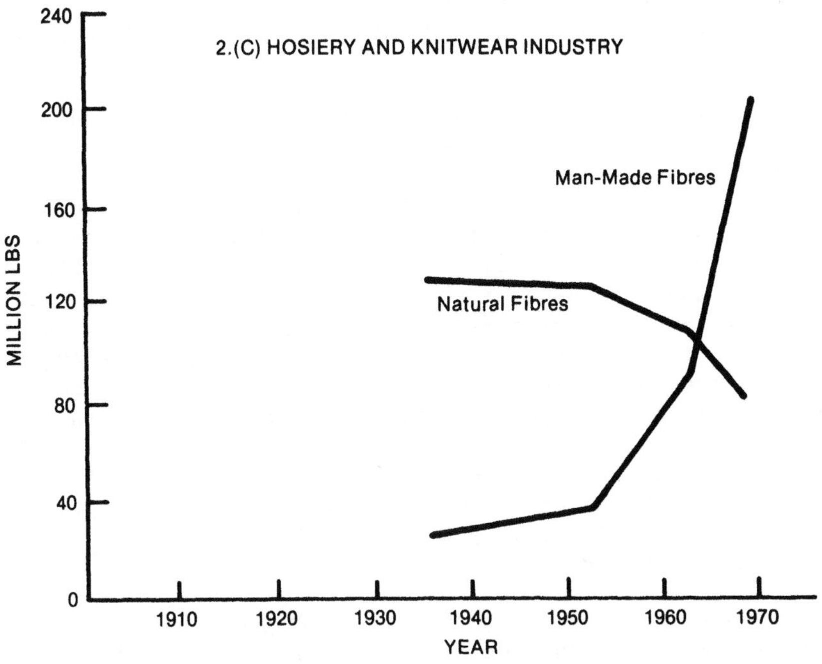

Figure 2. Consumption of Man-Made Fibres

of technology transfer in the technological development of the textile industry, in both the traditional and the new sectors of the industry.

If we consider first the traditional sector of the industry it appears that in all three of the sectors considered, spinning, weaving and knitting, the level of innovative activity with regard to the introduction of new processing methods has been fairly low; also in the first two sectors this has been accompanied by a poor economic record, the cotton industry having been in decline since the beginning of the first World War and the wool textile industry having remained static. Several factors have contributed to this situation. At various times both the cotton industry and the wool textile industry have found themselves challenged by foreign competition in world markets which they were unable to meet, and were consequently forced to concentrate their efforts in the home market. In the case of the cotton industry this has been aggravated by a rising level of imports of cotton goods to this country which has resulted in a sharp decline in the industry.

It has been suggested that the highly fragmented structure of the industry and the existence of a large number of small specialised units has hindered the industry's economic and technological development. Size is not generally held to be a causal factor for inventive activity, but this is usually related to the assumption of a high level of competition in a growth industry. However, it seems likely that in this instance the fragmented structure of the industry and the contraction which it has suffered have together hindered both economic recovery and innovative activity and that these factors have consequently restricted the opportunity for technology within these sectors.

On the other hand, within the new sectors of the industry the development of both man-made fibres and non-woven fabrics has involved a considerable degree of technology from such industries as electric lamp manufacturing, paper manufacturing and chemicals, while in all three cases, man-made fibres, non-woven fabrics and warp knitting there has been a fairly high level of innovative activity, this being related to the search for new markets and uses for their products in different fields of textiles and centering largely on the development of their own specific technologies.

In summarizing the situation it appears that such development as has occurred within the British textile industry with regard to the adoption of a scientific base has not been via the traditional sectors of the industry. Neither would it appear to have resulted from the direct impact of science on the industry. Rather, it appears to have occurred through the medium of other science-based industries, for example the chemical and polymer industries, and the transfer of technology from these areas to the production of textile materials, this being apparent both in the development of man-made fibres and non-woven fibres.

Hence, it appears that a vital role is played by technology transfer in the transition from a craft to a science based industry, through the substitution of technologies developed in other science based industries for existing technologies.

THE CRITICAL ROLE OF COMMUNICATION IN TECHNOLOGY TRANSFER

George W. Tressel

Battelle Memorial Institute
Columbus, Ohio 43201

Despite our best efforts the process of industrial technology transfer largely depends upon a critical and random diffusion of ideas into the private sector. In the United States some 18 billion dollars per year are spent by the federal government on research and development. A primary justification of this expenditure is its contribution to the solution of contemporary problems...energy, pollution, transportation, social planning, etc. Yet the fact remains that the diffusion process is halting at best, and a broad gap exists between the language and goals of the research community and the day-to-day trials of the industrial environment.

The information systems of the scientific and academic communities are largely self-centered. They provide an effective means to document and store the results of today's research ...as well as indexing and retrieval techniques which make this knowledge available for future research activity. However the major federal information systems are far less effective in assisting with the selection and transfer of new ideas into the industrial sector.

The problem is far more difficult. Instead of a concentrated and well-defined group of peers with similar goals and language, the "target audience" is large and scattered, poorly defined, and comprises a broad spectrum of goals and interests. Its principal information source is likely to be trade gossip and salesmen rather than technical journals, and its decisions are weighed against markets, costs, politics and prejudice...as well as technical virtue.

It is our contention that inappropriate language and distribution channels present a formidable communication obstacle which should be recognized and investigated. We believe that in the industrial environment ideas must be selected and "sold" to potential users in much the same manner that new products are developed and sold to potential customers. Addressing this need the United States Department of Commerce, through a joint effort between the Economic Development Administration and the National Technical Information Service (NTIS), contracted with the Communication Research Laboratory of Battelle Memorial Institute to conduct an exploratory study to develop and demonstrate the effect of better communication on the industrial utilization of one particular backlog of technology, the enormous storehouse of government-originated and owned patents. Here is a body of technology that has already passed a preliminary review (both technical and legal) and which NTIS felt sure held great untapped industrial value. The communication system which resulted proved highly successful and, we believe, carries strong implications regarding both the appropriate agents and techniques for technology transfer.

Battelle's hypothesis suggested that a basic weakness in the technology transfer process centers about the "communication mismatch". There is a critical difference in language, perspective, and evaluation criteria that separates R&D personnel from industrial management. Unless this communication gulf can be bridged, new technology must diffuse slowly and haltingly between the two communities.

Battelle proposed to explore this hypothesis by developing a system to (1) identify patent technology of potential value to the industrial sector, and (2) develop an initial system to communicate this technology to industrial management in the language and through the channels with which they are familiar.

The contract called for exploration of this communication system and evidence regarding its effectiveness and acceptance (or rejection) by industrial representatives. First, we proposed selection by people who know the needs of industry. Battelle is one of the world's largest contract research organizations--an independent technical firm comprising thousands of sophisticated research workers in almost every imaginable field, ideally equipped to evaluate technology and its potential for use by industry. However, useful technology is not enough! The key to effective technology transfer rests on communication; one cannot adopt what one does not know.

Furthermore, effective communication must reach the right person, the industrial manager who controls the course of his company's development, seeks new technology and competitive position, and who makes the decisions regarding adoption or rejection of new ideas. It was Battelle's premise that new ideas must be publicized and sold in a manner analogous to the introduction of new products. Following the same analogy, the new ideas must have credibility. They must be selected, evaluated, and presented so as to more than hold their own in the market place of new ideas. And they must be communicated effectively, using the kind of channels that reach an audience of top industrial management and presenting the finest government technology in the language and style appropriate to this audience.

Obviously highly technical descriptions and technical communication channels would be both inappropriate and ineffective in reaching this goal. An innovative approach to communicating the technology was called for and developed over the course of a one-year exploratory study. The results of this project far exceeded the initial expectations.

In this initial exploration it was expected that it might prove possible to generate serious interest in one or two patents, but it seemed most unlikely that any serious discussions of licensing would develop during the time that an initial system was being developed. In fact, however, industry has shown overwhelming enthusiasm for the new approach, and even some licensing occurred. A small initial test group of patents covered a variety of subject areas, and the first six months of communication effort produced definite industrial interest in almost all of the test group. Thousands of patent reprints were mailed in response to requests from companies throughout both the United States and other countries. Most of the requests have come from industrial managers, many at the level of President, Vice President, and Corporate Planner.

By the end of the demonstration project some 65 companies were undertaking detailed consideration of the new technologies and 21 organizations had requested information on specific licensing conditions. At least one firm had completed a licensing agreement, another was conducting a cost analysis preliminary to adopting the new technology and there was indication of several others approaching this stage. The success of this project is significant not only to the handling and licensing of government patents but also to a multitude of related questions of technology transfer and the communication of new ideas.

THE BASIC PROBLEMS OF COMMUNICATING NEW TECHNOLOGY

We believe that there are two principal blocks to successful technology information transfer.

1. Decisions are made at a management level where time is at a premium and interest is general rather than technical, therefore credibility of the material is critical. As we begin to sell new ideas it is vitally important that our potential customers come to believe in the quality of the ideas, to believe that they are worth exploring even though many may not relate directly to today's problems and may, in fact, often be far afield from the immediate area of interest. We believe that managers at the level where major decisions are made have a broad and far-ranging curiosity, that they appreciate the synergism of good ideas regardless of their direct pertinence, and that such persons are eager to explore new material if they feel that it had serious potential. It is therefore more important to have a high proportion of good ideas even if a few potential "gems" are missed along the way.

2. Good material is often lost in the "paper blizzard". Persons at the management level are bombarded with paper. Their time is valuable, and the competition for attention is intense. They demand a concise, articulate presentation, and they respond to brevity, force, and attractive display. It was our challenge to select the best material, then package and present it in a most concise and attractive manner through channels which would effectively reach the management audience.

The system which we developed includes four stages: selection of material; "packaging" for the particular audience; dissemination through appropriate distribution channels; and successive filtering of inquiries.

Selection

Review

Determine whether or not the technology described in recent patents warrants industrial consideration--a technical content decision, with no attempt to determine whether the patents are legally sound licensing prospects.

Patents were grossly categorized into subject areas corresponding to departments at Battelle and distributed to their technical representatives for review. These departments include some 1200 available professional scientists, engaged in almost every area of applied research. Thus, they are not only in contact with industrial needs, but also have a feel for the practical development difficulty which may be involved.

In each case we allowed only a half hour for review and this initial decision. If there were doubt, the idea was rejected. We were not concerned with the ones we might miss--only that the remaining items had value.

Management Summary

Prepare a brief description of the idea and its merits.

Promising patents were discussed with other staff members. If the reviewers found a particular patent acceptable, they prepared a management summary form for the Battelle Communication Research Laboratory. This form provided, in elementary technical terms, a capsule statement of the idea, possible applications, and advantages over current techniques (as well as possible problems). We allowed one to two hours for this process.

The rejection rate was quite significant. Our initial test included patents from three agencies. Acceptance averaged 1 in 7. This experience reflects a limited sample, of course, and we are not sure that it can be extrapolated to larger samples and other areas.

Design of the Basic Management Bulletin

We had initially explored means to exploit a number of existing communication channels. In each case we were able to take advantage of established mechanisms and patterns to reach the type of person who is our "target". It was our belief that a wide variety of such channels are available, already established and proven at great expense and effort. It is both wasteful and ineffective to attempt to develop a parallel channel; say, by establishing a new mailing list.

For dissemination we chose to "piggy-back" our messages, distributing basic material to editors of magazines commonly read by managers and through "newsletters" specifically designed for inclusion with established news material or mailing to established audiences. In every such attempt, the response has been heartening. Magazine editors have received our material with enthusiasm. The resulting publication has varied, but in all cases it has produced a visible response from our audience.

Design News ran five articles based upon Basic Management Bulletins. These articles are keyed to a response card asking for further information. The first two articles alone produced over 600 reports; a response which the editor of *Design News* considers excellent.

Still more significant, we believe, is the level of the response. A significant proportion represents the managers and decision makers we seek. Program publicity and general articles have appeared in numerous publications circulated to R&D management such as: *ALERT*, *Industry Week*, *Trademark and Copyright Journal*, *Boardroom Reports*, *Take Five*, *Washington Science Trends*, *R&D News Report*, *Inside R&D*, and *TWA Ambassador*.

The first publication to be actually circulated and tested was a newsletter. Here again we sought to take advantage of an already established and identified audience--"piggy-backing" on a mailing of the Metals and Ceramics Information Center. We chose items generally related to the materials field, but included several items quite far removed--one relating to bacteria counting, for example.

The newsletter was accompanied by a "bingo" reply card asking for further information. The resulting 12% response was far beyond our expectation and we are still getting responses--even though the mailing occurred two years ago! One-third of the response was from President, Vice President, or Manager! A significant portion of the responses included highly favorable comments:

"The format is great and a big help for the less technically oriented"	(Co. President)
"Tech-Highlights is an excellent format!"	(Co. President)
"Absolutely A-1. Action oriented, clear pictorial, uncrowded information. Thanks"	(Consultant)
"Great idea"	(Co. President)
"Enjoyed reviewing bulletin #1, look forward to seeing your future bulletins"	(Co. Exec. VP)

"Very good, succinct reviews"	(Mgr. Accident Resch)
"An excellent improvement in your services"	(Q C Mgr.)
"This is a very valuable service and it is greatly appreciated. Thank you!"	(Patent Attorney)

Every idea was of serious interest--even those that we considered marginal (the bacteria counter and heparin treatment, for example).

A second test, to verify the validity of this experience, was even more encouraging. In May 1973 a similar mailing was sent to an NTIS mailing list. The results were still more impressive in terms of the management audience reached, probably reflecting the selectivity of this paid (approximately thirty-five dollars per year) subscription.

Responses averaged 18% and of these two-thirds were President, Vice President, or Manager! In both tests of such mailing we received a large percentage of hand-written notes congratulating us on the program, format, ideas, and style. There can be no question that industry welcomes new ideas and the NTIS program.

Filtering

It was obvious at an early state that our hypothesis regarding the "communication gap" is valid. Both the quantity of response and the overwhelming favorable comments indicate that industrial management is seriously seeking new technology, and is highly appreciative of material which is responsive to their needs and interests.

As a result, we turned our attention toward extending the communication system. It was clearly necessary to develop a response system which would continue to supply detailed information as needed, and make the transition from general interest to specific discussions of the technology and its licensing potential. At the same time we tried to act as a buffer between the inventor and the inquiry--building a system that answers and encourages while it filters out the casual interest.

Inquiries were separated into four categories according to the nature of the request, and the response called for: requests for (a) general information; (b) idea support; (c) additional technical information; and (d) licensing information. A standard response format was adopted for each of these areas.

Each response was designed to both answer the request and encourage further consideration. While initial response was mechanical, promising inquiries were followed by personal phone calls and detailed support. Throughout the process we attempted to sustain interest by supplying a summary of recent work, the latest state of development, related activity, publications references, etc.

During this minimal exploratory project, over twenty organizations were referred to government agencies for discussions of licensing terms. Thus the basic need for "targeted" communication seems well demonstrated. We believe, however, that there is a further need for personal intervention by professional "facilitators" when the industrial manager begins to seriously weigh problems of cost and technical difficulty. We know far too little about the role of the technology "champion" within industry and problems which he must overcome. Past research has been retrospective and subject to the euphoria of hindsight. It is also easier in retrospect to examine successes than failures, so we cannot presume to judge the validity of industry's decision process in this area.

We do know the complexity of the review and the elaborate trade-offs of cost, difficulty and expectation. Without far more detailed (and statistical) knowledge of the decision process, we can only speculate on the potential impact of technical assistance during this stage.

A communication system of the kind described here could provide both the means to identify companies at this stage and the opportunity to follow their deliberations. This seems a very promising direction for future research.

REGULATORY BARRIERS TO TECHNOLOGICAL INNOVATION: SOME EXAMPLES

Stephen Feinman

Gellman Research Associates, Inc.
Philadelphia, PA

Government regulation of the marketplace is as old as government itself. Inscriptions on clay tell of Urukagina, the King of Lagash on the banks of the Euphrates, who set forth prices and wages as well as other economic matters around 2425 B.C.[1] A thousand years later, the rulers of Babylon were fixing interest rates, requiring contracts and trying civil cases of economic disputes.[2] An early example of regulatory intervention which may have helped as well as hindered technological innovation in the Edict on Price, promulgated by the Roman Emperor Diocletian in A.D. 301.[3] The edict set the wages and prices to be paid for the production of commodities. In addition, the edict required that producers sell the cities of the empire certain minimum amounts of food, hardware and fuel. Penalties for not complying with the edict included: castration, crucificion or being sold into slavery.

A cursory analysis of the supply and demand functions of the Roman Empire indicates that capital saving innovations might lead to increased profitability under such wage and price controls. In addition, to a lesser degree, labor saving technological change might also be expected to increase the profitability of these goods. Under such duress as the economic edicts of the emperors, the merchants of the late Roman period exceeded all previous civilizations in exploiting the natural resources of their world.[4] Through vast building schemes and intense practical improvements in mining, agriculture and transportation, the Roman entrepreneur extracted the last silver nugget from Britain, the last fish from Galilee and the last stalk of grain from Roumania.[5]

Throughout the long centuries of decline after the fall of Rome, regulation and innovation kept on apace.[6] Government intervention, whether civil or ecclesiastical, continued right through the Medieval Period and on into the Renaissance. The hastening or hindering of technological change by this intervention varied, of course, with the situation and the times. A fine example of such intervention influencing technological change by forcing an international transfer is seen in the case of the early printers of Mainz. Here it was the ecclesiastical authorities of the Roman Church which caused the intervention.

> The authorities of the Church now began to take the ground that the reading of the Scriptures by individuals was not to be permitted, and that the Bible was to be given to the community only through the interpretation of the Church. At the same time, the authority of the Church was exerted to repress, or at least to restrict, the operations of the printing-press, and to bring printers and publishers under a close ecclesiastical supervision and censorship. It was now, however, too late to stand between the printing-press and the people. Large portions of the community had become accustomed to a wide circulation of books and to the selection without restriction of such reading matter as might be placed within their reach, and this privilege they were no longer willing to forego.
>
> It was, nevertheless, true that in certain countries, particularly in Italy and in France, the censorship of the Church was strong enough seriously to hamper and interfere with publishing undertakings and to check the natural development of literary production. Even in Italy, however, the critical spirit was found to be too strong to be entirely crushed out, and from Venice, the most important of the Italian publishing centres, it proved possible to secure for the productions of the printing-press a circulation that was practically independent of the censorship of Rome.
>
> The typesetters of Mainz, driven from their printing-offices by the heavy hand of the Church, journeyed throughout the world, carrying their new knowledge and training and they were able to give to many communities the means of education and enlightenment through which the great revolt against the Church was finally instituted. The work of the printers, checked for the time in Mainz, took shape promptly in Strasburg, and from there was taken down the Rhine to Cologne, and in a few years was also in active operation in Basel, Augsburg, Ulm, and Nuremberg. In 1464, as elsewhere described,

> German printers carried their invention into Italy and erected the first Italian printing-press in Subiaco. And in 1470, also, through Germans, the work of the printers began in Paris.[7]

The colonial policies of the British Empire in the colonial history of the United States can also be interpreted as influencing technological change. British policy fostered the development of basic industries because of the abundance of raw materials.[8] However, it was clear that the "purpose of the government when colonies were established, (was) to make them subservient to the growth of English commerce and manufacturers."[9] The British policy would on the one hand, tend to stimulate technological change for basic industries. On the other hand, the policy would tend to inhibit technological change aimed at the consumer market.

The colonial policies of other nations also regulated the marketplace and at the same time influenced technological change.

> The object of the colonial policy of Great Britian, to engross the trade of the colonies and to stimulate the consumption of English manufacturers in their markets, differed in detail but not in principle from that of other European countries. The commercial policy of Holland, which governed to some extent the early history of New York and Delaware, was, like other industrial legislation of that progressive country, in some respects more liberal than that of England. But previous to the repeal of her navigation acts, under the monopolies granted her chartered trading companies, commerce was restricted and manufactures were regulated as carefully as in the British possessions. The "Freedoms and Exemptions" of the New Amsterdam settlers forbade their making any woolen, linen, or cotton cloth, or weaving any other stuffs, on pain of banishment and other arbitrary punishment, but this law either was not enforced or soon was abrogated. The policy of France, controlling what was destined to be the central territory of the American Republic, differed from that of England in regard to manufactures, because her industrial interests also were different. The staple manufactures of France even at that time catered to the wants of more luxurious consumption and were not so well suited for the Indian and colonial trade, or so cheaply produced, as those of England. The fur traders of Canada were dependent on the British colonies for many of the supplies they bartered. So the Canadian governors, like the earliest Virginia

> governors, actively encouraged manufactures. The royal instructions to the intendant of New France, dated March 27, 1665, direct him to "observe that the establishment of manufacturers and the attraction thither of fabricators of articles essential to the purposes of life constitute one of the great wants of Canada." Twenty years later the colonial minister of France wrote to the authorities in the new settlements: "Nothing of greater importance than to accustom them (the colonists) to industry, and means must be adopted to establish manufactures suitable to the country." A few years earlier the indendant of the province negotiated with New England for shipwrights, mill mechanics and other skilled tradesmen. In Louisiana, too, the authorities were favorably disposed toward manufacturing industries.[10]

We have briefly considered in what way the colonial policies of various nations might have influenced technological change in the American colonies. Domestic policies of these nations also served to influence technological change at home.

The role of the French government in the manufacture of glass is such an example.

> During the ministry of the celebrated Colbert, some French artists, who while residing in the Venetian state had acquired a knowledge of the process used at Murano for the making of plate glass, returned to France in the hope of profitably pursuing the manufacture in their native country. Such an event falling in with the views of Monsieur Colbert, who was anxious by every means to extend the useful arts within the kingdom, these artists were in the year 1665 established with privileges at Tourlaville near Cherbourg, and an advance of money was made to them from the public coffers to assist in the formation of their establishment. The plates made by this company were blown, after the system used in the Venetian manufactories.
>
> It was not until 1688 that the beautiful art of casting plates of glass was invented by a manufacturer named Thevart, who, obtaining a patent for the invention to continue in force during thirty years, established a company and erected works in Paris, where plates were cast of the then extraordinary dimensions of eighty-four inches long by fifty inches wide, a size which excited universal astonishment and admiration. The expense of conducting such a manufactory in

> the metropolis was, however, so great, that the establishment was transferred to St. Gobain in Picardy, where the undertaking was prosecuted, not without considerable opposition from the more ancient association.
>
> To accommodate the disputes between these rival establishments, Thevart's company was bound not to cast any plates whose dimensions should be less than sixty inches in length and forty inches in breadth. The largest piece that had then been produced by blowing did not exceed fifty inches in its largest dimension. This arrangement failed to produce harmony between the rivals; but in 1695 that end was effectually answered by uniting both companies under the same charter -- not however, as the issue proved, to their mutual advantage; -- for, possibly owing to a want of the salutary spur of competition, the company declined in prosperity with such rapidity, that in two years from the junction the united body was in a state of insolvency, obliged to discharge most of its workmen, and to abandon many of its furnaces.[11]

The above example shows government intervention in several forms. First, the government desired to promote the technology imported from Venice by using public funds to establish the manufacture of glass. Second, the government intervened, limiting competition, by not allowing Thevart to cast glass in sizes which would compete with the Venetian process. Finally, in an effort to eliminate competition altogether and perhaps foster the manufacture of glass and technological change, the companies were forced to merge. The outcome of the latter, was an initial reduction in sales and within two years, the insolvency of the company.

Technological change in the glass industry in Great Britain was impeded in the early 19th Century by the imposition of additional duties on glass manufacturers in 1812.

> It is principally owing to these restrictions that so much foreign glass is now brought into this country in the face of what may be considered an amply protective duty. Foreign manufacturers are allowed to make any and every article out of that quality of glass which will most cheaply and advantageously answer the end, while our own artists are forbidden to form certain objects, except with more costly materials, which pay the higher ratio of duty. Nor is the restriction only commercially

> wrong, since it forms matter of just complaint on the part of chemists, that they are unable to procure utinsils fitted for effecting many of the nicer operations connected with their science, because the due protection of the revenue is thought to require that such utinsils shall be formed out of that quality of glass which, apart from all consideration of prices, is otherwise, from its properties, really unfited for the purpose . . . "Whenever the measure (removal of the duties) shall be accomplished, it can hardly fail to induce such an extension of the manufacture as will prove generally beneficial to the community."[13]

The impact of the duty was to inhibit the growth of the glass manufacturing industry in England. In addition, it would seem that the duty, as well as the imposition of materials standards by the government, at least influenced the direction and nature of the technology employed in the domestic manufacture of glass.

The above material has served to indicate that government intervention through regulation has influenced technological change over the centuries. Therefore, when we talk of the relationship between government regulation and technological change is is one which has regularly occurred through history, but not been directly confronted. In the remainder of this paper, we will consider for a number of limited cases, how regulatory barriers have influenced the process of innovation. In a recent report prepared by GRA,[14] a number of hypotheses have been identified in the literature concerning the relationship between economic regulation and technological innovation. These hypothesis will be stated and then illustrative examples concerning each hypothesis, or, combination of hypotheses, will be presented. These examples will serve to identify some of the regulatory barriers to technological change. The hypotheses are:

> There clearly is a relationship between economic regulation and technological innovation (ERTI).
>
> The ERTI relationship generally has profound implications for entrepreneurs in regulated industries.
>
> The ERTI relationship often has spillover effects for suppliers to regulated industries; these effects may profoundly influence or determine their propensity to innovate.

The ERTI relationship sometimes thwarts technological innovation, sometimes promotes it, and, perhaps most often, distorts the innovative drives of enterprises touched by the relationship either directly or indirectly.

Where there are multiple layers of economic regulation being applied the ERTI relationship is very great with the highest probability being that innovation is stifled more effectively than where there is just one set of regulations.

The existence of a regulatory lag effects the ERTI relationship and discourages certain types of innovation even while promoting others.

Where the regulated industries are wholly or principally made up of nationalized enterprises, the nature of the ERTI relationship is substantially different than where private firms dominate the scene.

National policy objectives can often be served through exploitation of the ERTI relationship.

Manipulation of the ERTI relationship by government, especially when accompanied by government financing of the development of technology, stimulate innovation in regulated industries.

Where there has been severely restricted entry into a regulated industry, relaxation of the barriers will trigger great R&D and innovation activity.

Immunity from anti-trust restraints concomitant with economic regulation is not sufficient to stimulate innovation in regulated industries and in many circumstances will have an opposite effect.

Market structure is a powerful factor in determing whether vertical integration in regulated industries will stimulate or discourage technological innovation.

Rate-of-return regulation very likely has the effect of encouraging investment in capital-intensive technology.

The structure of subsidy applied to a regulated industry can influence technological development and innovation.

UNITED STATES EXAMPLES FROM THE LITERATURE

Transportation

For rail transport, it is rate regulation that has most often been found to impede or distort innovation. It is by this basic mechanism that technological innovation initially has been impacted, as in the case of Trailer-on-Flat-Car (TOFC) freight transportation.

TOFC is an interesting case in which the technology and service had proven popular and was starting to grow as early as 1926.[15] The service quickly gained acceptance and was rapidly expanding in the late 1920's[16] and early 1930's until an Interstate Commerce Commission (ICC) decision in 1931.[17] The ICC "initiated an investigation on its own motion, into the rates, charges, rules regulations and practices of common carriers by railroad . . . incident to the use of container equipment . . ., which interrupted the trend in container service development. Many feel that this caused a setback in piggyback operations."[18] As a result of this action of the ICC, the Senate Committee on Interstate and Foreign Commerce concluded, "This resulted in the end of container service for that era . . ." and, "The 1931 decision, because of a ritualistic interpretation of the Interstate Commerce Act, denied the benefits of innovation to carriers and shippers to our national detriment."[19]

It was not until 1964, with the decision in the New Haven case,[20] in which the ICC gave approval to certain operations, that piggyback carloadings started increasing rapidly.[21] Between 1931 and 1954, the ICC made a number of decisions at first favorable to TOFC, then unfavorable. Josephine Ayre thus asserts: "The end result was that piggyback operation had been set back, in spite of the two favorable ICC decisions in 1936. Piggyback service was nominal for a period thereafter. Thus, each time the ICC rendered an unfavorable decision or engaged in another extensive investigation, piggyback development was arrested for the time being."[22]

The history of TOFC certainly confirms that the ICC utilize rate regulation in a manner that impedes or distorts technological innovation. But, rate regulation is not the only regulatory parameter that is noticeable in the history of TOFC. As previously indicated, the ICC conducted a number of investigations into the issues surrounding TOFC. In this connection, GRA has suggested that a ". . . powerful influence on transport innovation is the delay in innovating caused by regulatory review, which frequently causes significant time to elapse between the conception and the exploitation of an innovation."[23] He further asserts, that ". . . regulatory delay impinges on the process of innovation for regulated carriers largely by linking the application of new technology with the need to publish new and often conceptually different tariffs governing the use of such technology."[24]

In the area of waterborne transport, the Maritime Administration (MarAd) expected to spend some $9MM in 1965 for R&D[25] in areas ranging from automated ships to hydrofoils. Unfortunately, any technological innovations that derive from the research sponsored by the Maritime Administration may not be "promoted" into use in the subsidized steamship industry, which is subsidized under the Merchant Marine Act of 1936. For, as James Robert McCaul asserts,[26]

> The present operating subsidy does not provide incentive to invest in labor-saving innovations such as automated engine room controls. Any saving that is realized through such an investment simply reduces labor cost and hence the operating subsidy. Put another way, there is a zero return on investment. It should also be noted that, unlike cost-saving innovations by public utilities, as soon as a cost-saving device is introduced, the subsidy decreases. There is no "regulatory lag" such as that which prompts utilities to innovate even when such innovation will ultimately force a general rate reduction and wipe out the cost gain. The utility enjoys excess profit for some time, and such lag encourages them to innovate. In the case of the subsidized maritime carriers, however, the subsidy reduction is simultaneous with the cost-saving innovation.
>
> If the innovation reduces a cost that is non-subsidized, such as cargo-handling costs, the level of subsidy will not be affected. However, the recapture clause provides that half the excess profits (i.e., return in excess of 10% of capital necessarily employed) be returned to the federal government and the remaining half must be deposited in a special reserve fund and cannot be distributed in stockholders' dividends. Hence, the innovative carrier must either return the "excess profits" to MarAd or put them in storage.

With regard to rate regulation as it influences the propensity to innovate in highway transport, Gellman in 1971 notes that in no specific instance have highway carriers sought explicit rate approvals from the ICC for the introduction of new major technology.[27] Indications are given that the highway carrier requires new cost-saving innovations, which the industry and its suppliers do not seem to have developed.

The literature concerning inland water transport was found, in most cases, not to be cognizant of the ERTI relationship. The journals did not provide relevant literature on the subject; in fact, there was only one item identified that gave even limited coverage:

> For carriers operating on the inland waterways of the United States technological innovation has been somewhat limited in recent years, partly because some of the regulations that have been applied were designed for an earlier technological environment. An important example is the provision of the Interstate Commerce Act that exempts from economic regulation movements of bulk commodities where "not more than thre such commodities" are carried in a single tow. In recent years, Towboats of up to 8,000 horsepower have become available, yet common carrier barge operators have little opportunity to use this modern, efficient equipment since they cannot compete with unregulated and private carriers by hauling more than three different commodities at one time.
>
> Other government-imposed limits on technological development in inland waterway transportation relate to the size and draft of vessels, which are in turn largely determined by channel depths and lock sizes, and to the subsidy to water carriers inherent in the federal provision and maintenance of the waterways. The implications for technological development of these governmental policies are not considered further here.[28]

Communications

Microwave technological knowledge is at least 60 years old. Research and development in microwave relay transmission began during the 1930's and continued into World War II, during which time a significant breakthrough occurred in the development of the Klystron high-frequency transmitting tube. As soon as the war ended, applications of the new technology became obvious.

During the war, development of microwave technology had not progressed sufficiently far that the process of innovation had reached the production phase. Indeed, in 1946, introduction to the market of a microwave communications system awaited additional research. Many firms, both large and small, common carrier and non-common carrier, sought to enter this promising field. For example, Western Union constructed an experimental microwave route between New York and Philadelphia. The established monopolist, American Telephone and Telegraph (AT&T), correctly perceived the efforts of the intruding firms as a threat to the sanctity of their market. AT&T met the challenge of the independent systems by conducting a massive two-stage innovative effort between 1946 and 1950, leading to creation of a nationwide microwave relay system, the TD-2. AT&T carried out a "crash" program to make the technology operational quickly.[29] Shepherd describes the program as:

> ...extensive and costly, and some specific expenditures no doubt yielded a low social return, even though they evidently generated high private returns to the Bell System by helping to assure exclusivity in this crucial area. The development was telescoped into about three years, and the Bell System had acted quickly enough to take over virtually the entire domestic microwave carrier field.[30]

The Federal Communications Commission (FCC) played a critical role in this process of "preemptive" innovation. The regulatory commission impeded the attempt by Western Union to develop its system -- it refused Western Union permission to carry television programs over the system.[31] In addition,

> ...AT&T unremittingly refused to interconnect with rival microwave systems. As on other issues, the refusals were not supported by quantitative evidence about quality of service and other marginal costs and benefits that might be involved. By the period 1949-50, the Bell System had succeeded in maneuvering the FCC into converting the microwave field -- with much potential for fruitful competition -- into a total monopoly, not only of transmission operations but also of equipment manufacturing. Indeed, control extended even further. The FCC excluded all private microwave until 1959.[32]

In effect, the FCC's abdication of control over AT&T resulted in massive and unusually fast-paced efforts to outrace all other competitors through steps in the process of innovation. AT&T won the race and the ensuing era of FCC-condoned monopoly was characterized by reversion to the "evolutionary" pace of innovation.[33] The significant point is that during the postwar era, the form, nature, and vigor of research and application of microwave technology was most definitely influenced by FCC regulatory policy and decisions (or lack thereof).

Since its emergence in 1949 as a means of improving television reception in rural areas, the regulation of Cable Antenna Television (CATV) has primarily been the responsibility of local government.[34] Interest in the regulation of CATV at the federal level was not manifest until 1959, at which time the FCC determined that it did not have the jurisdiction to regulate CATV. Since then, of course, the FCC has revised this position. From 1968 to the present, the FCC has changed its policy on CATV from one of protecting UHF/UHF broadcasting to one of promoting the development of CATV and the development of a national wire system. As the regulatory history of this policy reversal has been considered elsewhere, the present discussion will center upon the interplay of economic regulation at the hands of each level of political jurisdiction.

The responsibility for CATV regulation fell to local municipalities primarily because of the abdication of regulatory authority by both the state and federal governments which were unprepared to cope with or consider the complex and changing technologies. The local municipalities, however, often myopically viewed the franchising of CATV as simply a general revenue source that could be incorporated into the operating budget, and which would not require the municipality to provide any direct services. However, in the eyes of many, the control of CATV franchises at the local level has not been satisfactory. A commonly held view is that "as regulators of cable, the local government, generally speaking, has failed in almost every respect to protect and promote the public interest in the new medium."[35] The failure of CATV regulation at the local level has been attributed to various institutional factors inherent in local government. A number of these factors will be outlined in the ensuing discussion. However, the most publicized one has been the not infrequent willingness of certain local officials to accept bribes or extort funds in exchange for the award of a cable franchise in the municipality.[36]

Major causes of disenchantment with the local franchise method of regulation relate mainly to the procedures for review and issuance of permits. These procedures have led to an inconsistent cable system, without adequate protection of the public interest. For instance, adjacent municipalities may have systems with differing numbers of channels. Often the municipalities provide lease terms in excess of the system's accounting life. Further, the uncoordinated regulation of CATV can lead to a disaggregated system of franchises, which in Pennsylvania, for example, could lead to some 2,400 separate franchises. Local regulation of CATV does not provide for an agency to coordinate or regulate interconnections. Most important, the municipality often does not possess the technical or economic expertise necessary to evaluate the full ramifications of a decision in response to a franchise application. At the local level it is difficult to maintain a technically competent regulatory staff since a lease will often extend over terms of several administrations and this hardly justified a significant steady regulators payroll.

The arguments in favor of state regulation have gone to the correction of these deficiencies at the local level. State allocation of franchise areas can provide a more coordinated cable system. In fact, the state as regulator can promote interconnection. Expertise in the technology, economics, and regulation and their interrelationships can be funded more adequately and continuously at the state level, since licensing and other regulations will be more of an ongoing process at the state level. Further, the federal government's record for working successfully with local governments has not been particularly good. Proponents of state regulation suggest that state agencies would have better insight into the needs and desires of the totality of local communities, whereas a federal regulatory agency has neither the staff nor the ability or interest to be aware of the needs and desires at the level of the relatively small community.

In 1965, the FCC, moving to protect broadcasting interests, decided it did have jurisdiction over CATV relative to the importation of distant signals. The Commission's attitude of protectionism towards broadcasting interests has transitioned to one of promotion of CATV technology. In 1973, the FCC issued a new set of regulations. The new policy calls for peaceful coexistance between CATV and over-the-air broadcasting, promoting the former while protecting the latter. One of the current policies, and possible reason for such federal regulation, is the promotion of a national cable network, which requires a coordinated effort and sound technical standards.

It is apparent that the municipal government cannot perform effectively as a regulatory authority in this field. However, the primary reasons are inherent in the form of government rather than a propensity of local officials to "assimilate" funds. Municipalities cannot form an integrated state-wide CATV network with compatible technical standards, quality standards, rate structure, and the like. In the event of nonperformance by the local franchiseholder, the municipality is often at a loss in obtaining relief for those individuals affected, as well as in recovering anticipated revenues. Further, any judicial relief sought by a municipality would apply only to itself and would not affect the operation or obtaining of franchises in other municipalities by the CATV enterprise in default. Finally, the municipality, as a regulator of, and at the same time as a business partner of the CATV firm will find it most difficult to separate regulatory considerations from revenue considerations.

The state, as the next level of government, could, because of its broader purview relative to the institutional factors outlined above, play a significant role in CATV regulation. But, for some of the same reasons outlined above for local government, it cannot provide a coordinated national CATV system. Voluntary harmonious action among states is highly unlikely as far as interconnections, technical standards, and the like are concerned. Thus, the development of a national CATV system that is technically consistent, and that maintains a minimum level of service, must be coordinated if not regulated at the federal level. But what degree of regulation is applicable? That, of course, is a question that will be debated for years to come and that is outside the realm of this discussion. However, the interplay between local, state, and federal regulation of CATV under the recent FCC rules is clear. The FCC will set certain minimum requirements for franchising and will establish methods for determining and making rates known and set standards for programing. Other levels of government, either states or municipalities, may be left with a number of areas to regulate. But the mode of regulation has clearly changed from that established in the 1950's and early 1960's. The FCC and the state governments have become increasingly active, and the municipalities have been dislodged as the primary regulators of CATV.

UNITED KINGDOM EXAMPLES FROM THE LITERATURE

Britain represents an extreme position in regulation and nationalization. Therefore, problems associated with the promotion, distortion of thwarting of technology in the three industries are largely viewed as intragovernmental problems. Regulation of the industries in their totality is accepted with little question. The confrontation between the regulated and the regulators is generally shielded from view because it is usually a confrontation between government entities. The usual monopoly position of the government precludes concern for competition, entry/exit, rate of return, and numerous other parameters focused upon in the American literature. Nevertheless, compared with the literature of the four other countries (Canada, France, West Germany, and Japan), the British material provides considerably more insight regarding the ERTI relationship.

The United Kingdom items generally deal with the general concept of regulation through nationalization. In this respect,

Christopher Layton said, "A special case of the key problem of transfer of technology from development to market is the state-owned industries and research facilities."[37] The principal problem referred to here is the inability to move technology from the R&D phase to the marketing and diffusion phase of the process of innovation. In the aircraft industry, development and marketing do take place in one organization. The problem is to create a genuine commercial relationship with the customer, the government, so that the industry is impelled by valid commercial drives."[38] "Commercial drives" refers to incentives to innovate which, it is impled, are in shorter supply under nationalization. In terms of the United States, those incentives in the regulated industries might include regulatory lag, profits realizable through working of the Averch-Johnson effect, competition, etc.

Specifically with respect to nationalization, S. N. Chatterji has said, "Public enterprises, particularly in the United Kingdom context, have not shown greater ability to innovate than private enterprises."[39] Unfortunately, he does not support this argument with data. Neither does H. Speight who observes that competition under certain conditions can foster innovation:

> "Insofar as competition affects innovation, <u>a priori</u> reasoning leads to the probable conclusion that what matters is the degree of concentration of the output in the industry . . . The situation most conducive to innovation is that of a few large firms, or more or less equal size, existing in competition with each other and/or exposed to potential competition from new entrants in the market."[40]

Sir Alex Cairncross' views of the problems of technological innovation in the United Kingdom are stated thus:

> "Looking at Government Policy towards innovation in Britain since the war, I am tempted to argue, provocatively and dogmatically, that the problem was misconceived, the strategy mistaken, the tactics unsatisfactory and yet that none of this made much difference since the pace was set by an unfavourable social climate over which the Government had little control. . . Concentration on research and development is less helpful to innovation than concentration on industrial efficiency, for true industrial efficiency must embrace the ability to innovate successfully. . . The greater the area of the economy which is owned or controlled by the government, the greater almost by definition must be its role in technological development."[41]

John C. Duckworth has considered the role of government in the process of innovation and has noted that:

> "Historically, Government has taken direct action to encourage innovations in those areas where it has assumed an executive function."[42] With respect to the problems encountered with innovation in the United Kingdom, he states, ". . .there is little doubt that in the post-war years too much emphasis was placed on 'science,' and more latterly 'technology.' without a full appreciation of the financial and other resources needed for engineering, design, production and marketing of products and processes. Unfortunately, this trend coincided with the national philosophy which had grown up, in the years we could afford it, of the superior status of cultural, rather than productive, activities."[43]

C. F. Carter and B. B. Williams have studied some 250 firms looking for the "influences of investment on innovation." They have made some specific observations concerning the nationalized industries which are noteworthy:

> "Innovation is likely to be helped by . . . the absence of expectations of violent changes of conditions (including sudden and considerable changes of Government policy) . . . We have suggested that the tendency to vary the conditions under which nationalized industries operate, to fit the short-term variations of national circumstances, is probably harmful to innovation in those industries."[44]

In most cases, the United Kingdom literature that specifically addresses transportation, communications, and the energy utilities does not explicitly consider the ERTI relationship. However, some insights can be obtained from the implicit recognition of the ERTI relationship that is found in some of the industry-oriented materials. Prominent among these is Stephen Wheatcroft's Air Transport Policy,[45] which uniquely addresses several specific relevant issues.

> The most obvious consequence of this obligation (the Civil Aviation Act of 1946) is that the introduction of new aircraft is an expensive undertaking and extra costs are therefore imposed upon an airline with innovating obligations. . . But less obvious than these direct aircraft introduction costs are the indirect influences upon the industry of a constant and internationally competitive pressure towards innovation. For the major flag carriers in international air transport, the costs associated with support for national

> aircraft industries are far greater than the direct ones arising from the introduction of new aircraft; there are also all the costs arising from a high rate of obsolescence. There is, in effect, a special cost penalty for operating in the first division of the international air transport industry.

Thus Wheatcroft, alone among British authors, raised the question at least indirectly, of subsidy to British air carriers, nationalized and private, in order to support technological innovation in commercial transport aircraft. Wheatcroft also directs attention to the international market for domestically -- and internationally -- produced transport aircraft and suggests international economic regulation as a means of ameliorating what he perceives to be too rapid technological innovation.

Wheatcroft later turned the issue of aircraft development around to focus upon the direct relationship between airlines and aircraft producers and the connection to regulation and policy:

> The relationship between our airlines and the aircraft manufacturing industry is the root problem of a clear aviation policy. The reason for this is that whereas we could undoubtedly continue to be a major air transport nation without manufacturing our own aeroplanes, it is highly unlikely that we could continue to be a major producer of civil aircraft unless this activity were supported by British airline operations. British aircraft manufacturers would find it extremely difficult to sell transport aircraft to foreign airlines, particularly in the face of fierce American competition, unless the initial introduction and operational development of their aircraft were undertaken by one of our own airlines. It is for this reason that aircraft manufacturing policy is so closely related to air transport policy.[46]

J. B. Hogg has indicated that the regulation of competition between nationalized and private air transport has hindered innovation. Specifically, he has stated that "although the number of carriers on any one air route may be limited, competition ensured by freedom of entry will hold down the level of charges and will require firms to seek the benefits of technological advances and effective marketing. . .[47] In much the same manner, D. H. Aldercroft held that lack of competitive forces in the railroad industry distorted technological innovation especially with regard to the change from steam power to dieselization or electrification.[48]

Primarily, the literature discussed the need for government intervention to ensure the development of alternative low-cost sources of power.[49] In one instance it was even noted that it is the statutory obligation of electricity authorities "to generate electricity abundently and cheaply."[50] If government intervention is necessary to develop alternative sources of energy, it will undoubtedly influence the direction and rate of technological innovation, either one way or the other. Additionally, the electrical authority obligation "to generate electricity abundantly and cheaply" implies the need for such public authorities to be sensitive to technological possibilities in general and to cost-saving innovations in particular.

CANADIAN EXAMPLES FROM THE LITERATURE

The items identified in the non-industry specific literature in Canada are primarily concerned with the overall implications of science policy for the Dominion. In this respect, the articles are not directly related to the ERTI relationship. However, in reviewing these items' contents, some imply the existence of the ERTI relationship. For example, O. J. Firestone has indicated that "a tax program aimed at high employment. . . (decreases) the resistance of labor and management to the risk of technological change and correspondingly relaxes the grip of restrictive practices."[51]

In regard to science policy in general, Gilles Paquet said, "The Canadian government has used both grants and tax incentives to induce industry to engage in scientific activities to a greater extent."[52] In his concluding remarks in "Taxation and Science Policy," he further stated that "carefully designed and monitored assistance programs are agreed by academe, government and industry as necessary for an effective government effort to induce scientific research leading to innovation."[53]

In an argument that implicitly supports Paquet and Firestone, Dennis C. Mueller and John E. Tilton conclude that R&D costs to achieve successful market entry have risen to become a major obstacle in the process of innovation.[54] However, they also indicate that the mechanism that best protects the innovating firm is patent policy. In this regard, they have stated that "occasionally, the innovating firm has an airtight patent position and prevents other firms from entering the industry or adopting the process." In their article, Mueller and Tilton, however, place the impact of economic regulation on technological innovation into the market. It can be concluded from this literature that there is some degree of recognition in Canada that the process of innovation does exist in terms other than simply R&D. Other literature in the non-industry specific category recognizes that certain tax policies and subsidy policies utilized by the Canadian government can induce technological innovation in both regulated and unregulated industries.

Two critics of Canadian transport policy are K. W. Studnicki-Gizbert and H. M. Romoff. Romoff has indicated that "inhibiting action has been overregulating or misregulating the actual operations of the railways because of the inability of regulatory policy and procedures to catch up with rapid technological changes."[55] Romoff further indicates that the proper regulatory policy consonant with the economic realities of 1970, would involve a very substantial deregulation in the railroad industry and the recognition that railroads should be allowed to function in a manner analogous to other large-scale industries.

The most informative article[56] on transport in Canada was the one prepared by K. W. Studnicki-Gizbert. In this article, Studnicki-Gizbert presents a general analysis of regulatory policy options. In the second part, he relates some regulatory experiences in the field of transport with reference to the framework laid out in the first part of his article. Some of the more interesting aspects of the article are the conjectures the author makes: (a) "the stabilizing effect of regulation and economies of scale where such are achieved with the help of regulators should produce, at least, some favorable conditions for long term R&D efforts"; (b) "rate-of-return regulations tend to have unfavorable effects for two reasons: (1) they restrict the size of the pay-offs, (2) by providing bias for the investment in tangible assets they tend to affect adversely the building up of intangibles"; (c) "some regulatory practices encourage excessive rigidity in the operating and financing patterns of the industry with the consequent investments and innovations being channeled not necessarily into the areas of the highest payoff"; (d) "service competition which tends to develop when rate competition is restricted tends to bias investments into quality-improving rather than cost-decreasing areas."[57]

With respect to air transport, Terry Gow has taken the position that the rate of introduction of new technology by a nationalized enterprise has a negative impact on a firm competing with that nationalized entity. In particular, Gow is concerned about the relationship between Air Canada, a government enterprise, and the privately owned C P Air (Canadian Pacific). These two airlines are engaged in a limited competition in Canada. However, regulation of C P Air by the government has placed some stringent requirements upon the private entrepreneur compared to the restrictions upon the government owned air transport operation. Gow's principal complaint is that C P Air's route pattern and seating capacity is tied directly to the number of seats and flights that Air Canada offers between certain cities.

It seems that Air Canada has a definite advantage in obtaining investment funds to speed the introduction of new aircraft into service. However, Gow contends that the ability of Air Canada to introduce such new technology with a minimal effort and without undergoing the risk taken by private enterprise in the introduction of new technology will severely impede the ability of C P Air to provide a competitive standard of service. He contends that the capacity-limiting agreements by which C P Air is constrained through government regulation will decrease (at least relatively) the number of seats and flights on domestic routes that C P Air can offer when Air Canada introduces any new type of aircraft which are larger than those previously flown. The necessity of C P Air to introduce a similar type of aircraft to remain competitive will force them to fewer aircraft and lower frequencies, thus reducing the effective competition between the two lines. Gow indicates that the restrictive practices of the government monopoly against private enterprise will not allow competition to develop as it should with innovations in cost and quality of service.

Conclusions

Again, the objective of the study was to survey and analyze the literature concerning the relationship between economic regulation and technological innovation in three regulated industries that has been published since World War II in six industrialized nations. The countries surveyed were the United States, Canada, Great Britain, France, West Germany, and Japan; the industries specifically considered were transportation, communication, and the energy utilities. In addition, material that related to the economic regulation of specifically regulated industries as a group was also studied.

At all times, it is necessary to keep in mind that the relatively small quantity of "surveyable" literature in itself indicates that the ERTI relationship has not been much recognized, much less considered in depth by analysts of these industries and by economists in general. This, in turn, likely reflects a general motion that economic regulation is neutral as to technology. This hypothesis is also supported by the fact that in the few items which do recognize an explicit ERTI relationship, the conclusion is usually that economic regulation is not neutral as to technology which idea is more often than not identified as going against the conventional wisdom. Primarily, such literature holds that economic regulation actually impedes or distorts technological innovation. In contrast, there is a rarely-expressed view that economic regulation has promoted technological innovation, though not always in a "desirable" and "timely" fashion.

Relative to specific issues, the extent to which government support for innovation is a concomitant of economic regulation was considered to a limited extent in the literature. In both the United States and Great Britain, instances were cited in which the innovative activities of regulated industries were supported with government resources. The commitment in the United Kingdom, at least in relative terms, appears to be greater in part because the regulated industries in Britain are largely nationalized.

The interrelationships between economic regulation applied at various levels of government and their respective relationships to technological innovation were considered only in the context of the communications industry. Indeed, this issue was considered solely in the literature dealing with the development of CATV technology in the United States where it was held that multi-level regulation impedes the diffusion and utilization of technology.

The literature surveyed indicates that the propensity to innovate in regulated industries is often influenced by the character and degree of economic regulation to which they are subjected. Where regulation impinges upon the ability of the regulated industry or firm to introduce new technology, such as where investment or financing is subject to review and approval, this inevitably has a dampening effect on the firm's or industry's propensity to innovate. This point was made especially clear in connection with innovations whose value could not be fully realized because of material delays in market introduction resulting from the regulatory process itself. Rate-of-return regulation was cited as being especially permicious where the opportunity existed for cost-reducing innovations even though there was some evidence to the contrary. Such regulation also was often held in the literature to be an inducement for the regulated to employ more capital-intensive technology than was otherwise warranted. All in all, economic regulation was found to have a generally detrimental effect on technological innovation by regulated industries as well as by firms supplying them.

The literature surveyed was rarely concerned with such matters as antitrust regulation, industrial concentration, and similar issues. The most significant exception is discussion of the impact of vertical and horizontal integration upon technological innovation in regulated industries and such discussion was largely centered around the position of the American Telephone and Telegraph Company in the United States communications industry. The general conclusion is that vertical integration appears to be a stifling influence where the technological innovation propensities of a regulated industry are concerned. Vertical integration distorts the process of innovation by "forcing" the process to serve the objectives of the regulated entity which often has substantial monopoly power which it seeks to preserve with various possible results such as an inflated rate base, undue technological complexity, or other means which tend to limit competition.

The relationship between economic regulation and technological innovation has been recognized in limited degree in each of the six countries whose literature was surveyed. The bulk of the material concerning the ERTI relationshp was found to have been published in the United States and this importantly grows out of the amount and complexity of economic regulation found in this country as compared with others. It also follows, not unreasonably, that the process of innovation is better understood in the United States than in other countries even though that understanding is far from comprehensive or complete with respect to any single aspect of regulated industry.

REFERENCES

1. G. Roux, Ancient Iraq (London: Allen and Unwin, 1964), p. 118 ff.

2. G. R. Driver and J. C. Miles, The Babylonian Laws (London: Oxford University Press, 1960), pp. 87-95.

3. W. Enssline, "The Reforms of Diocletian," in The Cambridge Ancient History, ed: J. B. Bury (London: Cambridge, 1939), 12:405.

4. M. Rostovtzeff, The Social and Economic History of the Roman Empire, 2nd ed. (London: Oxford University Press), 2:505 ff.

5. William White, Jr., "Finance," in The Catacombs and the Colosseum: A History of the Later Roman Empire, eds: S. Benko and J. J. O'Rourke (Philadelphia: Judson Press, 1971), pp. 218-36.

6. Lynn White, Jr., Medieval Technology and Social Change (London: Oxford University Press, 1962), pp. 129-34.

7. George Haver Putnam, Books and Their Makers During the Middle Ages (New York: Hillary House, 1962), 1:370-72.

8. Victor S. Clark, History of Manufacturers in the United States, vol 1: 1607 to 1860 (New York: McGraw Hill, 1929), p. 8.

9. Ibid, p. 14.

10. Ibid, p. 15.

11. Dionysius Lardner, The Cabinet Cyclopaedia: A Treatise on the Progressive Improvement and Present State of the Manufacture of Porcelain and Glass (London: A. & R. Spottiswoode, 1832), pp. 136-37.

12. Ibid, pp. 143-47.

13. Ibid, p. 143.

14. Gellman Research Associates, Inc., Economic Regulation and Technological Innovation: A Cross-National Literature Survey and Analysis (Jenkintown, Pennsylvania: Gellman Research Associates, Inc., (January 1974).

15. Eugene D. Anderson and Dickson R. Loos, "Piggyback Plans," Boston College Industrial and Commercial Law Review 3 (Spring 1962): 336.

16. Ibid.

17. Josephine Ayre, "History and Regulation of Trailer-on-Flatcar Movement," Highway Research Record 153 (1967): 2.

18. Ibid.

19. Ibid, p. 4.

20. Interstate Commerce Commission, Movement of Highway Trailers by Rail, Docket No. 31375, 293 ICC 93 (July 30, 1954).

21. Ayre, "History and Regulation of Trailer-on-Flatcar Movement," p. 9.

22. Ibid, p. 12.

23. Aaron J. Gellman, "Surface Freight Transportation," in Technological Change in Regulated Industries, ed: William M. Capron (Washington: Brookings Institution, 1971), p. 174.

24. Ibid, p. 175.

25. Richard J. Barber, "Technological Change in American Transportation: The Role of Government Action," Virginia Law Review 50 (June 1964): 878.

26. James Robert McCaul, "The Direct Maritime Subsidy Programs: An Analysis and Proposal for Change" (Ph.D. dissertation, University of Maryland, 1971), pp. 143-44.

27. Gellman, "Surface Freight Transportation," p. 179.

28. Ibid, p. 178.

29. William G. Shepherd, "The Competitive Margin in Communications," in Technological Change in Regulated Industries, ed: William M. Capron (Washington: Brookings Institution, 1971), pp. 113-14; Harry M. Trebing, "Common Carrier Regulation -- The Silent Crisis," Law and Contemporary Problems 34 (April 1970): 308; "The Development of the TD-X and TD-2 Microwave Radio Relay Systems in Bell Telephone Laboratories," cited by Harry M. Trebing, "Common Carrier Regulation -- The Silent Crisis," Law and Contemporary Problems 34 (April 1970): 308.

30. Shepherd, "The Competitive Margin in Communications," p. 114.

31. Stuart L. Mathison and Philip M. Walker, Computers and Telecommunications: Issues in Public Policy (Englewood Cliffs, New Jersey: Prentice-Hall, 1970), p. 178.

32. Shepherd, "The Competitive Margin in Communications," p. 114.

33. Ibid, pp. 114-15; Trebing, "Common Carrier Regulation -- The Silent Crisis," p. 308.

34. Roscoe L. Barrow and Daniel J. Manelli, "Communications Technology -- A Forecast of Change (Part I)," Law and Contemporary Problems (Spring 1969): 205-43.

35. Stephen R. Barnett, "State, Federal, and Local Regulation of Cable Television," Notre Dame Lawyer 47 (April 1972): 691.

36. Ibid.

37. Christopher Layton, Ten Innovations (London: Allen and Unwin, 1972), p. 4.

38. Ibid, p. 15.

39. S. N. Chatterji, "The Process of Innovation" (MSc thesis, Imperial College of Science and Technology, 1972, pp. 24-42.

40. H. Speight, Economics and Industrial Efficiency (London: Macmillan, 1967), pp. 241-47.

41. Sir Alex Cairncross, "Government and Innovation," New Scientist (September 2, 1971): 502, 504-5.

42. John Duckworth, "The Role of Government," in Technological Innovation and the Economy, ed: Maurice Goldsmith (London: Wiley, 1970), p. 111.

43. Ibid, p. 114.

44. C. F. Carter and B. R. Williams, Investment in Innovation (London: Oxford University Press, 1958), p. 144.

45. Stephen Wheatcroft, Air Transport Policy (London: Michael Joseph Limited, 1964).

46. Ibid, pp. 180-81.

47. J. B. Hogg, "Government Policy and the Department of British Air Transport" (MS thesis, London University, 1972).

48. D. H. Aldercroft, Innovation in Railways (London: London School of Economics, January 1967).

49. W. G. Jensen, Energy and the Economy of Nations (Oxfordshire: G. T. Foulis and Company, Ltd., 1970), Sections I and V.

50. J. L. Gray, "Economies of Scale -- Generation of Electrical Power," in Economics and Technical Change, ed: E. M. Huyh-Jones (Oxford: Basil Blackwell, 1969), pp. 99-112.

51. O. J. Firestone, Problems of Economic Growth (Ottawa: University of Ottawa Press, 1965).

52. Gilles Paquet, "Taxation and Science Policy," Canadian Tax Journal (September-October 1971): 429-37.

53. Ibid.

54. Dennis C. Muller and John E. Tilton, "Research and Development Costs as a Barrier to Entry," Canadian Journal of Economics (November 1969): 570-79.

55. H. M. Romoff, "Cybernetics and Government Regulation," Rail International, Number 5 (May 1970): 348-52.

56. K. W. Studnicki-Gizbert, "Regulatory Policy Options in Transport," in Papers of the Twelfth Annual Meeting, Transportation Research Forum (Oxford, Indiana: Richard B. Cross, 1971), pp. 1-30.

57. Terry Gow, "The Future of Air Regulation Policy -- The Airline Viewpoint," in Papers of the Thirteenth Annual Meeting, Transportation Research Forum (Oxford, Indiana: Richard B. Cross, 1972), pp. 75-81.

PART III: PUBLIC TECHNOLOGY

This part is divided into three areas: the first is on experiences of remote sensing technology; the second relates to management information systems and their incorporation into criminal justice communities; the third examines Technology Transfer to local jurisdictions.

The paper by Mason and Spann describes potential applications of remote sensing technology to decision and policy-making in the public sector and documents observations about different mechanisms for transferring the technology from its original context to the decision contexts of state, regional, and local agencies. The paper reviews the concepts of remote sensing technologies, describes different types of technology transfer experiences, and provides some observations about the relative successes of these experiences.

Dean Merrill's paper on "Accelerating Reform in the Courts Through Technology Transfer" describes the successful transfer of a computer based management information system to prosecutors throughout the United States.

What are the reasons behind the successful transfer of this system? What are some of the traditional impediments to transferring technology in the criminal justice community, and how has the PROMIS transfer package overcome these problems?

The PROMIS system is even more impressive when one looks at some of its additional benefits:

> Generating statistics on office work load and performance;
>
> Monitoring evenhandedness and consistency in the exercise of prosecutive discretion;
>
> Making it possible to control and alleviate scheduling and logistical impediments to the adjudication of cases;
>
> Providing a rich data base of case and defendant information which can be used to analyze and research problems in the prosecutive system.

Carlson's paper which follows relates how U.S. state and local governments are organizing to capture benefits of R&D. The utilization of new technology in local and state governments in the United States requires the aggregation of this normally large and fragmented market. This can be accomplished by the definition of performance requirements and specifications common to many localities so as to be large enough to be attractive to would be bidders. Firms who would hope to enter this marketplace with products or services must be helped to make R&D and investment decisions based on such aggregated requirements. This form of technology transfer, emphasizing product development by reducing the uncertainty in the supplier/user interface, is performed by Public Technology Incorporated, which operates in the middle ground between supply by industry and demand by state and local governments.

The paper by Bill Carey discusses technological transfer from federal laboratories. According to Carey, in the U. S. economy, technology is transferred very effectively in the private sector but ineffectively in the public or intergovernmental sector. Innovation is not sold as such but is embedded in the performance characteristics of the product. Technology alone could not have brought it off, but technology combined with managerial and marketing know-how is what made the difference.

Bill Raney's paper examines the essential factors that govern military technology transfer within the military system with some comparison to how it works in commercial practice. He also discusses the problems in doing internal transfer within the military and then proceeds to describe the essential features to successful technology transfer as he found them.

The last two articles in this section deal with military technology transfer to the civilian sector. The Udis article is based on interviews and is fairly qualitative as opposed to the Bar-Zakay article which is more of a factor analysis. The principle object of the Udis study was to throw new light on problems of military to civilian transfer of resources. The basic interview was designed for organizations forced to adjust to a reduced level of dependence on military expenditures and the consequent need to develop civil market alternatives. The field work consisted of a series of interviews with industrial executives, government officials, university professors and journalists.

According to Bar-Zakay, the government of Israel was aware of the potential of technology transfer (TT) and in 1969 decided to commission the Ministry of Defence and the Ministry of Commerce and Industry to examine the possibilities of transferring new technologies already existing in research organizations of the Ministry of Defence to the civilian sector. The research project had two main objectives:

> To recommend government policies which would improve the process in the future by analyzing past cases of technology transfer and
>
> To induce three successful transfers in real time in order to indicate to the civilian sector in Israel the benefits of TT in order to compare findings with those reached in the framework of the first objective.

REMOTE SENSING TECHNOLOGY TRANSFER TO THE PUBLIC SECTOR

Robert M. Mason and G. William Spann

Metrics, Inc.
Atlanta, Georgia 30339

Introduction

The purpose of this paper is to describe potential applications of remote sensing technology to decision and policy-making in the public sector and to document observations about different mechanisms for transferring the technology from its original context to the decision contexts of state, regional, and local agencies. The paper reviews the concepts of remote sensing technologies, describes different types of technology transfer experiences, and provides some observations about the relative successes of these experiences.

Remote sensing generally is taken to mean the remote collection, analysis, and presentation of electromagentic spectrum data on the earth's surface. The data normally are from the visible and infrared portions of the spectrum, although the ultra-violet region also has been utilized, and data collection is accomplished by specialized optics and electromagnetic sensors in high and low altitude aircraft and in satellites.

Applications of remote sensing include land use mapping, crop forecasting, and ecological studies. Remote sensing techniques can be used to aid highway and pipeline route selection, forecast tax revenue (from land use inventories), and to pinpoint areas requiring insect control. The application of these techniques thus can improve public policy and decision-making by providing low-cost information on the availability and utilization of natural resources, on the impact of development activities, and on the likely environmental impact of proposed projects.

Background

Remote sensing generally refers to the acquisition of aerial photography and/or digital data for the purpose of performing some type of earth resource analysis. Both aircraft and, more recently, spacecraft are used to collect remote sensor data. LANDSAT is a spacecraft which offers the only continuing source of remote sensing data. This section describes the LANDSAT system first and most extensively, but also describes other remote sensor platforms.

LANDSAT

LANDSAT (formerly the Earth Resources Technology Satellite, or ERTS) was launched by NASA on July 23, 1972, into a near polar orbit.[1] From an orbital altitude of approximately 570 miles, it relays data to one of three receiving stations in the U.S. or one of several foreign receiving stations. The sensor complement on LANDSAT is such that a swath of the earth 115 miles wide is viewed on each pass. The entire earth can be imaged every eighteen days. Recently LANDSAT--II has joined LANDSAT--I in orbit so that a spot on the earth can be imaged every nine days. Most of the experimental results reported thus far are from LANDSAT--I data, but LANDSAT--II results should prove similar since the sensors are identical.

There are two types of sensors on board the satellite, a return beam videcon (RBV) system and a multispectral scanner. The return beam videcon system consists of three television cameras which collect data in three different portions of the visible spectrum. The multispectral scanner (MSS) consists of four sensors which record the intensity of reflected light from a point on the earth in four spectral bands, the green and the red portions of the visible spectrum and two bands in the near infrared. Each of these systems has an onboard tape recorder for storing data taken over areas not within range of a ground receiving station. The present LANDSAT sensors do not sense heat (thermal infrared), but a fifth channel in the thermal infrared tentatively is planned for inclusion on the MSS on LANDSAT--C scheduled for launch in 1978.

LANDSAT has a third, but lesser known, capability in its data collection system (DCS). The DCS serves as a relay for data obtained with ground-based sensors. The ground equipment consists of a data collection platform (DCP) which has mounted on it a radio transmitter and some type of measuring instrumentation. This instrumentation could measure water quality, water depth, snow pack or other desired variable. Typically these DCP's are located in remote or inaccessible areas where regular visitation would be extremely difficult. When the LANDSAT passes within range of one of the DCP's, data are transmitted to the LANDSAT for relay to one of the ground receiving stations along with the RBV and MSS data. DCP data are frequently used in conjunction with the RBV or MSS data.

Shortly after launch of LANDSAT--I, a problem developed in the power supply powering the RBV system, necessitating the shutting down of the RBV system in order not to jeopardize the entire mission.[2] However, the MSS and its tape recorder, as well as the DCS, has worked continuously for almost three years, almost two years longer than the design life of LANDSAT--I. Therefore, almost all of the useful results from LANDSAT have been derived from the MSS system, occasionally supplemented by data from the DCS.

Since most of the results obtained from LANDSAT--I have come from the MSS, a brief description of this subsystem and its data products is appropriate. Figure 1 shows a portion of the electromagnetic spectrum. LANDSAT band 4 takes data in the green portion of the visible spectrum, band 5 in the red portion of the visible spectrum, and bands 6 and 7 in the near infrared. Cultural features are most readily identifiable in bands 4 and 5, whereas bands 6 and 7 give the most information concerning the natural environment. Usually three or four bands are used when making an investigation using LANDSAT data. The instantaneous field of view of the sensor is 57 meters by 79 meters, or approximately 1.1 acres.

As LANDSAT passes over an area of interest, light reflected from the surface of the earth is recorded simultaneously in each of the four MSS bands. These data are digitized (i.e., converted to digital form) and relayed to a ground receiving station via radio link. (If the satellite is out of range of a ground receiving station, the data are stored on the onboard tape recorder for later transmission to the ground.) After the data are received on the ground, two types of products are produced: (A) computer compatible tapes which can be further processed to produce thematic maps and (B) photographic products. Photographic products generally consist of a black and white photograph for each band of data and a color infrared composit made by combining bands 4, 5 and 7.

The photographic products typically are produced at scales of 1:1,000,000, 1:500,000 and 1:250,000. Generally, five-to-ten acre parcels can be recognized in the photographs. Computer generated thematic maps can be produced at scales up to 1:24,000 with individual one acre "objects" often recognizable. Photographic products are most suitable for regional-scale studies, with each photograph covering an area 115 miles by 115 miles.

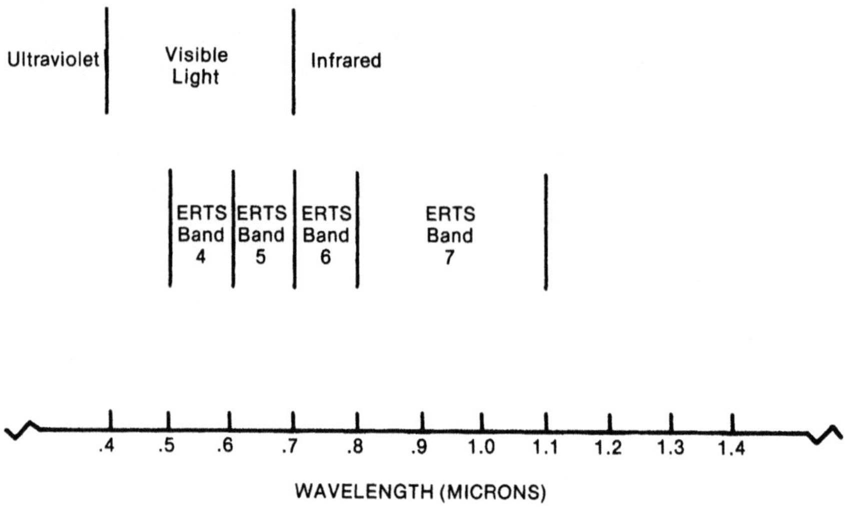

Figure 1. A Portion of the Electromagnetic Spectrum

More detailed studies, even down to the local level, can be carried out using the computer data. Significant results have been obtained using both types of data from LANDSAT.

Frequently LANDSAT data are supplemented by high altitude (60,000 ft.) vertical aerial photography and/or low altitude photography.[5] These photographic missions generally include blacks and white and color infrared imagery at scales of approximately 1:120,000 (for the 60,000 ft. photography) and, possibly, multispectral photography. The multispectral photography is similar to the data recorded by the LANDSAT MSS except that it is recorded on film. Multispectral scanners with up to twenty-four channels are sometimes flown on high and low altitude aircraft but their complexity and the costs of data reduction inhibit their widespread use.

A major portion of the Skylab missions was devoted to earth resources photography and data collection. Several camera systems as well as thirteen channel multispectral scanner were on board. These data while valuable, are not available on a continuing basis since Skylab has completed its mission.

The above sensors and complex computer analysis methods form the technology base for what is generally referred to as remote sensing. Spacecraft (LANDSAT and Skylab) and aircraft (high and low altitude) provide data in both digital (MSS) and analog (photographic) form.

LANDSAT Data Users

In order to assure widespread experimentation with use of the LANDSAT data, NASA stimulated several hundred investigations in a variety of disciplines. These investigations took place during the first one or two years of LANDSAT-I. In addition to providing the ERTS data products to the investigators, funds for research and supportive studies were provided.[3,4] It is not surprising, therefore, that much enthusiasm for LANDSAT-type data exists among these investigators. The true test of the usefulness of this technology rests on its adoption by users who were not funded to conduct experiments and/or demonstration projects.

The Earth Resources Observation System (EROS) Data Center was established by the Department of Interior at Sioux Falls, S.D., to distribute the data products from LANDSAT (and other sources) to the general public at the cost of reproducing these projects. Black and white photographs from ERTS are available at a scale of 1:1,000,000 for \$2 to \$3. Color infrared composites are available at a cost of about \$12 at the same scale. Almost since the launch of LANDSAT, the EROS Data Center has been deluged with requests for information and orders for the data products.

Some statistics supplied by the EROS Data Center indicate the tremendous interest on the part of the non-NASA funded investigators in the LANDSAT data: During the period October 1973 through July 1974, there were approximately 5000 customer contacts per month by EROS Data Center staff members. To be sure, some of these inquiries were prompted by curiosity only. However, it is reasonable to assume that a significant number of these customers were genuinely interested in the remote sensor data and wished to acquire useful information.

There are other indications of the benefits to be derived from use of the LANDSAT data. These are the active state programs for utilization of the LANDSAT data in those states not funded by NASA. For example, in Georgia, there are three agencies which have had ongoing projects for applying LANDSAT technology to state programs almost since the launch of LANDSAT-I. The Earth and Water Division of the Georgia Department of Natural Resources has pursued a program of utilization of the LANDSAT photography. These photographic products have been used in the preparation of geologic maps and to produce LANDSAT mosaics of the state. The Planning and Research Division of the Georgia Department of Natural Resources has been investigating photographic products from both satellite and aircraft and digital processing of LANDSAT data for use in their own program.

The Engineering Experiment Station (EES) at the Georgia Institute of Technology has also had an internally funded program utilizing LANDSAT and other remotely sensed data since 1972. In addition to using the photographic products, EES has developed, without NASA funding, the capability for computer processing the LANDSAT CCT's to produce thematic maps. During 1973-74 an active project of remote sensing technology transfer to state and local agencies was carried out using internal funds. During this project many state, regional, and local agencies were contacted concerning their problems to which remote sensing technology might be applied. A complete explanation of the types of data available and its potential usefulness was explained. In addition to these meetings, seminars and a short course on the applications of remote sensing were presented. Total attendance was approximately 200 persons. Since developing these capabilities EES has received funding from NASA/Marshall Space Flight Center for a cooperative research program with the Georgia Department of Natural Resources and other state agencies.

Not only do domestic agencies have programs for the use of LANDSAT data but many foreign countries are also using the data. Some governments obtain the data directly from NASA, whereas others get data from the EROS Data Center. Several countries, however, have invested millions of dollars in their own ground receiving stations. Canada and Brazil are two countries which have completed or nearly completed stations. Other countries including Japan and Italy are considering building ground receiving stations. We can be sure these commitments were not made without complete consideration of the potential costs and benefits.

REMOTE SENSING APPLICATIONS

As an earth observation platform for capturing earth resources data, LANDSAT is unique in a number of ways. LANDSAT imagery provides a synoptic view not otherwise obtainable except at considerable expense. One ERTS image covers an area 115 mi x 115 mi or approximately 13,000 square miles; this is an area larger than eight of the states. Large scale phenomena can be obtained directly on the ERTS photographic products. For example, the areal extent of forest fire burns can be rapidly and accurately mapped from LANDSAT imagery.[5]

LANDSAT imagery can be used to study dynamic phenomena because of the repetitive nature of its coverage. Each point on the surface of the earth can be imaged at least every eighteen days (clouds permitting) (with two satellites currently operating this becomes nine days.) Because of orbit overlaps many areas north and south of the equator are imaged more frequently. Available LANDSAT data permitted mapping the extent of the Mississippi River floods in 1973. Also the extent of snow cover can be accurately mapped and these data, when combined with snow depth statistics, can be used to estimate water supplies in the growing season.[6] Dynamic phenomina of short duration may not necessarily be imaged by LANDSAT, however.

The altitude of LANDSAT, approximately 570 miles, is another advantage in many instances. The nearly vertical imaging of the earth provides photographic products with low distortion. Because of its altitude and its high geometric fidelity, LANDSAT images have been used to revise nautical and aeronautical charts. Maps of many countries have been revised because of the new information provided by LANDSAT. Photomosaics of the entire United States also have been prepared.[7]

All of this information provided by LANDSAT possibly could have been obtained from conventional sources. However, the costs would have been prohibitive, if in fact there are sufficient capabilities world-wide for gathering these data. LANDSAT, therefore, is unique in providing these capabilities at a cost easily affordable by the U.S. and other countries.

LANDSAT data have been used in a variety of natural resource and environmental surveys. The data are most useful to resource managers for measuring physical parameters necessary for the planning process. For example, a range manager needs information on the vigor and extent of grasslands in order to plan the proper grazing population for his area of responsibility. LANDSAT data could become an integral part of the planning process by providing timely inputs concerning the physical parameters of interest.[8]

Symposia sponsored by Goddard Space Flight Center (GSFC) on significant results obtained from LANDSAT were held in March and December 1973(4). Many of the participants of these symposia were asked to serve on panels to prepare discipline summary reports outlining the applicability of ERTS to their disciplines. The disciplines covered by these reports include:

Agriculture, Forestry, Range Resources

Mineral Resources, Geological Structure, and Landform Surveys

Environment Surveys

Water Resources

Land Use Mapping

Marine Resources and Ocean Surveys

Multidisciplinary/Regional Resource Surveys

These disciplines are representative of the wide range of uses to which the LANDSAT data have been put. Interested readers are referred to the GSFC symposia proceedings.[4]

Since these investigations were funded by NASA, they were largely devoted to research. The authors' experiences have been more directed toward education of users and transfer of the technology to users as well as the solution of problems. The technology transfer experiences will be described in the next section. However, this section is concluded by briefly describing a few projects where the users have funded their own remote sensing investigations.

High altitude color infrared photographs were used to survey the ecosystems and cultural features along 500 miles of proposed pipeline routes from an off shore deep crater port to the refinery. Since these areas were predominantly marsh, field investigation would have been impractical. Remote sensing provided the quickest, and possibly the only, method for surveying the area.[9]

A county engineering department and planning department funded an investigation of several alternatives for producing and updating county land use maps. Also included in this study was an evaluation of two alternative information storage and retrieval systems. The study concluded that remote sensing, primarily photography, would be useful in producing and updating the land use maps.[10]

A regional planning commission in a major urban area was concerned with annually updating a development pattern map. Without frequent updating the map would soon be useless in such a rapidly growing area. Multiple remote sensing methods including high and low altitude photography and computer analysis of LANDSAT data were investigated.[11,12]

All of these projects have two things in common: all relied heavily on remote sensor data and all were funded entirely by the users. In these instances, at least, the use of remote sensing has been adopted by the sponsoring agencies. However, not all of these agencies as yet have developed the internal capabilities for utilizing remote sensing. Consequently, technology transfer is a continuing need.

TECHNOLOGY TRANSFER EXPERIENCES

The authors have experience in four types of technology transfer projects: seminars, short courses, surveys, and consulting projects. This section summarizes these experiences and includes a brief description of the National Science Foundation sponsored experiments in remote sensing technology transfer at the NASA/National Space Technology Laboratories.

The capability to transfer technology varies considerably with the structure of the transfer instrument. For example, a consulting project is potentially an excellent method for transferring technology to users. However, if the user agency does not participate directly in the project with the consultant, it is unlikely that any technology will be transferred to the user. The remainder of this section is devoted to an examination of the various technology transfer methods. The next section contains observations about the relative effectiveness of the alternative methods.

Surveys can be a mechanism for transferring technology. A written questionnaire circulated to users or potential users of remote sensing can serve to increase awareness of the technology. Properly drawn questionnaires can also lead to user interest in getting additional information about applications of their technology to their particular needs. Obviously there is a greater possibility of information transfer when the survey is conducted in person--either in conjunction with or following a written questionnaire. In the author's experience remote sensing questionnaires circulated to potential users who have little or no knowledge of the subject raise more questions than they provide answers. Thus while they do not necessarily transfer technology directly, surveys can promote the transfer of technology by other mechanisms.

Seminars are another possible mechanism for the transfer of remote sensing technology to users. Seminars may be considered as including any meeting in which current research and applications are discussed with a combination of other researchers in the field and those users who may be interested in applying the technology to their own problems. If the seminar is devoted exclusively to one subject, such as remote sensing, the audience is likely to be composed of individuals who already have some familiarity with the subject. However, if remote sensing is but one of many subjects covered, it is likely that potential users will be reached who have little or no previous knowledge of the subject area.

In the past most seminars devoted exclusively to remote sensing have tended to draw only those individuals already interested in remote sensing such as researchers. This pattern may be changing, however. At the Earth Resources Survey Symposium sponsored by NASA in Houston, Texas June 8-12, 1975 a significant percentage of the participants (possibly a majority) consisted of individuals from state, regional, local, and foreign governments as well as private firms who desired to use remote sensing for solving their operational problems.

In the authors' experience, presentations given to audiences at multi-subject seminars have evoked more comments and questions from the audience than those presentations prepared for remote sensing symposia. We conclude that the general level of knowledge of remote sensing capabilities has been quite low until recently. Also the multi-subject seminar has in the past been a better remote sensing technology transfer forum than remote sensing symposia.

Short courses have been used extensively by universities, and to a limited extent, by the EROS Data Center for remote sensing technology transfer. These courses range from a few days to several weeks in duration. The longer courses are more likely to include lab experiments, project work, and individual data analyses than are the shorter course. While the lab sessions and projects provide the opportunity for substantial interaction between the students and instructors, the setting is artifical. Students are probably working on problems with which they have only limited familiarity, and time constraints inhibit the learning process.

The above drawbacks not withstanding, properly prepared short courses do provide an opportunity for "ahnds on" experience in the use of remote sensor data. Neither of the previously discussed transfer mechanisms provided this opportunity.

Properly conducted consulting projects can result in the efficient transfer of remote sensing technology to a client. However, if the client does not participate directly in the project, little or no technology will be transferred--the client will receive only a report and/or presentation of the results. The authors have been involved in consulting projects of both types. In those projects where alternatives were discussed and/or results were presented in a report, it is felt that relatively little technology was transferred. The level of awareness on the part of the client was increased, but this probably could have been accomplished by other means.

In an ongoing consulting project in which the clients are actively involved in all phases of the work, significant accomplishments in technology transfer are occurring. The project is being conducted for a regional planning agency in a larger metropolitan area. The purpose is to investigate several alternative schemes for annually updating a development patterns (land use) map. Several remote sensing alternatives are being considered. As consultants, we are providing direction to the project, handling logistics for the project, and making recommendations concerning data sources, needed research, and possible results.

From the beginning the emphasis has been on maximum possible remote sensing technology transfer to the client. The project will not make remote sensing "experts" of the clients, but indications are that significant increases in client understanding are taking place. In addition, the major experimental portion of the project provides for direct client participation in all phases.

The experimental part of the project involves use of interactive color display and processing equipment for analyzing LANDSAT computer compatible tapes to map land use and detect changes in land use. The General Electric Image 100 system at Kennedy Space Center (KSC) was used in the preliminary analysis. The Image 100 system at the EROS Data Center is to be used for testing three alternative updating methods involving LANDSAT data in the second phase of the project. Four members of the client's staff accompanied the consultant to KSC for the initial analysis which were largely performed by the clients' staff. It is anticipated that two or three staff members will accompany the consultant to the EROS Data Center.

This project is not complete at this time. However, we believe that it will be one of the most successful remote sensing technology transfer experiences in which the authors have been directly involved.

Until recently, no large scale remote sensing technology transfer effort had been undertaken in this country. The projects funded by NASA were primarily research oriented. The EROS Data Center has conducted several short courses in remote sensing techniques but it has only recently begun an organized technology transfer program. The most advanced large-scale transfer program to date is probably the Mississippi/Louisiana technology transfer experiment funded by NSF with expertise provided largely by NASA/ National Space Technology Laboratories at Bay St. Louis Mississippi.

The projects were begun in mid-1974 program evaluations indicate that substantial progress is being made. For example, at the third quarterly meeting of the Joint Policy Council of the Consortium for Technology Transfer (composed of representatives from NSF, NASA, Louisiana, and Mississippi) held April 28, 1975, a number of completed and continuing cooperative efforts with state/regional/local agencies were reported. Louisiana reported ten problems encountered by state agencies in which the Technology Transfer Office of the State Science Foundation had been able to assist. In addition, tours and/or briefings were given to nine agencies personnel. These problems and briefings were primarily concerned with remote sensing applications.

The Mississippi Office of Science and Technology reported on fourteen projects involving numerous state agencies with technology being transferred from various federal agencies. Again the primary emphasis of these projects related to remote sensing capabilities.

While these projects have had some organizational and growth pains, significant progress toward the goal of technology transfer has been achieved. Both participants and observers of the project have pronounced it successful. For the most part the success seems to arise from the <u>direct</u> interaction of the users and the technologists. Based on these successes, it is likely that the scope of the transfer process will be expanded to include other states and/or groups of states.

OBSERVATIONS AND CONCLUSIONS

The problem of transferring remote sensing technology to aid public decision- and policy-making has some of the elements of a classical technology transfer problem: the potential user of the technology may be unaware of what potential applications exist, lacking in understanding of the scope and limitations of the technical capabilities, and unskilled in the use of the technologies. In tracing a case of remote sensing technology transfer, one can often observe three distinct steps in the technology transfer process: awareness of potential applications, understanding of requirements and capabilities, and skill in applying and using the technology. The first or first and second steps may be undertaken without a commitment to a full skill transfer.

Consequently, examinations of the relative merits of particular mechanisms for transferring the NASA-developed remote sensing technologies to the potential public users requires that the expected results of the transfer be specified. For example, the desired results may be simply a transfer of the awareness of the potential applications of the technology, and an evaluation of the transfer mechanism in terms of how well remote sensing technology skills are practiced in the new context would be inappropriate.

The technology transfer process conceptually can involve three separate and distinct roles: the potential user of the technology, a funder of the technology transfer activities, and a performer of the research or transfer activities. Figure 2 is a diagram showing how these roles may overlap.

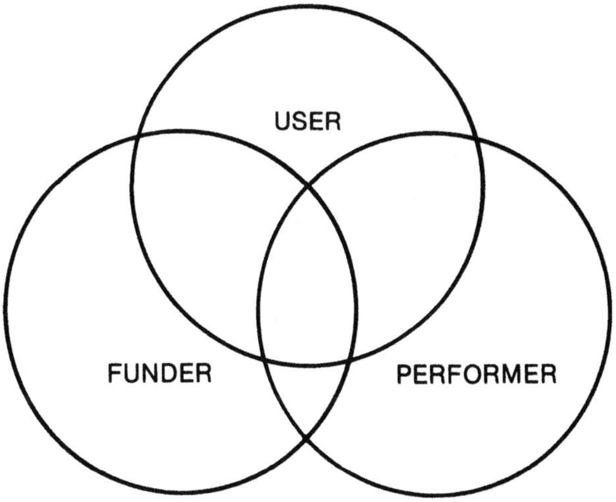

Figure 2. Possible Role Relationships in the Technology Transfer Process

The experience of the National Science Foundation's Research Applied to National Need (RANN) program suggests that the most effective technology transfer takes place where the three roles overlap, that is, when the user is also the performer of the activity and the one providing the funds to support the effort.[14] The transfer process is less effective when there are two separate agencies/organizations (funder) performer and user, funder/user and performer, or user/performer and funder. The least effective situation occurs when the roles of funder, user, and performer are fulfilled by separate organizations or agencies.

Operationally, however, one observes that at least some technology transfer must take place before a potential user is willing to support the technology transfer activities which lead to the full understanding and skill required for complete realization of the potential applications. This observation, coupled with the empirically-based judgments in Table I, suggest the following possible strategies for transferring remote sensing technology:

1. Survey (sponsored by a central or state-level government) of possible users and/or sponsored presentations of remote sensing potential applications at multi-subject symposia;

2. Sponsored (e.g., by government and/or professional organizations) short courses for the potential users identified in step 1; and

3. Subsequent separate participatory consulting projects, sponsored by the individual users (if the number of users are few) or a large-scale project analogous to the NSF experiment (if there are several potential users).

In summary, remote sensing technology has significant potential for aiding public policy- and decision-making, particularly resource utilization policy and decisions. Several methods can be effective for various stages in the technology transfer process, and the authors' experiences suggest a desirable sequential strategy for technology transfer which utilizes a mix of transfer mechanisms.

Table 1. Observations on Comparative Effectiveness of Alternative Technology Transfer Methods*

	CRITERION			
	AWARENESS	UNDERSTANDING	SKILL	COST
METHOD				
SURVEY				
Interview	2	1	1	4
Written	3	2	1	5
SEMINAR				
Remote Sensing	3	3	2	4
Multi-Subject	4	2	2	4
SHORT COURSE				
Lecture Only	3	2	3	4
Lecture and Lab	4	3	4	3
CONSULTING				
Non-Participation	4	4	3	3
User Participates	4	4	5	3
NSF EXPERIMENT	5	4	4	1

*Rated on a Scale from 1 to 5, with 5 = Excellent/Outstanding (Most Effective) and 1 = Least Desirable (Least Effective or Most Costly)

REFERENCES

1. NASA Press Kit No: 74-329, January 14, 1975 and many other articles.

2. Reported by NASA personnel at Goddard Space Flight Center Symposium in March 1973 and other places.

3. Proceedings of the Ninth International Symposium on Remote Sensing of Environment, University of Michigan, April 1974.

4. Symposia on Significant Results Obtained from the Earth Resources Technology Satellite, NASA SP-327, March 1973 and Dec 1973, Goddard Space Flight Center.

5. C. Winikka et al., "Applications of Remote Sensing in Arizona State Government," Proceedings of the Eighth International Symposium on Remote Sensing of Environment, University of Michigan, September 1972.

6. James C. Barnes, et al., "Use of Satellite Data for Mapping Snow Cover in the Western United States, "Management and Utilization of Remote Sensing Data, American Society of Photogrammetry, Sioux Falls, S.D., Oct. 1973, p. 166.

7. Alden P. Colvocoress, "The ERTS Image Format as the Basis for a Map Series," Ibid, p. 142.

8. Merle P. Meyer, et al., "Remote Sensing Applications to Northern Great Plains Resource Management," Ibid, p. 593.

9. Unpublished Metrics study for a private client.

10. G. William Spann, METRICS, INC., "Proposed Aerial Photo-mapping Program for Cobb County," Final Report, August 26, 1974.

11. G. William Spann, METRICS, INC., "Use of Remote Sensing Data for Land Use Mapping" Final Report, Prepared for the Atlanta Regional Commission, December 1974.

12. Atlanta Regional Commission, "Land Use Study Design" ARC Working Paper, December 1974.

13. Information available from EROS Data Center, Sioux Falls, S.D.

14. Personal communication with Dr. Thomas P. Anderson, Office of Systems Analysis and Integration (RANN), National Science Foundation.

ACCELERATING REFORM IN THE COURTS THROUGH TECHNOLOGY TRANSFER

Dean C. Merrill

Institute for Law and Social Research
Washington, D.C.

Introduction

This paper describes the successful transfer of a computer based management information system to prosecutors throughout the United States. The system known as PROMIS (Prosecutor's Management Information System)[1] has been designated as an exemplary project of the Law Enforcement Assistance Administration of the U.S. Department of Justice. Such designation is reserved for criminal justice programs judged outstanding, worthy of national attention, and suitable for adoption by other communities.

PROMIS has been made available to interested prosecutors since August 1974, and currently is operational in three jurisdictions: Washington, D.C.; Cobb County, Georgia; and Los Angeles County, California. It is presently being implemented in nine other jurisdictions.

What are the reasons behind the successful transfer of this system? Which components of the transfer package convince prosecutors to take the big step toward automating their operations? What are some of the traditional impediments of transferring technology in the criminal justice community, and how has the PROMIS transfer package overcome these problems?

Prosecutorial Environment

Before attempting to address these questions, it is important first to appreciate the environment in which the prosecutor operates and to identify the problems that PROMIS addresses.

What better way to describe the dilemma of the criminal justice system than to present a typical case and track its handling today.

On January 15, 1974, at 10:30 p.m., a 43-year-old male is walking through an alley in a large city when he is approached by two persons, one of whom is carrying a pistol. The victim is ordered to empty his pockets and hand over his wallet. After taking one hundred dollars, the man with the pistol, strikes the victim twice on the head with the revolver. Bleeding profusely, the victim still manages to scream for help. By chance, another citizen hears the cry and summons a police officer, who apprehends the assailant with the pistol. The other assailant escapes.

The arrested suspect is taken to the police station and booked for armed robbery and assault. He gives his name as John T. Jones. Although the defendant has two cases currently pending in the court system for prior crimes under the name John Johnson, the police and prosecutors do not realize it since Mr. Johnson is using an alias this time. The next morning, the court, unaware of the other pending cases, releases John T. Jones on his own recognizance pending trial on the new charges.

Meanwhile, the victim is hospitalized and treated for severe head lacerations and a fractured skull, and is told he must remain in the hospital for a month. The eyewitness who summoned the police has stated that he will testify against the defendant. A subpoena is sent to the victim and eyewitness informing them that trial will be held on October 10, 1974. On the 10th of October, both the victim and the witness are notified that the trial has been postponed for two weeks until October 24, 1974. On that date the victim and witness come to court and wait for the trial to begin. After waiting for four hours they are told that the defense counsel has a schedule conflict and the case is postponed for one month.

Prior to the rescheduled trial, the eyewitness is confused about the trial date. He calls the prosecutor's office and asks the current status of the case. He is told that without having the court docket number there is no way to answer his question. Frustrated, the witness hangs up and decides not to pursue the matter any further.

On the day of trial, the prosecutor reviews the case for the first time fifteen minutes before trial. He has three other cases to prepare during the day. Present in court are the arresting police officer and victim. The eyewitness has not appeared by the time trial is scheduled to begin. Since the eyewitness is the only one who can identify the defendant as having robbed and assaulted the victim, the prosecutor asks for a postponement. However, the court does not grant the government's request, and the charges against John T. Jones are dropped.

Soon thereafter, the same defendant commits yet another crime.

The processing of this case is not an exception to the way prosecutors in large urban centers handle their case loads. The prosecutor must dispose of thousands of cases every year. Because of inadequate staffing, the lack of a rapid methods for identifying high priority cases, and insufficient management consciousness, case backlogs grow inexorably. Cases are accepted and disposed of without any sense of direction. Prosecutors fight to acquire additional staff with little success.

The result of all this is the mass-produced, "assembly line" prosecutor's office in which cases are dealt with rapidly, anonymously, and with minimum accountability. And, perhaps not suprisingly, the public has become increasingly frustrated and demoralized about the criminal court system.

Recognizing the environment in which the prosecutor currently operates, let's take the case previously described and see how an information system such as PROMIS can improve the operations of the prosecutor.

The same situation exists as before, up to the point where the suspect is booked. Using the PROMIS system, the prosecutor can determine whether any other cases are pending against the defendant through a defendant identification number based on the suspect's fingerprints. The prosecutor can thus link the suspect to the two other cases pending against him, regardless of any alias he may have used upon arrest.

Furthermore, the prosecutor can note the type of pretrial release the defendant has received for the previous alleged crimes. He can notify the prosecutor handling the other cases that the defendant has been rearrested, thus facilitating plea negotiations, or at least permitting consolidation of efforts to dispose of the defendant's multiple cases. This information is available even before official charges are filed with the court based on the latest arrest. Armed with this information, the prosecutor can recommend to the court a type of pretrial status that is more in line with the defendant's probable threat to the community.

The seriousness of the crime[2] and the gravity of the defendant's criminal history[3] are evaluated using a predetermined ranking system. The seriousness of the crime is measured in terms of the degree of harm done to society rather than in terms of the legal nomenclature. In this case, an individual was assaulted and hospitalized and the rating of the crime would reflect the serious injury that was involved, in addition to the amount of money stolen. The gravity of the defendant's criminal history is assessed by factors such as frequency of prior arrests, the number of previous arrests for crimes against persons, and the use of aliases. As disposition data becomes more readily available, conviction data will also be taken into account.

The system automatically generates subpoenas to the victim and eyewitness and a notification to the arresting police officer, informing them of the trial date. If the trial will occur too soon to permit mailing the subpoenas, the names of all appropriate persons will be automatically flagged by the system for telephone notification.

If the eyewitness calls the prosecutor's office for information about the case in which he is to testify, the witness's name is all that is needed to determine immediately the status of the case and when it is scheduled for trial.

Several days before the trial, the prosecutor receives a print-out of all cases scheduled for that day. The cases are listed in order of priority according to the rating schemes explained before. The prosecutor will then decide which cases are the most important and which ones he would like to prepare specially for trial. The case we are using as an example here would be flagged as high priority, since the offense involved personal injury and an offender who has a serious criminal history. Because the case is chosen for special preparation, the witnesses would be individually contacted and the case would go to trial on its merits rather than being short circuited by administrative inefficiencies.

Based on this case example alone, one may wonder why every big city prosecutor does not implement such a system. President Ford took note of this problem in his first presidential speech on crime, when he described the need to "assign priority cases of habitual criminals and expedite the process by which they are brought to justice."[4] More recently, President Ford had this to say about priorities in the reform of the criminal justice system:

> "Effective deterrence to law-breaking is currently lacking, in part because our criminal justice system simply does not operate effectively.

"A logical place to begin discussion of such improvement is the prosecutor's office, for it is there that important decisions are made as to which offenders should be prosecuted, what cases should be brought to trial, when plea bargains should be struck and how scarce judicial resources should be allocated. Many prosecutors' offices currently lack the manpower or management devices to make those decisions correctly. Prosecutors often lack information on a defendant's criminal history and thus cannot identify habitual criminals who should be tried by experienced prosecutors and, if convicted, sent to prison. In too many cases, they lack efficient systems to monitor the status of the numerous cases they handle. If improved management techniques could be made available to prosecutors, the likelihood of swift and sure punishment for crime would be substantially increased."[5]

The PROMIS system is even more impressive when one looks at some of its additional benefits:

- generating statistics on office work load and performance;

- monitoring evenhandedness and consistency in the exercise of prosecutive discretion;

- making it possible to control and alleviate scheduling and logistical impediments to the adjudication of cases;

- providing a rich data base of case and defandant information which can be used to analyze and research problems in the prosecutive system.

History of PROMIS

The history of PROMIS demonstrates its evolution into a transferable product. The system was initially designed, developed, and implemented under Law Enforcement Assistance Administration (LEAA) funding for the Superior Court Division of the United States Attorney's Office for the District of Columbia.

In 1972, a year after PROMIS became operational, the LEAA administrator sent a letter to 1,300 district attorneys throughout the nation recommending PROMIS for their consideration. The decision to recommend PROMIS to other jurisdictions was prompted by the fact that a 25% increase in convictions resulted in

Washington, D. C., for offenders identified by PROMIS as having serious criminal histories.

PROMIS was not then available as a transferable product. It had been developed for a particular prosecution system and was written in a programming language supported by a very limited number of computer manufacturers. Therefore, LEAA awarded a grant to the Institute for Law and Social Research (INSLAW) to redesign the system and reprogram it in American National Standards Institute Common Business Oriented Language (ANSI/COBOL) for transfer to other jurisdictions. This language allows the potential users of PROMIS flexibility to implement the system on a variety of manufacturers' hardware. After the newly designed system was complete, INSLAW began the PROMIS transfer effort.

Pitfalls to Systems Transfer

The transfer package was carefully designed to bridge the communications gap between technology and the user, the prosecuting attorney; in addition, it overcomes many of the pitfalls usually encountered when transferring computer technology, particularly within the public sector.

These pitfalls to technology transfer are common to many computer based information systems transfer efforts. No matter how exceptional the quality of the product, the potential user may be faced with the following problems:

- comprehending the concepts which the system supports;
- employing new categories of personnel to implement and monitor the system, such as systems analysts;
- obtaining funds to support the transfer effort;
- planning an unfamiliar project requiring strict time schedules, special funding, and rapid procurement of services and hardware;
- using contractors or consultants for the first time; and
- justifying costs and benefits of the system to local legislatures.

These problems are aggravated by conditions peculiar to the prosecutive environment, such as the following:

- Effective advocacy on a case-by-case basis places a premium on recognizing the unique aspects of individual cases. This orientation militates against the search by management for common attributes or patterns in overall work flow.

- Preoccupation with advocacy based on concrete facts in individual cases overwhelms any tendency to contemplate abstractions about systems and procedures.

- The politically volatile nature of the office prompts many prosecutors to seek short-term, highly visible improvements that can quickly be translated into votes, instead of concentrating on longer term, less visible improvements in systems and procedures.

- The inadequacy of resources in the large urban prosecution agencies often discourages any thought about long-term projects for improvements.

The PROMIS Transfer Package

In view of these problems, it is remarkable that a sophisticated computer based information system like PROMIS has been transferred successfully numerous times in so brief a period. NASA studies[6] have indicated that technology transfer is most successful through the movement of the people who are intimately familiar with the technology. However, this is not always practical and alternative methods must be applied.

Technical briefs and communication of ideas and concepts are important ingredients for successful transfer, but again should not be the only mechanisms used in leading a user to make the decision to implement existing technology. In the 1972 *Directory of Automated Criminal Justice Information Systems*[7] alone, there are 454 separately defined systems representing 153 jurisdictions in the United States. It would be unreasonable to expect a busy prosecutor to review these systems and choose one for implementation.

The role of the Institute for Law and Social Research in accomplishing the goal of transferring PROMIS is to perform what a recent National Science Foundation (NSF) report, *Technology Transfer and Utilization*,[8] terms "a complex brokerage process" which serves as "the catalyst to help match the needs to the technologies." The PROMIS transfer plan conforms to the stated recommendations of the NSF report, which calls for "shifting the focus of Federal concern from *simply telling* commercial users and local governments about promising technologies to actually *transforming technical information into ultimate uses* that fulfill public or private economic and social needs." (Emphasis added.)

The PROMIS transfer package contains the following components, which attempt to overcome the initial pitfalls of transfer. PROMIS is offered to interested prosecutors at no cost.

1. PROMIS Briefing Series

INSLAW has prepared a series of 21 briefing papers to explain to nontechnical audiences, such as prosecutors, court administrators, criminal justice planners, and members of the bar, the underlying concepts of management and organization inherent in PROMIS. It is expected that these briefings will assist jurisdictions to evaluate and, when appropriate, implement PROMIS in part or whole. Subjects include a general overview of PROMIS, its role in case screening, its use in identifying deficiencies in legal training, improving witness management supporting forms and procedures, security and privacy considerations, criminal justice research capabilities, cost and benefit analysis and so forth.

2. PROMIS Video Presentation

Twenty minute color videotape and 16mm film presentations on PROMIS for nontechnical audiences have been developed, presenting in documentary fashion, the major concepts and management uses of PROMIS.

3. PROMIS Software Documentation

A four-volume set of technical documentation has been developed. The series includes:

- System Overview - Intended for prosecutors, court administrators, and other potential users of PROMIS including computer systems analysts, this volume contains a general description of PROMIS capabilities and their relationship to the prosecutive process.

- System and Program Descriptions - Intended for computer systems analysts and programmers, this volume contains system flow charts and narratives by module, program descriptions, file and record descriptions, and a data element dictionary.

- Data Preparation Guide - Intended for data collection, coding, input, verification, and editing personnel, this volume defines the coding conventions, source documents, turnaround documents, input transactions, editing and error correction procedures, daily execution instructions, purging instructions, and procedures for updating indexes.

- Software Implementation Guide - Intended for computer systems analysts and programmers in jurisdictions which have decided to install the PROMIS software, this volume provides a description of the tape product containing the software and checklists of tasks for testing, modifying, and installing PROMIS.

4. PROMIS Computer Software

The software includes the computer source programs, copy libraries, sample indexes, and test data for testing the software.

5. PROMIS Technical Assistance

Technical assistance includes: (a) special seminars and conferences for computer systems personnel and such non-technical personnel as lawyers and court administrators; (b) on-site visits to advise interested potential users on the feasibility of transfer and on modifications and installation; (c) presentation of briefings at regional and national meetings of prosecuting attorneys and other groups; and (d) help to interested jurisdictions in:

- writing applications to obtain funds;
- writing a request for proposal to attract bids from private industry to install PROMIS;
- establishing criteria for a jurisdiction to select a contractor;
- helping jurisdictions conduct bidders conferences;
- reviewing progress reports;
- providing on-site and telephone technical assistance to solve contractor or user problems during implementation.

6. PROMIS Users Group

An essential component of the PROMIS transfer package is the formation of a Users Group which provides a valuable forum for discussion of implementation problems and coordination of necessary changes in concepts and operation. INSLAW, as administrator of the Users Group, is the central repository of all documentation on changes and modifications in PROMIS concepts and software. The Users Group includes 15 members representing jurisdictions either operating or implementing PROMIS or planning such implementations.

Meetings enable participants to exchange experiences, failures, successes, problems, and solutions. In addition, the Users Group is a mechanism for transferring enhancements made to PROMIS by one particular jurisdiction to another. The members of the Users Group meet three or four times a year for one or two days depending on the subject matter to be discussed.

How the PROMIS Transfer Package Functions

An important aspect of the transfer process is the method used to combine these components into an effective package which enhances transferability of the PROMIS technology. The mechanisms listed above are used individually as well as in combination, depending upon the needs of the potential user. Perhaps an example of an actual transfer of PROMIS may demonstrate how the transfer mechanism operates.

The New Orleans, Louisiana Parish District Attorney's Office (NODA) expressed an interest in developing an automated information system to monitor a yearly case load of approximately 16,000 criminal cases. The District Attorney serves a community of 538,000 people and has 31 assistant prosecutors.

The New Orleans District Attorney contacted INSLAW, and a set of briefing papers was forwarded to him for review. Shortly thereafter, representatives of NODA's office visited INSLAW in Washington, D.C., and a briefing and tour of the U.S. Attorney's Office, where PROMIS is operating, was conducted. In addition, a representative of NODA was invited to attend the PROMIS Users Group meeting. Technical assistance visits were made to New Orleans to perform a preliminary feasibility study. Discussions with the District Attorney led to the decision that PROMIS could be transferred to New Orleans Parish, would meet the needs of the District Attorney, and could be transferred at a cost which would be appropriate for federal funding.

INSLAW provided NODA with copies of several PROMIS grant applications from other jurisdictions which had received funds to implement PROMIS. Together with NODA, INSLAW helped prepare a draft grant application. Although the content of the grant application was tailored to New Orleans, many of the task plans for implementation were adapted directly from the sample grant applications. INSLAW then met with the federal funding agency (U.S. Department of Justice, LEAA) and NODA and informally resolved questions on cost projections and time schedules for the PROMIS implementation. This review process has benefited the funding agency in several PROMIS transfers because users had been quoted excessive costs by contractors. In these instances, the cost reduction finally negotiated to implement PROMIS was as much as one-half the original estimate.

Once the grant was awarded, INSLAW aided NODA in preparing a request for proposal (RFP) to solicit bids from contractors to perform the implementation. Again, sample RFPs used by other jurisdictions were made available to NODA.

Subsequently, INSLAW conducted a bidders' conference with NODA and helped evaluate the bids from private contractors. Once a contractor was selected by NODA using the criteria INSLAW provided, the software and related system documentation were provided to New Orleans Parish. In addition, INSLAW helped to evaluate two prospective computer centers in New Orleans and made recommendations on which would best serve the interests of NODA and the PROMIS transfer.

INSLAW continues to monitor this implementation effort and provides technical assistance to both the contractor and the District Attorney. However, INSLAW's primary role is to be a "counselor" to the user, in the case the New Orleans District Attorney. INSLAW is available to aid the District Attorney whenever problems or doubts arise. Since INSLAW has no contractual ties with the contractor, it can operate independently of the client/contractor relationship and provide valuable advice to the prosecutor.

This approach to technology transfer, using the originator of the technology in a brokerage function, has led to the successful transfer of PROMIS to Los Angles County, California; Cobb County, Georgia: and the State of Rhode Island. Figure 1 lists the jurisdictions that have implemented PROMIS or are in the process of transfer, and shows the relative populations that these jurisdictions serve.

The transfer of PROMIS has been successful even with a wide disparity in prosecutor office size, criminal procedures, court/prosecutor relations, centralization and decentralization of case processing, and computer hardware.

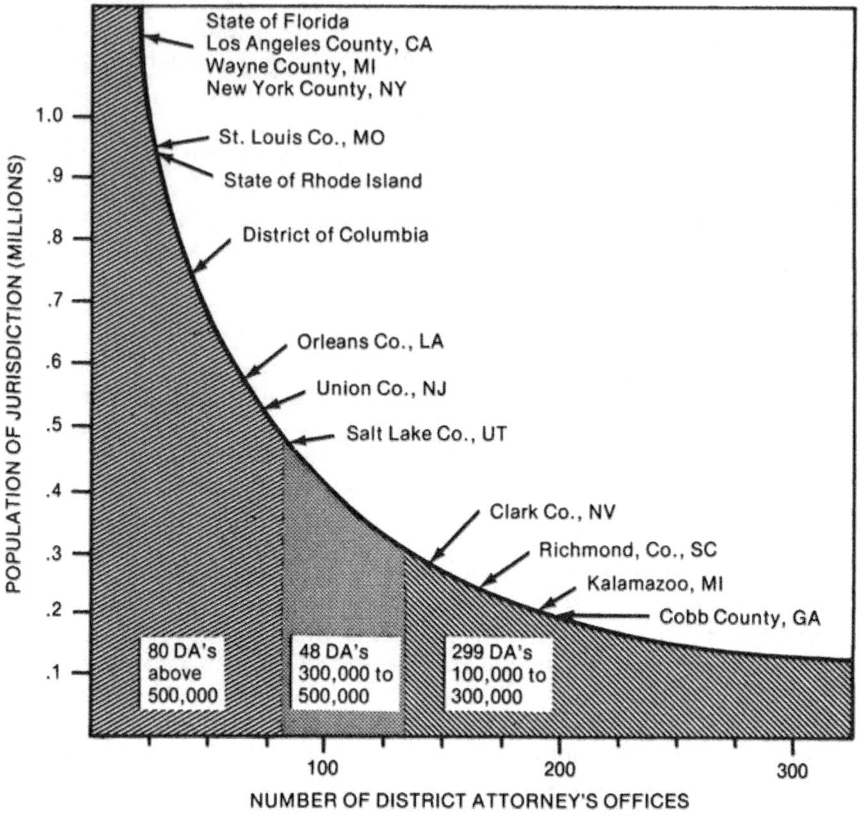

Figure 1. 347 Largest District Attorneys' Offices by Population of Jurisdiction

To summarize the transfer package itself, three essential components of the PROMIS package make it a unique example of technology transfer:

1. A complete package of documentation describing the product is made available to the user. This includes conceptual documentation which the prosecutor can relate to and understand. In addition, the package includes detailed technical documentation as well as implementation guidelines and procedures.

2. The originator of the technology acts in a brokerage role and does not actually implement the system. Implementation is accomplished by a variety of local contractors who can implement the system and tailor it to the user. This approach also allows the user and contractor to take credit for implementing the system, to dispel any feelings that "it was not invented here."

3. The entire transfer package is offered at no cost to an implementing jurisdiction.

Future Developments of the Transfer Package

The obsolescence of computer information system technology is a factor that must be addressed when attempting to transfer a system such as PROMIS. If the software remains static, its utility may depreciate rapidly with time. This situation is caused in part by a fast moving computer technology market characterized by new hardware and software developments. These may include more sophisticated data entry devices, compilers, and minicomputers. The improvement in data entry devices already has been accommodated by designing PROMIS to be independent of data collection and entry procedures. (In fact, the number of data entry device types that are being used is approximately equal to the number of jurisdictions implementing PROMIS.) Avoiding options and programming methods which are unique to a particular manufacturer by writing PROMIS in ANSI/COBAL has diminished the problem of hardware obsolescence and incompatibility among various manufacturers' compilers.

The rising popularity of minicomputers currently is being addressed by INSLAW. Plans are being made to modify PROMIS to operate on minicomputers that support ANSI/COBOL compilers, thus allowing users a broader choice of hardware. They will have options to use time-sharing computer services or buy or lease a minicomputer.

Along with this hardware independence, there still remains a need to enhance the product so that it will become even more attractive to prospective users as the system is transferred from one jurisdiction to the next. In the PROMIS package this is the function of the Users Group. Any new applications developed are placed in the pool of products available to an implementing jurisdiction. For example, the Los Angeles County District Attorney will be developing an on-line data entry capability to handle the decentralization of data collection. The software and conceptual design are available at no cost to another jurisdiction wishing to have the same capability. Another example is that the Rhode Island Attorney General's Office handles only felonies and then only after probable cause is found by a grand jury. The modifications made by Rhode Island to the software will be made available to other prosecutors having the same limited jurisdictional scope as the Rhode Island Attorney General.

In contrast to a system that may become outdated is one that is too advanced for certain users. Inherent in the concept of the PROMIS transfer package is that parts of the system may be implemented in manual form if total automation is not warranted. In these cases many of the concepts, forms, and procedures required for implementing automated PROMIS could be transferred without the software itself. In fact, INSLAW is currently developing a manual (non-automated) version of PROMIS to make available to smaller jurisdictions the underlying concepts used in PROMIS at a lower operating cost. Also, in some states (e.g., New Mexico) the manual version of PROMIS will be used in smaller offices and the automated version in the larger offices to develop a unified set of criminal justice statistics.

Looking beyond the day-to-day operational uses of the PROMIS data, there are important possibilities for long-term research that can prove useful to the improvement of the entire criminal justice system. These include cross-jurisdictional research using the common data base structures developed in a variety of jurisdictions as a result of the PROMIS transfer effort. The PROMIS data base includes over 170 separate data elements on each case in a particular jurisdiction (See Appendix A for a summary of the data elements). In Washington, D.C., the first jurisdiction which implemented PROMIS, there are over 70,000 criminal cases stored on magnetic tape. The data base grows at a rate of 17,000 cases a year.

In Washington, D.C., a three-year research project, currently in its second year, is using PROMIS data to investigate six major problem areas: prosecution performance, police-prosecutor relations, judicial decision making, plea negotiations, speedy trial and patterns of criminal behavior. The research methodology, statistical packages, and the conclusions reached by analyzing the data will be made available by INSLAW to other jurisdictions wishing to embark on a similar research effort.

These additions to the PROMIS transfer package will broaden the scope of technology transfer and provide continuing support to the users of PROMIS.

Further developments in the PROMIS arsenal of transfer mechanisms will include a cost and benefit analysis. This will provide jurisdictions with an ability to estimate costs and benefits of such transfer, and to document and explain those facts to local legislative bodies which must provide operating funds.

The underlying PROMIS concepts and even the software itself may have transfer implications beyond the scope of the court and prosecution environment. Case management in any public law environment where there are thousands of cases to be handled can be affected by programs and ideas such as those contained in PROMIS.

For example, authorities on the public regulatory process, such as Kenneth Culp Davis,[9] and scholars of the criminal prosecution process, such as the late Herbert L. Packer,[10] have noted the close similarities in the decision-making processes of regulation and criminal prosecution. In both sectors of public law, most dispositions result from the exercise of administrative discretion in accordance with informal rules and procedures. The concepts addressed by PROMIS in the criminal justice sector are potentially relevant to the regulatory environment, including the development of:

- mechanisms for routinely documenting and statistically analyzing reasons for discretionary decisions;

- a means for feeding back to enforcement agencies information concerning legal or evidentiary deficiencies and differences in priorities between enforcement and litigation components:

- techniques for assigning litigation resources to more important cases and monitoring evenhandedness of discretionary decisions;

- empirical techniques to analyze case flow and decision making for the purpose of evaluating the performance of individual components (enforcement, litigation, and adjudication) as well as overall system effecitveness, speed, and equity; and

- techniques for formulating and revising enforcement policies and rules based on empirical analysis of operations.

Conclusions

The PROMIS transfer experience clearly demonstrates that a key to successful technology transfer is the establishment of a dialogue between the originator of the technology and the potential user. This open communication has been advanced by the brokerage role played by the Institute for Law and Social Research during the implementation of PROMIS. The methodology used in the PROMIS transfer effort may itself be transferred and contribute to the continuing discussion of how best to transfer technology.

APPENDIX A

SUMMARY OF DATA ELEMENTS IN PROMIS FOR EACH CASE

Information about the accused or defendant. Name, alias, sex, race, date of birth, address, facts about prior arrests and convictions, and employment status. If judged appropriate, additional data may be added, such as information about alcohol or drug abuse. Some of this information is used to rate the gravity of the case based on the defendant's criminal history.

Information about the crime. The date, time, and place of the crime; the number of persons involved; and a numerical rating reflecting the gravity of the crime in terms of the amount and degree of personal injury, property damage or loss, and intimidation.

Information about the arrest. The date, time, and place of the arrest, the type of arrest, and the identity of the arresting officers.

Information about criminal charges. The charges originally placed by the police against the arrestee, the charges actually filed in court against the defendant, the reasons for changes in the charges by the prosecutor, the penal statute for the charge, the FBI Uniform Crime Report Code for the charge, and the national standard (Project SEARCH) Code for the charge.

Information about court events. The dates of every court event in a case from arraignment through motion hearing, continuance hearing, final disposition, and sentencing; the names of the principals involved in each event, including the defense and prosecution attorneys and judges; and the outcomes of the events and the reasons therefore.

Information about witnesses. The names and addresses of all witnesses, the prosecutor's assessment of whether the witnesses are essential to the case, and any indications of reluctance to testify by the witnesses.

REFERENCES

1. See generally William A. Hamilton and Charles R. Work, "The Prosecutor's Role in the Urban Court System: The Case for Management Consciousness," The Journal of Criminal Law and Criminology" 64 (1973) 183; William A. Hamilton, "Modern Management for the Prosecutor," The Prosecutor 7 (1971) 472; Frederick G. Watts and Charles R. Work, "Developing an Automated Information System for the Prosecutor," American Criminology Law Quarterly 9 (1970); Charles R. Work, "A Prosecutor Guide to Automation," The Prosecutor 7 (1971) 479; Dean C. Merrill, "Using the PROMIS Tracking System for Criminal Justice Evaluation," Proceedings of the International Symposium on Criminal Justice Information and Statistics System (1972) 231.

2. See T. Sellin & M. Wolfgang, The Measurement of Delinquency (1964). The modifications made to the Sellin-Wolfgang scale were minor.

3. See D. Gottfredson & R. Beverly, Development and Operational Use of Prediction Methods in Correctional Work, 1962 (Proceedings of the Social Statistics Section of the American Statistical Association, Washington, D.C., 1962); D. Gottfredson & J. Bonds, A Manual for Intake Base Expectancy Scoring, April 1, 1961 (Form CDC--BEGIA) (California Department of Corrections, Research Division, Sacramento); Gottfredson & Ballard, Differences in Parole Decisions Associated With Decision-Makers, 3 J. Res. in Crime & Delinq. 112 (1966). Scale modifications were minor.

4. President Gerald R. Ford (Address to the 81st Annual Convention of the International Association of Chiefs of Police, Washington Hilton Hotel, Washington, D.C., September 24, 1974).

5. President Gerald R. Ford (Message to the 94th-1st Congress of the United States, Thursday, June 19, 1975).

6. Sang Joon Hanh and others, AID/NASA Pilot Project for Technology Transfer to a Developing Nation, Republic of Korea, Korea Institute of Science and Technology, 1972. Robert E. Roberts and others, Economic Impact of Stimulated Technology Activity, Kansas City, Midwest Research Institute, 1971.

7. 1972 Directory of Automatic Criminal Justice Information Systems, Law Enforcement Assistance Administration, Washington, D.C.: U.S. Dept. of Justice, 1972.

8. National Academy of Engineering, Technology Transfer and Utilization (Washington: National Science Foundation, 1974), p. 9.

9. Kenneth Culp Davis. Discretionary Justice: A Preliminary Inquiry. Chicago: Louisiana State University Press, 1969.

10. Herbert L. Packer. The Limits of Criminal Sanction, Stanford, CA: Stanford University Press, 1968.

ORGANIZING U.S. STATE AND LOCAL GOVERNMENTS TO CAPTURE THE BENEFITS OF R&D

Joseph M. Carlson

Public Technology, Incorporated
Washington, D.C.

Introduction

The utilization of new technology in local and state governments in the United States requires the aggregation of this normally large and fragmented market, through the definition of performance requirements and specifications common to a segment of the market large enough to be attractive. Firms who would hope to enter this marketplace with products or services must be helped to make R&D and investment decisions based on such aggregated requirements. This form of technology transfer, emphasizing product development by reducing the uncertainty in the supplier/user interface, is performed by Public Technology, which operates in the middle ground between supply and demand. For products involving complex technology, for which applied R&D and product development expenditure is required, this middle ground role is particularly important. The specific nature of the interface assistance must be carefully tailored to relate to the specific case at hand, and is dependent upon the area of governmental service delivery, the nature of the technology, pricing issues, complexity of the technology, and many other factors.

Background - Capital/Labor Substitution and the Need for Innovation

In the United States, inflation and reduced output combine to produce serious effects on all sectors of the economy. Regional, state, and local governmental units are experiencing severe impacts of this recession, and face serious problems of maintaining their fiscal health. Property taxes, the primary revenue source for local governments, suffer because new contruction has been largely curtailed, while at the state level the combined sources of income, sales, and excise taxes also produce less additional revenue. Large urban areas are particularly hard hit because of the increasing costs of welfare and unemployment compensation without offsetting revenue sources.

R&D Expenditure

This financial picture combines with a traditional pattern whereby the expenditures of state and local governments, because of the service-oriented fundtions they perform for their citizens, are highly labor-intensive. This fact points clearly to the need for innovation in the use of more technology as a substitute for labor in those areas where such a tradeoff seems to make sense. If one examines the likelihood of capital/labor substitution, the overall trends in the U.S. are not comforting. The reason is that R&D expenditures, one of the best indices of the development of new technology, are in major proportion devoted to space, national defense, and other areas not directly associated with the problems of state and local government. As one measure of this direction, one can look at the expenditure of R&D-performing industry compared to the purchases of state and local government. Those industries which expend the largest absolute amounts on R&D -- typically chemicals, aircraft and missiles, electrical and nonelectrical machinery, and so on, sell little of their output to state and local governments. Put differently, state and local units purchase few goods and services from the industries that account for more than 80% of total industrial R&D. If one assumes that states and localities benefit from R&D performed by an industry in direct proportion to their purchases from that industry, only 1.2% of the 1970 U.S. industrial R&D expenditure, which totaled over $17.8 billion, resulted in direct benefit to state and local governments in the form of improved products and services.[1]

While this calculation ignores the substantial spin-off benefits of R&D which occur in some technical areas, it still indicates that state and local units could stand to profit from activities which would more accurately focus R&D directly on their needs.

Labor-Intensity of Public Services

The labor-intensity of local units is illustrated by the fact that labor costs are approximately 50% of all local government expenditures.* This figure rises to 68% of local expenditure when one considers only current operations accounts (excluding debt service, capital outlay, insurance, and transfer payments).[2]

The fire and police functions of local governments have both been major targets for the introduction of new technology. In examining local government expenditure for these services, a recent survey found that 1974 annual expenditures for police services totaled over $2.5 billion. Of this total, approximately $80 million, or 3.1% was for capital outlay expenditure, as compared to 87.5% for wages, salaries and fringe benefits.

Expenditures for the fire services show a similar pattern. Of 1974 expenditures totaling over $1.65 billion, 3% were for capital outlay, 91% for wages, salaries, and fringe benefits.

The ratio in refuse collection and disposal increases noticeably, with 10% of total 1974 expenditures of about $650 million going for capital outlay.[3]

---

* The total size of this marketplace is large and growing. In 1970, state and local governments' purchases of goods and services accounted for 12.5% of GNP. Further, this percentage has been growing steadily; from 7.6% in 1955 to 12.5% in 1970, to 12.9% in 1972. Expenditures for equipment in 1970 totaled $2.8 billion as shown in the following table.

Expenditures for Equipment
1970
($ in Millions)

States	$ 870
Local Governments	
(Municipalities $722)	1,898
Total State and Local	$2,768

State and local government expenditures for all durable goods were $5.8 billion in 1970, and expenditures for non-durables were $7.7 billion in the same year. Total purchases of goods and services were $22.5 billion in 1970.

In the U.S., a decision last year to extend the overtime provisions of the Fair Labor Standards Act to uniformed fire and police personnel highlight the cost implications of the labor-intensive makeup of local government. An appeal to this decision is now before the U.S. Supreme Court; however, the extension of overtime pay benefits to this additional body of workers means police and firemen are to be paid overtime for all on duty hours in excess of 60 per week beginning in 1975; this is reduced to 58 hours in 1976, and 56 hours in 1977. Because of the peculiarities of fire duty schedules, implementation of this provision will become very costly.

Against this background of traditionally low capital expenditure levels (those normally associated with the purchase of R&D-intensive goods and services), high labor-intensity, and rising labor costs, the need for innovation and the careful introduction of new technology stands out clearly.

Structural Relationships and Technology Development

The use of new technology is obviously affected by the structural relationships and market forces that advance or retard the rate of innovation. In the U.S., the federal government has been looked upon to provide stimulus, often through experimental programs, to reduce perceived barriers to the introduction of new technology. This has produced certain new programs, aimed at technical services provision and market aggregation, which will be described in more detail. The role of government as regulator, concerned with assuring the public health and safety, has also strongly affected the introduction of new technology. New requirements have resulted in the development of so-called "legislated markets" for advanced pollution monitoring and control instrumentation and equipment, advanced structural analysis procedures and techniques, and a wide range of solid waste handling and disposal techniques. At the same time, increasingly complex and stringent rules for worker safety, materials handling, building codes, and analysis of environmental impacts has made market entry (or the maintenance of market shares) more difficult and expensive. Governments are coupling such regulatory forces with more complex procurement procedures designed to assure fair competition and incorporating such requirements as environmental impact analysis, product liability requirements, and performance guarantees. As a writer in Fortune magazine recently put it, "Decisions about how to raise money and where to build plants are made only after a close look at federal and state tax laws and the constantly changing investment-tax credit. How to dispose of waste, how to advertise, what new products to market, how much to reveal about profitability -- all these are shared by the government in its capacity as regulator."[4]

Another aspect of the structural relationships that exist in the technology-development community is that state and local governments conduct relatively little R&D themselves -- they are largely dependent on the federal government or private industry to take the lead in new product or service development. The close ties in the R&D community between federal government, industry, and universities have thus far tended to exclude another partner -- state and local governments -- from the process of R&D planning, priority setting, and requirements definition. Accordingly, the supporting systems, such as scientific and technical information processing, which are a vital part of the R&D process, likewise reflect an imbalance of attention paid to the needs of state and local units.[5] Clearly, there are notable exceptions. In some areas where operational responsibility lay clearly with non-federal governments from the start, they have played a stronger role. In the federal road and highway construction program, state governments have been involved in the process of assessing technological needs, R&D planning, and in the utilization of R&D results. In the most often-used example, American agriculture, state and county officials have been heavily involved in research and the dissemination of results. In the agriculture case, colleges and universities, concerned with the specific problems of particular geographic and climatic conditions of their regions, have been responsive to local needs.

Private industry, understandably most concerned with the large, aggregated market afforded by the federal government, particularly in the fields of national defense, space and aeronautics and atomic energy, has put forth its greatest efforts in response to these requirements. Firms developing advanced capabilities, by virtue of meeting these demanding requirements, face higher uncertainty in turning their talents to addressing the problems and needs of state and local governments. What sort of mechanisms, then are available to address this situation and to help direct greater attention to the problems of those units of government which are now farthest removed from a position of influence in the national R&D pattern.

Mechanisms for Innovation Incentive

In 1971, Professional Engineer, the magazine of the American Society of Professional Engineers, devoted an issue to technology and the cities. The situation was summarized as follows:[5] "Historically, the cities may have been the cradle of technology, but there is a growing consensus that the cities today are facing 20th century problems with an awful lot of 19th century technology. From fire alarm systems and fire fighting equipment through solid waste disposal and centralized traffic control systems, technology at the municipal level is a challenge-and-opportunity scene for engineering applications in practically every field or discipline."

In a 1975 review, the editors conclude: "Four years later, the basic problems and opportunities remain. But over that same period the full scope and nature of technology transfer have come into much clearer focus. Essentially, what has been recognized is that technology will not transfer itself to cities or to other countries any more than the knowledge and skill of job-terminated engineers in high-technology industries can be automatically transferred to other industries. Given the barriers (political, financial, administrative, etc.) to the application of advanced technology to municipal needs, it is a wonder that the cities have achieved any technology problem solving at all."

The changes that have emerged in the past 4 to 5 years have been in two areas: the development of means to support the internal science and technology capacity and understanding of state and local governments, and attempts to incentivize or otherwise encourage private industry to turn its attention to this market.

Building Internal Capacity

There have been many programs recently instituted in the United States, aimed at the development and institutionalization of increased science and technology capability in local government. One of the key experiments in this area, sponsored by the National Science Foundation's Experimental Research and Development Incentives Program is known as the Urban Technology System. This is a nationwide experiment carried out by Public Technology, to test a variety of mechnisms designed to overcome barriers which have stood in the way of urban technology transfer in the past. Public Technology is the organizing force to provide central management for the program.

The Urban Technology System experiment consists of a network of 27 technology agents placed in randomly selected municipal and county governments in the 50,000 to 500,000 population range throughout the U.S. PTI, universities, non-profit research institutes, federal laboratories, and private industry, constitute a network of technical backup organizations to provide research and scientific support to the technology agents and governments to which they are assigned. The task of the agents, who are located in the central offices of the local government jurisdictions, is to define and assemble technology-oriented needs, opportunities and problems, and to link these with federal, industrial, and academic resources which can bring to bear possible solutions to these problems. This experiment, carried out over a three year period, is intended to stimulate additional private sector investment in technological problems of state and local units, as well as to support the growth of an internal science and technology capability with local governments. Problems developed within the UTS network, as previously indicated, will be exposed to a variety of organizations possessing relevant technological resources.

A key objective of the program, in addition to stimulating additional investment, is to carefully evaluate whether this method of providing additional technical capacity to local governments is effective. To this end, the experiment is carefully instrumented for evaluation, and uses a control group of cities, which have received no organized external science and technology advice, against the test sites in which technology agents are located for purposes of comparison.

The experiment was initiated with a one-year planning period, and the 27 technology agents went on-site in their respective jurisdictions in July 1974. At this still early date in the program, it appears that we have been successful in developing generic problems of common interest to many jurisdictions, and that some of the experimental assumptions about the ability to aggregate the market and to define common needs are valid. As the experiment progresses, we will be looking very closely at the extent of industrial involvement, to determine whether this is a viable mechanism to encourage private investment which would not otherwise take place.

Stimulating Private Investment

The introduction to the cities of new products and services incorporating advanced technology, has traditionally been accomplished primarily by vendors and consultants. Both sources have played roles of stimulating technical innovation, generally as embodied in new products and services, over the past several years. However, cities have generally not been left with a residual means of rationally evaluating opportunities and making choices between competing technologies. Vendors frequently have specified hardware products for well-known and well-defined uses, and consultants have offered analysis or design options for individual projects. When discrete purchases of design projects are completed, the consultants and vendors have departed, leaving the cities without continuity of technical capacity and the ability to replicate an engineering design option in future projects without virtually duplicating their original expense.

Concurrently, high technology industry has generally approached cities as a potential market for the consumption of already-developed hardware and software. Seemingly mundane problems of local governments, such as fire prevention, pothole patching, equipment maintenance, and vehicle routing have frequently not been seen by industry as commercially attractive or demanding of technological solutions. Further, the diversity of markets including piecemeal pricing and purchasing together with loosely defined specifications, have inhibited the aggregation of demand in this marketplace, and have deterred industry from making necessary investment decisions to develop new products and services specifically for this market. As a result, industry has frequently said to cities, "You people should buy what we sell," rather than "What do you need that we can make for you?" The idea of the decentralized and disaggregated market is further compounded by the proliferation of government jurisdictions in the United States. Counties, municipalities, states, metropolitan councils of government, special districts and regional consortiums all constitute potential buyers and make up a constantly shifting target at which to aim new products and services.

The Role of Public Technology, Incorporated

Within this fragmented situation, an organization has been created which can act in the middle ground, to provide a focus for the aggregation of state and local government needs, to be brought to the attention of high technology firms as an investment opportunity. Public Technology attempts to provide private industry with the kind of information necessary to reduce their uncertainty in R&D investment decisions, and to help such firms gather the kind of information necessary to logically evaluate the potential for market entry.

The starting point for Public Technology (PTI) in this began in 1970 by working with public officials from 80 local jurisdictions to undertake the task of building a national R&D agenda targeted to addressing common technology-related issues. That agenda is being continually expanded. A collective effort was mounted to match technology to user needs, attempting to achieve early results. The basic notion was that given the low level of state and local government-sponsored R&D activities, it was possible to collectively finance the development of technology, directed specifically to the problems and needs of state and local government, and carried out by an organization sponsored by, and working on behalf of, these users themselves.

The issues addressed on the agenda were pointed to needs geared to the day-to-day problems of local government operations. Emerging out of a series of meetings were problem statements and operational requirements for products and services such as permanent, long-lasting street patching material, a mathematical model to assist in locating fire stations, and an automated fire pumper which could release the vehicle operator for firefighting duties, and many other problems.

In this and other agenda-building activities, the first objective is the explicit definition of problems, whether hardware or software-oriented, that are susceptible to a technological solution. The next step is the explicit definition of performance results to be sought within time and cost boundaries.

The basic approach is to spell out the problem in detail, assess the market potential in state and local government, develop estimates of the technical and cost feasibility of the available solutions, survey the state-of-the-art, and define the desired system and performance attributes of the proposed innovations.

By proceeding in this way PTI has provided an institutional setting which makes it possible for its member jurisdictions to share the costs and benefits of development programs. Concurrent with planning, organizing, and staffing each specific development project, PTI forms a User Requirements Committee. Members of this committee are chosen from those jurisdictions having particular interests in the project and each member must have personal knowledge of one or more facets of the problem. The committee reviews or provides technical, operational, and economic requirements and specifications as well as guidance during design, market data, performance evaluation criteria, and field test and demonstration programs.

Dealing with Risk and Uncertainty

As noted in a previous section on R&D expenditure patterns, a "macro" look at U.S. R&D indicates that high technology industry, which does the greatest percentage of research and development work, delivers little of its output to state and local government markets. More specifically, the following table shows that only five of the industry groups with significant R&D expenditure sell more than 10% of their output directly to this sector.

R&D PERFORMING INDUSTRIES AND STATE AND LOCAL MARKETS

Industry	1970 R&D ($ in Millions)	Estimated % of Total Sales to State and Local Government Market
Food	196	1.2
Textiles & Apparel	64	.7-2.9 range
Lumber & Furniture	24	*
Paper	119	*4.8-5.7 range
Chemicals	1182	
Industrial	(1075)	3.9-5.8 range
Drugs	(486)	5.0
Other	(250)	*(paints)

Industry	1970 R&D ($ in Millions)	Estimated % of Total Sales to State and Local Government Market
Petroleum	608	5.2-5.3 range
Rubber	238	5.2
Stone, Clay & Glass	188	*5.5 (glass)
Primary Metals	265	8.0-8.2 range
Ferrous	(131)	
Nonferrous	(134)	
Fabricated Metals	183	*3.0-4.5 range
Machinery	1727	1.4-7.7 range
Electrical Equipment	4324	1.7-4.9 range
Motor Vehicle Transportation & Equipment	1475	1.6-3.7 range
Aircraft & Missiles	5173	.3-.4 range
Instruments	694	1.6-6.1 range
Other Manufacturing	98	3.9
Nonmanufacturing	669	
TOTAL	$17858	

* Indicates those R&D performers where outputs consumed by State and Local governments are high (over 10%)

At the level of the individual firm, it has been PTI's experience that "high technology" R&D performers, typically large firms in the aerospace/defense sector, encounter great difficulty in dealing with the risk and uncertainty associated with entering a new marketplace. A key factor in their analysis has been the calculation of a reasonable payback period to recover engineering, prototype development, and market penetration costs. A major role for PTI has been to help reduce such uncertainty by providing experience and tested data for estimating time-to-achieve-profitability.

In cases experienced to date, we have found that a break-even point may take three to five years to achieve in this marketplace. Corporate new-product planning, when armed with validly-based estimates, can set reasonable objectives for investment and cash flow, and avoid unreasonable expectations which might result from experience in other market sectors.

Providing market surveys, securing direct, face-to-face access to key state and local government officials, knowledge of the relevant experience of other firms, and insight into the budgetary and procurement lead-times and cycles of state and local government, are all factors which PTI can clarify to aid in the calculation of expected return on investment. As a simple example, the fiscal years of various governments in the U.S. are non-uniform. In some areas of the country, fiscal years end in June, others in December, still others in September and April. Anticipated purchases must be included in budgets whose preparation begins from 3 to 6 months in advance of fiscal-year-end. Timing of new product introduction and marketing must take this into account, since failure to meet a critical date could result in more than 18 months delay in budget approval and procurement. While a seemingly simple factor, knowledge of marketplace custom and tradition is sometimes acquired only at great cost and frustration by high technology firms considering new market entry.

Acting in this way to manage risk and uncertainty is a key component of PTI's strategy. It would appear that high technology firms in Europe, as well the U.S. could profit by developing a greater understanding of the factors which determine a reasonable time to achieve return on investment. It is our hope that cooperation and mutual interest can develop along this line, all pointed toward the goal of increasing the level of R&D investment in the problems and needs of the public sector.

Over the years, the application of this methodology has begun to result in a flow of products and services to utility to state and local government. Some examples of these development results will serve to help illustrate the application of this methodology, and how it has been used in some specific cases to stimulate the involvement of high technology industry in the state and local government marketplace.

Firefighters Breathing System

One of the highest priority problems indicated to PTI by local governments is the need for an improved firefighter's breathing system. Firefighting is one of the most hazardous occupations in the United States. On a national average, 47% of the nation's active firefighters will sustain some injury during the course of a work year. Of these injuries, 10% will be caused by inhalation of smoke, toxic fumes, or breathing oxygen deficient atmospheres. Each year the number of synthetic materials which produce poisonous gas when burned increases. Many of the gases and reagents used and transported for industrial processes are highly poisonous and deadly if inhaled. Yearly, approximately 115 firemen are disabled by lung and brain damage caused by inadequate respiratory protection.

The National Aeronautics and Space Administration, which sponsored PTI's work on development of this problem, made a commitment based on their expertise in developing portable life support systems, as demonstrated by the breathing system which allowed the astronauts to perform their scientific mission on the lunar surface.

The system ultimately developed through the efforts of NASA, PTI and the Scott Aviation Company, is a lighter weight compressed air system. Through the incorporation of aerospace materials and construction techniques it was possible to produce a unit that offered the same compressed air storage capacity as present equipment, vastly improved human factors, and still effected a weight savings of almost 40%. This weight reduction, coupled with such innovations as a lumbar support pack frame, bubble type face piece, and low breathing resistant regulators allow the firefighter to perform his work in hazardous environments much more comfortably and safely. The system is currently being tested in actual firefighting use in the fire departments of Houston, New York, and Los Angeles. Following the six-month field test program, Scott Aviation Company plans to make commercially available a breathing system based on the NASA technology.

Energy Conservation.

After surveying the state-of-the-art, PTI is working with the Grumman Aerospace Corporation to demonstrate new techniques leading to the alteration of heating, ventilation, and air conditioning (HVAC) systems in public buildings. The prospects for significantly reducing fuel consumption levels are great. These techniques, beginning with an "energy audit" of public buildings, which identifies the facilities with highest energy savings potential, followed by engineering or operational changes in the HVAC systems, are now being put into practice in two states and several cities. In addition, PTI has prepared a communications package which assists state and local administrators in developing an energy conservation program. The package addresses energy conservation measures for public buildings, residential and commercial buildings, transportation, and electric utilities.

Two kinds of measures are recommended: those which reduce energy consumption in government operations and facilities; and those actions by which governments can control energy consumption in the private sector of the community.

PROBEYE Infrared Viewer

In another development project, a device called"PROBEYE", developed by the Hughes Aircraft Company, has been designed to meet a serious firefighting problem with the following components:

1. Detection of first order fires through the heat radiated or conducted through walls and floors.

2. Detection and location of fire or smoke victims in dark or smoke-filled environments.

3. Providing orientation to firefighters in identifying the physical characteristics of dark or smoke-filled rooms (doors, window, furniture, and other obstacles).

4. Identifying residual hidden "hot spots" during mop-up or overhaul operations.

The device produced in response to these needs is a portable infrared detector that gives a clear view of objects under conditions of no light and dense smoke. Any object above the temperature of absolute zero emits energy in the infrared range. The amount of energy that is radiated is dependent upon the temperature, mass, and physical makeup of the object. This radiation is long wave compared to visible light. Because of its long wave length, it is able to penetrate through some substances, particularly smoke, which tend to absorb visible light.

The infrared technology for this device was developed by the Hughes Aircraft Company as part of a weapons system for the Department of Defense. This system, in its military application, was highly sophisticated and very costly. For fire service operations it was necessary for Hughes to redesign the unit to reduce its cost and simplify its operation while maintaining its basic capabilities. The process of technology transfer was then one of defining the problem, seeking out the Hughes device as a potential solution, redesigning to meet the cost constraints of the marketplace, and providing the necessary information to reach a positive decision to enter the municipal marketplace.

Hughes Aircraft Company sensed that there was a market for their infrared imaging device in the fire service, but they had no knowledge of the problems which firefighters encountered, the market size, or price elasticity of demand for such a device.

PTI provided a mechanism by which the user community could communicate to the manufacturer their needs and requirements for such a device. PTI was instrumental in establishing contact between Hughes and the user community. It was through this contact that the users began to perceive that a device existed which could solve many of their operational problems, and that Hughes realized that there was sizable market for their device in the fire service.

Once Hughes had established what was felt to be the optimum position in price/performance tradeoffs, PTI surveyed the market for the device to aid Hughes in reaching a production decision and began a campaign to build awareness of the product at all levels of city administration. A pricing decision was reached which offered the device to the fire service at significantly less cost than the hardware for military application.

This was due to the "de-engineering" done to reduce the sophistication of the system, and also because of the price sensitivity range in the marketplace.

In adapting this technology to state and local government, relatively little technical development beyond that performed for the Defense Department device was required. The main thrust of the transfer effort was to acquaint Hughes with the municipal marketplace and to make the ultimate users aware that such a device existed and that it was a useful tool in firefighting operations.

Automated Flow Control System

Yet another case involves a development for the standard fire pumper apparatus to provide the fire service with a capability to directly control the water flow at the nozzle. The safety and effectiveness of firefighting operations are increased significantly by the use of this system.

The method used currently by firefighters for regulating water flow is for the nozzleman or company officer to hand signal or radio the engineer stationed at the pumper. However, this method gives slow or inaccurate response to rapidly changing conditions, ties the engineer to the pumper, and can create conditions which are hazardous to personnel.

Grumman Aerospace Corporation in conjunction with Public Technology, and its local government User Requirements Committee, designed and developed a system, to the requirements specified by the Committee, for automating the water flow control function of the pumper apparatus. Grumman Allied Industries, Inc. is producing and marketing the system to local governments.

The Automated Flow Control System, designed in direct response to a local government need, and in accordance with performance requirements stated by fire service personnel, was supported by demand analyses and marketing support provided by PTI.

Grumman was easily able to overcome the technical problems which arose during the development of the system. Not so easily overcome have been the factors arising from operating in an unfamiliar marketplace. Penetrating an unfamiliar market justifiably produced an uncertain reaction by corporate management. PTI assisted Grumman in penetrating the market by creating awareness of the product in local governments, by providing local government budget information to Grumman, and educating Grumman's management and marketing personnel about local governments.

Field test programs in two cities and regional demonstrations throughout the U.S., arranged by PTI, have assisted in marketing the device, as has the preparation of a product awareness package tailored to the information needs of local government management, procurement, and budget officials.

Fire Insurance-Introducing Structural Change

A previous section of this paper spoke about the structural relationships in the U.S. which affect the direction of R&D spending and the formation of R&D policy. In the area of fire insurance, Public Technology has been able to begin effecting institutional change of the sort that directly addresses barriers to innovation and the introduction of new technology. In the U.S. the Insurance Services Office provides guidelines and a schedule which is widely used by the major fire insurance companies to grade the fire protection capability of cities. This rating is then used as part of a basis on which rates for residential fire insurance premiums will be established. In the past, the grading manuals have based their measure of fire protection adequacy on the proximity between fire houses and the property at risk. There was no consideration of the time necessary to arrive at the fire scene, including street networks; an arbitrary distance factor was the only criterion for fire station location. The grading schedule also acted to penalize the introduction of other new firefighting technologies--it required that a certain quantity of water had to be deliverable to a fire and gave no recognition to the pumping capacity of mini-pumpers. There are many other examples of the outdated and arbitrary provisions of the grading schedule, which acted to inhibit innovation and maintain the status quo. Public Technology was able, acting with the National Association of Insurance Commissioners, to negotiate with the ISO to change many key provisions of the grading schedule, issued in 1974. These included a recognition that the schedule was not intended as a planning guide for local fire protection, and was not a "standard" for evaluating fire defenses. Similiarly, public fire flow requirements were reduced for buildings which had automatic sprinkler systems. Also, certain water supply and fire department requirements were reduced for small cities, and the pumping capacity of mini-pumpers was specifically recognized by allowing credit for their use as reserve apparatus.

In summary, this case outlines an attempt to influence the regulatory and rate-making sector of the economy to directly confront institutional constraints which have retarded technological change and the use of new management techniques.

The Brokerage Function

The opportunities for transferring new technologies into municipal governments have in some cases been met more quickly in Europe than in the U.S. Near Boston, an American company is now building a pilot plant operation which marries their technology with a materials handling and incerator system under license from a Swedish firm. The system has been is use in European cities for years. Fire protection and fire response has been conducted for some time in European cities in ways just now being evaluated in the U.S. Obviously, there is a need for more communication and providing a basis for evaluation for technologies developed by all the Atlantic partners. It is the intent of this paper to describe the characteristics of the situation which call for the use of new technology, the existing patterns of expenditure and decision-making relative to R&D, the structural and institutional framework in which they are made, and how Public Technology has been able to enter this area with some success. PTI was created because the emphasis on urban problems in the U.S. was lacking a critical focal element--the provision and transfer of new technology. It was intended to act as an aggregator of problems and markets, yet as an organization which could talk with equal understanding and credibility to both buyer and seller--to city officials who were dissatisfied and sometimes distrusting of the traditional vendor and consultant, and to the industry executive who needs to understand a marketplace perceived as fragmented and difficult. President Ford, in a recent interview, commented that "We have to adjust our society to the development of technology, which means that we have to do something about our major metropolitan areas." He added, "We have to learn to master science for the benefit of every detail of our life."[6]

If we attempt to carry out even part of this challenge, a new level of communications and comprehension is necessary on both sides if our best talents are to be applied to our local problems in a way that their results can be applied, accepted, and trusted.

REFERENCES

1. Blair, John F., "Industry, Innovation, and the Municipal Market", The Franklin Institute Research Laboratories, October 15, 1973, p. 2-5.

2. Public Technology, "Final Report: Public Sector Technology Innovation Process", December 8, 1972, p. 16.

3. Lewin, David, "Expenditure, Compensation, and Employment Data in Police, Fire, and Refuse Collection and Disposal Departments", The 1975 Municipal Year Book, International City Management Association, 1975, p. 39.

4. Guzzardi, Walter, Jr., "Putting the Cuffs on Capitalism", Fortune, April, 1975, p. 105.

5. See "Technology Transfer and Utilization: Recommendations for Redirecting Emphasis and Correcting Imbalance", National Academy of Engineering, Washington, D.C., 1974.

6. "How President Ford Views the System", Fortune, April, 1975, p. 81.

TECHNOLOGY TRANSFER: EXPANDED USES OF FEDERAL LABORATORIES

William D. Carey

American Association for the Advancement of Science
Washington, D.C.

The subject of technology transfer has sustained an unbelievable number of national and international conferences, and I suspect that this conference will not put an end to the matter. What we must all hope is that we can do a little to clarify the problem, and not add to the confusion. Sometimes I think that our working premises are mistaken, in that some of us tend to imagine a huge reservior of technological applications held back by a dam, and that if we could only open the gates the great and thirsting desert would bloom. I hope that we have become mature enough to put aside that romantic illusion, and that instead we understand that technology is limited, that it is not a solution by itself, that it is one partner in a large company of solutions -- some of which are more important than the technological factor -- and that the process of adapting and retrofitting available technology to different uses has its own time scale, and that we cannot force its speed of diffusion except at some risk. But we are impatient, and it can be argued that if man were not impatient we would see very little change or progress.

In the United States economy, technology is transferred very effectively in the private sector, but very ineffectively in the public or intergovernmental sector. The reason, I believe, is that in normal transactions between buyers and sellers the innovation is embedded in the product itself, and the mode of transfer is very simply the sales or marketing mechanism which provides a comparative choice within parameters of customer needs, price elasticity, and market competition. Innovation is not sold as innovation, but is embedded in the performance characteristics of the product. In this sense, it would appear that the economic function of technical innovation is to stimulate market activity by both creating and meeting demand, and it goes a long way to explain the vitality and the scale of the American industrial economy. Technology alone could not have brought it off, but technology combined with managerial and marketing know-how is what made the difference.

It is a very different matter when the problem is to transfer technology between levels of government -- between the federal government and the state, county, and local governments. The reasons are to be found in what I have already said. In the first place, we are not pursuing innovation, under government's auspices, for the same reasons we find in a market economy. We do it to fulfill a governmental mission. Spin-off is an afterthought, not a forethought. Moreover, the federal government approaches the state and local governments with existing technology which it is prepared to share, not with new technology which was designed from the beginning to fit state and local needs. In other words, the user was not present when the technology was defined and pursued. To put it another way, federal technology was undertaken without the close familiarization with state and local users and requirements -- a difference which does not exist in the market economy. And finally, the federal purveyors of technology transfer must behave only as catalysts or agents of transfer, without the skills or the motives in management and marketing which are so basic to the diffusion of innovation in the market economy.

Now let us speak about the potential of the federal government's laboratories and research and development centers, as delivery systems for technology transfer. The scale and the mix of these facilities is extremely impressive. Over 500 laboratories, employing some 120,000 scientists and engineers, are scattered through 32 of the 50 American states. They range from very large and sophisticated centers to relatively small and specialized facilities. They do not function within a centrally managed network structure, but instead are dedicated to -- and administered by -- different government departments and agencies which are charged variously with missions of national defense, or energy, or health, or agriculture, or natural resources, or transportation. Their combined annual expenditures are in the range of $7 billion. However one looks at it, this is a massive technological enterprise held in public ownership and until very recently dedicated exclusively to the purposes of the central government. The question is how, in a rapidly-changing society, this technological capacity should be used for wider benefits, and whether the federal laboratories have a high or only a marginal role in technology transfer. The evidence to date is most charitably described as inconclusive. It is inconclusive because the function of technology transfer is not a paramount function, but a residual one at the bottom, or close to it, of the laboratories' priorities. It is inconclusive also because even where the federal laboratories have tried technology transfer, the success stories are few and hard to find. It is inconclusive because the laboratories operate under severe constraints of manpower and money, and because there has been far more talk, more committees, more meetings and symposia, and more studies, than there has been action.

But the potential for transferring technology via the federal laboratory delivery system is no illusion. When we narrow our focus to the Department of Defense group of laboratories we find in place a consortium of some 25 installations working under a joint agreement to find opportunities to transfer technology. Within this subset of the larger family of federal laboratories, some 100 projects have been under way involving 20 different end users at an outlay of $12 million. While in terms of the Department of Defense budget this isn't very much, nevertheless, it is a beginning. We find a spectrum of applications of defense technology to problems of mine safety, air traffic control, passenger vehicle safety, medical instrumentation, fire fighting, law enforcement, rehabilitation of paraplegics, and medical diagnosis. We find some of the defense laboratories involved in joint research on pollution control and abatement with civilian agencies and state governments. So there is a beginning. It is enough to confirm the potential of the federal laboratories as useful partners in technology transfer with other sectors of government, even though the scale is modest. It has been enough to persuade high policy makers to expand the defense laboratory consortium to a federal laboratory consortium by adding the laboratories of the National Aeronautics and Space Administration, the Energy Research and Development Administration, and the Department of Commerce.

Yet, the process is painfully slow and anecdotal. I have seen an evaluation by Sherman Gee which is worth sharing in part:

> "Although there is room for an expanded DOD effort, there exist other constraining influences. One is the absence of incentives on the part of DOD laboratory managers to become involved in technology transfer activities. No extra recognition or credit can be expected, and only the personal satisfaction of having helped alleviate some of our social ills is offered . . . Technology transfer is viewed all too often as having little more than nuisance value to the busy line manager. . . .
>
> "DOD technology transfer to date has been oriented mainly toward other federal, state, and local government

> institutions as potential technology users, with insufficient attention to industry. This . . . stems partially from trying to avoid situations which may create conflicts of interest. . . . The transfer of publicly-owned technology to the private sector is where the great promise of DOD technology transfer lies."

Some additional light is shed on the problem in a memorandum dated June 14, 1974 from the chief research and development officer of the Department of Defense, setting forth guidelines to govern non-defense work in DOD labs and R&D facilities. I quote:

> "The expenditure of in-house effort in any one laboratory shall be limited to 3% of the professional personnel . . . unless express approval of the parent Military Department is granted to exceed this limit.
>
> The DOD commitment to support the brokerage function at the National Science Foundation shall not exceed 2 man-years per year through Fiscal Year 1976, subject to the continued willingness of the Military Departments to absorb the costs."

A memorandum like that from the high throne certainly does not send a thrill of motivation or encouragement to laboratory managers, and it bears out what I said earlier as to the low policy priority being given to the technology transfer role of the laboratories.

I consider it a strange and saddening state of mind, and I think it must soon change. A trickle of government-held technology into the civilian sector is not enough, especially at a time when the national economy is in recession and the forces of economic demand are too weak to trigger a normal flow of innovation from private industry. What will happen again is that government-financed research and development will continue to create new technology within the government system which will choke the pipelines and fail to accomplish diffusion within the larger economy. The technology mismatch between the haves and the have-nots in the American economy will continue to exist, and the taxpayers will continue to pay $7 to $8 billion per year for defense and other government technology which is locked up instead of being returned to them. And the internal contradiction, of course, is that the same government is committed to sharing technology and is busily creating intergovernmental networks and pass-through mechanisms and brokerage systems and encouraging potential users to queue up at the window for a ration of technology.

My own view of the future is somewhat different. I believe the time is approaching when the Federal laboratories and research centers will be -- and must be -- managed very differently. They must be assembled as a science and technology system, instead of as a galaxy of independent sub-systems each of which looks for its rations and quarters to one federal agency or another, and each of which follows prescribed missions like cargo ships, plying familiar trade routes. The laboratories represent a vast and diversified national resource, and it is in that sense that they should be integrated into a network and utilized flexibly for a variety of both public and private purposes. Regardless of which particular agency or national emergency brought individual research centers into being, or when, I believe we have reached the point where many of them are ripe to be reassembled into multipurpose clusters under program managers. They should compete, cluster with cluster, for major mission assignments and in the production of research results and diffusion payoffs. And they should not be restricted simply to doing government's own work. Instead, they should be national R&D enterprises in the complete sense of the term, capable of joint research and development with industrial organizations and state or local governments, because in the end this is the process by which technology and innovation are planned to meet user needs, and the route over which innovation travels fastest and most surely. In the course of time, some of the government laboratories might be hived-off and converted into lively institutes of technology which would be prime movers of regional development -- a strategy, if you will, of regional capacity-building.

In the shorter run, while we build up the nerve to think such unconventional thoughts, and while the federal laboratories remain balkanized, I believe that the emphasis should be upon technical assistance rather than upon the transfer of hard technology. I am speaking now of a consultative role to state, local, and other non-federal clients in advising on problems of choice in applying solutions to the problems of civil society. These are such problems as those of metropolitan transportation balance, solid waste disposal, setting and policing air and water quality standards, defining the permissable uses of endangered coastal zones, determining sites for major airports or energy facilities, assessing the mitigation options for limiting radiation leakage from nuclear power plants, defining the procurement and performance parameters of new technologies to be purchased on the open market, and so forth. This all comes under the head of capacity-building, of providing supportive technical assistance to units of government which do not have the experience or know-how to approach problems of technical, economic, and social complexity. If, in the course of providing this technical assistance, government-held technology can be passed on as well, so much the better.

So you see that for us in the States the existence of the great federal laboratories is not the panacea for technology transfer that it might seem. It is a complex matter, and this morning I have helped to complicate it even more. If there were fewer constraints on the federal laboratories, if the potential users were better able to define their problems and needs, if the R&D had been done in the first place with spin-off in mind -- there are many "ifs," and they are not helpful. We will make slow but measurable progress in technology transfer through the federal laboratories, but in my judgment there will be a wide gap between the potential of the delivery system and its actual achievements until new and more radical arrangements are made. And even then, I believe, the role of government in technology transfer will be only a minor piece of the action, with the market economy as the main theatre. But, as in everything else, where you stand depends on where you sit.

TRANSFER OF MILITARY TECHNOLOGY TO CIVILIAN NEEDS

William P. Raney

Office of Naval Research, Arlington, VA

It is always a pleasure to discuss one's vocation, and I should like to start my talk by pointing out that those engaged in research and development for the military are constantly in the business of technology transfer -- transfer in all directions. We seize the state of the art in civilian technology and use it where we can for military purposes; we work constantly at transferring new science and technology wherever we find it or create it, into military systems; and of late years we have been paying formal attention to the matter of transferring new military technology to civilian needs.

This last item is, of course, the nominal subject of my address. Much has been written about it; the literature is growing rapidly, and I suspect that most of you can glean useful details of the process more efficiently from the written reports than from listening to me talk. Thus, I plan to spend my time sketching the background, the context in which our formal system functions so that you can appreciate more fully why we have chosen to set up our system as it is. More importantly, I hope you will be able thus to see what parts of our system are applicable to your situation and what parts are not. There is no _a priori_ reason to believe that our system can serve as a good model when it is taken out of context and applied to some other complex of society and industry.

First I should like to describe briefly the essential factors that govern technology transfer within the military system, with some passing comparisons to how it works in commercial practice. The intent to create new technology to apply to military functional needs, and the utilization of some fraction of that new technology for the satisfaction of operating requirements is relatively easy to rationalize. Clear sequential arguments can be built up that cover actions ranging from the support of areas of basic research to the scheduling of training for the operators of new equipment. In practice, however, the actual implementation of introducing such new technology into systems is difficult, precisely because the system is so highly structured that an almost unmanageable number of constraints must be satisfied simultaneously. In industry, on the other hand, there may be real difficulty in working to a clearly defined goal in a carefully planned schedule, but that lack of rigidity in plan allows for useful progress by determined groups of individuals. All industries do it constantly as they develop new products for existing markets. And we all know that by suitable advertising campaigns it is possible to create new markets -- as in the garment industry. There are problems in the offing, I believe, in this traditional business of creating new markets; and the problems are akin to those of the military in the following sense. They have to do with worldwide concern for the environment, for the amount of energy consumption, for the safety of the consumer, and so forth. Thus in the commercial world there are more and more constraints that must be satisfied before the wisdom of introducing a new technological product is clear.

In the military system, the transfer of new technology to its ultimate application to military function is governed by the statements of military requirements for operational capability. These have to do with types of combat and readiness for combat, but they must also pay attention to the need to do training and routine peacetime operations. Thus almost all the functions normally associated with civilian activities must also be carried out by the military with the maximum efficiency and hopefully minimum cost. We are thus involved with feeding and housing and medical care and transportation and sewage treatment and waste disposal -- the list never stops. In terms of strictly military functions, we in the Navy like to think that our operations on and under the water, in the air, and with the Marine Corps on land give us the greatest spectrum to work and thus the broadest range of required technologies. It is not clear whether that state of affairs should engender pride in being able to do it, or some concern over the size of the problem. The requirements can clearly pull the introduction of new technology. Perversely they can also inhibit consideration of new technology that doesn't lend itself fairly neatly to any of the existing and well-understood military tasks. But whatever else they may do, the requirements do force us to live with the discipline of implementation, with logistics support for a new product, with training, and with the hazards that may affect people who are ordered to use the new equipment. That sort of discipline will be an asset in meeting the new constraints that appear to be affecting the commercial affairs of the country. In addition to covering the full gamut of activities, the military situation also has certain other features, the most important being the chance to try new technology under reasonably controlled conditions. We can thus arrange for large scale experiments with statistical follow-up that permits logical decisions about the value of new technology; and we are required to and can keep pretty good track of the costs involved in accepting new equipment.

The performers who are creating new technology for possible application all work toward the general satisfaction of the military requirements, but they do their work in several types of institutions. We have a large number of government laboratories in the Department of Defense. Their functions range from basic scientific research to engineering support of forces operating in the field. In the Navy laboratories alone there are over thirty thousand people paid with research and development funds. In addition, we let thousands of contracts each year with both universities and industrial firms for the performance of research and development tasks. Beyond this contract program, industry does a great deal of development work with its own funds and with a specially negotiated fraction of the purchase price of military equipment supplied by those firms. Some of those firms specialize in military equipment, but there are many whose main business is civilian, except for a division of the firm that does military work. In our system, there are some companies preferred for particular sorts of work, but the general climate is that companies make competitive bids for this government work and the government in turn must deal with all the companies in an even-handed manner to assure fairness in the competition. And finally, there are thousands of small companies that compete successfully for small jobs in support of the military. By government policy, small businesses get special attention and help in various forms from the government. These are the performers, and it is between and among these performers that we do our internal technology transfer.

Let me now list some of the problems we find in doing internal technology transfer, as examples of the difficulties that will appear in any transfer. First, we must generally establish some sort of proof of the claimed advantages of the new technology, whether they be in performance, or cost, or ease of maintenance. We struggle with uncertainties in the cost of the new items, and with great uncertainties in the cost of making the required changes in the logistics system. Regardless of cost, there are sure to be disturbances in the logistics and training systems. There are usually so many options of new technology to meet requirements that we find it very complicated to make a choice. New technology will upset the plans that already exist for the acquisition of equipment that uses the old technology. And the most intractable difficulty is that occasionally the new technology would require some sort of cultural change among the users in order to accept it. The introduction of aircraft into naval operations is perhaps the easiest example I can cite.

Many of these same facets of difficulty pertain to established commercial activities, where new products will upset production lines and distribution and maintenance systems. This applies unless the business is highly competitive and a clear case is possible for performance improvement or substantial cost savings -- or the business is small, deals in high technology items, and must depend on its wits and the generation of new markets for survival.

Another troublesome area is obviously common to both military and commercial operations. There must be some mechanism to carry out the implementation of technology introduction, and that mechanism can include such things as a public relations effort to stimulate the market and a customer service organization that can solve training problems, work out modifications to respond to an improved understanding of the customer's needs, and so forth. The transfer job is not done and cannot be done without such a capability to smooth the actual introduction of new material to the users.

Let me now compare the Department of Defense practices with those of other government agencies both national and local. There are two other large agencies that, like DoD, have their own laboratories and deal regularly with the creation and use of new technology, either in government organizations or through large efforts conducted in their behalf by industry. These are, of course, NASA (National Aeronautics & Space Administration), and ERDA (Energy Research and Development Administration) which has taken over many of the functions of the old AEC (Atomic Energy Commission). For both those agencies, the process is very similar to what I have described for the Department of Defense. Beyond these two, however, the other civil agencies are not generally in the business of <u>creating</u> new technology which is then passed on to a civil user, in either government or private sectors. Thus they lack in <u>apparat</u> for doing that job. In comparison, they tend to be arrangers, dispensers, connecters, or brokers of something. Further, they have tended to see the problems they deal with as being non-technical, or at least not dependent on hardware. Rather, their problems have appeared to be legal, or financial, or sociological, or political. Other governmental bodies, ranging from state down to local city governments, have not been in the habit of sponsoring technical efforts to solve their problems. Judging from the statements that occasionally appear in the press, the reaction of these smaller government bodies to the cost of creating technical solutions to their problems is generally one of shock and horror. Thus they, too, have no standing mechanism for taking care of the introduction of new technology, either as creators or as new users. It is quite possible, however, that some of the larger cities will find it expedient to sponsor a certain amount of original technical effort. By their sizes, they could. Recent population numbers show New York with 7.9 million within the city limits, Los Angeles with 2.8, Chicago with 3.4, and London with 7.6 million. Compare these with the Netherlands at 13.4 million, Sweden at 8.1, Denmark at 5.0, and Norway at 3.9. It is clear that if money must be spent on technical solutions to civil problems it will be, but it is also clear that there must exist in the civil sector organizational means to accept and put to use these new solutions.

Now that I have described the milieu in which technology transfer has to work, let me say a bit more about how we do it. Within the military services, there are many paths, so long as the essential features are satisfied. These paths include convincing potential users by hardware demonstration of the virtues of the new technology, by convincing the procurement headquarters organizations that they should require the use of certain new technologies in all new equipment, and sometimes by convincing industry that it is to their advantage to incorporate certain items of new technology in their equipment designs before the military issues any written requirement for the use of that technology. I will readily admit that this last path is sometimes a little chancey.

The introduction of new technology that has been developed by or for the military into the commercial market goes on all the time. We can count on the major industrial firms to seek new commercial markets for the technology that is being used in their military divisions, just as we try to make good military use of new technology that has appeared in the commercial sector. But that transfer doesn't always work well, for reasons ranging from unavailability of the appropriate people within the company who understand both the new technology and the new commercial market, to divisional jealousy and lack of communication, to occasional outright bad management. Thus, major industries know how to do it, or at least should know how to do it, and our special efforts at technology transfer simply amount to making it easier for them. On the other hand, there are many small businesses that could make important contributions to the economy that do not know how to do it. In such cases, our special efforts amount to teaching them how to do it, in telling them where the sources of information are, and in some cases suggesting what we think interesting civilian applications might be.

In making any transfer of technology from the milieu in which the technology was discovered or was developed for some purpose to a different milieu, there appear to be certain essential features, a common theme of this institute. I ask your patience in hearing my formulation of the essential features as we have found them in Navy experience:

a. An identifiable technology product, for which we see expanded application;

b. A mechanism for recognizing this expanded application and for supplying organized assistance to the new user. In all really successful cases I know about, this has involved personal contact of people experienced in the new technology with people who are familiar with the potential application;

c. A customer who has a need or a problem that he wants to solve badly enough to spend money on the solution and perhaps to change his ways so that he can use the new solution. Another class of client can be convinced or trained to believe that he wants such a new solution, whether or not he recognizes it initially;

d. A mechanism through which the client can focus on and define his problem so that he can be assured that it is amenable to a technical solutions rather than, say, a sociological solution;

e. And finally and crucially, a way for the client actually to do something about the introduction of the new technology. This may mean that he must create some sort of performing organization for the purpose.

Most of the formal activities in technology transfer in the Navy have to do with items b. and d., that is, with the business of supplying a contact point in the Navy that can work directly with a contact point among the potential users of the new technology. Thus we are able to provide both information and the essential element of personal contact between the two parties to the transfer. These methods are described at length in the literature. Many of the features of the instructions and regulations deal with specifics of the situation in the United States, particularly with the existence of large and competent government laboratories. We have, as you are aware, set up a consortium of government laboratories, almost half of which are Navy laboratories, and those laboratories have been given special permission to devote a fraction of the work force to the solution of civilian problems. In our system, that permission is necessary for the very existence of those organizations has been justified on the basis of the military need for the services of each of the employees. The areas in which Defense technology has been able to contribute to non-military problems is legion, and I would be happy to discourse on that subject at length after this lecture. What we cannot do, of course, is to create the customer perception of need or the means to make use of the help we can provide. Thus we stand ready to make the broadest possible public good out of the government investment in science, both through the general process of technology diffusion and, when we can identify matching interests, through the formal mechanism of technology transfer.

The central thing I wish to emphasize today is that the utilization of technology for new applications is a complex and ubiquitous process. The process has certain central features but the details of how it works depend on the technical, commercial, and governmental structure and traditional relationships. For each new situation in our country, or in any country, the process must be adjusted to the case at hand. I have been at some pains to describe the milieu in which our system functions in the hope that it will assist you in picking and choosing those parts of our technology transfer process that can be helpful. We are dealing with matters of substance in the transfer of technology, and we must all avoid the error of confusing the appearance of a formal system for transfer with the real thing.

EUROPEAN VIEWS ON THE TRANSFER OF TECHNOLOGY FROM MILITARY TO CIVIL USES

Bernard Udis

Director, Bureau of Economic Research
University of Colorado, Boulder, Colorado

Introduction

The material which follows was drawn from a study conducted in seven major industrialized countries of Western Europe during the Fall of 1972.[1] The principal objective was to throw new light on problems of military to civilian transfer of resources. While a variety of subjects are discussed in the full report, the section on technology transfer has been abstracted for this paper. The basic interview was designed for organizations forced to adjust to a reduced level of dependence on military expenditures and the consequent need to develop civil market alternatives. The field work consisted of a series of interviews with industrial executives, government officials, university professors and journalists. Table 1 provides the distribution of interviews by type of institution and country.

Table 1

DISTRIBUTION OF INTERVIEWS BY TYPE OF INSTITUTION AND COUNTRY

	TYPE OF INSTITUTION				
COUNTRY	COMPANIES	UNIVERSITIES AND RESEARCH ORGANIZATIONS	GOVERNMENT MINISTRIES	JOURNALISTS AND PRIVATE INDIVIDUALS	TOTAL PER COUNTRY
Britain	9	6	8	1	24
Sweden	8	3	9	0	20
Holland	3	0	4	0	7
Belgium	5	1	3	1	10
West Germany	13	1	6	2	22
Italy	11	4	1	1	17
France	5	2	11	1	19
Totals	54	17	42	6	119

Transfer of Ideas, Technology, and Persons

Spinoff

Potential spinoff of new technology or products from the military to civil sectors has repeatedly been stressed as a rationalization for military expeditures on high technology projects in many countries. The evidence is surely mixed on this point and it would be very hard to definitively lay the question to rest. The one thing that is clear is that in certain fields the existence of spinoff and the probability of further spinoff is much higher than in others. It must be recognized, however, that the major objective of military R&D lies in the military area. Rather divergent views were encountered in several countries concerning the appropriateness of considering civil spinoff as a rationale for military research endeavors. For example, a high official of French military R&D indicated his belief that in the long run, civilian money should be used for problems in which civilian solutions were sought. He preferred to concentrate military research in areas where the military payoff was likely to be large. In contrast the West German government appears to be consciously attempting to restrict its military R&D to those projects with a high probability of spinoff and to buy purely military R&D elsewhere. It was widely believed that most military research and development of necessity is concerned with military application. While there may be spinoff possibilities these usually occur only if the same qualities are required in other work. Military secrecy also constitutes an obstacle to ready transfer to civil sectors. There is also some belief that spinoff is more likely when organizations use their own funds and hence may be more motivated to look for the highest return on investment. For a similar reason spinoff is viewed as more likely in competitive than in government owned operations. Even with spinoff technically possible, little use has been made of it in civil markets.

The belief was fairly widespread that successful spinoff would have to be consciously planned or even forced. A group of Swedish government officials spoke of the possibility of what they called a "pump effect" which would apply to technical advance and spinoff. They envisioned this process as one in which people would be recruited and utilized in their government positions, later trained in marketing and other civil skills, and finally moved out into civil industry after a certain period of time. This process would provide openings for bright, new graduates, and give them an opportunity to perform their technical work in the military field and then later on also move into civil markets. Such a process would result in a kind of cross-fertilization over a period of years and might conceivably open up the doors between technical developments in the military and civil application.

The director of the British Atomic Energy Laboratories at Harwell saw little evidence of accidental spinoff. His view was that it was necessary to adopt a "cold-blooded, calculated" approach to industrial utilization. In such a process, solving a scientific or technical problem is only the start. The successful shift requires patience, time, and effort. He spoke of creating spinoff as a "conscious act of will." There was general agreement on the difficulty of successfully applying new basic knowledge. The bottleneck clearly is in the transfer of new information into a form useable for industry.

An English economist expressed strong views that there was no economic justification for many of the high technology projects which have been conducted in recent years. He went on to doubt the usefulness to society of additional innovations per se. A French governmental study also showed little useful transfer from large, high prestige R&D projects. A top French science official estimated that spinoff in all these large programs at most was in the range of 10-15%. He conceded that this might be large in an absolute sense. Also, large programs are large buyers from high technology sectors and this has provided a market for such industries and helps cut the costs and spread familiarity with high technology processes.

OECD officials expressed the view that high technology rarely moves to lower levels of technology within a given country but moves much more easily horizontally across national boundaries. They also doubted that military R&D was the cutting edge of scientific advance in most countries. The argument was that most of it is done in private industry anyway and if spinoff possibilities exist the companies doing the work would be those in the best position to use it. If in spite of this, there has been little transfer, the assumption must be made that there is little transferability or profitable civilian application.

Nevertheless, there are some areas of successful spinoff which should be noted. Many firms indicated that their military experience aided their quality control and systems integration work and led to more successful simulation. It was also noted that not all military research is used in the military. For example, the Dutch military research organization, (RVTNO), devotes about one-third of its operations to civil applications, such as air pollution, traffic control, etc. This has been going on for some time. Some also distinguish between spinoff from space work and from military work with the belief that space work which concentrates on coupling human beings with technology is more likely to be successful in technology transfer. In discussion of the most successful ways in which particular technical successes might be transferred the view seemed strong that success is more likely where an entire organization shifts, including its people. An example was given of the Stansaab firm in Sweden which successfully shifted from the production of an air warning system for the Swedish military to an air traffic control and hospital monitoring system which has been quite successful. Stansaab actually had been a division of the IT&T Swedish affiliate, Standard Radio & Telephone which was later split away from the parent firm. Stansaab executives indicated that spinoff must be "conscious and purposeful." It also requires that a firm choose areas in which it has an advantage rather than attempting to compete across the board with industrial giants.

Sometimes the spinoff is not immediately obvious, as for example in the location of a new university in the Swedish city of Linköping which was partly due to the location there of Saab production facilities. There was also an effort by the Swedish Materiel Command to study the benefits of participation in the Viggen Project for those contractors associated with the project.[2] Interestingly, large firms, like Philips and Bofors, had very little to report in the way of advances. Others however, saw it as a means for gaining interchange of technology, familiarity with new technology, and high quality standards, all of which might give them the skills to enter high technology international markets as serious competitors. The mini-computer which Saab developed for the Viggen advanced the state of miniaturization and also the art of data processing techniques and transmission. While the Swedish Defense Research Organization (FOA) has done very little non-military research, many of the highly trained people in Swedish industry and science came through that organization. It was stressed that the spinoff phenomenon is complex and more often involves processes rather than tangible products.

Some still feel that particular civil problems might receive quicker solutions if efforts were concentrated on the problem directly, but until now there has been no rallying cry nearly as effective with national legislatures as that of military security. In most countries some of these military funds have been applied in ways which will prove beneficial to society, but under these circumstances these funds to some extent were obtained under false pretenses. Those who have been relatively successful with spinoff emphasized the need to analyze the company's true capacities, the skills of its personnel, the capital equipment, etc. For example, VFW Fokker has aided the traffic control authorities in the city of Bremen, has developed simulation and training capabilities, has done some work in bio-medical and electronic areas to improve the operation of artifical limbs, and through its experience in "clean rooms," has been able to make contributions to environmental studies and materials technology. As noted above, a major question that such a company faces deals with the process of commercialization. The originating company might itself decide to produce some items or alternatively lease them for production by someone else, or sell the rights entirely. There is no requirement that the company actually produce in all of the new areas in which it innovates if it seems more appropriate to handle the introduction in some other way.

One of the under appreciated areas of spinoff apparently deals with the rapid transfer of advanced managerial skills and a classic case is the production under license of the F-104 American jet aircraft by Belgium, West Germany. Holland, and Italy. The current international collaboration to produce a multi-role combat aircraft under the management firm, Panavia, is also providing experience in the coordination of managerial skills.

Some Saab officials consider the Saab automobile an example of spinoff since aerospace people designed the initial model of the car. The British advanced railway passenger train has been developed by a combined team of aerospace and traditional railroad engineers. It involves a new suspension and braking system that permits a train to travel at 155mph on existing track. Critical to the success of the venture in the view of those familiar with it was the use of traditional railroad people by the new aerospace team. This is another example of a prime principle of success in spinoff -- to involve the user from the start.

Some officials of the Dutch applied research organization, TNO, noted that most defense R&D was done in the same organization which does other governmental R&D and most of it is done physically at the same locale. The Dutch basic research organization, ZWO, also is located in the same complex of buildings. Thus there is some encouragement to interchange. TNO management boards include representatives from industry, the technical universities and other government ministries. The presidents of the boards meet weekly in the central organization. There was also some belief that in larger European firms more interchange occurs between military and civil divisions than is the case in the U.S. In Britain the belief was stressed that defense interests are broader than simply those of arms and that occasionally military R&D supports fundamental research in a number of areas that are not immediately obvious as being in the narrowly defined military realm of interest. The Royal Aircraft Establishment at Farnborough has a long record of important basic contributions to the British aircraft industry, for example in the area of aerodynamic design. The Royal Aircraft Establishment has conducted the research while industry has done the detailed design and fabrication. The director of French military R&D also emphasized work in private company laboratories which he feels facilitates the transfer of any relevant technology to civil use.

Saab has transferred some of the skills developed in the Viggen autopilot to remote control of systems with maritime application such as the control of very large ships by small crews. As noted above most of the Viggen sub-contractors were large firms such as Ericsson, Philips, and Volvo, with appreciable civil markets. Only about 20% of Saab's activities are in aerospace. Volvo also has a small percentage of its total personnel engaged in aerospace. The percentage of such sales does not exceed about 7% of the company total. Most Swedish firms have gone a long way toward diversification and in their case it was somewhat easier since most of them had pre-existing civil markets to which to return. It was also pointed out in Germany that some of the military effort during the First World War created the skills which later were used to create the famous oceanliners, Europa and Bremen. Also, the Kiel Canal which was originally produced for military purposes has been put to many civil uses.

The one generalization which can be drawn from the discussion of spinoff is that to the extent to which military and space technology can be successfully transferred, it will be to sectors requiring similar high level technology. This of course constitutes a problem since it is hard to find comparable civil market applications and products. Most military and space products are designed with specific applications in those particular areas. Thus, civil application is likely to occur only when the underlying conditions are rather similar to those prevailing in the military and space environment. Often these conditions are not obvious which makes communication even more difficult between advanced technology firms and potential users in what appear to be low technology areas.

Methods for Technology Transfer

A commonly encountered view was that technology transfer is more often accomplished via a movement of persons between organizations or of information concerning components or processes rather than in the transfer of a particular product. This is difficult to measure yet it apparently occurs more frequently than people realize. It was noted in one meeting that "walls are porous between military and civilian divisions."

Therefore, to some extent, cutbacks in military spending may actually aid the transfer of technology through the transfer of individuals from military to civil organizations. An important spinoff is clearly the ability to manage large systems which may be important in areas of health, ecology, etc. An Italian aerospace firm considers itself a pilot project in advanced technology transfer since it operates a central research lab which works on civil applications. Italy is trying to pump technology into the south by influencing high technology firms to locate there. The success of the policy is still in doubt since the area offers principally large quantities of cheap and relatively unskilled labor.

The most frequently mentioned methods for technology transfer follow:

1. Subcontracting

It was often noted that the process of subcontracting constitutes an important method for the transfer of technology. The subcontractor was described as being located at the hub of a wheel, especially if he supplies basic materials and equipment to a variety of different industries. To the extent to which he is able to learn new skills and techniques he is in a strategic position to spread them.

2. Competition and Nationalization

There was occasionally a view that competition is the fastest way to discover what works technically and also provides incentives for its introduction into industry. Yet there is a common attitude in Europe that competition is too expensive a luxury to be afforded by small countries or companies. There was some active denial of the presumed virtues of competition. For example, in the U.K. some maintained that the nationalized British Coal Board had been instrumental in introducing modern mechanization and automation into an industry which would not have been possible under the form of private ownership which earlier prevailed with many smaller firms in the fractionalized market.

3. International Collaboration

The offshore procurement contracts and joint work on U.S. military equipment were often cited as major aids in technology transfer. Such programs as the Marshall Plan and NATO were also widely credited with positive technology transfer results. Such skills as quality control and production to close specifications and other managerial skills were acquired which laid the groundwork for the collaboration in high technology projects which are now underway.

4. Data Storage and Retrieval

While computerized systems of data storage and retrieval have received much publicity there is some concern that they really serve one another rather than serving active researchers. The problem of how to be useful without inundating the user with tons of irrelevant information has not yet been solved. Such processes were often viewed as wasteful. The consensus belief was that such systems must be much more carefully aimed in order, for example, to approximate the very successful methods of searching files of expired patents which goes on all the time. A French military research executive noted that most creative people don't work by sitting at their desks and pushing buttons to gain data but rather want to retain the right to go to the library and think as they flip through the pages of scientific journals. One serious technical problem results from the different meaning assigned to terms, both between scientists and across national boundaries. Another challenge is how to rid the files of redundant information.

It was generally agreed that spinoff rarely develops accidentally. It usually requires a plan and an organization which might, for example, utilize industrial conslutants. Some feel that personal immobility and inflexibility limits technology transfer in Europe. Others are concerned with the high degree of government in-house research and feel that the best way to have the advanced R&D transferred is to have it done in industry directly. That way one needn't worry over the "not invented here syndrome," or the transfer from government laboratory to industry. The Harwell people in Britain feel that they can take an economy-wide view and aid those industries that lack their own highly developed R&D capabilities. Housing and food were put forth as target industries. The hope is that Harwell can play the role of catalyst or funnel for technology.

There were some Swedish observers who wondered whether it might not be more efficient to use existing technology more effectively rather than developing brand new programs. Pure researchers were viewed as too far removed from day-to-day operations to appreciate society's needs or even the marketing needs of their own firms. In Italy the problem of getting research results out into industry was stressed and it was blamed largely upon the poor communications between Italian universities, research laboratories and industry. Apparently there is a universal obstacle to accepting or transferring scientific information between organizations. A research executive of the Pentagon complained of the difficulties he had experienced in trying to get other U.S. government agencies to accept the transfer of some surplus facilities of the Defense Department which appeared on the surface to be very appropriate to their uses and missions.

Aside from the transfer of facilities, an effort to transfer military technology to civil applications was begun in 1972 within the U.S. government with the establishment of a consortium of Defense Department laboratories. The consortium arose informally and reflected a belief that Defense Department technology and equipment could sometimes be effectively used to solve civil sector problems. By 1974 roughly 30 Defense Department laboratories were participating in the program and approximately $10 million of projects were conducted. The labs must be fully reimbursed for their work and such activities must not infringe on their mission requirements. The program apparently has been most effective in developing cooperation between the Pentagon and other federal agencies, somewhat less effective in dealing with state and local government, and least effective in dealings with the private sector. The consortium is linked with the Committee for Domestic Technology Transfer of the Federal Council for Science and Technology via a Defense Department employee assigned to the National Science Foundation.

Obstacles to Technology Transfer

While opinions varied somewhat on the most effective methods for technology transfer, there was agreement on those factors which impeded it. These include the following:

1. Government Regulation

A number of Europeans felt that anti-trust laws in the U.S. have hindered technical advance by inhibiting communication between American high technology firms. A poor system of patent laws can also seriously block technical transfer. The assignment of patent protection for work done under government contract was identified as being in need of review. Occasionally the Mansfield Amendment in the U.S. was singled out as a potential clamp on technology transfer. Under its terms the Pentagon is prevented from doing much more than simply announcing what it has available. Apparently it is not able to demonstrate uses or engage in prototype development for civil application which the Europeans view as minimum steps in successful transfer procedure. There is debate however, about the extent to which the Mansfield Amendment really constitutes an obstacle. For example, a recent Arthur D. Little study observed:[3]

"To argue that it is alright for the DOD laboratories to engage in mission-connected basic and applied research, but that it is wrong to go to the expense of diffusing that knowledge, appears to mangle the intent and purpose of a straightforward provision of public law."

2. Competition Between Government Agencies

On occasion interdepartmental jealousies and competition over budget allocations tend to encourage each ministry to keep its own technical breakthroughs to itself.

3. Separation of Divisions

In some cases company decisions to dispose of divisions which are outgrowths of technology advance have prevented further cross-fertilization which might otherwise have developed between the divisions of the firm.

4. Post-War Political Agreements

This factor applies uniquely in West Germany. Officials of the West German aerospace industry and government complained that their industry was too small to be an effective partner in international collaboration or a market for the U.S. aerospace industry. In part the size of the German industry has been restricted by the offset arrangements which require German purchase of U.S. military equipment to partly offset the costs of maintaining American forces in Germany.

5. Structural Imbalance and Problems of Communication

It is structural imbalance which makes it difficult to transfer technology vertically between different levels of a nation's economy. The problem is to devise some means to communicate with industries utilizing lower levels of technology. There have been few signs of success in this area. It was also noted that on occasion the size of a firm is an important variable in the process of technical diffusion with the transfer easier to accomplish if the firm is large enough to operate both military and civil departments. In companies which are more specialized and which lack their own civil departments the first step in the process of diffusion is that much more difficult.

6. Problems of Commercialization and Fragmented Markets

Even if a company has developed what it considers to be a useful civilian product or application the question arises as to the most cost-effective path to commercialization. The alternatives are numerous and much rides on the particular approach selected. Should the firm work through others under a royalty or license scheme when a different type of firm may be necessary to utilize the results or produce a product? Should the production be shared with a partner? Should it be put into an affiliated company? In order to diversify successfully by itself a company must find a line of work complementary with that in which it is currently engaged. This is often a difficult task.

It was frequently observed that there is no single focal point in government with the breadth and capacity to know how to apply military skills to civil problems. Society is not yet organized to take advantage of the opportunities from the cross fertilization of ideas. Lack of standardization was often a subject of complaint since it tends to prevent the development of quantity production which would enable costs to be brought down in fragmented markets. This is especially a problem in public markets where there are a multiplicity of local governments and governmental units. As it was put by a Pentagon research official, "How can you transfer your fire technology when you must deal with 10,000 West Podunk fire companies?"

7. Customer Inability to Specify Needs

Another common complaint was that most civil sectors are unable to describe their own research needs and that their officials are inadequately trained to understand their own needs. The absence of this talent leads to the inadequate definition of civil problems which makes it very difficult to obtain a solution from the scientist "at the bench." It is tough to move from supplying a single expert buyer to meeting the needs of many uneducated buyers lacking in centralized purchasing facility. Firms face a difficult marketing problem. Such firms must break the habit of depending upon an able buyer who completely specifies the desired product characteristics. The serious problems of communication which exist between low technology users and high technology producers were often emphasized as a major difficulty. An obvious need is for a translator between the two groups. It was also noted that the costs of entering new markets are high and must be met each time a new market is in fact penetrated. Officials at the Harwell Laboratory in Britain noted that frequently they must do much of the firm's own work if a successful transfer of technology was to be effected.

8. Inadequate Infrastructure

Occasionally a useful technology is already available, such as the case of VTOL aircraft, yet existing major investments in airports distant from city centers and the absence of landing facilities in the center city have tended to postpone the introduction of VTOL aircraft.

9. Scale of Output

Modern military production in Europe now occurs in small batches, painstakingly produced. This requires a variety of high skills which are often difficult to shift from high quality job shop production to mass production of lower quality products. As a result, military know-how is difficult to commercialize in a production environment which is rather drastically different from that in which it evolved. Another problem particularly in Europe is that the national markets are often too small to permit efficient levels of output to be reached. This underscores the importance of export markets and international collaboration.

10. Specialized Resources

It becomes more difficult to transfer redundant military resources to other uses the more specialized they are. Also, highly specialized military equipment tends to involve high overhead resulting from the extreme requirements for quality control, environmental testing, etc. This leads to conflict with the necessity for civilian price competitiveness. It is thus difficult to serve both markets. It also seems apparent that there is a much higher investment in research and development work in military products than in civilian items although this generalization has to be treated with some caution, particularly in the case of electronics, which is more ubiquitous with specialization varying widely with the type of firm.

A distinction was drawn between two types of firms, both of which may be involved in military production. The first class essentially produces military products and its success is tied very closely with its military goals and ability to satisfy military customers. These firms work closely with defense ministries and in the U.S., for example, would include such companies as North American Rockwell, TRW, and Northrop. These are unlikely to develop civilian activities as they have specialized extremely in military work for the government. They are not likely to develop a civil orientation unless new civilian lines appear which require their specialized type of advanced technology. These firms contrast to others with civil market orientations but which also do military work. Here examples would include IBM and

Motorola. These have established a better equilibrium between high technology uses in both military and civil areas. It was also hypothesized that technological transfer within the latter type firms is much more likely to occur since with a foot in each camp they may have a greater motivation to seek it.

11. High Cost of Quality

It was pointed out that in aerospace work, "no task is so simple that it doesn't require your best efforts." This seems to characterize the high technology producers who have worked extensively for the military. Such firms try not to produce both military and civil goods in the same plant or on the same production line. It is apparently extremely difficult to mix complex and simple items in the process of production. Some aerospace executives view high costs as largely a result of "a bad habit of overspending." There seems to be general agreement however, that firms in this area tend to be motivated to do their best without respect to cost. There is also a tradition of having large numbers of people to interpret the many regulations and laws which govern government contracts in the military area in particular. Traditionally technical goals rather than cost considerations have been more important in the aerospace industry. Various officials of the Swedish government expressed serious doubt that military firms could shift as collective entities to successful roles in civil markets. They felt that while individuals often can shift gears, so to speak, organizations as such which have for example, developed excessive quality mindedness would be near impossible to change. The traditions of high production standards and quality in military systems have evolved principally because the buyer has been willing to pay to obtain such high performance capability. Such a circumstance is most rare in civilian markets.

12. Inadequate Marketing Skills

There were complaints about this in all countries visited but they were particularly pronounced in Italy and in Britain. The point was made repeatedly that R&D people have little contact with the market or the needs and preferences of customers. The question was frequently raised as to whether research and development could help in achieving cost reductions rather than being a source of cost inflation. Some executives believe that cost reduction provides a goal against which to measure the potential contribution of alternative development possibilities. In other words, new R&D investment must yield savings greater than the nominal productivity gains normally forthcoming in order to be worthwhile. It was also emphasized that new markets are typically won by the quality of marketing efforts rather than by new technology. In Britain in particular, there were frequent complaints that the government had tended to overestimate the importance of R&D and technological superiority instead of promoting the market for British industry. Recognition of the importance of the marketing effort and close contacts with customers was exhibited by the management of the British Atomic Energy Laboratory at Harwell which has concentrated very largely upon civilian applications up to and including the building of prototypes, determining existing market needs, and packaging. Some British executives complained that the brightest young men still go to work for the government since they consider government jobs to be more interesting and comfortable than winning markets for British industry. This is viewed as an important element in Britain's loss of competitiveness and reflects the belief of critics that marketing skills are more important than technological effort.

Transferability of People and Skills

Varied views were expressed concerning the ease with which highly trained people could be transferred from military to civil production. Each category of experience will be reviewed below.

1. Successful Experiences

The opinion was general among those who claimed to have experienced successful transfer that a broader basic and less specialized education enhanced the chances for successful transfer. This type of education was viewed as more common in Europe than in the United States whose approach to education was criticized as overspecialized. There were also some interesting examples of innovation in transfer. For example, a German Defense Ministry research laboratory transfers its scientists and engineers out into industry after five years. While there is some disagreement over the success of the program to train scientists in marketing at Harwell, all agreed that it was necessary for a scientist to have some view of the marketing problem, even if only in broad terms. In most European aerospace and electronics firms one only rarely encounters the separation of production into military and civil divisions. Of particular interest was the observation by a relatively high placed official of the German Defense Ministry that "if both cannot be produced together, then the weapons system was not well designed." In many cases the same functions are performed, the same components are used, etc. This is particularly true in electronics. On occasion there is a separation of production but it is more for security reasons than for reasons of technology. Parts or components that have been put into "black boxes" can surely go either way and do in the electronics case. The essential difference is the degree of technology implicit in the product rather than whether the product be designed for civil or military markets. There are also some differences between military and civil aircraft, for example, but these largely result from the fact that military aircraft usually operate at full capacity in terms of speed, payload, and general performance and therefore have a shorter useful life than civil aircraft. A very important question concerns the uniqueness of military specifications. To the extent that they are not unique it is obviously easier to transfer people who have worked on military items.

There was some disagreement on whether it is easier to shift higher skilled or lower skilled people. It was agreed however, that design engineers may be more difficult to shift than others. The German government maintains a liaison office to help transfer military personnel from the German armed forces into the civil aviation industry.

2. <u>Qualified Experience with the Successful Transferability of People</u>

It was occasionally noted that mobility is less frequent than it would be in terms of technological possibilities. This reflects the reluctance to move which is widely viewed as characteristic of European workers, including high technology personnel. Those who urge the shifting of the individual as the most effective way to transfer technology note that technical publications most often record successes but only rarely failures. It is the individual who knows both sides of the picture and he is unlikely to pursue an avenue which has already been proven a failure in another context. Occasionally obstacles to transfer are due to economic factors rather than to some technical bar to movement. Thus, in a large British aerospace firm there was little personnel transfer because of salary differentials between plants located in different regions, with most workers reluctant to leave jobs in the plants in the high wage areas.

The low level of social mobility in Britain and the still powerful role of the "old boys'" school add to the difficulties of movement into a new organization. Another subtle obstacle to transfer is found arising from differences in approach rather than from strictly technical obstacles. It is often a new point of view rather than special characteristics of a piece of apparatus which make adjustment to change difficult. Some now feel that the useful life "at the bench" of a scientist is about 5-6 years, and that surely after about ten years his work as a creative engineer or scientist is over. One British firm is taking promising men at that stage of their career and shipping them to the Harvard Business school for a six month conversion course in management.

Some new development work in high technology areas is rather similar between military and civil products. The most pronounced differences are apparently found in marketing and sales with the civil markets often more difficult. Civil work is occasionally just as demanding as military work, particularly in electronics. Some switching is difficult to do however, without some degree of retraining. Obviously much depends on the particular occupation involved and its specialized nature. Research on the nature of the component elements in different occupations in terms of skills, personality, and talent, might cast more light on this subject.

3. Negative Views on the Transferability of People

Even among those with serious doubts on transferability it was often specified that the military-civil dichotomy was not crucial but rather other elements which frequently make transfer difficult. Such elements contribute to the formation of a unique approach to work tasks which requires great effort to overcome. An aircraft producer in the Netherlands stressed the enormous attention paid to safety in producing civil aircraft. This concentration reflects many factors; for example, the governmental concern with a reliable civil aviation, the much larger number of flying hours for civil as compared with military aircraft and the consequent more frequent number of takeoffs and landings, the absence of in-flight escape devices for civil passengers, etc. The same source also noted that even among aircraft producers specialization often follows along size of aircraft lines which makes a shift to the production of aircraft of significantly different size very difficult.

Interindustry shifts by a firm are even more difficult to achieve and for those with experience primarily as military producers a new unfamiliar concern with cost consciousness and marketing is often required. Such firms also must be able to adapt to longer production runs and perhaps more automated processes. Since less skilled hand work is required in most civil production it is often necessary to convince workers shifting to civil work that they aren't suffering a reduction in status. Jobs carrying the same title in different industries frequently involve widely differing activities and responsibilities.

A general conclusion was that it is much easier to transfer persons as individuals than to convert existing organizations.[4] The fabrication of military products was viewed as requiring a "military product concept." Thus, when a person is transferred to a civil organization he must be transformed, as it were, to leave behind ideas and ways of thinking which are appropriate only for military work. Other parallels were drawn which stressed the importance of different approaches, even aside from any military-civil dichotomy. Thus, persons with experience in central research laboratories often have important orientations and attitudes which must be changed if they are to function effectively in a product development laboratory. It was viewed as more difficult to build new and perhaps contrary demands on top of old ones than to effect a complete shift. This is why the prevailing view stressed the difficulty involved in requiring employees to frequently shift between military and civil product lines. Such a requirement was described as requiring "split personalities."

REFERENCES

1. Bernard Udis, Adjustment of High Technology Organizations to Reduced Military Spending: The Western European Experience, Revised February 1975. Prepared for the National Science Foundation under Research Grant, No. GI-34932

2. Aspects of Spin-off: A Study of the Impact of Concorde and the Advanced Passenger Train on Their Supplier Firms (London: Centre for the Study of Industrial Innovation, October 1971).

3. William D. Carey, Intergovernmental Uses of Federal R&D Centers and Laboratories: Report to the Council of State Governments (Lexington, Kentucky: The Council of State Governments, April, 1973), p. 5.

4. Amitai Etzioni, "Societal Turnability: A Theoretical Treatment:, pp. 337-382 and Graham T. Allison, "Organizational and Administrative Factors Affecting Shifts in Defense Expenditures," pp. 289-335, in Bernard Udis (ed.), The Economic Consequences of Reduced Military Spending (Lexington, Massachusetts: D.C. Heath, 1973).

Technology Transfer from the Defense to the Civilian Sector in Israel--Methodology and Findings

Samuel N. Bar-Zakay*
Tel-Aviv University, Israel

INTRODUCTION

The conditions of the State of Israel are such that a large proportion of the national budget is devoted to defense requirements. Under such conditions it seems that the civilian economy could benefit from the reservoir of scientific and technological developments accumulated in the defense effort. In principle, this situation exists in many other countries.[1,2] In Israel however there are unique features of the problem. For example in Israel civilian--industrial research and development (R&D) is generally in its infancy and thus a large percentage of the total defense R&D is performed in the defense sector. This is in contrast to the U.S. where most of the defense R&D is performed in the civilian sector.

The Government of Israel was aware of the potential of technology transfer (TT) and in 1969 decided to commission the Ministry of Defense and the Ministry of Commerce and Industry to examine the possibilities of transferring new technologies already existing in research organizations of the Ministry of Defense to the civilian sector.**

---

* The author acted as Project Leader.

** Government Decision No. 882 of August 3, 1969 regarding the organization and management of scientific research.

Various committees discussed this subject, and they all reached the conclusion that a thorough study should be conducted in order to examine the entire complex of problems and possibilities relevant to TT in Israel.

In 1973 the Ministry of Defense, the Ministry of Commerce Industry and Development, as well as the Prime Minister's Office via the National Council for Research and Development initiated such a study to be carried out at Tel-Aviv University. A steering committee* was appointed to guide the study. During the two years of the project, the committee held fifteen meetings with the research staff.

The sponsors of the project made two basic assumptions:

The defense sector develops a large number of technologies which are suitable for civilian use and which are not available to the civilian sector. Transfer of these technologies to the civilian sector would bring about economic and other advantages to the national economy.

It is both possible and desirable to influence this process and to increase its magnitude.

The research project had two main objectives:

To recommend government policies which would improve the process in the future by analysing past cases of technology transfer (TT).

To induce three successful transfers in real time in order to indicate to the civilian sector in Israel the benefits of TT and in order to compare findings with those reached in the framework of the above objective.

Two research teams were set up, both of which made extensive use of consultants for various purposes. The two teams started from the same conceptual model described below, but diverged in order to approach the subject from two complementary research angles. Towards the end of the project they converged in order to compare findings, draw conclusions and make recommendations. Team A concentrated on past cases of TT, examining them by quantitative statistical methods. Team B tried to induce three successful transfer cases in real time, examining them with a case-study approach. The two teams worked independently but met regularly for interdisciplinary discussions.

---

* The Chairman of the Steering Committee was Israel Roth, Executive Vice-President of Israel Aircraft Industries.

The teams were comprised as follows:

Team A -- an economist, a statistician and a sociologist

Team B -- three engineers

The Center for Technological and Interdisciplinary Forecasting (CTIF) at Tel-Aviv University being a national, non-profit research centre with an applied orientation, outlined the objectives of the research so that their achievement would permit the formulation of TT policy.[1] The final report of the CTIF contained 485 pages. It is obvious that this paper cannot go into all the details. Instead, we will try to draw attention to items that may be of interest to the international community of scholars of the technology transfer process, namely:

The pilot use of the specific statistical techniques in the field of technology transfer.*

With the Technology Transfer Model providing the conceptual framework, the idea of diverging from the model into two separate research courses and then converging for the purpose of drawing integrated conclusions.

CONCEPTUAL FRAMEWORK

"When scientific or technological information generated and/or used in one context is re-evaluated and/or implemented in a different context, the process is called technology transfer."[4] Bar-Zakay developed this definition into a Technology Transfer Model.[5] Briefly as can be seen in Figure 1, the model views the process of TT as a four-step operation in which the participants are a donor and a recipient.

While the model in Figure 1 is qualitative, an effort was made in this study to quantify the various components and to examine their relevance to the success or failure of a TT case.

---

* Similar statistical techniques have been used to study success and failure of industrial innovations in the course of project Sappho.[1,3] The innovation field is closely related but not identical to technology transfer. Obviously, the Sappho project did not start from the same conceptual model. Careful analysis would reveal that the conclusions of project Sappho substantiate the findings of this study and vice versa.

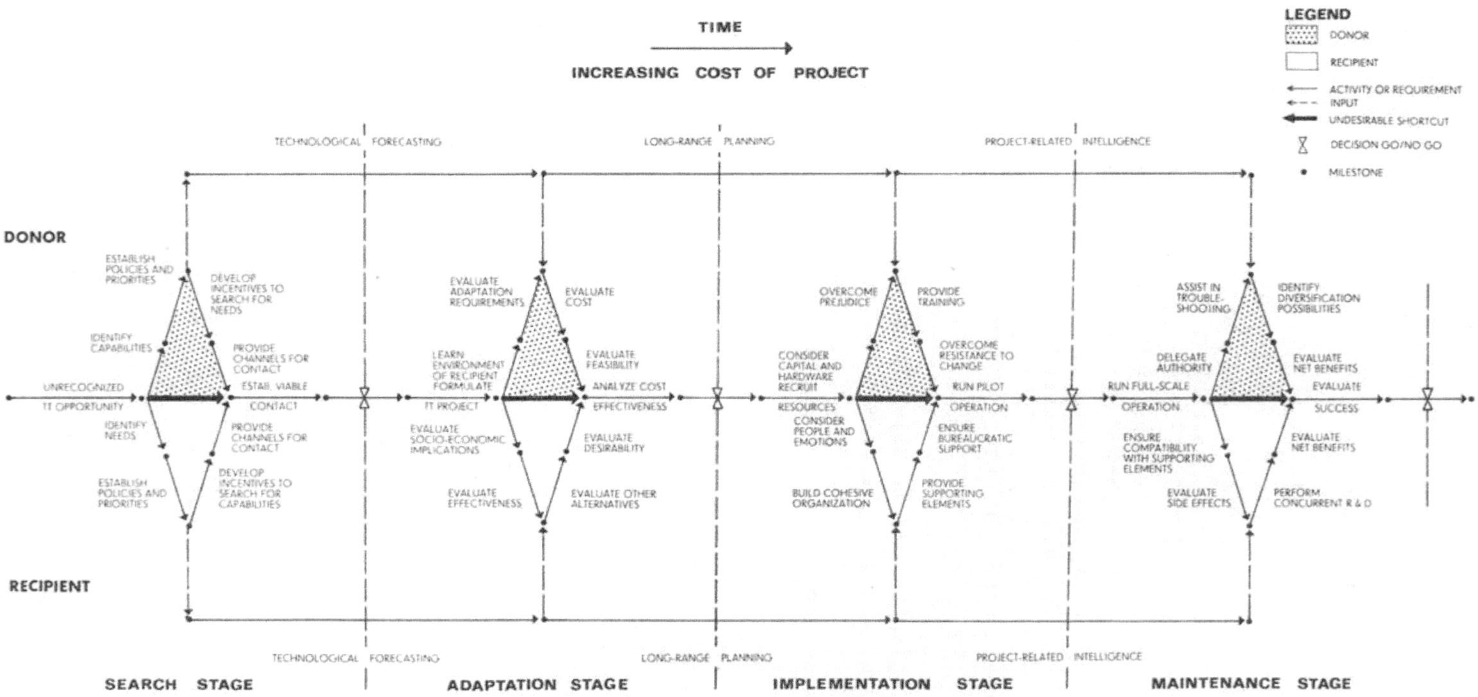

TECHNOLOGY TRANSFER MODEL

FIGURE 1

In the course of the project various new terms were coined, for example Order Transfer and Proper Transfer. In the first type the donor (here the defense sector) orders goods and services from the recipient (here the civilian sector) and TT is essential to ensure compliance with the order. In the second type, namely Proper Transfer, TT takes place for its own sake--with or without payment--and is not connected with any order from the defense sector. It was found in the course of the project that during the last ten years the ratio of Order versus Proper Transfers was high in Israel and therefore it was practical to make this decision.

Another set of terms distinguished between high level success, low level success and failure. High level success means that the transferred technology is implemented in the recipient plant in a product used for civilian purposes. Low level success means that the transferred technology is implemented in the recipient plant in a product which is used for defense purposes (but not necessarily in the same product which was originally ordered). A failure means that a TT began to take place but was not actually accomplished due to difficulties involved in the TT process (and not due to external reasons).

The relative importance of the various TT types, from the point of view of a broader utilization of the defense budget in general and the defense R&D in particular with emphasis on genuine spin-off is as follows:

	High Level Success	Low Level Success
Order	Second	Fourth
Proper	First	Third

TEAM A: PROCEDURE AND FINDINGS

With the conceptual framework, Team A assumed that:

1. A finite number of variables in the TT process could be identified.

2. Data on these variables could be gathered from the total population of transfer cases or from a sample.

3. A success measure (output measure) for TT cases could be developed.

Components of the model (Figure 1) were translated into operational variables which encourage or hinder TT.* Data were collected and statistically analysed to find its relevance to the success measure as will be shown here.

Team A visited about 200 industrial plants in the defense and civilian sectors and identified a large number of TT cases which took place during the last ten years in Israel. For various reasons, a sample of only 67 cases was used for the statistical analysis.** Two questionnaires--a donor form and a recipient form--were compiled to obtain data regarding the operational variables and these questionnaires were completed in extensive interviews.

Two statistical methods were applied:

1. Factor Analysis

2. Stepwise Discriminant Analysis

The reasons for choosing factor analysis for this purpose were outlined in the first paper on this project[1] and will be mentioned here only briefly:

1. The use of factors reduces the amount of variables to be handled without loss of information.

2. The use of factors could result in policy recommendations of a general type (built of details but more encompassing) and could enable decision makers to interpret the policy in their own environment.

---

* The list of variables with their ranking is given in the Appendix. It is beyond the scope of this paper to describe in detail the translation process. For example, it was decided that the questions with which it was determined whether the donor has a TT policy were: a) does the donor advertise the know-how it has for transfer? b) does the donor have a list of criteria for evaluating the capability of a recipient plant to perform TT successfully? Attention is drawn to the fact that questions which received the same answer were deleted from the statistical analysis. We are aware of the difficulties of performing factor analysis with ranked variables rather than continuous ones but hope that a more elaborate analysis will be made in the future.

** One of the reasons for not including all TT cases which were identified was that, in some cases, the donor reported the transfer whilst the recipient did not approve of the information, or vice versa.

Variables were factor-analysed separately for donors and recipients. The success variable was not included in these analyses. For obvious reasons it is desirable to analyse the connection between the factors involved in the TT process on the one hand and success on the other. The factors connected with success/failure do not necessarily have to be the same for donor and recipient since some of the variables are specific and relevant to one side and not the other. The use of stepwise discriminant analysis helps in translating the findings to a list of conclusions (and, later on, recommendations) directed towards increasing the probability of achieving success in the TT process.

FINDINGS OF TEAM A

Tables 1 and 2 present the factor matrix (after rotation)* for donors and recipients respectively. The input consists of data on 18 variables (success variable excluded) and the sample size is 67 TT cases. A computer programme for factor analysis was used.[6]

From the donor's analysis four factors were obtained which accounted for 52% of the total variance. From the recipients' analysis three factors were obtained which accounted for 41% of the total variance.

---

* Only high loadings have been shown.

TABLE 1 - FACTORS OF THE DONORS

	Variables	Factor 1 Sophistication	Factor 2 Willingness	Factor 3 Mutuality	Factor 4 Efficiency
01	Does an R&D Dept. exist?	78			
02	Extent of change induced in Recipients' plant as a result of the transfer				57
03	Confirmation of transfer			76	
04	Transfer type			46	
05	Co-operation of donor in the process			48	
06	Initiation of contact			59	
07	Form of interaction for the transfer				
08	Extent of planning of transfer				54
09	Complexity of the technology				36
10	Extent of planning & forecasting	89			
11	Availability of donor's know-how for "potential transfers"	88			
12	Method of communicating information between parties				47

TABLE 1 (Cont'd)

Variables	Factor 1 Sophistication	Factor 2 Willingness	Factor 3 Mutuality	Factor 4 Efficiency
13 Donor's use of incentives for encouraging transfer			73	
14 Availability of a list of "potential technologies"		65		
15 Availability of advanced training to enhance transfers		81		
16 Advertising of donor's know-how		82		
17 Availability of criteria to evaluate potential recipient's capabilities	60		51	
18 Attitude of personnel in donor's plant towards transfer		74		
Proportion of the Total Variance	18.74%	14.69%	11.17%	7.63%
Eigenvalues	3.37	2.65	2.01	1.37

Total number of transfers = 67

TABLE 2 - FACTORS OF THE RECIPIENTS

	Variables	Factor 1 Sophistication	Factor 2 Efficiency	Factor 3 Mutuality
01	Does an R&D Dept. exist?	69		
02	Number of persons with academic training in the plant	92		
03	Export level	58		
04	Import level	60		
05	Extent of change induced in the recipient's plant as a result of the transfer		71	
06	Confirmation of transfer		35	
07	Transfer type			68
08	Co-operation of the donor in the process			33
09	Initiation of contact			74
10	Form of interaction		54	
11	Extent of planning of the transfer		53	
12	Complexity of the technology		39	
13	Changes in manpower accompanying the transfer		34	
14	Search for alternatives to implement the transfer		32	

TABLE 2 (Cont'd)

Variables	Factor 1 Sophistication	Factor 2 Efficiency	Factor 3 Mutuality
15 Extent of planning and forecasting	61		
16 Availability of donor's know-how for "potential transfers:		36	
17 Number of employees in plant	88		
18 Proportion of academic personnel		46	
Proportion of the Total Variance	21.54%	13.30%	6.29%
Eigenvalues	3.88	2.39	1.13

Total number of transfers = 67

The Sophistication Factor was obtained in both analyses. This factor refers mainly to the existence of R&D and forecasting activities. For the recipient this factor includes the size of the plant (import and export levels, number of employees) and it implies the ability to seek out and absorb new developments.

The Efficiency Factor was obtained in both analyses. It refers mainly to the extent of planning the transfer. The extent of change induced in the recipient plant is connected both with the complexity of the transferred technology and with the preparation of the transfer. This factor implies the degree of serious involvement of the participants in the TT process.

The Mutuality Factor was obtained in both analyses. It takes its meaning mainly from mutual initiation of the contract and co-operation of the donor in the process. For the donor it also includes the use of incentives to encourage transfers. This factor implies common motivation of both sides for participation in the process.

The Willingness Factor is unique to the donor and takes its meaning from the availability of a list of "potential technologies," and availability of advanced training to enhance transfers and promotion of know-how. Coupled with this there is a favorable attitude in the donor's personnel towards the transfer.

Next, the way in which the various factors are differentially connected with success was examined. Stepwise discriminant analysis (SDA) was performed on the factor scores according to two groups--success and failure.*

DONORS--SDA

Out of the four factors, only factor 3 contributed significantly to the correct classification of success and failure. In other words, factor 3 entered in the first step (F=21.9, where the F-value corresponding to a signficance level of 5% is 3.14):

---

* Although we give two types of success (high and low level), there is no significant difference between these two types from the point of view of stepwise discriminant analysis. Therefore, we have combined the two types of success into one group for the purpose of this short paper.

TABLE NO. 3

Groups	Programme Decision "Failure"	"Success"	Total
Failure	4	2	6
Success	4	57	61
Total	8	59	67

Independently of the distribution into groups of success and failure, the program classification was right in 61 out of 67 cases (91%). A random classification without information on either factors or distribution can be right in 33 to 34 cases on average (50%). The conclusion is that factor 3 contains relevant information for the distribution between failure and success.

For the donors the variables included in factor 3-(Mutuality) are connected with the success of the TT. In other words, there is a higher probability for success when both parties are aware of the occurrence of the process; when the donor actively participates in the process and encourages it by using incentives for TT in its plants; when the contact is mutually initiated and when criteria to evaluate the potential recipient's capabilities are available with the donor.

RECIPIENTS--SDA

For the recipients, two factors contributed significantly to the right classification. Factor 2 entered in the first step (F=12.9, where the F-value corresponding to a significance level of 5% is 3.14):

TABLE NO. 4

Groups	Programme Decision "Failure"	"Success"	Total
Failure	4	2	6
Success	6	55	61
Total	10	57	67

The second factor which added significantly to the right classification was factor 1 which entered in the second step (F=6.8, where the F-value corresponding to a significance level of 5% is 3.14). The contribution of the remaining factor was insignificant. The final classification was as follows:

TABLE NO. 5

Groups	Programme Decision "Failure"	"Success"	Total
Failure	4	2	6
Success	1	60	61
Total	5	62	67

Independently of the distribution into groups of success and failure the program classification was right in 64 out of 67 cases (96%), as opposed to 50% in a random classification. Therefore, the conclusion is that factors 2 and 1 contain relevant information for the distribution between failure and success.

For the recipients both factors 2 and 1-(Efficiency & Sophistication) are connected with the success of the transfer. There is a high probability of success when the recipient plant seriously prepares for the transfer and when it is committed to it by inducing various types of changes in the plant. At the same time, a high level of sophistication--namely the conducting of R&D as well as planning and forecasting activities, coupled with a large-size plant with high levels of import/export--increases the probability of accomplishing a successful TT.

SUMMARY OF FINDINGS OF TEAM A

1. The distribution of the 67 cases was as follows:

	High Level Success	Low Level Success	Failure
Order	30	26	3
Proper	4	1	3

2. For the donors four factors were obtained--Sophistication, Efficiency, Mutuality and Willingness. Success is connected with variables included in the Mutuality Factor.

3. For the recipients three factors were obtained--Sophistication, Efficiency and Mutuality. Success is connected with variables included in the Efficiency and Sophistication Factors.

TEAM B: PROCEDURE AND FINDINGS

The objective of Team B was to induce and to analyze the performance of three transfers in real time, in order to present to the civilian sector successes which would increase its interest in the process. Team B examined the process as it unfolded and compared findings with those of Team A, thus adding a further point of view to the data collected from past TT cases. The decision to concentrate on a few cases only, rather than to spread efforts over a larger number of cases, was made in accordance with conclusions drawn by NASA[7].

Work on this objective was divided into three stages in accordance with the first two stages of the TT Model (Figure 1):

First--Team B prepared a list of technologies available in the defense sector which might be suitable for the civilian sector, i.e., "potential technologies." In order to uncover these "potential technologies," Team B visited the large industrial plants of the defense sector which carried out R&D. Liason officers were appointed in these plants whose job was:

- to examine the "potential technologies" suggested by the professional personnel in the plants and to give clearance in the name of the management to transfer them to the civilian sector;

- to be the connecting link between the CTIF and the recipient plants on the one hand and the defense plants on the other.

As the project had to begin at some point, the team fixed an arbitrary deadline and closed the list when 37 "potential technologies" were available.

The CTIF then distributed letters, together with the list of 37 "potential technologies," to 520[8] industrial plants in Israel employing fifty people or more. The "potential technologies" were also advertised through other channels--such as interviews with top managers of eleven holding companies in the civilian sector and through professional experts in various industrial branches in the civilian sector. By the end of this stage, 77 civilian industrial plants had expressed interest in one or more of the technologies out of the 37 listed.

In brief, the first stage comprised the following steps:

- uncover "potential technologies" in the defense sector
- obtain detailed technical and economic information about these "potential technologies"
- obtain security and commercial clearance
- uncover the population of civilian plants and distribute the "potential technologies" amongst them
- classify the requests from the civilian plants and supply additional information about the "potential technologies"

Secondly--Out of the 77 applications, three were chosen for the experiment.

This second stage comprised the following steps:

- establish contact between the interested civilian plants and the liason officers in the defense plants
- advance the contacts with simultaneous analysis in order to choose the candidates for the three transfer experiments
- follow closely the transfer process in the three plants until the signing of the contract

Thirdly--Team B analysed the findings of its observations within the conceptual framework of the TT model (Figure 1).

In the course of the research various secondary objectives were also studied. These included analysis of the attitude of the managements of the defense plants to the whole TT project; the attitude of the managements of the civilian plants to the proposals made to them and so on.

SUMMARY OF FINDINGS OF TEAM B

1. 77 civilian plants expressed interest in the TT suggestions. Contacts were made between the defense sector and several of these plants.

2. The success of TT depends to a large extent on a preliminary preparation of detailed technical and economic information about "potential technologies" and the conditions for their transfer. At present, this preliminary preparation is far from satisfactory.

3. The success of TT depends to a large extent on the appointment of "contact men" in the donor plants whose job it is a) to uncover "potential technologies" b) to handle their transfer to the civilian plants. At present, such a function does not exist in many defense plants.

4. The civilian sector is interested in TT from the defense sector. In order to realize this interest, continuous flow of information between donor and recipient is necessary above and beyond the flow which exists today. It is also essential that both sides should be fully aware of the importance of TT and its economic potential.

5. As a result of the single successful experiment (out of the three which were tried) the recipient was able to fill a major export order and benefit economically from the successful technology transfer. The donor received a fee commensurate with his effort.

SUMMARY OF FINDINGS

The findings of the two teams are very similar*, as can be seen in the following comaprison:

TEAM A	TEAM B
It was discovered that in order to ensure success as opposed to failure, the following conditions are important:	It was discovered that two out of three technology transfer cases failed for the following reasons:
DONORS	DONORS
Mutuality -both donor and recipient are aware of the existence of the transfer. -incentives are given by the donor to its personnel to encourage the transfer. -initiation of contacts is mutual.	-were less ready to transfer technology, although they were willing to sell equipment and services. -do not give sufficient incentives to their personnel to encourage the transfer. -CTIF on behalf of the recipients was the initiator of the process. -do not have systematic and established criteria to evaluate recipients.
-donor has criteria for evaluating the capability of recipient to absorb transfer. -donor is actively involved in the process.	-do not encourage the transfer process, but sometimes hinder or disturb it.
RECIPIENTS	RECIPIENTS
Efficiency-induce changes in the production process, the structure of organization and the training of personnel. -the connection between the two parties takes the form of a contract.	-of three experiments only one was successful where extensive changes were induced in the structure of organization and in the training of personnel. -a contract was signed only in the successful transfer. In the other two cases, in spite of recipient's willingness to sign, this was blocked by the donor.

TEAM A		TEAM B
	-there is a detailed plan of the transfer.	-only in the successful case was there a detailed plan of the process.
Sophistication	-the level of sophistication of recipient plant is high when there is a distinct R&D department, a planning and forecasting function, a large number of staff with academic training, high level of exports and imports, large number of employees.	-the level of sophistication of the three recipients participating in the experiment, as measured by the criteria mentioned by Team A, was low--for example, none of the three plants had a distinct R&D department.

The above is based on:	The above is based on:
1) Factor Analysis of a sample of 67 cases; an analysis which identified the factors characterising TT: Donors-sophistication, willingness, mutuality, efficiency. Recipients-sophistication, efficiency, mutuality.	1) Initiation of three TT cases of a Proper type and their follow-up in real time.
2) Stepwise Discriminant Analysis applied to the above groups of factors and transfer cases.	2) The suggestion of 37 technologies for transfer from the Donors in a letter to 520 plants to which 77 plants replied.

* A priori there is of course a qualitative difference between findings derived from statistical analysis and those derived from a case study.

EPILOGUE

Conclusions from this work can be drawn in various cross sections:

a) At the beginning of this project the potential value of translating factors into policy decisions was suggested. This can now be demonstrated*: Factor "Sophistication" implied that more advanced R&D capability of the recipient would increase the probability of TT success. Therefore, it was suggested that the government should formulate policies which would encourage technology transfer and research & development simultaneously. The above recommendation may take various shapes and forms in different levels of government. It would enable decision makers to interpret the policy in their own environment.

It may be mentioned here that the above recommendation is in line with the setting up of the Experimental Technology Incentives Program (ETIP) at the National Bureau of Standards (U.S.A.). The ETIP program encourages TT and R&D simultaneously.[9]

b) From the TT Model (Figure 1) point of view, it may be said that what was concluded intuitively and qualitatively at the time of writing the Model[5] has been proven here. Namely that "Mutuality" is essential for the success of technology transfer. The Donor and the Recipient must perform certain activities. Short cuts lead to failures.

c) Finally, it may be suggested that the techniques which were used here could be applied to other types of technology transfer such as technology transfer to developing countries[10] or to technology transfer between developed countries (U.S.-Russia, U.S.-China, etc.). Although methodological difficulties as analysis over time, analysis with additional variables, ratio of the number of variables to the sample size, etc. will always be with us, it seems that the field of TT has come of age for some systematic comparative analysis of various types of technology transfer.

---

* As was mentioned in the introduction to this paper, details of the final recommendations to the Israeli government will not be given here for various reasons.

APPENDIX

LIST OF VARIABLES INCLUDED IN THE FACTOR ANALYSIS

	Variables for the donor	Coding
01	Does an R&D Dept. exist?	1. none 2. small department (1-3 persons) 3. large department (over 4 persons)
02	Extent of change induced in Recipient's plant as a result of the transfer	1. no change 2. minor change (training only) 3. medium change (training and change in equipment) 4. new process (change in equipment and layout, recruitment of professional manpower, and production of a new product)
03	Confirmation of Transfer occurrence. (Criterion: both Recipient and Donor agreed that there actually was a transfer)	1. both parties deny 2. one party denies 3. difficult to assess (mixed feelings) 4. one party confirms 5. both parties confirm
04	Transfer type	1. Order-accompanies an order for goods and services by the Donor from the Recipient 2. Proper-transfer is either for payment or without payment but not tied up with any order
05	Co-operation of Donor in the process	1. hinders 2. passive 3. encourages
06	Initiation of contact	1. defense sector 2. civilian sector 3. both
07	Form of interaction for the transfer	1. informal 2. order 3. contract

Variables for the donor	Coding
08 Extent of planning of transfer	1. no plan 2. outline 3. detailed
09 Complexity of the technology	1. very simple 2. simple 3. complex
10 Extent of planning and forecasting functions	1. none 2. planning only 3. planning and forecasting (long-range planning)
11 Availability of Donor's know-how for potential transfers (as perceived by Donor)	1. none 2. very little 3. medium 4. high
12 Method of communicating between the parties	1. verbal description (telephone) 2. explanatory material 3. demonstrations 4. blue prints 5. loaning of manpower
13 Donor's use of incentives at his plant for encouraging transfer	1. none 2. rare 3. infrequent 4. frequent 5. constant
14 Availability of a list of potential technologies for transfer	1. none 2. outlined list 3. detailed list
15 Availability of advanced training to enhance transfers (Indicators: library; participation in conferences; investment in dispersion of know-how)	1. none 2. 1 indicator 3. 2 indicators 4. 3 indicators 5. 4 indicators
16 Advertising of Donor's know-how in the civilian sector	1. none 2. sporadic 3. regular

	Variables for donor	Coding
17	Availability of criteria at Donor's plant to evaluate potential Recipient's capabilities, (Criteria: technological proficiency; turnover; science-based industry; experience in field of technology; subsidized plant working with defense sector; reasonable period for fulfillment of orders	1. none 2. 1-2 criteria 3. 3-4 criteria 4. 5-6 criteria 5. 7 or more criteria
18	Attitude of personnel in Donor's plant towards Transfer	1. strong objection 2. objection 3. indifference 4. encouraging 5. strongly encouraging

	Variables for the recipient	Coding
01	Does an R&D Dept. exist?	1. none 2. small department (1-3 persons) 3. large department (over 4 persons)
02	Number of persons with academic training in plant	none at all and over
03	Export level (in proportion to the total production level)	1. none 2. small (up to 20%) 3. medium (20-60%) 4. high (60-80%) 5. very high (80% and over)
04	Import level (in proportion to the total production level)	1. none 2. small (up to 20%) 3. medium (20-60%) 4. high (60-80%) 5. very high (80% and over)
05	Extent of change induced in the recipient's plant as a result of the transfer	1. no change 2. minor change (training only) 3. medium change (training and change in equipment) 4. new process (change in equipment and layout--recruitment of professional manpower as well as new product)
06	Confirmation of transfer occurence. (Criterion: both recipient and donor agreed that there actually was a transfer)	1. both parties deny 2. one party denies 3. difficult to assess (mixed feelings) 4. one party confirms 5. both parties confirm
07	Transfer type	1. Order--accompanies an order for goods and services by the donor from the recipient 2. Proper--transfer is either for payment or without payment but not tied up with any order

	Variables for the recipient	Coding
08	Co-operation of donor in process	1. hinders 2. passive 3. encourages
09	Initiation of contact	1. defense sector 2. civilian sector 3. both
10	Form of interaction	1. informal 2. order 3. contract
11	Extent of planning of the transfer	1. no plan 2. outline 3. detailed
12	Complexity of the technology	1. very simple 2. simple 3. complex
13	Changes in manpower deriving from the transfer	1. none 2. minor--training of personnel 3. medium--retraining of personnel 4. major--recruitment of additional skilled manpower 5. new personnel
14	Search for alternatives to the technology transfer	1. none 2. superficial 3. partial 4. extensive
15	Extent of planning and forecasting functions	1. none 2. planning only 3. planning and forecasting (long-range planning)
16	Availability of donor's know-how for potential transfers (as perceived by the recipient)	1. none 2. very little 3. medium 4. high
17	Number of employees in plant	One and more

	Variables for the recipient	Coding
18	Proportion of academic personnel to total number of employees	None and more

REFERENCES

1. Bar-Zakay, Samuel N. et. al. "Technology Transfer from the Defence to the Civilian Sector in Israel," in Davidson, H.F., Cetron, M.J., and Goldhar, J.D., (eds.) Technology Transfer, NATO Advanced Study Institute, Noordhoff International Publishing, Leiden, The Netherlands, 1974, pp. 371-386.

2. Ibid., the Appendix.

3. "Success and Failure in Industrial Innovation: Report on Project Sappho" by the Science Policy Research Unit, University of Sussex, published by the Centre for the Study of Industrial Innovation, London, February 1972. Also see other publications by Paul Jervis, Roy Rothwell and others from the Science Policy Research Unit. For example in the book mentioned in reference (1).

4. Bar-Zakay, Samuel N., "Policymaking and Technology Transfer--The Need for National Thinking Laboratories," Policy Science, Vol. 2, No. 3, Elsevier, 1971.

5. Bar-Zakay, S.N., "Technology Transfer Model," in Technological Forecasting and Science Change, Vol 2, No. 3/4, 1971. American Elsevier Publishing Co., Inc., New York, 1971. This model was also published in: Industrial Research and Development News, United Nations Industrial Development Organization, Vienna, Vol. VI, No. 3, 1972, and Boltein Extraordinario, Ministerior De Industria Y Comercio, No. 1, Julio 1973, Ecuador.

6. For a basic description of Factor Analysis see Rummel, R.J., "Understanding Factor Analysis," Journal of Conflict Resolution, Volume XI, No. 4, 1968. For more details see Harman, H.H., Modern Factor Analysis, University Press, 1967.

7. The Technology Utilization Office which was set up by NASA (National Aeronautics and Space Administration) for the purpose of inducing technology transfer was engaged in various technology transfer activities, simultaneously decreasing in scope and increasing in intensity. Out of its experience, the Technology Utilization Office came to the conclusion that the more intensive the treatment of the transfer, the greater its chances of success. See Hamilton, Jeffrey T., "Technology Transfer--and the U.S. Space Program," in OMEGA, The International Journal of Management Science, Vol. 3, No. 1, 1975.

8. NASA has used for several years the Tech. Briefs to induce TT by mailing lists of potential technologies. Data on their response level can be found in the work of Wright, Philip, "Government Efforts to Facilitate Technical Transfer: The NASA Experience," edited by William H. Gruber and Donald G. Marquis, The M.I.T. Press, Massachusetts, 1969.

9. Berke, Joseph G., "Procurement--The Pull Side of Technology Transfer," at the Fifth Intersociety Conference on Environmental Systems, July 21-24, 1974, San Francisco.

10. See reference (1) Bar-Zakay, Samuel N., "Technology Transfer in Developing Countries," pp. 511-535.

PART IV: INTERNATIONAL TECHNOLOGY TRANSFER

The first two articles by Baranson and Hayden have very "penetrating insights" into transferring technology to the People's Republic of China and the Soviet Bloc countries, respectively. Baranson discussed the manner by which the People's Republic of China purchased independent plants from Japan. He states that Japanese trading companies have played a leading role in seeking out business opportunities for Japanese companies and in establishing initial contracts with the Chinese trading corporations. The experiences of Japanese firms reveal some important insights for China's industrial priorities and technology acquisition strategies.

By using special case studies of U.S. corporation experience, Hayden discusses the central question of why and how do U.S. firms transfer industrial technology to Socialist enterprises.

Two articles dealing with barriers to international technology transfer were given by Trainor and Rinne. Trainor discusses problems in transferring foreign military technology to the United States. Rinne, on the other hand, examines means for holding back for security reasons, information in nuclear energy areas which the U.S. does not want to transfer to foreign countries. Trainor's paper describes problems involved in transferring technology to the U.S., and uses four case histories to illustrate the problems of technology transfer.

The problems presented by security considerations to the transfer of nuclear energy technology are examined by Rinne. The paper outlines the nuclear fuel cycle, evaluates the terrorist threat, provides examples of security barriers and notes current approaches to transferring technology in the nuclear energy area.

The paper by Boggio of the European Common Market covers a number of actions that the Market Commission has taken or is planning to take which directly or indirectly promote the interchange of scientific and technology know-how and a partial assessment of the degree of their effect.

The article by Rolf Piekarz of the National Science Foundation discusses the research program relating to determining the effects of international technology transfer on the U.S. economy. It describes the public policy setting, the information needs generated by this setting, and current and planned research.

PEOPLE'S REPUBLIC OF CHINA'S PURCHASES OF INDUSTRIAL PLANTS FROM JAPAN

Jack Baranson

Developing World Industry and Technology
Washington, DC

Japanese trade with the People's Republic* of China was reopened in 1959 and has continued to expand since 1963, when the first package plant was sold to China.[1] Japanese trading companies have played a leading role in seeking out business opportunities for Japanese companies and in establishing initial contacts with the Chinese trading corporations. The experiences of Japanese firms reveal some important insights for China's industrial priorities and technology acquisition and transfer strategies.[2]

CHINA'S INDUSTRIAL PRIORITIES

Trade with China in the export of capital equipment was resumed in late 1972, following the inward-turning period of the Cultural Revolution (1966-69). There had been a period in the mid-1960s (1963-65) when Japan sold up to $30 million in package plants. In the period August 1972 to April 1973, Japanese firms sold identical plants totalling near $200 million in value. As of April 1973 there were several hundred million dollars of additional plant purchases under negotiation (Figure 1).

* Article is based upon a visit to Japan in April 1973 and discussions with Japanese industrial firms and Government officials.

Negotiated 1963-1965

- Vinylon Plant (20.0)
- Acetylene Gas Generating Plant (3.0)
- Air Liquefying Plant (1.7)
- Oil-pressure Equipment Manufacturing Plant (1.8)
- Wire Drawing Plant (.5)

Negotiated Since August 1972

- Thermal Power Plant (17.3)
- Offshore Oil Riggs (10.0)
- Ocean Cargo Vessels (19.2)
- Ethylene and Butadiene Plant (11.5)
- Ethylene Plant (34.6)
- Dredging Equipment (15.4)
- Acryl Monomer Plant (- -)
- Polyvinal and Polybutadiene Plant (3.8)
- Urea Plant (42.0)

Under Negotiation (as of April 1973)

- Steel Plant (192.3 to 230.8)
- Steel Rolling Mill (Over 385.0)
- Ethylene glycol/oxide and acrylic (- -)
- Ethylene plant (- -)
- Synthetic Fiber Plant (- -)
- Methanol Plant (- -)
- Maleic Anhydride Plant (- -)
- Alpha Olefin Industrial Detergent Plant (- -)
- Foundry (1.9)
- Thermal Power Plant (133.5)
- Polyester Plant (76.3)
- Pulp Plant (3.8)
- Color Television Studio (2.3)
- Polyester Plant (- -)
- Color Television Tube Manufacturing (19.1)

SOURCE: Japan Planning Agency.

Figure 1
SALES NEGOTIATIONS BETWEEN JAPAN AND THE PEOPLE'S REPUBLIC OF CHINA FOR INDUSTRIAL EQUIPMENT AND PACKAGE PLANT
(In U.S. million dollars)

Exchange missions between Japan and China have reflected stated priorities and related needs: electronics (including computers, TV, and measuring instruments), construction equipment, machine tools, chemicals, steel, oil (exploration and refining), automotive, shipbuilding and textiles.

In the steel sector, China is now negotiating with Kawasaki Steel and Nippon Steel for a 3-million ton hot strip mill and a 1-million ton cold strip mill at a cost approaching $400 million. Both Japanese steel makers have developed their own technology to produce electrolytic steel plates and proposed agreements will undoubtedly include substantial technical assistance. In the textile fields, the Chinese want to shift from natural to synthetic fibers as a much less costly way of providing its population with cheap textiles. The Chinese also want to shift from conventional basic processes for the manufacture of fertilizer bases to the more advanced petroleum oil processes that will also yield synthetic resins and rubber chemicals.

Energy and transport are two other designated priority areas. In the energy field, the Chinese are negotiating with Japan for 250-600 megawatt thermal power plants and have either purchased or are negotiating with various countries (Canada, U.K., Germany, and Japan) for 25 to 30 additional jet-turbine generators in the 9 to 20 megawatt range. In the transport field, the Chinese are interested in expanding port facilities and in purchasing ocean cargo vessels. Sector goals to expand port facilities are reflected in negotiations for the purchase of dredging equipment. They are also purchasing in commercial lots tank trucks and refrigerator units to transport liquified gas. The Chinese have such widespread needs for truck transport, they are even willing to import second-hand equipment. In the communications field they are interested in the expanded use of color television (color TV transmission station and color TV tube manufacturing equipment).

Following President Nixon's visit to China, Japanese business interests were anxious to reinforce and expand their sales of plant and equipment to the People's Republic of China. The Chinese undoubtedly exploited intensification of competition both in expanding technical contacts and in enhancing their bargaining position by playing off one set of businessmen against another. Japanese firms believe they have certain inmate advantages in the Chinese market over their European and American competitors. Culturally and psychologically, they consider themselves more closely attuned to Chinese modes of thinking and ways of doing business. The Japanese believe they are more willing to carry out business transactions based upon mutual understanding, rather than the letter of the contract to which Europeans and Americans are more accustomed. Japanese businessmen also feel they better understand the Chinese mode of arriving at decisions through the process of consensus, which they consider very similar to their own industrial organization culture. This includes the interaction between government and enterprise, which is so thoroughly integrated in China. Japanese firms believe these insights and affinities give them an edge over their European and American counterparts; the Japanese trading firms visualize themselves as advantaged intermediaries in the China trade.

The Japanese further believe that their industrial products, manufacturing techniques, and even managerial style is more suited to China's needs and conditions than are several categories of American and European equipment and production systems. They believe their machine tools are more closely attuned to the work habits and cultural affinities of Chinese operations (controls at the right level, for example). Japanese firms have a "natural" advantage in high bulk-to-value, because of their geographic proximity to China. But they realize they face heavier competition in high technology goods. As for production techniques, technical people note that Japan had gone through a similar stage of industrialization in the early 1950s, and they were therefore more familiar with small-scale techniques and manufacturing requirements under rudimentary conditions. This is one reason, they argue, why Japanese technicians are able to respond and adapt to Chinese needs and conditions more readily than Europeans and North Americans. This is particularly true of technicians from small-to-medium-size Japanese enterprises.

Whether or not these self-images of their potential role and advantage in the China trade are valid, Japanese businessmen and government officials seem intent upon maintaining and extending their place in the China market. This drive has been intensified by the prospects of mounting trade barriers to European and American markets. Japanese businessmen were seriously disturbed by President Nixon's visit and its implication for substantially expanded United States inroads into the Chinese market by American industrial firms.

There have been several cases where American technology has been sold through Japanese intermediaries. A $20 million agreement was signed with Asabi Chemical, a licensee of Standard Oil of Ohio for the purchase of a synthetic fiber acrylon plant.[3] The new plant will increase ten-fold China's synthetic fiber output capability ---at present, China has a single small plant producing 10,000 metric tons a year. The new plant is part of a newly developed integrated chemical complex to which this plant will furnish by-products such as propylene. Under the Asabi agreement, Sohio for a $6 million fee agreed to furnish process technology and proprietary rights to their newest catalyst equipment, which has decided economic and environmental control advantages over previous equipment. Design engineering and equipment procurement will be carried out by Niigata Engineering and The Chori Trading Company. Asabi will train the Chinese engineers and technicians in Japan and financing is through the Export-Import Bank of Japan. The plant will produce 110 million pounds of fiber a year and is scheduled to be completed by 1976. Other U.S. technology has been sold indirectly in two recent cases through a Japanese firm (Toyo Engineering). One was a thousand metric ton-per-day ammonia plant using "Kellogg" technology, and the other a 300,000 metric ton-per-year ethylene plant using the "Lummus" process. In both cases, a lumpsum payment was made to the American company, in lieu of licensing fees.

TECHNOLOGY ACQUISITION MODES

Following initial contacts, Japanese company representatives are invited to Peking to make full presentations on the performance and maintenance characteristics of their product line. Japanese firms are asked to choose preferably items in which they own the industrial proprietary rights and in which they have a technological lead. In the automotive field, Japanese companies indicate the Chinese have requested little in the way of technical assistance following sales agreements for such items as bulldozers and trucks -- other than the training of a few Chinese technicians in Japan in maintenance and repair procedures.

The Chinese have two principal motivations in developing their technical information base. From a commercial standpoint, it considerably enhances their bargaining position on price negotiations, including their ability to break down purchases to advantageous elements. The other reason is to acquire production know-how outside the traditional licensing and investment mold. There are six discernible modes the Chinese have used to acquire technical know-how that will now be examined.

<u>Single purchases of industrial samples</u>, either at trade and through other sources has been a general practice for a decade or more. Japanese firms have noted that the Chinese have purchased a relatively large number of single sample equipment without any follow-on orders. Many of these firms are now reluctant to send "high technology" items on this basis. A recurrent Japanese visitor to the Canton Fair has observed continued improvement each year in Chinese machine tools, and

he attributes some of these improvements to copying Japanese prototypes.

A second acquisition made is through technical presentations by individual companies at Peking industrial fairs, in which several Western European and Canadian companies also have participated. During these sessions -- and particularly in follow-on sales negotiations -- there has been intensive probing into the technical performance and manufacturing techniques along the lines described and analyzed earlier. During these encounters, the Chinese provide only the roughest indications of their needs and leave it to foreign firms to supply vast quantities of data containing product standards and specifications. This tactic supplies the Chinese with substantial technical information which they might not otherwise obtain.

A third mode is through the interchange of industrial technical missions. Chinese teams visiting Japan have covered mainly the priority areas outlined earlier. They consist of from anywhere between 8 and 45 members and stay from 4 to 6 weeks. During that time they may visit as many as a hundred plants. The Chinese seem principally concerned with collecting technical information and do not place any orders while in Japan. These visits add significant dimension to paper learning upon which isolated Chinese technicians have had to rely heavily in the past. This includes observation of equipment in operation and related aspects of production organization and management. Several Chinese teams were particularly interested in learning how organization and management changed as the small-sized firm evolved to larger scale operations. The Chinese also showed interest in every minute detail they can obtain on how a part is fabricated, materials specifications, and equipment utilization. The automotive mission (45 members, 40 days) was interested in auto-engine processing lines (at Toyota, Komatsu, Nissan-Diesel, and Isuzu), forging operations (at Toyota, Hino, and Nissan) and foundry techniques (Nissan-Diesel). The visiting team members appeared to be largely interested in "fundamentals." In one case, for example, the Chinese team members asked for complete plans to build up an integrated foundry, including construction costs, plant layout, time estimates, and technical details on processing methods. The Chinese also have asked Japanese truck manufacturers for complete sets of data on vehicle fabrication.

The fourth acquisition mode is through "technical training" agreements associated with the sale of equipment. Under these sales agreements, Chinese technicians are trained in Japanese plants for specified periods. Hitachi agreed to train 15 technicians in their shipyards over a three-month period. Komatsu (a manufacturer of road construction equipment, diesel engines and heavy machine tools) trained 25 engineers for three months in engine repair and maintenance. This group of Chinese engineers was probably assigned to train others in China to carry out diesel engine maintenance and repair. Nissan also offered to train Chinese technicians in after-sales servicing of their vehicles. Presumably, such agreements accompany any sizeable sale of trucks or other automotive and construction equipment.

The fifth mode is technical support associated with automotive parts exports negotiated by the People's Republic of China as offsets to foreign exchange costs for automotive vehicle imports. For example, Toyota agreed to take a small quantity of accessory tools (about $38,000) for equipping new Toyota cars sold in Japan for delivery in July 1973. Komatsu also is considering imports of Chinese-made tool boxes as accessories in bulldozers and other construction equipment in amounts that could reach $10 million a year as partial offset payment for Komatsu imports into China. In order to assure that such equipment meets international standards, Japanese firms would have to provide designs, production engineering and other technical support.

The purchase of package plants is the sixth and most comprehensive mode of acquiring industrial technology. This mode is chosen in priority areas where the Chinese want to make a quantum jump in production know-how in a minimal time. A special agency has been reconstituted to negotiate these package plant purchases -- the China National Technical Import Corporation. The new agreements provide for complete plant installation, including the preparation, plant design, procurement and installation of equipment, supply of "know-how," training of technicians, and technical support during the run-in period. In most cases, the Chinese are insisting in guaranteed performance levels by the seller (volume of output and quality of production). This raises a considerable dilemma for Japanese firms, since (a) the Chinese in most cases are insisting on doing their own site preparation; (b) they have asked that certain items be procured from Chinese sources; and (c) in connection with plant installation and run-in, they have continued to limit both the number of foreign technicians permitted into China and the time period which they may remain.

The Chinese have adopted a more flexible attitude toward payments for technology and know-how. In the past, they have consistently refused to pay royalties, licensing fees, or technical service charges. They now recognize they must pay for industrial proprietary rights, but they do insist on a lump sum payment over and above hardware costs. They are also willing to

INDUSTRIAL OBJECTIVE	TECHNICAL INFORMATION REQUIREMENT	TECHNICAL ACQUISITION MODES
Purchase End-Product	• Performance Characteristics • Maintenance and Repair • Replacement parts Manufacture	• Discussion in Connection with Equipment Purchase • Training in Repair and Maintenance as Part of Sales Contract
Manufacturing	• Operation Characteristics of Factory Equipment • Production Organization and Management (Quality Control, Material Flow, Cost Analysis, Etc.)	• Discussions in Connection with Equipment Purchases and at Trade Fairs • Interchange of Industrial Technical Missions • Technical Support through Run-in Phase in Connection with Package Plant Purchase
Industrial Design and Engineering	• Production and Process Engineering (Machine Loading, Process Sheets, Materials Standards and Specifications) • Plant Layout and Site Preparation	• Deeper Probing into Production Organization and Management, Particularly in Connection with Package Plant Sales • Tracing through Steps of Supplier's Own Industrial Development • Inquiries into Metallurgy and Equipment Design • Reverse Engineering Analysis

Figure 2. Technology Acquisition Objectives, Requirements, and Modes

pay limited technical service fees for time spent in China by Japanese technicians. Chinese purchasing authorities also have agreed to honor industrial property rights. This includes clauses that they will pay an additional know-how fee, if they wish to "copy" a purchased plant. They have also accepted restrictions on building duplicate plants abroad. In earlier days, the Chinese insisted on minute price breakdown for every single item in a package plant, but they have now come to realize it is not necessary to do this in order to secure competitive price quotations. They do continue to insist on complete sets of data on plant layout, manpower requirements, and everything else connected with operating and maintaining the purchased facility.

A major objective behind stipulations in purchase agreements requiring intensive technical encounter, including the furnishing of detailed technical information, apparently are aimed at acquiring industrial design and engineering capabilities leading to self-reliant, and self-sustaining systems (see Figure 2).

CONCLUDING REMARKS

The Chinese have further extended their trade negotiations for capital goods and package plants to Canada and Western Europe, and more recently have begun direct negotiations with American firms beyond the initial purchases of jet transports from Boeing and earth satellite stations from RCA and Western Electric. This wide casting of the purchase net is apparently part of China's technology acquisition strategy. It is apparently designed to acquire advanced technology along with design engineering capabilities on highly favorable terms.

REFERENCES

1. For a survey of Japan's trade relation with the PRC, see Japan External Trade Organization (JETRO), How To Approach the China Market (Tokyo, 1972).

2. For background material, see William W. Whitson, "China's Quest for Technology," Problems of Communism (July-August 1973), pp. 16-30.

3. Chemical and Engineering News (May 14, 1973), p. 3.

U.S. CORPORATE EXPERIENCE IN TRANSFERRING INDUSTRIAL TECHNOLOGY TO THE SOVIET BLOC

Eric W. Hayden

Bank of America
New York, NY

Before the 1970's, Soviet Europe was a geographic area unknown to most U.S. firms. A combination of Cold War tensions and Socialist autarky prevented more than a superficial commercial interface. Today, however, political relations have warmed, the Socialist economies have re-assessed their economic philosophies, and commercial relations between U.S. firms and Eastern nations are assuming a new importance.* For the average U.S. firm, the Soviet bloc offers the attraction of an untapped market. For the bloc nations, the U.S. is a source of products as well as a means for improving their industrial output and making that output internationally competitive. The growing commercial relationship has involved the sale by U.S. manufacturing and engineering firms of goods, turn-key plants, patent rights, technical know-how and services, and production technology. This paper will assess one aspect of this commercial flow, the transfer of industrial technology to the Eastern bloc through sustained enterprise-to-enterprise relationships.

---

* Trade between the U.S. and the Soviet bloc began its "trade-off" in the 1970's, particularly in 1972, the year President Nixon met in Moscow with Chairman Brezhnev. That year, trade turnover was over $1.1 billion, nearly double what it was in 1971. In each of the two subsequent years, 1973 and 1974, turnover has been well over $2 billion.

Using specific case studies of U.S. corporate experience, the paper will be directed at answering this central question: Why and how do U.S. firms transfer industrial technology to Socialist enterprises?** In assessing why, our perspective will be primarily that of the particular firm; i.e., what gains it anticipates from dealing with Socialist nations where development plans are carefully set far in advance, local currencies are not convertible and hard currency reserves are scarce, wholly-owned Western subsidiaries are prescribed and joint equity arrangements with Westerners are being explored only gently. Besides the firm's point of view, however, we will also consider what specific development requirements prompted the recipient to enter into the particular relationship. And in assessing how a firm transfers its technology, our focus will be on the nature and complexity of the technology as well as on such practical aspects of the transfer process as the actual transfer mode used and the negotiating leverage available to the U.S. firm.

Before turning to the case studies, however, our first task is to clarify what is meant by "technology" and by "sustained enterprise-to-enterprise relationships."

Perhaps the concept of technology is best introduced with the saying attributed to the ancient Chinese philospher Confucius: "If you give a man a fish, he will have his dinner; but if you teach him to fish, he will never starve." In other words, technology is knowledge. In the industrial world, technology is that knowledge necessary to produce industrial materials, components, and end-products.

Several important distinctions must be made in defining and explaining "technology." The first is between technology and the manufacturing rights which patents protect. These rights are sold by one firm to another through "patent licenses," with payment most frequently made in the form of a royalty on production or on sales. However, sale of a patent license does not comprise the transfer of the manufacturing knowledge necessary to put into actual production the rights granted. This point will become clearer as the discussion progresses.

** In the Socialist economies, there are no "firms" or "companies" as we in the West know them. Instead, suppliers of goods and services are called "enterprises," a word we will use throughout when referring to Eastern European manufacturing, processing, or distributing entities. "Firms," whether small proprietorships or giant industrial corporations, are owned by individual shareholders. "Enterprises," in keeping with Marxist-Leninist prohibition against private property, are owned by the "State" and, indirectly, by all the people.

Another differentiation is between science and technology. The former organizes and explains data on the basis of theoretical relationships; the latter translates science into practical use. Consider, for example, the thermodynamic principle of the internal combustion engine. Technology is the specific application of that scientific principle to solving particular problems; e.g., the development of a certain type of gasoline engine to meet a special local requirement.

Likewise, technology must not be confused with "R&D." R&D is generally considered by most industries to account for less than 20% of the total costs of "technology." The rest is represented by those expenditures necessary to convert the laboratory findings into actual product of marketable products.

In making a similar point, John Tilton differentiates between the innovative process, invention, and innovation. The innovative process combines the basic and applied research steps necessary before commercial production is feasible. Invention represents the development of the first workable model of the new product or process. And innovation is the practical dimension of the evolution, the commercial production or the invention.[1] The Japanese, for example, excel in recognizing and putting into efficient commercial production the laboratory findings of others. One observer has called the Japanese habit of buying others' R&D results "the biggest bargain sale in business history." For about three billion dollars, or about one-tenth of what the United States alone now spend annually for R&D, the Japanese have acquired from others the best of the world's R&D results.

Having made these distinctions, we can further refine our definition of technology. More specifically, it is the quantum of knowledge by which such inputs as patent rights, scientific principle, and R&D are translated into production of marketable items. This quantum comprises two parts: the "engineering documentation" and the "manufacturing techniques." The latter are the human implementation of the written instructions contained in the former.

The engineering documentation consists of such data as: plant layout and designs; equipment requirements (either by brand name or necessary capacity); product design information (e.g., blueprints and drawings); and such additional information as materials standards and specifications, process sheets specifying factors like temperatures, pressures, tolerances, metallurgical formulae, and instructions on production sequence and assembly steps. This documentation, or "know-how," may be sold by one firm to another via a "know-how license." However, a know-how license does not comprise the complete technology package. The information contained in the documentation is useless - as many

East European purchasers of know-how licenses have discovered through bitter experience - without the second element of the technology quantum.

This second element is the production methods, techniques, and systems necessary for the application of the engineering data;* e.g., manufacturing processes such as welding, casting, or batching; tooling; scheduling; quality control; equipment inspection, maintenance, and repair; personnel training and qualification; product inspect; trouble-shooting and problem solving; and packaging and storing. These manufacturing techniques perform the vital task of transforming the physical items - drawings, equipment, materials specifications, and so on - into actual production capability.

In transferring manufacturing methods, techniques, and systems, the supplier is transferring what might be called its "human knowledge." This human knowledge is gained from practical applications of the engineering documentation; but it cannot possibly be included in the actual drawings and specifications sheets. As Denis Goulet notes about technology transfer, "It is something far more dynamic than the mere handing over of plans, blueprints, or manuals."[3] We can expand upon this observation, noting that the dynamic input consists of the in-house production techniques without which the documentation may be useless. In large measure, this part of the technology quantum is intangible, representing the firm's organizational ability in developing and integrating engineering, scheduling, machining, and quality control standards. Transfer of this type of knowledge involves a much closer and longer-term relationship than that involved in the simple sale of a patent or even a know-how license. Instead, it requires sustained enterprise-to-enterprise relationship through which the recipient can acquire the latest production techniques which can be duplicated in its own plants under the supplier's guarantee that the design and quality of final product will be internationally competitive.

Within the broad area of "East-West trade," we can generalize two broad categories of inter-firm relationship. The first is the classic, short-term relationship in which one entity sells another a product, license, or an entire plant, including the start-up assistance necessary to put that plant on-stream. The seller is

---

* For simplicity, the production methods, techniques, and systems will usually be referred to henceforth as "production techniques."

paid in currency or unrelated* products, and the relationship is terminated upon completion of the immediate transaction. The second type of interfirm relationship involves an extended form of interface. Unlike the first variety, this relationship goes beyond a "one-shot" encounter and may even involve, in certain cases, joint equity participation (e.g., in Romania, where a Western partner can own up to 49% of a manufacturing facility). More frequently, however, the relationship is one in which the Western partner has no equity interest. Instead, its long-term involvement is established through a commitment to provide current technology and to supply the recipient of that technology with any improvements in production methods which the supplier may develop during the course of the industrial cooperation agreement (typically five to fifteen years). In addition, the Western side may also commit its trademark rights and even agree to purchase part of the product produced by its Eastern partner.

The past decade of East-West commercial relations shows that the East Europeans are more inclined to experiment with the second type of interfirm relationship while the Soviets prefer the first. East Europe does not have the raw material wealth or gold reserves of the U.S.S.R. to pay for Western goods, equipment or plants through "one-shot" deals. Furthermore, foreign trade is more important to most East European** nations than it is to the Soviet Union. Hence, the need to obtain modern production technology on a continuing basis to compete in international markets is more crucial to the East Europeans than it is to the Soviets. Accordingly, the Soviet Union has generally restricted consideration of long-term interfirm relationships to the extractive industry,*** preferring to limit arrangements in the manufacturing sector to "one-shot" transactions.

These different preferences of Soviet versus East European partners are delineated in Figure 1; they will be elaborated upon in our case study analysis.

---

* i.e., not produced under the license of or in the plant provided by the supplier firm.

** i.e., Bulgaria, Czechoslovakia, GDR, Hungary, Poland, and Romania.

*** Because the focus in this paper is on the manufacturing sector, we do not consider arrangements being discussed to develop natural resources in the Soviet Union, such as the North Star and Yakutsk.

RELATIONSHIP

	ONE-SHOT	LONG-TERM		
Definition:	Sale of Equipment, License and/or Plant for Cash or Unrelated Products	Provision of Technical Assistance and/or Trademarks for Cash and/or Purchase of Resultant Products		
Duration:	Termination upon Completion	Usually 5-15 Years		
Content:	Contract for Design, Manufacture and/or Delivery of Equipment	Model A Technical Assistance (T.A.) Only	Model B T.A. + Trademark Rights	Model C T.A. + Trademark Rights + Resultant Product Purchase
Examples:	Swindell-Dressler and the Kama River Truck Plant in the Soviet Union	General Tire in Romania	Honeywell in Poland	International Harvester in Poland

DEEPENING INDUSTRIAL COOPERATION →

Figure 1. COMMERCIAL DEALINGS

The importance with which East Europe views the transfer of manufacturing technology through extended enterprise-to-enterprise relationships is exemplified by the experience of Clark Equipment Company, a large American producer of materials handling equipment. Early in its negotiations with Poland for the sale of the firm's axle manufacturing technology, Clark was explicitly told by the Polish negotiators that they were not interested in acquiring only a "license" (by which the Poles meant a know-how license). They went on to cite the case of the British firm Leyland Motors which, several years earlier, had sold Poland the technical documentation to manufacture certain engines. To the chagrin of the Poles, however, they were unable to translate the technical data into practical production capability. Where the Poles had failed, they came to realize, was in not demanding that their British counterpart become an actual production partner rather than simply a vendor of blueprints. In short, the production capability the Poles needed was possible only through a longer-term association than that permitted by the exchange of documents and cash.

The Polish attitude toward interfirm relationships with Western partners is generally mirrored through most of East Europe. That is, experience has taught these nations that the "human knowledge" aspect of the technology quantum cannot possibly be transferred in the short time frame permitted under the one-shot transaction. In contrast, however, stands the Soviet Union, as yet reluctant to permit the intimate interfirm association being explored by its neighbors. Illustrative of the Soviet practice is the participation, of the American company Swindell-Dressler in the Soviet Union's Kama River truck project.

Swindell-Dressler is acting as a subcontractor on the project, responsible for overall design of the plant's foundry but supplying only some of the necessary equipment. The Soviets are their own general contractor for both the foundry and the entire truck plant. Furthermore, the Soviets retain responsibility for plant construction and equipment installation. In view of Swindell's engineering and procurement role, there is little opportunity for a transfer of actual production techniques. This is not, of course, to suggest that nothing in the way of human knowledge is passing to the Soviets. For instance, 125 Soviet engineers have been located in Pittsburgh for at least two years, observing preparation of the foundry designs and manufacture of certain equipment. It is only natural to assume that they are learning something during their stay, both in terms of design engineering as well as the more general management of U.S. firms.

However, the point here - and it will become more obvious as we consider the East European example - is that there is no conscious effort on the part of the U.S. partner to transfer its technology. There is no contractual provision for on-going technical assistance beyond the turn-key period necessary to design and erect the truck facility. There is absolutely no provision that Swindell-Dressler be a long-term partner, one interested in assuring that the Soviets do, in fact, learn the latest in design and production techniques; nor is there any commitment by the American party that the Russian plant be an efficient operation and one whose out-put is internationally competitive. Instead, once Swindell's subcontracting responsibility ends - i.e., once the equipment is operational - its association with the Kama River authorities officially terminates.

As already noted, Western experience in East Europe suggests a different pattern of industrial cooperation. Compared to the decade-old experience of West European competitor firms, U.S. corporate involvement in such sustained relationships is a recent phenomonon of only the past three or four years. Nonetheless, the experience to-date of companies does provide some basis on which observation may be made about the pattern this avenue of commercial exchange has assumed; specifically, how and why they are effected.

As Figure 1 suggests, the principal modes by which U.S. firms have entered into sustained non-equity relationships with East European partners are three: Model A, a technical assistance agreement; Model B, technical assistance and trademark rights; and Model C, a combination of technical assistance, trademark rights, and resultant product purchase. The three elements involved - technical assistance, trademark rights, and product purchase commitment - will be briefly considered below, after which some of the practical aspects of each particular model will be assayed.

A <u>technical assistance</u> agreement provides for the transfer to the recipient of the supplier's patent rights, design specifications, and manufacturing techniques for the particular product or products involved. The manufacturing technique - or the "human know-how" - are the most important part of the technology package. They are typically transferred through the dual mechanism of training Eastern technical specialists in one of the supplier's facilities and of periodic visits by U.S. engineers to the Eastern facility. An on-going technical assistance obligation also calls for the supplier to keep its flow of technology up-to-date throughout the life of the agreement by furnishing all available engineering changes covering design modifications and production improvements. This obligation is usually limited, however, to providing that information which has actually been put into commercial production by the supplier firm; this relieves the firm of the obligation to transfer data or technology which has not yet passed from the drawing boards or the laboratory to the production line.

The granting of trademark rights is typically provided under the explicit provision that the product be manufactured in accordance with technical information and production methods prescribed by the supplier. Obviously of paramount concern here is the Western firm's desire to protect its product reputation. Consequently, the supplier will require periodic inspection of products, reserving the right to deny the Eastern party authorization to the trademark whenever the latter's quality control procedures or production standards fall below those that the supplier judges to be minimally acceptable. By committing its logo, the Western firm is, in effect, guaranteeing to its Eastern partner that the final product manufactured will be as good in every respect as a product coming off the supplier's assembly line. This is of great psychological and practical importance to the Eastern recipient, who is thereby assured the receipt of the latest in design information and production techniques. As suggested in the introduction to this article, one of the primary reasons East European have turned Westward for technology is to develop an internationally competitive production capability.

A purchase commitment by the supplier guarantees the recipient another highly prized advantage: a hard currency buyer. The Western side usually agrees to purchase a certain minimum quantity of product at an agreed upon price (e.g., a percentage of its own selling price, FOB ex-U.S. works). One frequent method of effecting the purchase arrangement is by allowing the Eastern party exclusive sales within the Eastern bloc nations. In exchange for this limitation on its own marketing efforts, the supplier then receives a royalty (i.e., percentage on a pre-established sales price) on all items produced but not purchased for its own international marketing network. As a concomitant, the Western partner is usually given exclusive rights to non-Eastern bloc markets. Markets in which the Eastern partner has clearing account arrangements - e.g., several Middle Eastern nations - may be left open to the individual marketing efforts of each partner, with the Western party receiving a royalty on all items successfully marketed by the Eastern partner.

The specific mode of corporation - i.e., Model A, B, or C - adopted for the transfer is a function of at least two factors: why the firm entered into the arrangement; and the degree of negotiating leverage available to the U.S. firm. This will become more apparent in the following pages as we look at each model - in reverse order, progressing from the most complicated (Model C) to the least complicated (Model A). The discussion of each model will focus on the actual experiences of U.S.

corporations.

Model C

For the firm actively seeking a low-cost European production source, an arrangement with an Esastern partner willing to undertake all capital costs can be an attractive alternative to constructing a new facility in Western Europe. Likewise, selling production techniques to East Europe may be a means of entering an otherwise closed market. For instance, the firm may be having difficulty overcoming any one of several trace barriers; e.g., East Europe's shortage of hard currency; the area's lack of familiarity with U.S. firms; or its proximity to traditional and well-established West European vendors. Whether it be to establish a cheaper production source, to penetrate a new market, or a combination of both, the U.S. firm may be willing to acquiesce to the Eastern partner's desire to acquire not only the Western technology but also the firm's logo, in addition to its commitment to purchase part of the finished product; i.e., enter into a Model C arrangement. One firm entering into such an arrangement is International Harvester Company (IH).

In mid-1972, IH signed a ten-year cooperation agreement with Poland, an agreement whereby the U.S. firm assists its Polish partner in manufacturing IH bulldozers, loaders, and pipelayers. The agreement is especially opportune for Poland in view of the nation's current modernization and expansion of its local production of construction equipment. As part of this concerted effort, Poland has in recent years entered into a variety of similar agreements with several Western manufacturers; e.g., Jones Cranes and Coles Cranes, both of England, to manufacture mechanical and hydraulic cranes; Setter of West Germany to produce concrete mixers; Menck, the West German division of the American firm Koehring for hydraulic excavators; and the U.S.'s Clark Equipment for rear axle production. Part of the purpose of such agreements has been to develop a local source of equipment for alleviating such construction shortages as housing, shops, schools, and hospitals. Alleviating such shortages is part of the government's program to raise and improve local living standards. As important as meeting domestic needs has been the second purpose of Poland's industrial cooperation agreements in the construction machinery area; to increase exports. The Polish Ministry of the Machine industry envisages that its exports to the West resulting from cooperation agreements will represent as much as 30% of the Ministry's total exports in 1975.[4]

The technology package being transferred to Poland by IH comprises the following elements: dimensions; metallurgical specifications; tooling and machining techniques; quality control systems; and assembly methods. The main difficulties the U.S. firm is facing in effecting the transplant are: lack of worker tooling and machining skills; poor quality control and supervisory procedures at the management level; and generally poor worker motivations. Poor skills and inefficient quality control and supervisory procedures have been easier for IH to rectify than worker indifference. For IH, it has been an exercise in patience, having to cajole and exhort each individual worker that his respective contribution, however small, will affect the quality of final product.

Despite these obstacles to effective technology absorption, the Polish product, currently produced under IH's rigid supervision, does meet the firm's own quality standards. Furthermore, IH is confident that in time the close supervision now necessary will no longer be required. This optimism is based partially on the fact that the management of the Polish enterprise is determined to manufacture a product identical to the one coming off IH's U.S. facilities. Another reason contributing to IH's confidence is the fact that the Polish engineers and management personnel are not in the least resentful of or resistent to the semi-management role being assumed in their own facility by IH personnel. And the third reason relates directly to the U.S. firm itself: the ability and willingness of its transfer agents as well as the overriding purpose prompting the firm to enter into this arrangement in the first place.

In the past eight to ten years, IH has confronted an increasing desire by many nations to whom it has traditionally sold its construction equipment to develop their own indigenous production capabilities. In response to this changing attitude, IH has tried to leap-frog the other five or six international firms in this oligopolistic industry and retain its share of the market by establishing overseas production facilities. But of its 30-odd overseas facilities, the one in Poland is the first in which the firm has never had any equity. What prompted the firm to alter its traditional method of international investment?

The reasons are essentially two. First, the project was seen as a market entry vehicle. As a manufacturer of bulldozers, payloaders, and pipelayers, Poland offered IH no product market. But when Poland proposed buying IH's production technology, the U.S. firm saw an excellent opportunity for market penetration: i.e., as a means of selling whole vehicles until the local facility became fully operational; of selling those components not locally manufactured but which would be necessary for the final assembled vehicles; and of selling replacement parts until such time as they, too, were produced within Poland. For instance, as part of the overall agreement, Poland was obliged to purchase $1.5 million worth of components in the first three years of the contract. For this initial purchase, Poland obtained U.S. Export-Import Bank financing. To accommodate the growing component requirements, as anticipated by IH, Poland placed another order in 1974, this time for $6 million worth of parts.

Second, besides being a market entry vehicle, the arrangement has proved to be an important manufacturing facility for IH. As the world demand for construction equipment has soared in the past three years, IH has been unable to satisfy its international customers with existing production levels. Its world-wide construction equipment sales, for example, in 1973 surpassed those of 1972 by as much as 25%. This trend was mirrored throughout all corporate product divisions, so that as 1974 began, the company had the largest unfilled backlog - $1.7 billion - in its history.[5] In addition, with almost 75% of its corporate earnings derived from overseas activities, the firm was increasingly anxious for overseas capital expansion, especially to accommodate what its chairman calls IH's single largest overseas market, Western Europe. And the beauty of the arrangement with Poland has been that IH was spared any capital outlay in either expanding a West European facility or erecting a new one. In short, it has been able to avail itself of an extant Polish facility which the Poles have equipped with the latest equipment suggested by their American partners.

So rapidly has Poland acquired the IH technology, and so impressed is IH with the quality of finished product, that the Polish facility has become a crucial part of the firm's international marketing strategy. As one IH executive has commented, the Polish partner is an "absolutely first-class source which is going to be one of our main manufacturers of components, replacement parts, and final products for all our markets, especially Western Europe." In fact, in mid-1973, a year after the initial agreement was signed, IH extended the line of bulldozers being manufactured so that Poland might become the firm's main European source for components to be assembled by its UK facility. And by 1978, IH expects that the facility will be producing as many as 1,500 finished units annually, representing an invoice value of $100 million. IH will profit whether it purchases the product for its own market or whether its Polish partner markets them within the Eastern bloc territory assigned it. If the firm buys the product from Poland, it does so at a yearly re-negotiable price which is always 10% less than its U.S. production costs for the same product. And if Poland either keeps the product or sells it, IH receives a certain royalty fee.

Model B

Not every firm feels the need to buttress its own manufacturing capability with Eastern-made goods, even as a quid pro quo for entering a new market. Likewise, not every firm is looking for a cheaper production source. To the Eastern partner, however, the Western firm's commitment to purchase final product provides a source of hard currency without requiring a commitment to learn Western marketing techniques and without necessitating an investment in establishing an overseas marketing organization. Consequently, most would-be Eastern purchasers of Western technology bring pressure to bear on a prospective Western partner to commit to purchasing part of the final product. Whether the firm is able to withstand the pressure - at the risk of losing the opportunity to enter into a relationship with the Eastern side - is a function of the firm's negotiating leverage. This leverage, in turn, depends on the proprietary nature of its technological asset. That is, if there are no other available sources from which the Eastern side can obtain the technology, the leverage belongs to the firm owning the particular technology. The type of arrangement for which it opts will depend on its reason for entering into the agreement.

One U.S. firm which was able to leverage its technology in dictating the type of long-term relationship in an Eastern country is Honeywell. In late 1973 the firm entered into a cooperation agreement with Poland to transfer its technology to manufacture part of an industrial process control system. Included in the agreement was Honeywell's trademark. Excluded, however, was any commitment by the U.S. firm to purchase part of the finished product from Poland. In short, a Model B arrangement was established.

The importance of the electronics industry within Poland is suggested by the fact that the 1971-75 plan calls for a doubling of output of all products falling under this classification; e.g., computer and computer peripherals; automation, measuring, and process control systems and equipment; and electronic apparatus and components. One means of realizing this two-fold expansion has been through various cooperation schemes with Western firms, notably West German, French, British, and, most recently, American. From the West, Poland has acquired technology to manufacture such various items as resistors, radio transformers, hybrid circuits, integrated linear circuits, magnetic disks, silicon rectifiers, and so on. In part, this expansion is intended to contribute to the improvement of local production of such consumer goods as radios, TVs, record players, etc. Much of it, however, is aimed at enhancing national industrial production capacity by producing elements to be used in industrial facilities. For instance, the process control system purchased from Honeywell is to play an important part in outfitting the series of petrochemical facilities either being or about to be erected in Poland.[6]

Honeywell's agreement with Poland is actually two-fold. The first agreement calls for the production of the firm's Vutronik line of recorders and controllers; the second provides for the manufacture by Poland of the firm's electronic pressure transmitter. The former agreement was signed with Honeywell's Scottish subsidiary, the firm's main overseas manufacturer of the particular product line. The latter arrangement is completely American: the technology was developed, put into commercial production, and will be transferred solely by a Honeywell U.S. division. As such, it is of direct concern to this analysis of American technology transfer.

The transmitter consists of two elements, a silicon sensor and a circuit board amplifier, each of which is contained within its own cast-iron housing. The documentation being transferred includes the dimensions, tolerances, and metallurgical composition of the housings and their respective component parts, excluding the sensor. The metallurgy involved is especially critical in view of the extreme temperatures to which the transmitter is subjected in a typical refinery. The production knowledge being transferred consists of quality control procedures, assembly techniques, and, most especially, how to manufacture the circuit board; i.e., how to solder, etch, measure output, and keep a clean and orderly production area.

According to Honeywell, the sensor portion of the device is the only such electronic detector-transmitter being commercially produced by any firm in the world. All other pressure measuring instruments operate on a mechanical, or pneumatic, principle. The heart of the sensor is a silicon chip - a tiny piece of crystallized, polished silicon, about one-sixth of an inch square and containing up to 10,000 microscopic transistors - diffused into boron in a "wheat-stone bridge" pattern. The advantage of the device is that it is a solid state component. In the absence of any moving parts, the need to recalibrate, repair, or replace broken parts is obviated; as a result, not only are costly equipment shut-downs avoided, but flow is also more accurately measured. The revolutionary feature of the device, which makes it proprietary to Honeywell, is its extreme sensitivity to the slightest change in pressure, such as those occurring in a refinery pipeline.

Because of the proprietary nature of the technology involved in the silicon sensor, Honeywell rejected Poland's understandable interest in acquiring the capability to duplicate manufacture of the sensor. However, Honeywell did agree to transfer the sensor technology in 1979. At that time through a technical assistance arrangement, the firm will provide the Poles with the 1974 state-of-the-art in silicon diffusion technology.

More important from our particular point of view, Honeywell was also able to reject the Poles' demand that Honeywell agrees to purchase part of the finished product. In contrast to IH, Honeywell saw no need to increase its supply capability for this particular product. Poland had little choice but to accept Honeywell's refusal both to transfer its sensor technology and to purchase any of the final product. There was no other manufacturer from which the Poles might receive another proposal to play against Honeywell's. Furthermore, Poland wanted the latest in pressure transmitters. And except for the sensor device, it is learning how to manufacture that item. Furthermore, until Poland learns to manufacture the sensor itself, Honeywell has committed itself to selling as many of the sensors as Poland needs for the units it produces.

While Honeywell would not commit to buying finished product, it did, however, permit the Poles use of the Honeywell trademark. Granting its logo was part of the strategy behind the firm's decision to enter into the cooperation arrangement: increase its visibility - and, hopefully - sales within the Soviet bloc. Thus, letting the Poles produce and sell within that bloc products bearing the Honeywell label would, presumably, make its name better known in a market which has been for years dominated by West European electronics firms.

The arrangement is also attractive to Honeywell for other reasons. First, it will take Poland up to eighteen months to manufacture the Vutronik panels and the pressure transmitter. Prior to that time, however, Poland has several petro-chemical and copper smelting plants coming on-stream, all of which require industrial process control systems. Because the commitment has been made to develop a Polish control system using Honeywell technology, it is logical that any system installed prior to the development of the Polish system be compatible with that system. As a result, Honeywell anticipates by mid-1976 having sold Poland up to $5 million worth of components for the Vutronik panels and the transmitter.

The second attraction to Honeywell of the cooperation deal is that even after Pnefal develops its own ability to manufacture the Honeywell products, it will still have to buy the silicon sensor, at least until it begins producing its own device sometime after 1979. And third is the royalty income Honeywell will be earning throughout the five-year agreement on all units produced by Poland.

Fourth, and finally, Honeywell sees the agreement as giving the firm the foot-hold within the Polish market that has for so long eluded it. As Poland expands its electronics industry for both consumer and industrial products, Honeywell hopes that its demonstrated willingness "to cooperate" with the Polish electronics community will give it the inside track on future sales.

Model A

The Model A type of cooperation is most readily exercised by those firms which are in the business of selling technology per se; i.e., for which a large portion of corporate earnings comes from the sale of production knowledge rather than the sale of products. Because they do not market their own products overseas, such firms are seldom interested in acquiring products in payment for their technology; nor is there any advantage to them in granting their trademark rights. Rather, they generally limit their relationship to a simple technical assistance agreement.

General Tire (GT) transfers technology on what the company calls "a total and complete basis;" i.e., technology for all the tires manufactured by the firm, whether truck, passenger, off-the-road, or bicycle, whether tube or tubeless, whether diagonal or radial. Its technology package consists of such documentation as tire dimensions, stock preparation formulae (e.g., amounts and types of resins, rubber, carbon black, and other additives), and temperatures and duration of vulcanization; plus production techniques and process information relating to compounding, milling and mixing, calendering, extruding, beading, actual tire building, curing, final finishing, and, above all, quality control.

Throughout the negotiations with Romania, the Romanians pressed GT to assume an equity position in the project as well as to extend its trademark and to purchase part of the finished product. On all three counts, however, General resisted. From the outset, GT saw the Romanian project only in terms of its being a source of fees, both supervisory (i.e., for setting up and equipping the facility, for which the U.S. firm has received $2.5 million) and technological (GT is charging the Romanians $500,000 per year over ten years to keep them abreast of the latest technological changes in tire production). The firm had no need to supplement its already sizeable overseas production of tires. Nor did it want to commit itself to the close quality control supervision which a trademark agreement would necessitate.

The Romanians hinted on several occasions that GT would lose the contract because of its stand on all three counts. At least once, the firm questioned whether it might have to re-consider its position. However, during the extensive period of time during which the negotiations took place, GT was able to learn that its competitors on the project were no more interested than it was in assuming an equity position, in extending their trademarks, or in purchasing part of the product. Thus, as negotiations progressed, the Romanians had little choice. If they were to acquire Western tire technology, they would have to do so through a simple technical assistance contract, devoid of an accompanying trademark agreement or guaranteed sales outlet. In short, the negotiating leverage belonged to the firm rather than the purchaser.

In view of their interest in obtaining the most modern, up-to-date technology with which to develop internationally competitive products, most East European recipients would generally prefer a Model C arrangement, i.e., one in which they not only acquire the latest in technology but also supplier cooperation in marketing the finished product. The Eastern side's negotiating leverage may lie in the fact that, for reasons already cited, it has not been buying products from the U.S. firm. Therefore, the American side realizes that if it is to do any business with the particular nation, its only option may well be some form of industrial cooperation. However, as we have also seen, the negotiating leverage is not always one-sided; i.e., the ultimate negotiating leverage can belong to the prospective U.S. partner. This depends of course, both on the reasons prompting the firm to cooperate with an Eastern enterprise as well as on the proprietary nature of its technology.

From our case studies, there is no indication that one model of transfer is preferred by the U.S. side. If the firm wants a cheaper manufacturing source, or if it is using the cooperation vehicle as a market entry vehicle, a Model C arrangement is most likely. In these instances, negotiations with the Eastern side will concentrate on such factors as the particular product technology involved, market restrictions, and the financial terms of the cooperation.

But if the firm has a proprietary technology unavailable from other suppliers, it will more likely insist on a Model A or B arrangement. The firm's success in prevailing upon the Eastern side to accept an A or B cooperation depends on how badly the prospective recipient wants the particular technology: e.g., if the Eastern party can obtain comparable technology from another source on terms more to its liking (i.e., Model C), it might decide that the particular technology being offered is not worth entering into an A or B arrangement. However, assuming that the Eastern side will accept something less than a C arrangement, whether as A or B cooperation is realized is mainly a function of the requirements of the transferring firm. Royalties from an otherwise closed or limited market may make extension of trademark rights attractive from the firm's point of view. But when the firm is in the business of selling its industrial production techniques, it may be unwilling to provide more than its technology.

Regardless, however, of the particular type of industrial cooperation arrangement adopted, one striking fact emerges from the experience of U.S. firms which have explored this avenue of international trade. While the U.S. side is never given explicit management functions in a non-equity venture, it is almost invariably expected to play an active role in the day-to-day manufacturing operations of the enterprise; e.g., in the training, production scheduling, and quality control procedures. Even when there is a trademark or product purchase agreement, the U.S. firms have found that the degree of influence they are permitted to exercise within the particular production facility far exceeds that which they would normally require. In short, there is no attitude on the Eastern part that "we know it all." Rather, they have evidenced a determination to avail themselves in every possible way of the technological capabilities of their American industrial partners. This attitude is in contrast to that which corporate experience suggests in dealing with the Soviet Union.

REFERENCES

1. John E. Tilton, International Diffusion of Technology: The Case of Semiconductors (Washington, D.C., The Brookings Institution, 1971), p. 4.

2. James Abegglen, "Needed: New Strategies for Japanese Companies," paper also published in Japanese language in President Magazine (January 1972), p. 3.

3. Denis Goulet, "Exporting Technology to the Third World," Perspectives on Development and Social Change 2 (January 1974), p. 10.

4. Poland, Ministry of Machine Industry, Poland-1973, 1974, p. 15.

5. "Reaping Profits Around the World," Financial World 140 (23 January 1974): 23.

6. See, for example, "Poland: Refinery Plans," Eastwest Markets (29 July 1974): 8

BARRIERS TO THE TRANSFER OF MILITARY SYSTEMS TECHNOLOGY TO THE UNITED STATES

Richard J. Trainor

U. S. Department of the Army
Washington, DC

Introduction

There is, today, a very high level of interest in the subject of technology transfer. Much of the recent interest is sparked by a desire to use technology transferred to a developing country or a lesser developed country as a catalyst to increase the pace of that country's development. However, this effort is swamped by the technology that is transferred between developed nations. Until the mid 1960's, much of this transfer has been from the United States to countries in Western Europe. However, in recent years the United States has become a net importer of technology in many industries and has lost much of its lead in key high technology industries such as computers, heavy electronics and aerospace.[1] This paper describes problems involved in transferring technology to the United States. Four case histories are used to illustrate the problems of technology transfer. The first two projects (MBT-70 and MALLARD) were joint international developments and the latter two (RATAC and SHORAD) involved the "Americanization" of weapon systems developed in Europe. The many value judgments are those of the author, who was personally involved in all four programs, and do not necessarily reflect the views of the U.S. Army.

MBT-70

Project Initiation

The Main Battle Tank-70 (MBT-70) received by its name because it was to be introduced into the operational inventory of the

United States and the Federal Republic of Germany (FRG) by the beginning of the year 1970. The program began unofficially in 1961 with discussions at the ministerial level on the feasibility of a joint tank development program. The initial German reaction was to suggest that the United States adopt their main battle tank, the LEOPARD. However, the United States Secretary of Defense, Robert S. McNamara, continued to press for a bilateral development program and a formal joint agreement was signed on August 1, 1963. The agreement was signed by the Secretary of Defense and the FRG Defense Minister Von Hassel.

In officially announcing the award of the development contract to General Motors, Mr. McNamara said:

> I am convinced that the joint defense efforts of this sort with our NATO Allies are important and can be highly beneficial to all concerned. The pooling of ideas and sharing of cost should make for better production at a lower expense on identical items of equipment in our inventory, simplify maintenance and support problems, and exemplify the cooperation which is essential to NATO success.[2]

Demise of MBT-70

The agreement of 1963 called for the estimated $80 million cooperative development program to be shared on a 50-50 basis, leading to a model incorporating the best of the United States and German concepts, for production in both countries. It was not until 1965 that the large management structure got moving and produced the first design, whereupon the cost estimate increased to $138 million. In 1966, the U.S. Deputy Secretary of Defense recognized a one year slip in production from December 1969 to December 1970. (The MBT-70 would still be produced in 1970, but just barely so.)

By August 1969, it was generally agreed that the cost of the joint program had increased to slightly over $300 million. Further, the $300 million did not include related unilateral projects or selected supporting efforts. By 1969, the cost estimates for these additional tasks were estimated at about $115 million. In January 1970, the United States and FRG terminated the joint development effort. The U.S. elected to continue unilateral development of an austere variant of the MBT-70. The austere variant was characterized by Congress as being too sophisticated, complex and costly and it was terminated by Congress in December 1971.

MBT-70 Problem Areas

Viewed in retrospect, most of the problems of the MBT-70 were not uniquely related to the bilateral development features of the program. However, most of its problems were exacerbated by its joint development features.

Specific problems that are generally recognized as contributing to the demise of the MBT-70 are the following:

Lack of U.S. Military Commitment. The role of the military in managing and controlling the program was created in an era of financial plenty by Minister Von Hassel and Mr. McNamara. The Secretary of the Army, Deputy Secretary of Defense, and Secretary of Defense (all civilians and all presidential appointees) figured prominently in its birth. The United States military regarded the MBT-70 as a gift from afar, but did not appear to feel that they had total responsibility for, or control of, the program until years later.

Precedent Setting. The MBT-70 was felt to be a program that was to establish a precedent for other major bilateral joint development programs. The feared potential collateral damage to unspecified future programs tended to create rigidity in early negotiations at a time when flexibility and trust were especially required.

Oversophistication of Requirement. In retrospect, it is easy to see that the original requirement was undesirably sophisticated. For example, the early designs had a combined gun-missile, automatic loader, a chemical-biological-nuclear warning and protection system, automatic fire detection system, requirement to fire accurately while moving, a "pop-up" auxiliary weapon station and a driver's remote control television for driving while submerged during river-crossing operations.

It is difficult to ascribe any of the specific items of sophistication to the joint features of the program. However, the aspect of a 50-50 development cost sharing surely did cause some of the designers to ignore the occasional early voices of concern with regard to system sophistication. Additionally, the apparent unwillingness of either country to compromise resulted in designs that tried to appease both design groups. The result was further complexity.

Overoptimism on Unit Costs and Weights. The very early cost and weight estimates (in 1963 and 1964) were influenced by early parametric design studies conducted by a U.S. company who had never designed or produced a tank or similar vehicle. These early designs resulted in an estimate that a high quality tank could be built within a weight of 35 short tons. Early cost estimates tended to be based on a cost per pound or cost per ton using much less sophisticated tanks as the basis of the estimate. By 1965, the development and production cost estimates began to grow both due to substantial weight growth and a growing realization that the MBT-70 was greatly more complex on a per pound basis than contemporary tanks. By the time of its cancellation, the MBT-70 prototypes weighed over 35 tons, a growth of over 40,000 pounds from early estimates. Exacerbating these already serious problems was a gradual recognition that the planned production quantities and production rates were incompatible with shrinking Army budgets and programs.

National Pride. The German people have been properly proud of their industrial design and production capabilities for decades. The German tank of World War II was clearly superior to counterpart American designs, especially in firepower. In a similar vein the German Army has been justifiably proud of their knowledge of tank warfare, since the days of Generals Guderian and Rommel. The Germans had a different view from the Americans as to what constituted the ideal tank. Their confidence in their industry and army probably made it especially difficult for them to compromise on the subject of tank design. An example of this was in the selection of a gun system. The United States chose a combination of 152mm high velocity gun missile combination while FRG preferred a smaller caliber gun system without an in-bore missile. Neither side would compromise and the result was an agreement that each country would produce the tank with its own firepower system. The selection of the firepower system clearly had substantial influence on other aspects of the design, from the turret to the automatic loader. Based on 20:20 hindsight, the Germans appear to have taken the more logical course. The American successor system, currently under development, does not have a gun-missile system.

Business Policies. There were numerous policy and procedural differences that affected the MBT-70 program. For example, in Germany the contractors were allowed more independent action and were freer from Government control than was the case in the United States. While in many respects this freedom was desirable it did cause delays in negotiations between the two governments. Testing procedures were also different in the United States and Germany. The United States concentrates on extensive component testing while the German policy gives greater emphasis to system-level testing. The result was that considerable time was lost early in the program negotiating design changes and procedures for their validation.

No Pressing Need. Many would argue with this problem. However, throughout the development cycle of the MBT-70, the United States was producing a tank, the M60A1, widely regarded as the best in the world. Similarly, the Germans were producing and enjoying foreign sales of their LEOPARD tank. There was no solid evidence of Soviet advances in tank technology that would force an extremely high schedule priority on the MBT-70 program. As a consequence, there was a tendency for the two countries to attempt to redesign the system more than would have been the case if there had been a higher priority on system deployment.

Metric System. An early impasse was reached on the use of metric versus English units. The compromise was finally reached after referral to the Secretary/Minister level. The English system would be used for United States development components and metric for German developed components. Metric fasteners would be used at the interface between English and metric components. These negotiations took time and delayed the beginning of detail design.

Organizational/Geographical Considerations. Organization structures and geographical considerations were both problems in and of themselves, and were simultaneously a reflection of some of the problems previously described. For example, Major General Burba (the second United States program manager) was headquartered in Washington, D.C. and wearing this hat, reported to the Chief of Staff, Army. Wearing his other hat as project manager General Burba reported to the Commanding General of the Army Materiel Command, also located in the Washington area. However, the main MBT-70 work force was located near Detroit, Michigan.

When one considers the organizational problems in context of geography, security precaution, and occasional language barriers, it would seem that program delay and associated cost growth would be the inevitable result. Such was the case although language barriers had less than expected adverse impact and were not difficult to work around.

MALLARD

Project Initiation

Project MALLARD was to be a large scale communication digital communication system involving a combination of radios, microwave and satellites. MALLARD was to be capable of voice and message traffic with emphasis on the latter.

Project MALLARD began officially on April 6, 1967, when the

Deputy Secretary of Defense signed the tripartite Memorandum of Understanding (MOU) for the United States. Australia and Canada had signed a few days earlier. MALLARD was originally a British idea, but the project began without British participation as they held out unsuccessfully for a commitment for a fixed percentage of MALLARD production. The MOU had the following key features:

- Each participating government would have the opportunity to compete for a value of production equal to at least that governments inventory requirement.

- Research and development effort would be shared on a basis proportional to their financial contribution.

- Patent rights would be shared by participating countries.

After the signing of the MOU, negotiations with the British continued and they signed a revised MOU in August 1967. The revision was considered very favorable to the British in that it allowed all participants to compete for up to 50 percent of the total requirement without penalty. The result was that the British were in a position to compete for production of a considerable amount of equipment destined for deployment with United States troops.

Project Termination

By 1969, less than two years after the project initiation, the MALLARD was showing early signs of being in trouble. Congress in reviewing the fiscal 1970 Appropriations Request asked that the Department of Defense consider the discontinuance of United States participation in Project MALLARD.[3] The Chief of Staff, Army, General Westmoreland, directed a special high level in-house review of MALLARD by a board of three star general officers. This Senior Officer Materiel Review Board (SOMRB) asked the program manager to address the impact of slipping the deployment date of MALLARD by three to five years.[4] Naturally the other participating nations became worried and directed numerous inquiries to various officials in the Department of Defense.

The 'coup de grace' was performed on October 3, 1970, by Deputy Secretary of Defense David Packard, by memorandum dated October 3, 1970 which read in part:

> I have reluctantly decided to initiate termination of U.S. participation in the MALLARD program. However, I am convinced, after nearly a year of unsuccessful attempts to overcome Congressional objection to this project that only a strong program fully supported both within the Department of Defense and by the Congress can succeed in providing effective tactical communications for our 1980 forces.[5]

So about three years after it started, this ambitious multinational development and production program was dead. The following paragraphs synopsize the key problems that led to its demise.

Source of Requirement

It is a generally accepted postulate of weapon system development that the user must perceive a true operational requirement and state explicitly the nature of that requirement. In the case of MALLARD, the source of the concept was an international R&D community composed of representatives of the United States, Britain, Canada and Australia. The user representative was brought "on board" somewhat later. This lessened early involvement of the user representative was probably a factor of the early demise of the system.

Unity of Requirement Community

Tne United States Army tends to be branch oriented with respect to stating and defending its needs. The Armor, Infantry and Artillery branches tend to exhibit considerable solidarity when one of its weapon systems are subjected to criticism. The MALLARD program was defended by the Signal Branch, and this branch does not demonstrate the "clout" typical of the combat arms. The problem was undoubtedly compounded by the difficulty in con conceptualizing a complex electronic system.

Requirement Not Specific

The requirement for MALLARD was stated in a very general form. It did not specify frequencies line capacities, computer capacities and did not specify exactly how MALLARD would interoperate with related electronic systems. The problem of system interface was aggravated by a lack of strong central control of the design of these related systems.

Resources Not Specified

With respect to resource requirements, MALLARD was also quite non-specific. There was no agreed-to estimate of total R&D cost, total procurement cost, a phase-in schedule or how the overall communication system was expected to operate during the long phase-in period.

Other Military Services Not Sufficiently Involved

MALLARD was intended to involve the other U.S. military services as well as Australia, Canada and Great Britain. The level of involvement of the other services is reflected by the number of full-time members assigned to the project office. By June 30, 1969, the Army had assigned 109 personnel, the Air Force, 13, the Navy 1 and the Marine Corps 1. It is not implied that the other services should have provided equal manpower. The Army was to be the largest user and was executive agent for the United States.

NATO Interface

A war in Europe would probably be the circumstance that would allow a large communication system such as MALLARD to most easily justify its existence. Such a war would involve our NATO allies such as the Federal Republic of Germany, and in fact, MALLARD would be deployed on German soil. Yet Germany was not involved in the MALLARD Program. Canada suggested that MALLARD be offered to NATO as a cooperative project. Later, Great Britain suggested that the Federal Republic of Germany be included as a fifth partner. Nothing came of these suggestions. As a result of the lack of NATO involvement, Project MALLARD never had to deal with language barriers or English-Metric units of measure. However, the Deputy Secretary of Defense, in the following extract clearly indicates the priorities for MALLARD were improperly placed:

> The need for better tactical communications remain great. We must now proceed to organize a new program which will accomplish this goal. In planning the new program we should hold in mind that our primary objective is effective intercommunication between the forces of the U.S. Military Services. Our next priority should be interoperability with the communications systems of major NATO forces.[6]

Organizational Structure

The organizational structure for MALLARD was complicated. The complex structure was undoubtedly a result of the involvement of four nations and four services within the United States. This complex structure probably contributed to the lack of discernable progress during the first two years of the MALLARD Program. As the program started to get into trouble, the authority of the MALLARD Program Manager was effectively diminished as higher level staff offices became increasingly involved in program detail.

Congressional Attitudes

Some reviewers of military programs are inclined to attribute the lack of success of the MALLARD Program simply to lack of Congressional support. The earlier paragraphs provide evidence that MALLARD's problems could not be overcome by increased briefings certainly true that by 1969-1970, the Congressional attitude toward MALLARD was decidedly unfriendly. By 1969, slippages and cost overruns in the MBT-70 program were beginning to create a MALLARD backlash in congress and contributed to the early death of MALLARD.

RATAC

In the previous paragraphs, the problem related to joint international development of nearly designed equipment has been explored. The French RATAC radar provides an opportunity to review the problems of two other means of transferring technology to the United States. The RATAC system first transferred technology to the United States by direct purchase of equipment and next by the process of modifying this French radar so that it could be produced in the United States to modified U.S. specifications.

Project Initiation

The Vietnam War created an urgent need to replace the existing ground surveillance radar, the AN/TPS-25. The French RATAC ground surveillance radar showed promise of providing the required level of performance. Accordingly, the United States Army proposed a 60 day loan of the RATAC for testing. After the test, the Army decided on a two phase program. First, as time was urgent, it was decided to satisfy the requirement in Vietnam by direct purchase of the French radars. It was planned to buy 24 radar sets from the French subsidiary of International Telephone and Telegraph. The second part of the RATAC plan was to Americanize the RATAC to meet United States military and production standards. The Americanized RATAC (AN/TPS-58A) was intended to satisfy the remainder of the United States Army's world-wide needs for this class of ground surveillance radar.

Results Achieved - 24 Sets for Vietnam

The 24 sets cost $6 million (50 percent) more than initially estimated. Schedule performance was a key factor and most of the radars were delivered with only minor schedule slippage. The radar reliability was less than expected and less than claimed by the manufacturer, but was about as good as contemporary U.S. electronic equipment. Overall the RATAC radar for Vietnam was considered to represent a successful transfer of technology.

Results Achieved - Americanization of RATAC

The Americanization program resulted in 100 percent cost overrun. The first unit was promised 26 months after contract approval and was delivered 45 months after go-ahead. Reliability has been less than satisfactory. Overall, the Americanization of the RATAC is viewed by many as a mistake

The following paragraphs will highlight some of the problems experienced in Americanizing the RATAC.

Record Disclosure

Federal procurement regulations require examination of the contractor's financial records as a pre-condition to the payment of development costs. The French Ministry of Defense refused and the United States Department of Defense relented and granted an exception to policy.

Data Acquisition

The United States purchase included purchase of foreign government proprietary data rights. However, much to the surprise of the Department of Defense, the United States agreement did not include proprietary data rights of foreign companies. The proprietary data was later offered for an additional $1.4 million, but the offer was refused. Additional problems were encountered in defining what constituted data and what constituted tooling. For example, printed circuit boards are regarded as tooling by the French, but this is not the case in the United States.

Metric to English Conversion

An early decision was made to translate production drawings from French to English. Additionally, it was decided to dual dimension (inch and metric) the drawings. This latter decision turned out to be costly, unnecessary and counter-productive in that the double dimensions created confusion and errors in choosing dimensions from the drawings.

Production Standards, Reliability and Quality Control

The French production process for RATAC was optimized for very low rate production by American standards and involved many hand-fit parts. Consequently, the lack of complete interchangeability of parts for RATAC created problems. The lack of quality control standards led to an inability to predict the frequency of component and subsystem failures. The Americanized RATAC has performed below expectations with respect to reliability.

Environment

"Redesign was required resulting from the more severe environmental requirements of the United States. As an example, moisture proofing was required to satisfy United States conditions of worldwide deployment. Limited deployment of French Forces and equipment preclude this requirement."[7]

A specific example of redesign required to meet United States situation and useful life tests involved printed circuit boards. Meeting United States standards required an increase in the radius of the wire and this, in turn required a redesign of the circuit board layout. Meeting the United States environmental standards required a total redesign of the circuit boards.

SHORAD

Project Initiation

In the early 1960's, the United States Army initiated development of a high performance missile air defense system called MAULER. The MAULER missile was to be guided to its target by a radar and therefore was an all-weather system. This program was suspended in 1963. After the MAULER cancellation, Great Britain, who had intended to procure the MAULER, initiated their own development program, RAPIER. The RAPIER system was later to add an all-weather radar and the all weather version is now known as RAPIER/BLINDFIRE. A French firm, Thomson-CSF, in 1964 initiated development of a short range air defense system (SHORAD) under a contract with the Republic of South Africa. A German effort to develop a SHORAD system began in 1962 and led to a fair weather SHORAD system called ROLAND I and later to an all-weather system called ROLAND II. The United States Army, after the MAULER cancellation concentrated its low altitude, short range air defense efforts on daylight, fair weather systems. A United States requirement for an all-weather SHORAD system finally emerged in 1973. This led to a competition for a SHORAD contract by four United States contract teams, three of whom are United States licensees for the RAPIER/BLINDFIRE, CROTALE and ROLAND respectively. A development contract was awarded early in 1975 to Hughes Aircraft, the U.S. licensee for the ROLAND system.

SHORAD Potential Problem Areas

The SHORAD program is at an early development stage. Accordingly, some of the presently perceived problems will surely prove to be imaginary. Just as certain new and real problems will rise to take their place.

Congressional Attitude

The United States Congress has, for many years, exhibited a natural and pronounced preference for products produced in the United States. In 1931, during the depression, Congress passed legislation requiring the government to buy from U.S. manufacturers unless there were overriding considerations to the contrary. While there have been many exceptions to the Buy American Act the existence of the legislation is an important barrier to the widespread importation of weapon systems technology.

The failure of both the MBT-70 and the MALLARD were blamed, in part, on their international origins. While such blame was misplaced, especially in the cases of MALLARD, it did establish an unfavorable political climate when the U.S. Army began to discuss the potential of an off-shore procurement of a SHORAD system. However, in the meantime, Congress has become increasingly concerned about the magnitude of research and development costs for major weapon systems. Of special and well publicized concern has been the tendency toward R&D cost overrun of many of these systems. The desire to share the R&D burden by modifying a foreign system as opposed to financing a new American development has been a key factor in the noticeable softening in Congressional attitudes during the past 2-4 years.

Electronic Countermeasures

There is concern in the United States that sale of a SHORAD candidate system to a third country, especially one that is not a United States ally, might lessen the usefulness of the system to us. If one of the systems should be subject to detailed examination by technicians of a potential enemy it certainly would improve that country's ability to develop countermeasures to the SHORAD system. As a consequence prospective contractors were required to address possible system compromises and to propose modifications as necessary. However, third country sales considerations were not allowed to eliminate a SHORAD system from the competition.

Extent of Americanization

As indicated earlier there is concern at all organizational levels with the extent of Americanization. The RATAC program is an example of a system where Americanization can get out of hand. Following are a few concerns that relate specifically to SHORAD and the proposed position of the SHORAD program manager with respect to the potential problem areas.

The position of the program manager is that strong action and explicit pre-agreements by the program manager and the contractors can greatly moderate the problem of excessive Americanization of an already developed system. For example, the contractor will be responsible for translating all language and symbols and is responsible for traceability of tools and production processes. Configuration control will be the responsibility of the program manager and he intends to authorize very few changes to the overall design. If RAPIER/BLINDFIRE had been selected instead of ROLAND it would have been produced in English units. ROLAND will be produced in metric units. Therefore, dual dimensioning will not be required. The prime U.S. contractors will be required to obtain rights to data. In response to concern about parts support, the program manager has stated that there will be no critical SHORAD components procured off-shore. The contractors will be required to identify United States suppliers for all components. A surprisingly large number of these components are already being produced in the United States.

Required Changes to SHORAD Systems

In spite of a desire to make the absolute minimum number of changes to the foreign systems a few such changes have already been identified. They fall into roughly four categories; safety, statutory, performance and standardization. Following is an edited list of the nature of these changes. The changes are applicable to all three foreign systems unless otherwise noted. Considerations of security and proprietary data rights prevent specificity.

Safety Changes

Two of the foreign missiles are equipped with rocket motor firing squibs that do not meet United States safety specifications with respect to involuntary ignition of the rocket motor. One of the systems will require a change to the warhead arming circuit to provide a greater distance between the launcher and the missile when the warhead first becomes armed. Safety changes are considered mandatory by the U.S. Army.

Statutory Changes

The United States Army is assigned certain world-wide frequency allocations so that its systems may operate in peacetime without interfering with electronic equipment such as radios and televisions, in the vicinity of training areas. All of the foreign systems will require changes in the frequency selection of certain of their radiating electronic equipment. In addition to communication frequency changes, certain changes will be required to assure that SHORAD will be compatible with the standard American identification equipment (IFF) on friendly aircraft operating in the airspace to be defended by SHORAD.

Performance Changes

The basic precept for selection of a foreign developed SHORAD was to make minimum changes. However, SHORAD systems, as all other major systems, are measured against a Required Operational Capability (ROC). One of the systems required more agility to meet certain ROC specifications and this agility was to have been achieved by using a more powerful rocket propellant. The use of the more powerful propellant, in turn, would have required a change in another component used to guide the missile's flight.

One of the requirements stated in the ROC is that the system be capable of air transport in the United States Air Force C-141 aircraft and be capable of tactical operation shortly after the aircraft lands. The weight and height of the ROLAND vehicle exceed the allowable limits. For this reason, the ROLAND will be produced to operate from a standard United States Army vehicle more compatible with the size of the C-141.

Standardization Changes

The criteria for standardization changes are very broad, and include considerations of the production base and logistic supportability of the deployed SHORAD system. In general, standardization changes are not mandatory but will be made if they can be shown to result in overall cost savings.

Six standardization changes applicable to the foreign SHORAD systems have been identified.

1. Certain test equipment used with foreign SHORAD systems operate on the European standard frequency of 50 hertz. This equipment will be changed to the United States standard of 60 hertz to facilitate operation from United States power sources.

2. Standard United States radio communication equipment will be used instead of European equipment.

3. The RAPIER/BLINDFIRE will use a standard United States generator instead of the British generator. The use of the United States generator was expected to result in easier maintainability and lower cost.

4. The RAPIER/BLINDFIRE will be operated from a standard United States Army 1¼ ton truck instead of the British lorry.

5. The CROTALE vehicle is powered by a Hotchkiss gasoline engine. The Hotchkiss engine will be replaced by a diesel engine manufactured in the United States. This change is intended to eliminate reliance on foreign production of a key component, lessen the logistic burden, and reduce costs.

6. The auxiliary power units and air conditioners on one of the foreign systems will be replaced by standard United States models in interest of a lower logistic burden and lower procurement costs.

The six changes are the total identified to date. However, since these changes are not required by statute, safety or by the ROC, the list could change in the future. Any additions to this list can be expected to be subjected to a rather intense scrutiny.

Summary of Problem Areas

The problem areas applicable to the four cases studies are summarized under five major headings as shown in Table 1. Five out of 23 identified problem areas were in the category, National/ International Policies. These policies, stated or de facto, could be expected to create problems in any area of international technology transfer. However, it should be noted that in this category there was only one problem area, Congressional Attitudes, common to the two joint development programs. Congressmen in the United States seem to be opposed to joint development programs and those Congressional views were surely a factor in the cancellation of the MBT-70 and MALLARD programs.

A key deficiency area for the MBT-70 and MALLARD programs was in the Requirements Formulation Process. Four of the six identified problem areas were common to both systems. None of these problems appear to relate to problems of Americanization of RATAC or SHORAD. On the other hand, changes to the system to match unique United States military requirements are a problem exclusively associated with Americanization. (Unique United States military requirements are reflected in the original specifications for MBT-70 and MALLARD.) These requirements, while not contributing to system changes, have contributed to oversophistication.

Problems related to Organization/Policies/Procedures appear to be the only category of problems that are common to both joint development and Americanization. These problems do not appear to have been of fundamental importance in the MBT-70 program although they are at the heart of the RATAC Americanization troubles. MALLARD was cancelled too early to allow a determination of their significance in that program.

It should be noted that the list of problem areas or barriers do not correlate with any degree of precision to the more generally accepted barriers to innovation.[8] The nature of the products discussed is undoubtedly a key factor, since each involved a rather high level of technology.

TABLE 1

SUMMARY OF PROBLEM AREAS FOR FOUR MAJOR SYSTEMS

PROBLEM AREAS	MBT-70	MALLARD	RATAC	SHORAD
National/International Policies				
National Pride	X			
Precedent Setting	X			
NATO Interface Not Clarified		X		1/
Congressional Attitudes	X	X		X
Electronic Countermeasures				X
Requirements Formulation Process				
Weak Requirement Community		X		
Requirement Did Not Originate With User	X	X		
Requirement Not Specific		X		
No Pressing Need	X	X		
Lack of Commitment by Military	X	X		
Oversophistication	X	X		
Unique U.S. Requirements				
Environmental Requirements			X	X
Safety Changes				X
Statutory Changes				X
Performance Changes			X	X
Standardization Changes			X	X

1/ An agreed NATO position for SHORAD would probably be desirable but would not be critical as the area of influence of this system is restricted by the short range of its missiles.

TABLE 1 continued

Resource Requirements/Estimates				
Overoptimism on Perf & Costs	X	X	X	?
Resource Requirement Not Specified		X		
Organization/Policies/Procedures				
Business Policies/Practices	X		X	
Organizational/Geographical	X	X[2]		
Records/Data Rights			X	?
Metric to English Conversion	X		X	
Production Standards			X	X

Conclusions and Prognosis

The need for sharing of military research and development was important ten years ago and is even more important today. The potential advantages include better utilization of R&D resources, better equipment available at an earlier date, lower unit costs, improved logistic support and improved relationships between military allies. Yet realization of these advantages has proven difficult -- indeed, impossible in some instances. The United States has engaged in two major international development programs and each has been an abject failure. The problem areas related to the MBT-70 are believed to represent a fairly complete list. The list of problems of the MALLARD program is similar, though truncated by its early cancellation.

It is interesting -- and discouraging -- to note that the identified problem areas of the four systems examined do not fall into any set, predictable pattern. Most of the problems tend to apply to only one or two of the four systems studied. Most of the major problems was accentuated by the international flavor of the programs. However, the joint development feature of the MBT-70 or MALLARD programs cannot be identified as the principal reason for the failure of either system. Certainly in the case of MALLARD the problem was that the R&D program got started before the problem was specifically identified. It seems, in retrospect, that the MBT-70 was simply too large a technological bite to take at the time the requirement was defined. Other contemporary Army programs afflicted with a like-type illness (CHEYENNE and MAULER) were cancelled without any help from our allies. However, the international aspects of the MBT-70 program did appear to create a rigidity in the bureaucracy that ultimately was fatal. Perhaps a national program would have lent itself to

---

2 MALLARD was troubled by organizational problems; geography was not a major problem.

being restructured more easily.

One facet of technology transfer that came into focus as a result of the RATAC and SHORAD review is that the process of technology transfer is more difficult when the transfer is to a country which is technologically more advanced and whose technological infrastructure has a rigid, established way of doing business.

In spite of the problems with RATAC, Americanization seems to show considerable promise. The RATAC program, while only a qualified success, did not indicate many fundamental problem areas. It would appear that good attention to detail (data rights, production drawings, etc.) and considerable discipline in holding the number of changes to the absolute minimum should allow Americanization, or technology transfer from one developed nation to another, to succeed. The SHORAD program will certainly provide a key test of the concept. The next two years are especially critical for SHORAD.

Experience in the MBT-70 and MALLARD indicates that joint development programs of major systems have little to recommend them if one of the countries such as the United States is very technologically advanced. The problems are simply too many, too basic, but alternatives appear to be available. The more technologically advanced the partner, the worse the problems are likely to be. Joint development programs will, of necessity, continue and will be intensified for the European countries. They have no real choice considering the magnitude of the investment. The collaborative European development and procurement program for the military PANAVIA 200 close support aircraft, is one of the latest examples.

For the United States, it would appear there are at least two alternatives to joint development. The first and most preferable is to find a silent partner who is willing to spend a specified amount of development money in exchange for having an opportunity to influence the performance specifications and to get assurance that the hardware will be dimensionally compatible with his production base. The silent partner would not have a voice in the design details and would have to agree to a "best effort" with respect to performance specifications. This alternative obviously depends on some country sending money with agreement from the outset that its role in the management of the project would be minimal. Such a country may be difficult to find, but the United States could begin its search in the Mid-East or Japan.

The second alternative to joint development is interdependent development. The United States agrees to develop System X, such as an aircraft, to an agreed-to specification. In exchange, the other partner to the interdependent development agreement agrees to develop System Y, such as a howitzer. In concept this alternative is the development counterpart of production offset agreements. Each nation would be expected to produce the two different systems in their own country for their own use. Production for third country sales would have to be negotiated in advance. This alternative is not as efficient as the silent partner arrangement but is more likely to be attractive to a developed country.

Neither of the two alternatives outlined represent a panacea. One must ask in advance how a management plan will work as schedules slip, costs increase, and design specifications change. Such changes are simply the realities of defense weapon planning. If these alternatives will not stand the test, other alternatives must be searched out.

The world's weapon systems are rapidly increasing in cost and complexity. Greater international cooperation is the only answer to the maintenance of the technological leadership of the NATO alliance. Even though progress to date has been slow and painful, a careful review of our past mistakes should allow the nations of the western world to profitably share the benefits of each others inventiveness.

REFERENCES

1. Marvin J. Cetron, "Technology Transfer: Where We Stand Today" Davidson, Cetron, Goldhar, (eds) Technology Transfer Noordhoff, Leiden, 1974, p. 13.

2. David W. Coble, "How is the West Germany-American Main Battle Tank Program Coming Along?" Armed Forces Management, II-4, January 1965, p. 42.

3. Program Managers Significant Action Report, December 1969.

4. Ibid.

5. Honorable David Packard, Memorandum, subject: The MALLARD Program, dated 30 Oct 1970, p. 1.

6. Ibid.

7. Eli T. Reich, "U.S. Procurement and Production of Foreign Weapon Systems," December 1972, Appendix D, p. 6.

8. Marvin J. Cetron, "Technology Transfer: Where We Stand Today" Davidson, Cetron, Goldhar, (eds) Technology Transfer Noordhoff, Leiden, 1974, p. 17.

NUCLEAR ENERGY TECHNOLOGY TRANSFER: THE SECURITY BARRIERS

Robert L. Rinne

Sandia Laboratories
Livermore, California

Introduction

Energy technology has replaced space exploration as the glamour subject in research and development. A principal source of optimism that future energy demands can be met lies in the potential of nuclear energy. The two forms, fusion and fission, presently are the major focus of the energy research and development effort. The basic principles of both fission and fusion are understood; the development of these energy sources is being governed by solutions to various technologically related problems. For fusion power, considerable development is required just to demonstrate practical feasibility. With fission energy, emphasis is on developing the safety and security systems necessary before nuclear reactors can be placed in full service. The research and development in both areas is partially constrained by technology transfer issues. In the case of fusion, its relation to weapon development has produced national security barriers; for fission, international security requirements are present because of the possibility of theft or diversion of special nuclear materials (i.e., uranium-233, uranium-235 or plutonium) and sabotage.

In this paper, technology transfer is used as a generic classification of a broad spectrum of information dissemination. Basically, the interactions can be subdivided into three classes: (1) detailed exchanges between technical peer groups (in industry and at other research installations), (2) education of the public and their representatives, and (3) activities to move laboratory discoveries into applied applications. The third class has been the central point in many technology transfer investigations. Here problems that arise out of security questions in the first two classes will be examined.

If the nuclear energy program is to have successful development, then industry, universities and other research bodies must be kept abreast of the needs and requirements. However, national security is a barrier to the flow of information on some aspects of the fusion reactor program. This barrier results in occasional problems in adequately transferring information so that maximum support can be obtained. This technology transfer problem will be described in the next section. In the case of fission reactors, the security problems are more complex. The power plants and fuel may be subject to sabotage and theft. The capabilities to solve these security problems must be described in a clear and understandable manner so that governmental officials can make appropriate policy and funding decisions, and so that the public can choose whether nuclear energy is preferable over other alternatives. It is also desirable to adequately describe the strengths of the protective systems, called safeguard* systems so as to deter a terrorist incident. However, the information should not contain details of the safeguards measures which might be used to defeat them. Since the sabotage of a nuclear facility, or theft of nuclear fuels can have international implications, safeguards technology must be exchanged internationally, and international security must protect it. This exchange is clearly a complex technology transfer relationship and will be the subject of the principal portion of the body of this paper.

Since the early seventies, Sandia Laboratories** has been deeply involved in research and development on nuclear energy problems. The laboratories have major programs in fusion energy and in command, control, safety and security systems for nuclear weapons and nuclear materials. In this paper, relying heavily on Sandia's experience, several examples of nuclear energy technology transfer under security constraints will be described. The paper does not propose to give a definitive solution to these transfer problems. The intent is to help establish a dialogue for further developing procedures to enhance the flow of information where such barriers exist.

---

*Some confusion arises over the term safeguards. In recent years, it has been associated with several different concepts. There is the U.S. Safeguard ABM program. There are the "four safeguards" that support the Limited Test Ban Treaty (LTBT). And, there are the International Atomic Energy Agency (IAEA) "safeguards". These consist of agreements and rules mainly concerned with accountability of material. They have the objective of the prompt detection of diversion of nuclear material at a national level in support of the Non-Proliferation Treaty (NPT). Here the term is being applied in the broader context, defined in the draft, GENERIC ENVIRONMENTAL STATEMENT FOR MIXED OXIDES (GESMO): "safeguards measures are designed to deter, prevent or respond to (1) the unauthorized possession or use of significant quantities of nuclear materials through theft or diversion; and (2) sabotage of nuclear facilities. The safeguards program has as its objective achieving a level of protection against such acts to insure against significant increase in the overall risk of death, injury or property damage to the public from other causes beyond the control of the individual."

**Sandia Laboratories, a wholly owned subsidiary of the Western Electric Company, is a prime contractor to the U.S. Energy Research and Development Administration. The laboratories operate under a non-profit, no-fee contract. The major facilities are located at Albuquerque, New Mexico, and Livermore, California.

Fusion Energy Technology Transfer Constrained By National Security

The early development of nuclear technology was constrained by the strongest security classification program in U.S. history. However, in the three decades since the first successful fission explosion in the Trinity test near Alamogordo, New Mexico, a great deal of the information required to design a fission weapon (an atomic bomb) has been unclassified. President Eisenhower in December 1953, with his "Atoms for Peace" proposal, lifted the curtain on a great deal of what had been classified technology. Information on the chemistry and metallurgy of nuclear materials, critical masses, and other neutron properties has entered the public domain in order to further develop the nuclear power industry. As has been pointed out in numerous articles, most notably by Mason Willrich and Theodore B. Taylor,[1] the secret of the atomic bomb is no longer hidden from the world. While the principle of fission devices is unclassified, the basic concepts used in fusion devices (thermonuclear or H-bombs) are still classified. Just as much of the technology on fission weapons became open in order to further the development of nuclear power reactors, so may the information concerning fussion weapons become available in the development of controlled thermonuclear reactor (CTR) systems. However, at the present time there is the desire to maintain control of the secrets involved in thermonuclear explosives while finding the key to controlled release of fusion energy. It was felt until recently that such constraints would not hinder the development of a CTR system, because most approaches to control fusion were sufficiently remote from the means of achieving an explosive device. For example, the magnetic confinement machines have been considered to be without military value, and the flow of information between all nations involved in CTR research has been quite free. The major direction in the U.S. program now involves the use of the Tokomak design formulated in the Soviet Union. International exchanges and visits of laboratories throughout the world by CTR experts have been quite open.

The national security barrier has arisen out of the possible application of lasers to the fusion problem. Shortly after the development of the ruby laser in 1960 by T. H. Maiman at Hughes Aircraft Company in Malibu, California, computer calculations showed that a laser could be used to compress and heat a small pellet of hydrogen fuel to the conditions needed for power production. However, the calculations indicated that a laser producing hundreds of thousands of joules of energy would be needed to achieve thermonuclear conditions. In the early sixties, the maximum laser output was about one joule. Throughout the sixties, small groups explored the possibility of using lasers to achieve controlled fusion. In the late sixties, more refined calculations indicated that properly designed hydrogen pellets might be ignited with a lot less energy than the hundreds of thousands of joules predicted earlier. Recently, research on powerful electron beams (E-beams) at Sandia Laboratories has indicated that they also may be an efficient means of creating controlled thermonuclear reactions. These developments have led to a sizable laser and E-beam fusion effort. However, some of the techniques in both laser and E-beam fusion are related to weapon concepts or have potential weapon application. This has brought these approaches to a controlled thermonuclear reactor under the constraint of security classification.

The laser and E-beam fusion effort has generated a great deal of interest throughout the United States and the world. Not all the required research and development comes from within U.S. government-supported labs. Much of the subsystems developments comes from industry. Thus, means of communicating needs and the state-of-the-art outside established secure installations was required. Furthermore, due to the high visibility of the program, its potential importance and the high level of governmental funding, it was felt that a general review of the technology was necessary. Fortunately, only a small percent of the research is classified, and, thus, meaningful exchanges could be developed. In addition to actively participating in professional meetings, in February 1974 the U.S. Atomic Energy Commission sponsored an Industrial Laser Fusion Symposium at the Lawrence Livermore Laboratory. The purpose of the meeting was to review the AEC laser fusion and E-beam program for representatives of national laboratories, universities, industries and government. The objective of the review was to increase the general awareness of the AEC program among (1) research organizations in the field, (2) industrial organizations that could participate in the program and (3) governmental organizations responsible for sponsoring energy research. This awareness was accomplished by describing the goals and approaches being taken throughout the AEC program. Extensive documentation of current research and development at the various laboratories was supplied to all the attendees.

In cases such as the nuclear fusion program, where classification hinders the free transfer of technology, the major facilities involved must assume the responsibility for adequately informing the remainder of the community, including the general public as to the goals and needs of the program. Too often in such circumstances, the tendency is to hide behind the security fence and avoid work on informing others as to what is going on. In the end, the overall program suffers. Conferences, such as the Industrial Laser Fusion Symposium, are valuable in that they supply a general overview of the state-of-the-art and describe program goals and needs in terms to which the public and industry can appropriately respond. It is also recognized that, while generalized conferences are a very useful part of an overall information exchange program, they cannot be left to stand by themselves. Such symposiums do not replace professional exchanges and journals as the key element in transferring high technology. In the fusion program, there has been continuing exchanges through national and international meetings on topics related to laser and E-beam fusion. For example, there was the Conference on Laser Engineering and Applications in Washington, D.C., just last May where the latest developments in laser fusion were discussed.

Fission Energy Technology Transfer: The Nuclear Safeguards

The previous section demonstrated the manner in which national security can be a barrier to energy technology transfer. While this barrier poses a problem to fusion energy development, it is not insurmountable. Through the weapons R&D program, there has been considerable experience in transferring technology where national security classification inhibits free flow. Classification guidelines and appropriate communications channels are well established involving extensive integrated contractor networks including laboratories and industry.

With fission energy, the technology transfer program becomes much more complex. The fission energy systems are no longer confined to the research stage; they are ready for full development and deployment. This transition from proof-of-principle research to on-line service has been accompanied by the necessity to inform governmental officials and the general public of the risks and benefits if these fission systems are to be a viable alternative source of energy. The most important subjects of public concern are the operational and material safety and the prevention of sabotage or theft of nuclear facilities or fuel. The public and their representatives rightly demand evidence that fission reactors and the associated nuclear fuels are sufficiently protected from accident, sabotage and theft that they cannot become a threat to either life or property.

The process of informing the public of the technology developed to safeguard reactors and nuclear fuels must be conducted in such a manner that the effectiveness of those systems is not jeopardized. There is a similar dilemma in communicating needs and results with industry. The problem is one of appropriately controlling the transfer of information. This is a complicated task for several reasons. First, the potential for sabotage or theft must be identified. This includes an understanding of threat capabilities and the identification of the vulnerable portions of the reactor/fuel system. Second, safeguard systems must be designed that reduce the vulnerabilities. Third, the critical features must be determined which, if known to a potential threat, could be used to defeat the system. Only when this critical information has been identified can decisions be made regarding what technology should be transmitted to the public and industry in general. The technology transfer problem is further complicated by the necessity to exchange details of safeguard systems with all other countries undertaking nuclear power programs. This transfer calls for the development of appropriate international exchange and security agreements.

As noted above, the public needs information concerning the control and accountability and the physical protection of special nuclear material in transit or at fixed sites in order to make informed judgments on (1) the safety of the nuclear power program, and (2) the capability to prevent theft or sabotage. However, certain information could (a) significantly assist in planning and implementing an attempt to illegally obtain special nuclear material or sabotage, (b) enhance the credibility of a terrorist threat through the nuclear power program and increase the frequency of such threats. Thus, the general release of safeguards information could have an adverse effect. So the general guidelines in the U.S. for determining whether specific safeguards information is classified or unclassified are the following:

(1) Information concerning in-place materials control and accountability systems for specific sites which would provide significant assistance (a) in frustrating or delaying the detection of the response to threat or diversion, or (b) increasing the credibility or frequency of threats of nefarious use of SNM is classified;

(2) Information concerning physical security systems which would provide significant assistance in defeating the system is classified; and

(3) All other safeguards information including information already in the public domain or obtainable by visual access from uncontrolled areas is unclassified.

The following sections describe the technology transfer effort that is under way. In order to place that discussion in proper context, the basic nature of the fuel cycle and the terrorist threat that motivates the desire to protect it will be described. Some of the principal protective measures for material transportation and the extent that the technological details should be protected will be outlined. At the conclusion, methods of conducting exchanges of information at both the national and international level will be discussed.

The Fuel Cycle and the Terrorist Threat

The nuclear fuel cycle is a collection of facilities connected to one another by transportation links over which the appropriate materials must flow. The facilities include enrichment plants for upgrading the concentration of U-235 in natural uranium to the higher percentages required for various reactors; fuel fabrication plants in which the fuel materials are manufactured into the fuel rods for the reactor; the reactors themselves, where the conversion from nuclear power to electricity occurs; storage, points at which spent fuel or waste material are stored; and reprocessing plants, where spent fuel is processed to reclaim valuable elements from it, primarily plutonium. Figure 1 is a simplified outline of the fuel cycle. The safeguards program consists of two disjoint, but mutually supporting, parts: (1) the protection of fixed site facilities, and (2) the protection of the transportation links. While the objective for both parts is the same, the technologies involved can be quite different.

In the United States, as nuclear reactors are developed, there will be an ever-increasing number of shipments of special nuclear material. Figure 2 gives an estimate of the amounts of material that may be flowing and the number of shipments involved. This projection indicates that, within 10 years, 2 to 3 shipments a month of nuclear material capable of being fashioned into weapons may be moving between reactor fuel cycle facilities. Thus, there could be a tremendous increase in the availability and exposure of nuclear material due to the fuel cycle.

The nuclear fuel cycle may be an attractive terrorist target. As noted earlier, many have documented the relative ease with which one can build a fission device. Willrich and Taylor give a summary of the unclassified amounts of materials required for a nuclear explosive (Table I). When these quantities are compared with

TABLE I: Critical Masses of Some Materials in the Fuel Cycle

Material	Quantity
^{239}Pu	4.0 kg
^{235}U (93%)	11.5 kg
^{233}U	4.5 kg
PuO_2	10.0 kg
$^{233}UO_2$	10.0 kg

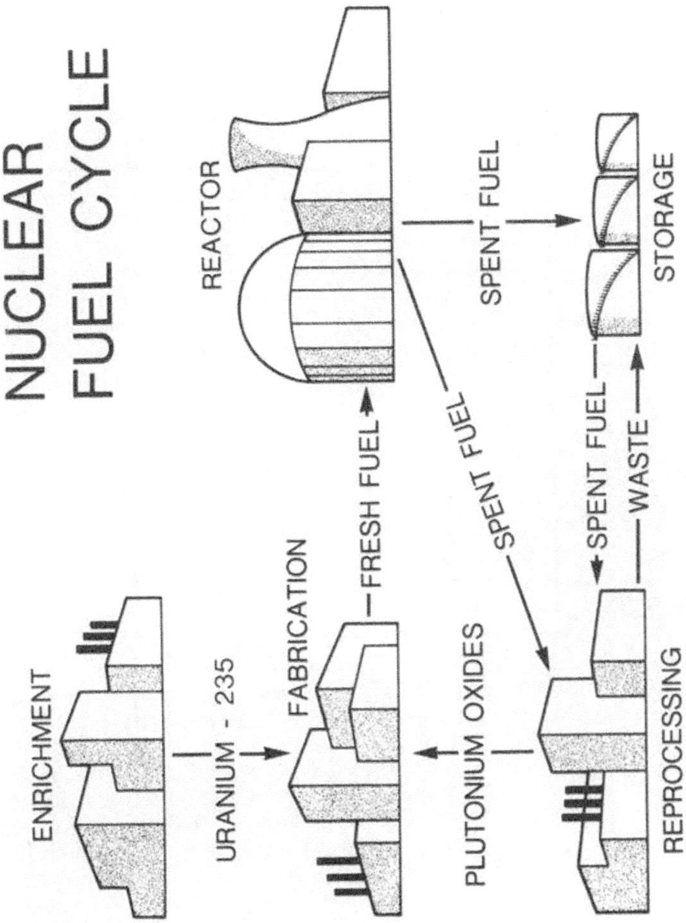
NUCLEAR
FUEL CYCLE
ENRICHMENT
URANIUM - 235
FABRICATION
FRESH FUEL
REACTOR
SPENT FUEL
SPENT FUEL
STORAGE
PLUTONIUM OXIDES
REPROCESSING
SPENT FUEL
WASTE

FIGURE 1

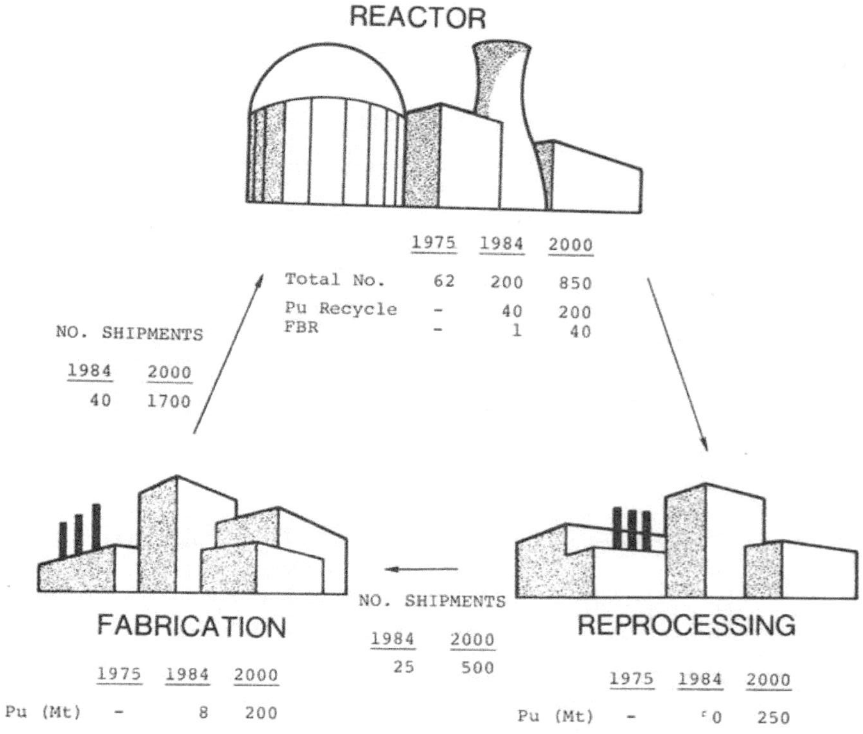
REACTOR
1975 1984 2000
Total No. 62 200 850
Pu Recycle - 40 200
FBR - 1 40
NO. SHIPMENTS
1984 2000
40 1700
FABRICATION
1975 1984 2000
Pu (Mt) - 8 200
NO. SHIPMENTS
1984 2000
25 500
REPROCESSING
1975 1984 2000
Pu (Mt) - 0 250

FIGURE II

TABLE II

Relative Numbers of Types of Terrorist Incidents

Time Period	Armed Attack	Bombings	Hijacking	Arson	Kidnapping	Sabotage	Sniping	Ambush	Seizure Occupation
1954-1958	44	90	10	2	32	3	9	8	2
1959-1963	35	111	23		19	2	15	2	1
1964-1968	21	117	11	11	5	4	1	1	
1969-1973	90	1265	300	11	116	11	4	6	18
TOTAL	190	1583	344	24	272	20	29	17	21

TABLE III

Examples of Nuclear-Related Incidents

Date	Place	Event
10/27/70	Orlando, FL	H-bomb threat; high school student hoax; demanded $1,000,000 and safe escort out of the country
9/71	Vernon, VT	Penetration past the guard towers and fences at the Vermont Yankee Nuclear Plant. The intruder wounded a night watchman and escaped.
12/7/71	Stanford, CA	Linear accelerator bombed by two dynamite explosions; $100,000 in damage
3/73	Argentina	Guerrilla groups occupation of a nuclear station
8/73	Arcadia, CA	Radioactive Iodine-131 capsules stolen from the hospital
2/19/74	Montague, MA	A 150 m meteorological tower bombed at a planned nuclear plant site in protest of nuclear power
4/17-22/74	Austria	Radioactive substances sprayed in a train compartment
Unknown	Bradwell, England	Attempted theft of 20 nuclear fuel rods

the projected material flows, one sees that within a few years there will be an annual flow of thousands of critical masses of material moving through the fuel cycle. From the standpoint of sabotage or as a toxic or radio-biological weapon, the problems are compounded due to the reduced quantities of material necessary to create a major incident.

In recent years, there has been a definite increase in the number and sophistication of terrorist acts. Table II summarizes the relative numbers of types of terrorist incidents over the last 20 years taken from a study prepared for Sandia by the Historical Evaluation and Research Organization on "The Terrorist and Sabotage Threat to United States Nuclear Programs." Terrorism groups cooperate with each other and may involve several countries. For example, members of a Japanese group attacked Lod Airport in Israel for an Arab organization. The lone Japanese survivor's release was demanded in the May 15, 1974 incident at Maalot, where Israeli children were held hostage. The level of sophistication in weapons, and the means of carrying out attacks is rapidly increasing. Terrorist groups outside the Rome Airport were found with anti-aircraft missiles. Aircraft, helicopters and electronic devices have been used by terrorists. The damage per attack is increasing. In general, terrorism uses violence to gain attention and exert political pressure, often by blackmail. The expansion of world-wide news coverage gives the terrorist the means to publicize their views to a huge audience. The acquisition of a nuclear weapon, nuclear materials or the sabotage of nuclear facilities would have dramatic effect and thus might appeal to the terrorist.

In the past, many have felt that underground groups were only interested in materials such as narcotics or gold, not uranium or plutonium. Some have claimed that terrorist groups are not interested in mass murder, for if they were, then why haven't they poisoned some city's water supply. There is the argument that killing people is not the terrorists's objective and may be counter productive to their goal by incensing public opinion against them. However, there have been recent terrorist acts that have extensively harmed individuals (i.e., the Munich-Olympic Village incident with 17 killed and the July 1972 Belfast bombings by the IRA resulting in about 150 casualties). Until recently, it has generally been believed that the technology required to build a nuclear device is too complex for any terrorist group to handle. There is also a broad public impression that there has never been a nuclear terrorist incident. But there is a lot more to cause concern than just the well-publicized possibilities of a nuclear terrorist. There have been several recent cases of unaccounted-for material, nuclear bomb hoaxes or radiological use. Table III describes several of these.

With the number of terrorist incidents increasing and the projection of sizable amounts of material flow, the concerns over properly protecting the nuclear fuel cycle are apropos.

Examples of the Security Barrier

The general policy on determining what is classified and what is unclassified was described earlier. It is clear that each point must be decided on a case-by-case basis. In order to understand the implications of this policy on technology transfer, several examples highlighting the security problem involved will now be described.

Adversary Analysis -- The usual first question in safeguard studies is "What is the threat?" There is no fixed answer. The threat is a function of the number of persons involved, the equipment used, the offensive and defensive armament, the knowledge, transportation available, motivation, training and planning. The possible number of attributes leads to hundreds of thousands of reasonable threat scenarios. In general, determining the effectiveness of a system against a given threat is inappropriate. The general philosophy of the analysis should be to determine the threat required to overcome a system of given effectiveness. The sequence is first to design what is felt to be a reasonably secure system, and then to determine the threat required to defeat that system. If the credibility of that threat is low, then confidence in the system is high. Otherwise, one uses the knowledge gained to redesign the system. The process involves the use of adversary simulation. The typical form is to take a team (or individual) without design involvement and supply them with an information package which may contain a range of detail about the objective under attack. The team then generates attack scenarios. The probabilities of successfully defeating the protective system are determined with the help of the system designers and through simulated field attacks. These studies identify vulnerabilities in the system and lead to recommended corrective actions which may, in turn, implement changes in the system itself. The results of such adversary simulations may identify serious shortcomings and indicate that extensive changes are needed. This requires the communications of the result of the experiment to a much larger community. For example, in reactor sabotage studies, adversary simulation may recommend certain technical changes in the safety and security procedures at the reactors. This information would need to be conveyed throughout the international community to those responsible for protecting these facilities. In communicating the information on what fixes are required, one does not want to give the general public the details of the scenario which lead to the need for the change. One would be giving out a blueprint for defeating a system. Thus, adversary simulation is an example where, in many cases, one wants to transfer the results of a study to a large audience but yet maintain control on the dissemination of the overall information.

Secure Vehicle Design -- The transportation portion of the nuclear fuel cycle may be the most vulnerable element. The necessity of having a safe, secure carrier is obvious, but the determination of the mode (i.e., aircraft, truck, rail, etc.) and carrier design is a complex task. Sandia Laboratories has been heavily involved in this program. The emphasis has been on trucks but many other modes are being examined as well. The design goals for a special nuclear material vehicle are listed in Table IV.

TABLE IV[2]

Feature	Goals
1. Immobilization system.	1. Provide controlled stop, resist release
2. Access denial.	2. Provide a variety of barriers to resist physical penetration. Intrusion penalties could provide additional deterrence
3. Driver protection	3. Provide an armored cab to protect occupants

The immobilization operation could be carried out in a number of ways, e.g., wheel locking systems, disabling the engine and/or drive train, or freezing the steering system. The trailer would be a vault on wheels. The cargo vault would be of penetration-resistant construction and contain intrusion-sensing devices coupled to penalty systems that would be severe but non-lethal. The driver and crew would be supplied with adequate protection so that they can assess the threat, initiate the immobilization and deterrent systems, and call for help.

From the exterior, the vehicle would not look unusual. This is not for camouflage purposes but does help reduce the social impact that high visibility vehicles might have. While the general features of the vehicle can be made public, detailed design information is classified. Knowledge of design details might significantly increase the vulnerability of the system.

For example, knowing the construction of the vault body could greatly reduce the expected access time. If the attacker knew the particular penalty agent used, such as a CS riot agent powder he could take proper precautions against them. Information of varying detail must be provided to the system manufacturers and operators, to the public and their representatives and to foreign governments with nuclear programs so that the movement of nuclear material will be acceptable, safe and secure. However, the flow of information must be internationally controlled so as not to compromise the systems.

Communications -- Communication is the vital link in a nuclear material transportation system. The communications network must be capable of handling a wide variety of information. It must carry routine check-ins, exchange information on weather and road conditions and take care of dispatching and scheduling the vehicles. In time of emergency, either an accident or an attack, it must be highly reliable and able to identify priorities. The system should be insensitive to atmospheric conditions and interference. It should be secure, jam-proof and not contain any dead zones. The Bell system has dead spots, and radiotelephones are not adequate. The development of the necessary system will involve extensive contact with the communications industry. In order to guarantee that the system is secure, protective measures will be required.

A safeguard system should have the capability to locate the special nuclear material containers even if they were removed from the carrier. This implies that systems which can communicate directly with the containers are desirable. One approach is the use of beacons or transponders. These would be similar to the devices used on aircraft to help locate them in case of an accident. The container's signal would be used to establish its location, and an adequate response force could be moved in to recover the material. The system must be reliable, jam-proof and not easily decoyed. It must be incorporated into the design of the container in such a manner that they cannot be easily destroyed or removed. Note that already the underground literature describes how to build a simple beacon finder.

The use of radio systems is not the only possible means for locating a mission vehicle or container. The possibilities of chemically tagging objects are being explored. Currently, animal sense of smell is two and three orders of magnitude better than the finest equipment. Trained animals have proven to be a good means of locating certain objects, especially where hidden in buildings. This technique has been successfully applied in search for explosives and narcotics through the use of dogs.

The applications to the safeguards program would be through "painting" a chemical on objects such as containers and training animals to seek out their unique smell. Another means of chemical tagging is the use of pheromones. These chemicals can be used to attract either animals or insects and might prove useful in finding hidden objects. The exact chemical compounds used must be protected so as to prevent the adversary from being able to decoy the tag.

Containers -- Explosive tests and simulated accidents are used to define, verify and demonstrate the level of container survivability. Such experiments, together with computer calculations, are used to predict the quantity of material release under various conditions. This information is combined with health models and safety statistics or adversary analysis to determine the consequence of an accident or sabotage event. The results are used to optimize container design and select preferred modes for transport. The results of the dispersal studies must be made public in such a manner so as to demonstrate the confinement capabilities of the containers. However, descriptions of the details for achieving breach of containers and the associated dispersion should not be broadly disseminated. Such information as explosive placement and their effects on dispersal must be protected.

The Transferring of Safeguards Technology

The theme throughout this discussion on the transfer of safeguards technology has been the necessity to provide means for information flow: (1) between nations with nuclear power programs, (2) between the industrial and research institutes that must develop and deploy safeguard systems, and (3) the general public and their representatives that ultimately must make the choice on whether nuclear energy is acceptable. This section describes the current safeguards technology transfer program and their shortcomings in each of these three areas.

In order to create an environment for constructive international exchanges on safeguards technology, Dixie Lee Ray, then Chairman of the U.S. Atomic Energy Commission, in a speech to the International Atomic Energy Agency in 1974 put the United States on record as willing to make available, on a selective basis, the results of our safeguards research and development effort. The U.S. exchange offer was motivated by a desire: (a) to lead all countries to increase their efforts and accept safeguards as necessary, (b) to reduce cost and deployment time by providing the results of the U.S. program, and (c) to acquire the technology that other nations have developed to protect their nuclear fuel cycles. The last of these emphasizes the two-way nature of the exchanges, for several countries have developed extensive safeguard systems and can teach the United States a great deal.

In order to promote the transfer of safeguards technology, the U.S. sponsored a series of bilateral exchanges. The meetings were designed to be non-political and non-commercial. They were strictly to exchange safeguards technology and not to discuss questions of source material supply or nuclear materials proliferation, per se. The countries involved thus far in the exchanges include the Federal Republic of Germany, the United Kingdom, France, the IAEA staff, the Netherlands, the European Community (EURATOM), Canada, Israel, Sweden, Egypt and Japan. These countries entered into bilateral agreements to protect the details of the safeguards information exchanged. The concerns of various nations over safeguards range from the economic consequences, to determining the dispersal of material in a sabotage act, to protection from sabotage, to training and implementation procedures, to methods for risk assessment and the evaluation of the effectiveness of protective systems. Several countries expressed concern over the release of safeguards details to the public. Some thought that the U.S. was lax in its protective policy and should institute more stringent controls. Thus, the technology transfer problem described here is well recognized and certainly has no set solution.

The delegations involved in the initial exchanges have been made up of governmental officials. Usually, these include mem bers of the nation's atomic energy commission, heads of security offices, scientific advisors and their scientific attache from the Washington Embassy. Generally, the delegations are accompanied by a member of ERDA's Division of International Security Affairs, personnel from the Nuclear Regulatory Commission (NRC), the State Department and the White House staff. Following a day of policy discussions in Washington, the delegations travel to Sandia Laboratories and Los Alamos Scientific Laboratory for technical briefings. Table V gives a typical agenda for the Sandia reviews. An agenda item which has proven to be extremely valuable to the success of these exchanges is the time given to the general discussion and formulation of future exchange plans. This provides an opportunity to identify where subsequent discussions have led to follow-up meetings between members of the appropriate research and development establishments.

The use of bilateral exchanges for technology transfer has several serious shortcomings. It has been found that protocol can hinder the flow of information. Often a request for further documentation must be coordinated and approved by ERDA's Washintgon headquarters, by other U.S. agencies, by the embassy of the country involved, and then the responsible agencies in the foreign country. At times, there has been a several-month delay in getting a paper transferred. Thus, it is extremely beneficial to exchange as much information as possible at the time of the visit. Careful preparation before the meetings and having available for distribution as much pertinent documentation as possible are extremely important to the success of the meetings. Even then, because of the level of officials involved, the transfer of technology is hindered by the lack of face-to-face contact among the researchers. How to improve this aspect of an exchange without the meeting becoming unwieldy requires further development of transfer techniques.

Another arena in which safeguards technology transfer is extremely important is with the industrial community. Those groups that must develop and produce safeguard systems and the power industries responsible for the implementation of the systems must be kept informed on the needs and results of the research laboratories. Development of exchange procedures are relatively recent. The first time the full scope of the AEC's research and development effort was openly discussed was at the 1973 winter meeting of the American Nuclear Society. This year ERDA arranged an exchange of its safeguards technology just prior to the Institute of Nuclear Materials Management annual meeting in June. Sandia Laboratories and the Los Alamos Scientific Laboratory held briefings and demonstrations on advanced physical protection systems and material accountability systems under development. The briefings and demonstrations were conducted at an unclassified level but with sufficient detail to identify the current trends for interested industrial participants. Table VI shows the agenda for these briefings. These briefings were followed up by further technical discussions at the INMM annual meeting in New Orleans. While these discussions are more constrained by security barriers than the bilateral exchanges, the freedom from diplomatic and travel difficulties leads, in general, to a better transfer of technology.

The third group to whom safeguards technology must be explained and demonstrated is the general public. They must receive an adequate explanation of the systems so as to make the final choice on the future of the nuclear power program. In the past, this transfer of information has been almost completely inadequate. The public has felt that information has been withheld not for security reasons but because it was not in the interest of those promoting nuclear energy. These credibility concerns underlie the recent division of the U.S. Atomic Energy Commission into an Energy Research and Development Administration and a Nuclear Regulatory Commission. The frequently used mode of presenting information through Congressional hearings and agency studies has often tended to be more confusing than beneficial. It is in this area of transferring information to the public that development of new techniques is most urgently needed.

TABLE V

A Typical Agenda for the Bilateral Exchanges

0800	Welcome Overview of Sandia's Role in Safeguards
0830	Visiting Delegation Statement
0900	Review of Protective System Concepts and the Means of their Evaluation
1000	Physical Protection of Nuclear Facilities
1100	Transportation Protection
1200	Lunch
1330	In-Plant Materials Control
1430	Response Capabilities
1530	Radioactive Material Dispersal Assessments
1630	General Discussion and Formulation of Future Exchange Plans

TABLE VI

Sandia Safeguards Briefing and Demonstration
June 17, 1975

0800	Welcome Overview of Sandia's Role in Safeguards
0815	ERDA Statement
0830	Protection Systems Concepts and Evaluations
0915	Transportation Protection
0945	Vehicle Display SNM Vehicle Cab Armor Unmodified Van Box SST Complete Winnebago with Communications Gear
1045	Facility Protection
1115	Adaptive Data System
1135	Tour-Test and Evaluation Site

REFERENCES

1. Willrich, Mason, and Taylor, Theodore B., Nuclear Theft: Risks and Safeguards, Ballinger Publishing Company, Cambridge, Massachusetts, 1974

2. Reed, R. E., Design Concepts Study of a Special Nuclear Material Cargo Vehicle, NUCLEAR TECHNOLOGY, Vol. 23, August 1974

EUROPEAN COMMUNITY POLICIES AND PROGRAMMES FAVOURING TECHNOLOGY TRANSFER

Giorgio Boggio

Commission of European Communities
Brussels, Belgium

The process of technology transfer, in the broad definition given in the context of this meeting, is favoured by the policies and programmes of the Commission of the European Communities in many ways, both among the member countries of the European Community and between the European Community and third countries.

A survey of the Commission's activities, which directly or indirectly promote the interchange of scientific and technical know-how, and an assessment of the degree of their effectiveness, would require a detailed investigation well beyond the scope of this paper.

I will however scan through a number of actions that the Commission has taken or is planning, about which I may expand in the course of the discussion if necessary.

To start with, I would like to discuss collaboration in the field of research and development at the European Community level.

A real milestone for common R&D policy was instituted by the Council of Ministers meeting of January 1974, which decided that a common policy should be developed for all sectors of science and technology with the exception of the military field and activities covered by industrial secrecy.

The development of such a common policy requires:

the co-ordination of national policies and the implementation of joint actions of common interest.

By co-ordination of the national policies, the Commission will attempt:

to eliminate unnecessary or unwarranted duplication of effort;

to avoid divergent tendencies contrary to the development of member states or the Community;

to improve efficiency and reduction of costs by task sharing, concentration of resources or research teams;

to harmonize gradually procedures for the formulation and implementation of R&D policies within the Community.

For this purpose, the examination and comparison of member states' national policies and the identification, analysis and comparison of their objectives will be progressively carried out.

All member countries have agreed to transmit the necessary information to the Commission at the appropriate time, and before adopting final decisions at national levels (with the exception of information militarily or industrially classified as secret).

With regard to common projects in the field of science and technology, the Council has emphasized that:

the choice of projects to be undertaken should be dictated essentially by the desire to fulfill the objectives of the Community and to meet their overall socio-economic needs in order to contribute to the development of a common policy on science and technology.

an appropriate approach should be adopted towards the whole range of available ways and means: direct projects, indirect projects, common concerted actions, etc., in an effort to ensure maximum effectiveness of tasks among the laboratories and research bodies in the Community and the member states.

whenever it proves necessary or desirable that non-member countries should be associated in these projects, steps should be taken to make this possible.

To assist the Council and the Commission in these tasks, a scientific and technical research committee "CREST" was created by the Council. CREST is a consultative body made up of senior officials of the nine member countries. CREST has to assist the Commission and the Council "to define objectives and ensure the development of a common policy in the field of science and technology." CREST now has under its authority specialized groups concerned with scientific and technical information and documentation, data processing, medical research, energy research, oceanology, town planning and housing, materials for chemical industrial equipment, and raw materials.

As it is intended, the common policy to be established should generate common projects only in those areas where the need for them exists.

In the definition of common R&D efforts, great attention will be attached to progressive removal of technical, fiscal, financial and legal barriers in harmony with the industrial policy, to contribute to the creation of the common European market and towards a real European industrial system.

In the definition and the implementation of common R&D efforts, close links will be established with industries to enable industry to participate in the phase of the preparation of such proposals for action and to give its timely piece of advice based on its experience and its knowledge.

In the frame of the implementation of the January 1974 Council Resolution, the Commission took part in the establishment of the European Science Foundation, which comprises the research councils and academies of fifteen European countries. ESF, created in November 1974, with headquarters in Strasburg, aims at the advancement of co-operation in basic research, the promotion of mobility of research workers, access to a free flow of ideas and information, better exploitation of existing unique research facilities, as well as the support of joint projects. Special links will be maintained with the European Communities.

Furthermore, the Commission contracted a feasibility study "Europe + 30" on the development of a Community instrument for technological forecasts and assessments; the study will be finished towards mid-1975.

Promotion of European co-operation extending beyond the Community borders and filling gaps existing in scientific as well as industrial research areas has been implemented by means of the COST (European Co-operation on Scientific and Technical Research) activities.

COST, which was set up by Council decision in 1970, and includes the nine Community countries, plus ten non-member countries, has selected as first approach co-operative action in seven fields of science and technology:

electronic computers, telecommunications, transport, oceanography, metereology, metallurgy and pollution.

As a specific example of successful international co-operation, the Nuclear Fusion Research Programme should be mentioned. All the non-military fusion research activities in the nine countries of the European Community are carried out in concertation by means of association contracts with the Commission. In this framework, plans are now being drawn for a large Tokamak-Type device entitled JET (Joint European Torus) which may be built under the 1976-80 programme.

Special mention is due to the intra-mural research activities carried out by the Joint Research Center (JRC) in the four establishments of ISPRA (Italy), Karlsruhe (Germany), Geel (Belgium) and Petten (Netherlands).

The JRC, which has now about 2000 employees, was created in the frame of the EURATOM treaty, and therefore started with an exclusively nuclear orientation. In 1973, when the Council of Ministers decided a four-years' research programme for the JRC, it authorized also the beginning of non-nuclear activities.

The ISPRA establishment, which is the largest one, devotes its efforts to a number of diversified sectors including nuclear safety, radioactive waste disposal, material research, environment protection, remote sensing of earth resources, utilization of nuclear-process-heat, primarily for the production of hydrogen by means of thermo-chemical processes, solar energy, standards and reference materials, information analysis and applied data processing, in addition to its role of technical assistance to the H.Q.'s departments and contractual work with private industries.

The other three JRC establishments are more specialized: Karlsruhe is mostly focusing on the study of transmanium elements, Geel is active in the field of nuclear measurements, and Petten's activities are essentially associated to a high flux reactor operation and material research.

In annex, a detailed breakdown of the European Community R&D programmes is reported. As it is shown, most of the R&D work is in line with and support to major policies (energy, agricultural, environmental, industrial and social policy).

I cannot talk about technology transfer without mentioning the Agreement for Co-operation between the United States and the European Community for Atomic Energy (EURATOM), since it has been an efficient instrument for the transfer to Europe of the US Light Water Reactor Technology. The Agreement, signed in 1958 and subsequently amended in the progress of its implementation, established a joint programme:

> To bring into operation within the European Community large-scale power plants using nuclear reactors of types of which research and development had been carried to an advanced stage in the United States. In the frame of this Joint Nuclear Power Programme, 3 reactors were built at Garigliano (Italy), Chooz (France) and Gundremmingen (Germany) for a total power of about 700 MW.
>
> The programme included exchange of information on the construction and operation of the plants as well as financial assistance from the Eximbank.
>
> To perform a joint research and development programme centered on US developed nuclear reactors. Particular mention is due to the Light Water Reactor Joint R&D Programme which lasted 10 years (1959-1969) with a budget of about 55 million dollars equally shared by the two parties.
>
> A joint US-EURATOM Board was set up in Brussels with the task of evaluating research programme proposals. The research carried out in the European Community was supported by EURATOM and reciprocally the research carried out in the United States was supported by the USAEC. All the research results were shared, and often exchange of visits and long-term assignments of scientists took place.
>
> To sell and lease Community special nuclear materials. In this frame, an agreement was also included for a EURATOM System of safeguards against possible diversion to non-peaceful uses of the nuclear materials made available by the United States.

Along with science and technology policies and programmes, the Commission also has been active in laying down policy guidelines in the field of energy and industrial sectors. An important and so badly needed "energy strategy", proposed by the Commission, has recently been approved by the Council of Ministers. This energy plan, dictated by the recent change in the Community's energy supply conditions, lays down medium and long term objectives to be pursued in order to avoid the risks of uncontrollable energy supply fluctuations. The Commission's energy strategy essentially would slow down the increase in the demand for oil, accelerate nuclear power growth, increase natural gas supply and encourage the Community coal industry.

As part of this overall strategy, a non-nuclear energy research and development programme has been submitted by the Commission to the Council to provide technical support to the action of diversification of available energy supply. The proposed energy R&D programme centers on energy conservation, production and utilization of hydrogen, solar energy, geothermal energy, and system analysis. This research programme will be performed extra-muros.

With regard to the industrial sector, a first programme for action on technological and industrial policy was adopted by the Council of Ministers in 1973. This programme made specific proposals and time-tables for their implementation. Such proposals called for removal of technical and technology transfer barriers to trade and concerted actions in the aircraft, shipbuilding, and computer sectors, in addition to the establishment of Community industrial development contracts.

The implementation of these proposals has been very slow so far, although some progress has been made and will gradually take place since common industrial policy is one of the most essential prerequisites for the full development of the Common Market.

Worth mentioning also is the actions underway for the elimination of technical barriers to trade. As customs barriers have been abolished between member countries of the Community, provisions to be complied with on a national level for use of industrial products are obstacles to Community-wide marketing. The Council has already adopted about 50 directives to harmonize product regulation, and at least as many are awaiting its decision. The products covered by these Community directives are motor-vehicles, tractors, chemical substances, building material and equipment, electrical appliances, measurement instruments, pressure vessels.

Different common policies are being developed for individual industrial sectors. I wish to mention two resolutions adopted last year by the Council concerning aircraft and applied data processing industries.

The aircraft industry resolution calls for the establishment of permanent procedures for consultation and concertation between the governments of the member states on the problems affecting this sector.

The data processing resolution authorizes the preparation, in the medium term, of a systematic Community programme to promote research into the industrial development and application of data processing. This programme would provide for the co-ordination of national promotion measures, together with Community financing for projects of common interest with the purpose of assuring by the end of this decade a viable and competitive European base industry.

Among the numerous actions the Commission has undertaken in the industrial policy area, I would like to recall for you the activities in the field of harmonizing company law, making possible the creation of European enterprises, and the patent law which will provide for a common procedure for the examination of patent applications and give a successful applicant the right to the grant of a patent in any or all of the participating states, which include some non-EC countries.

A direct contribution towards encouragement of innovation in industry is the Commission's proposal to grant industrial development contracts at the Community level. These contracts would have to be granted for projects aimed at developing new products or processes of a general economic or social interest. Assistance would be given by offering soft loans to finance the development up to the prototype stage. To do so, the Commission would use the services of the European Investment Bank, both to assess the proposals for contracts and to service the actual loans. The contracts would be offered for projects carried out in co-operation between firms for more than one member state.

In order to favour industrial co-operation across the borders of the Community member countries, the Commission created a Business Co-operation Center. More than 3000 Community firms have contacted the Center in the search of appropriate partners to consolidate their production and marketing capabilities.

In the area of environmental protection, a programme of action was adopted by the Council in 1973, defining objectives, principles, priorities and measures to be taken. As far as environmental quality objectives are concerned, the Commission has concentrated its initial effort on the quality of water. The Council adopted last November a directive on surface water used for the production of drinking water. The Commission is now working on directives for bathing water and seawater for breeding of shellfish as well as reduction of pollution caused by dangerous substances discharged into aquatic environment. A proposal for an air monitoring network has been sent to the Council as well as proposals for directives for highly polluting industries in the sectors of paper pulp, titanium dioxide and steel. Furthermore, work is carried out to present proposals in such fields as thermal waste, sulpur dioxide and nitrogen oxide.

In addition, efforts are devoted to promote measures to reduce ecological effects of modern techniques in agricultural applications, to avoid depletion of natural resources, for improvement of natural amenities and for town planning.

The Commission's environmental programme includes also a technical support by means of intra and extra-muros research efforts.

Another important area of Commission's activities relates to its commitment to aid to the Third World. The developing countries of major interest are the forty-five associated countries of Africa, Caribbean and Pacific oceans.

In the specific field of science and technology, three lines of actions are being explored:

co-ordination of national R&D projects aimed at development.

direct support of research programmes of regional significance.

support to the technological and scientific infrastructure of the developing countries.

In the specific field of the industrial co-operation with developing countries, the objective is to promote industrial development and diversification, and the establishment of new relations in order to facilitate transfer of technology and its adaptation to the specific local conditions and requirements.

Another Commission activity, which for its relevance to the theme of this symposium should also be introduced is information dissemination and management of industrial property rights arising from the Commission's research work.

The Treaties establishing the Coal and Steel Authority and EURATOM include provisions relating to information and patents resulting from financial aid for coal, steel and nuclear research.

In 1973 The Council of Ministers adopted provisions to cover areas of research other than the above now undertaken in the frame of the Common Market treaty.

According to such provisions, the Commission shall transmit the informations resulting from its R&D programmes to member states as well as to persons and undertakings which pursue, on the territory of a member state, a research or a production activity entitling them to access to such information, and whose interests coincide with those of the Community.

The patents obtained in the frame of programmes sponsored by the Commission shall be taken out by the Commission in the name of the Community, however, if an invention is the result of research done under contract, the contractor may be the owner of the patent if he so desires. In any case, the Commission shall obtain a free and non-exclusive licence with the right of sub-licences to the use of inventions.

Offers of licences are published in the Official Journal of the Commission.

In the field of dissemination of information, the Commission is in a phase of progressive expansion: In these last years, important steps have been taken towards effective and broad actions for scientific and technical information.

In 1971, the Council of Ministers adopted a resolution for:

the co-ordination of the activities of the member states in the field of information and documentation in science and technology.

the establishment of a European Computerized Network of Documentation and Information.

the development of information methodology and technology.

Among important activities, which should be noted in this field, are: a permanent inventory of agricultural research in the Community; joint contribution by member states to the FAO's world agricultural information system; several R&D inventories covering specialist centers and referral system for environmental information; operation of a metallurgy information system; link-up between the Community's nuclear information system and that of the International Atomic Energy Agency in Vienna.

A very significant plan of action was adopted by the Council of Ministers early this year, which decides to proceed from the exploratory to the experimental stage by setting up a number of evaluation and pilot projects, to enable a start to be made on launching an operational information network. The systems to be established will cover various sectors; furthermore, it envisages that studies will be devoted to specific problems of horizontal integration such as multilingual systems, standardization and training of specialists.

The plan aims to set up an experimental computer network by the end of 1976. This network, which may evolve from scratch or by integrating existing networks and systems, will use the most advanced technology available and offer a range of services without parallel in Europe.

I have covered a lot of territory in a carousel of politics and programmes which in some way or another do promote the transfer of technology. I am sure, however, that I told you only part of the story.

Technology transfer is favoured by all the elements of the Common Market, whether we deal with an education programme or industrial co-operation, or the search of solution to a common problem. There is a basic common approach: People from the Community member countries are brought together.

It is this international gathering, taking place every day for every activity of the Commission, that permits reciprocal understanding and appreciation to bring about successful joint undertakings, which lead to a strong and rewarding integration of the European Community.

European Community: Research and Development Programmes – Mid-1975 (million of U.A.*)

	Community Programmes intra muros (direct action)		Community Programmes extra muros (indirect action)	
	Funds	Period	Funds	Period
1. Energy policy				
Economical application of energy	–		11.38	75-78
Coal research (ECSC)	–		28.50	73-77
Nuclear energy (fission)				
– Recycling of plutonium in LWR	–		4.50	75-78
– Plutonium and transplutoniums	21.65		–	
– Treatment and storage of radioactive wastes	5.51		19.16	75-79
– Reactor safety	21.72		–	
– Control of fission material	5.40		–	
– Technical assistance for operators of nuclear power-stations	6.10	73-76	–	
– Dragon Agreement	–		10.63	73-76[1)2]
– Biology - Radiation protection	–		18.87	71-75[1)]
– Information Analysis Office	5.10		–	
– Nuclear energy (Fusion)	–		71.10	71-75[1)]
– Production and use of hydrogen	7.04		13.24	75-78
– Use of solar energy	2.04		17.50	75-78
– Use of geothermal energy	–		13.00	75-78
– Systems analysis	–		3.88	75-78
2. Agricultural policy				
Application of nuclear technology in agriculture	–		4.60	71-75[1)]
Research project on African swine fever	–		2.75	73-76
Agricultural research	–		10.30	75-78
3. Environmental policy				
Environmental research and development	15.85		6.30	75-75[1)]
4. Industrial policy				
High-temperature materials	3.60		–	
Material science	13.60			

*The Unit of Account (U.A.) is the dollar value before the 1971 devaluation.

European Community: Research and Development Programmes – Mid-1975 (million of U.A.*) (Continued)

	Community Programmes intra muros (direct action)		Community Programmes extra muros (indirect action)	
	Funds	Period	Funds	Period
Steel research (ECSC)	–		32.50	73-77
1st programme on data-processing	–		4.01	75-77[3)]
Programme on textile research			0.25	75-77
5. Social policy				
Industrial safety and medicine	–		11.00	73-77
Application of nuclear technology to medical research	–		1.01	71-75[1)]
6. Raw materials		73-76		
Remote sensing of earlier resources	1.42		–	
Recycling of raw materials	1.02		–	
7. Public service and scientific services				
Central Bureau for nuclear measurements	20.35		–	
Petten HFR Reactor	23.00		–	
Standards and Reference materials programme	6.20		–	
Community Bureau of References	1.36		1.9	73-75[1)]
Applied Informatics	6.05		–	
Information network (COST 11)	1.00		–	
Education and training	1.45		4.5	73-76
Action programme CIDST	–		6.64	75-77
8. Long-term forecasting				
"Europe plus 30"	–		0.5	74-75

1) The Commission has scheduled a proposal for an additional multiannual programme to the Council of Ministers in July 1975

2) The existing agreement expires on 3/31/76

3) Not yet decided upon by the Council of Ministers

*The Unit of Account (U.A.) is the dollar value before the 1971 devaluation.

ASSESSING EFFECTS OF INTERNATIONAL TECHNOLOGY TRANSFER ON THE U. S. ECONOMY

Rolf Piekarz

National Science Foundation
Washington, DC

Introduction

This paper discusses the research program relating to the effects of international technology transfer on the U. S. economy which is being funded and partly carried out by the Office of National R&D Assessment (RDA) in the National Science Foundation. It describes the public policy setting, the information needs generated by this setting, and RDA's current and planned research. The paper has two purposes. First, it describes one of a number of programs now going on internationally to obtain a better understanding of the effects of international transactions involving technology on national economic welfare. Examples of other programs are the OECD task forces on multinational enterprises, the UNCTAD studies on technology transfers to less developed countries and the UN Secretariat studies on multinational enterprises.[1] The second purpose is to obtain comments and suggestions about the RDA research program concerning the effects of international technology transfer on the U. S. economy.

The paper consists of three parts. The first section suggests that the growing attempts to discourage foreign licensing and direct investment reflect belief that such transactions have contributed importantly to U. S. economic difficulties. The second section indicates that information and analysis are lacking to either justify or refute such beliefs. The third section briefly describes the current and planned research of RDA with regard to the major gaps of knowledge.

Public Policy Concerns

During the past three years, the U. S. Congress and two Administrations have begun to consider legislation to subject foreign commercial transactions involving technology transfer to controls for reasons other than national security. Legislation, most notably the Burke-Hartke bill, has been introduced and discussed in hearings during two recent sessions of Congress to permit the President to place restrictions on foreign licensing and foreign direct investment.[2] Legislation has been proposed to place heavier taxes on incomes earned by firms from their foreign operations.[3] Two years ago the Internal Revenue Service proposed changes in its regulations to reduce the foreign tax credits permitted to U.S multinational enterprises by requiring the firms to allocate a portion of their U.S. R&D expenditures against foreign tax credits.[4] Most recently, legislation was introduced and hearings were held to restrict foreign direct investment in the United States.[5] At present, the Commerce Department is in process of setting up a reporting system to monitor all foreign direct investment into the country.[6]

These recent efforts represent a sharp change from the traditional United States laissez-faire attitude toward foreign licensing and foreign direct investment. The growing pressures to restrict and discourage these transactions, for reasons other than national security, probably reflect largely responses to two conditions. One is the performance of the U. S economy, especially in comparison to other nations, during the past decade or so. The other is widespread belief that U. S. technology may have contributed importantly to foreign economic capabilities.

Recent U. S. Economic Performance

In the past few years, the American public has become increasingly aware of the narrowing of U. S. economic leadership. Emergence of large scale travel and tourism have brought Americans into physical contact with the conditions in industrialized nations. Statistical quality of life indicators measuring physical well being such as life expectancy, diet, ownership of consumer durables, hours worked, presented in OECD and UN data, tend to substantiate these impressions.

On a more abstract basis, available macroeconomic data indicate U. S. output per man hour has tended to increase more slowly than for most other industrial nations. Table 1 shows that during 1953-1955 U. S. gross domestic product (GDP) per employed person at market price and current dollars was more than double for any other industrial nation, except Canada. By 1970-1972, the U. S. lead had, with the exception of Canada,

Table 1. Gross Domestic Product per Employed Person in Other Industrial Countries as a Fraction of the United States, 1953 through 1972, Selected Years. (Market Value in Current Prices and in U.S. Dollars at Current Exchange Rates)

GDP PER EMPLOYED PERSON AS A FRACTION OF U.S. GDP PER EMPLOYED PERSON

COUNTRY	1953-1955	1961-1963	1970-1972
United States	1.00	1.00	1.00
Canada	0.81	0.77	0.86
Japan	0.09	0.16	0.36
Belgium	0.42	0.43	0.61
France	0.41	0.47	0.62
Germany	0.24	0.41	0.65
Italy	0.21	0.27	0.42
Netherlands	0.30	0.38	NA
Norway	0.37	0.45	NA
United Kingdom	0.45	0.49	NA

Sources: OECD, Labor Force Statistics 1961-1972, Paris, 1974
OECD, Manpower Statistics 1950-1960, Paris, 1961
OECD, National Accounts of OECD Countries 1961-1972, Paris, 1974
OECD, National Accounts of OECD Countries 1960-1971, Paris, 1973
OECD, National Accounts of OECD Countries 1953-1969, Paris, 1971
OECD, National Accounts of OECD Countries 1950-1968, Paris, 1970

declined substantially. This narrowing reflects the greater increase in output per manhour for the production of services and manufactures among these other industrial nations. The United States has maintained its leadership position only for one major sector - agriculture.[7]

This sketch does not present a complete picture of U. S. output performance during the past two decades or so. Examination of the estimates of growth of U. S. output per man hour from 1899 through 1973 for selected sectors in Table 2, shows that during the past two decades growth of U. S. output per manhour has usually exceeded, especially in manufacturing and agriculture, the long term trend values. In addition, available information is insufficient to indicate whether the foreign trends of the past two decades represent a reliable basis for forecasts or whether they reflect a catch up of other nations and the high rate of U. S. involvement in conflicts and defense abroad.[8]

The U. S. experience during the past decade in foreign trade transactions has been even more upsetting. During the 1960's the U. S. balance of trade moved sharply from a substantial excess of exports over imports to fluctuations about an approximate balance, including some large deficits in the 1970's. As shown in Table 3 these events contrasted dramatically with the continuous large U. S. balance of trade surpluses which prevailed from the early years of the century through the mid 1960's.

In addition, as shown in Table 4 the value of the U. S. dollar against the currencies of most other industrial nations has depreciated markedly only over a few years. Again, this experience contrasts markedly with the relative stability, or even appreciation, of the U. S. dollar against other currencies throughout the post-World War II era.

Possible Contribution of U. S. Technology to the Performance of Foreign Economies

This relatively pessimistic picture of U. S. economic performance has been attributed to a number of causes including concentration of U. S. resources on national security and prestige, insufficient fixed capital formation, barriers to technological change, excessive growth of transfer payments. One set of explanations focuses on the following three claims. The technological outflow from the United States through foreign licensing and direct investment has contributed importantly to enhancing the economic capabilities of other countries, especially industrial nations. Large U. S. firms transferring this technology and foreign firms buying this technology have benefited

Table 2. U.S. Long-Term Private Economy Productivity Growth, 1899-1973, Total and Selected Sectors

SECTORS	(1) 1899-1966	(2) 1899-1919	(3) 1919-1953	(4) 1948-1966	(5) 1966-1973	(6) 1965-1971
(1) Private Economy	2.4	1.9	2.6	3.4	2.5	—
(2) Farm	2.4	0.0	2.7	5.6	3.3	—
(3) Manufacturing	2.6	1.2	3.1	3.1	3.5	—
(4) Non-Farm, Non-Manufacturing	—	—	—	2.8	1.7	2.5
(5) Transportation	3.5	2.3	4.3	4.0	—	2.9
(6) Communications and Public Utilities	4.4	4.3	4.0	5.8	—	4.2
(7) Trade	1.8	1.0	1.7	2.9	—	2.2
(8) Mining	2.8	1.4	3.1	4.3	—	2.8

Sources: (A) Columns (1)-(3) John W. Kendrick, Productivity Trends in the United States (Princeton: Princeton University Press, 1971); pp. 333-335, 362-364, 396-398,465-466, 596, 540, 581-582.
(B) Columns (4)-(5) except for line (4): John Kendrick, Postwar Productivity Trends in the United States, 1948-1969 (New York: Columbia University Press, 1973); pp. 243-244, 254-255, 260, 274-275, 326, 343, 351.
(C) Line (4) Columns (4)-(6): Third Annual Report of National Commission on Productivity (March 1974), op. cit., p. 38.
(D) Column (6) Lines (5)-(8): U.S. Department of Labor, Productivity and the Economy, Bulletin 1779, 1973, p. 6.

TABLE 3: AVERAGE ANNUAL U.S. IMPORTS AND EXPORTS FOR FIVE YEAR PERIODS BEGINNING 1900 THROUGH 1974*
(Millions of U.S. Dollars, F.O.B.)

	U.S. Imports	U.S. Exports	Ratio of Exports to Imports
1900-1904	919	1429	1.55
1905-1909	1221	1729	1.42
1910-1914	1609	2131	1.32
1921-1924**	2605	3347	1.28
1925-1929	4267	4990	1.17
1930-1934	1918	2337	1.22
1935-1939	2366	2872	1.22
1950-1954	10438	14281	1.37
1955-1959	13397	18212	1.36
1960-1964	16448	22678	1.38
1965-1969	28659	32443	1.13
1970-1974	62305	61395	0.99

* 1915-1919, 1940-1944, and 1945-1949 excluded because World Wars dictate foreign trade flows.

** 1920 deleted because large scale post World War I relief shipments dominate exports.

Source: Imports - 1900-1923, Dept. of Commerce, *U.S. Historical Statistics, Colonial Times to 1957,* Wash., D.C.

Imports - 1923-1968, Dept. of Commerce, *U.S. Exports and Imports 1923 to 1968,* Wash., D.C., 1970

Imports - 1969-1974, International Monetary Fund, *International Financial Statistics,* Wash., D.C., April 1975.

Exports - Same as above except *U.S. Exports and Imports* series begins in 1925.

Table 4:
INDEX OF EXCHANGE RATE OF THE U.S. DOLLAR AGAINST CURRENCIES OF OTHER INDUSTRIAL COUNTRIES, 1960-1974, SELECTED YEARS
(1958 Exchange Rate = 100)

Country	1968	1970	1971	1972	1973	1974
Canada	111	105	104	103	103	103
Japan	99	99	88	84	78	84
Belgium	101	100	90	88	83	72
France	101	113	106	104	96	91
Germany	96	87	78	77	65	58
Italy	100	100	95	93	97	104
Netherlands	96	95	86	85	75	66
Norway	100	100	94	93	80	73
Sweden	100	100	94	92	89	79
Switzerland	100	100	91	88	75	59
United Kingdom	117	117	110	119	120	119

Source: International Monetary Fund, *International Financial Statistics December 1967-December 1973* (May 1975) greatly from these transactions. But, U. S. employment and foreign trade, and thereby U. S. economic growth have been hurt greatly by these transactions. These three claims basically derive from a set of observations and not from any systematic coherent analysis.

During the 1960's, a number of Western Europeans, especially J. J. Servan-Schreiber and Christopher Layton, popularized the notion that U. S. enterprises were using their technological superiority to gain a larger share of the world market for manufacturers by setting up production abroad, especially in Western Europe.[9] This idea coincided with the rapid growth of U. S. foreign direct investment in Western Europe in such industries as automobiles, chemicals and pharmaceuticals, computers and electronics components, and petroleum refining. In addition, writers like Servan-Schreiber and Layton believed that expansion of production by U. S. firms represented the most dynamic element of European manufacturing for industries with the highest growth potential. Some governments, especially France, became fearful of domination by U. S. firms of the technologically progressive and most rapidly growing sectors of their economies. A few years later, some observers noted that Japanese capabilities, especially in consumer electronics, derived importantly from licensing technology from U. S. firms. This perception coincided with increased awareness about the large role of Japan in U. S. foreign royalty earnings and the major rise in U. S. imports of consumer electronics and autos from Japan.

Another widespread idea of 1960's has been that producing, at least partly, within Western European customs unions provides U. S. firms with larger sales and greater profits than through exports. This view gained prominence during the rapid rise of U. S. foreign direct investment in Western Europe which coincided with the formative years of European Economic Community and European Free Trade Association. Also, some observers have claimed that U. S. firms have used their technology to obtain a monopoly position and profits by setting up production facilities within less developed countries.[10] This proposition has coincided with growing efforts by less developed countries to mesh investment by foreign firms with domestic economic objectives and with increasing disillusionment in the United States regarding involvements abroad. Statements about large gains from international technology transfer do not always favor the U. S. firm. Some proponents have claimed that U. S. firms have received inadequate profits from their licensing of technology from foreign firms, especially from selling technology to the Japanese.

In recent years, U. S. labor unions have come to share these views about the causes and influences of the behavior of U. S.

firms.[11] In addition, prominence has been achieved by the idea that the elimination of U. S. foreign trade surpluses results largely from the gains in advanced technologies by other industrial nations -- a position advocated by Michael Boretsky.[12] These ideas, coupled with observations about U. S. firms transferring technology and production to less developed countries (e.g., Mexico, Singapore, Hong Kong, Korea) have resulted in the view held by a growing public that the enhancement of foreign capabilities from U. S. technology lowers U. S. exports, raises U. S. imports, and thereby eliminates U. S. jobs and hinders U. S. economic growth.

The unifying idea is the perception - by public officials, business executives, labor leaders, and the general public - that the creation, use, and disposition of technology play an important role in the growth of the economy. Domestic developments in defense and space programs have made everyone conscious that technology is a major factor in U. S. national security and international prestige. U. S. industries with the most rapid growth and international competitive advantage are ones characterized by a relatively high fraction of R&D to sales. These industries are electronics, aircraft, chemicals and pharmaceuticals, electrical and non-electrical machinery. In addition, research of the economics of technology during the past two decades has come up with two major findings. First, industrial R&D has a substantial pay-off in improved productivity.[13] Second, improved technology coupled with greater skills and reduced institutional barriers, has contributed importantly to economic growth during this century.[14]

Information Needs

The above mentioned observations pose three public policy issues. First, whether or under what conditions are foreign licensing and direct investment important sources of technologies for industrial economies? Second, when and how are foreign licensing and direct investment important sources for earnings and growth by firms? Third, to what extent and under what circumstances do foreign licensing and direct investment enhance or diminish national economic welfare?

Proposals of recent years to restrict foreign direct investment out of or into the United States tend to agree with claims that on the whole these transactions contribute importantly to foreign technology, the earnings of firms, and to U. S. unemployment and foreign trade imbalances. Suppose none, or possibly only one, of these conditions actually prevail; different policy options would then be optimal. For example, if foreign direct investment were found to contribute importantly to foreign technological capability without any major harm to U. S. economic welfare, U. S. officials then have added potential to obtain economic advantages (e.g., better trade terms on natural resources, lower trade barriers). In contrast, it may be that foreign licensing and direct investment contribute importantly to foreign technological capabilities at the expense of U. S. interests only under selected conditions (e.g., foreign restrictions on U. S. exports or foreign direct investment). Analogously, there may exist conditions where government measures could help foreign licensing or direct investment contribute importantly to U. S. technological capabilities. If so, more selective measures than have been recommended would be more appropriate.

To formulate and assess options effectively it is necessary to have more complete information and analysis about the situation. To develop a program for research, the necessary first step is to ask what is known and what are the major gaps in understanding.

What is Known[15]

Research to date has focused on foreign direct investment by U. S. firms. Known findings suggest that comprehensive restrictions on foreign licensing and direct investment by U. S. firms would not enhance U. S. economic welfare.

Available research has established that foreign countries obtain technology from U. S. foreign licensing and direct investment. The data and analysis suggest that U. S. industries spending relatively high amounts for R&D tend to be among the leading industries in foreign licensing and direct investment.

This association holds only in a general way.[16] Among the leading industries in foreign direct investment we find the following with high R&D intensity: radio, television, and communications; other electrical equipment; non-electric machinery; and, industrial chemicals. Notable high R&D intensity industries not among the leaders in foreign direct investment are aircraft and missiles, and instruments. Analogously, among industries with a high foreign direct investment propensity are found a few with only moderate R&D intensities: transport equipment (except aircraft); rubber products; and petroleum refining and extraction. These results tend to substantiate findings of selected studies which show that much of U. S. foreign direct investment does not involve either products or production processes where the United States has a substantial technological or resource superiority.

Available knowledge does not permit the conclusion that relatively unrestricted foreign licensing and direct investment into and out of the United States has resulted in a technology flow adverse to U. S. economic welfare. The empirical evidence shows that manufacturing industries with a high rate of foreign investment performance show a better foreign trade performance than do industries which license or invest abroad only in a limited way.[17] similarly, most studies examining the influence of U. S. foreign direct investment on U. S. employment show that on balance loss of jobs tend in general to be offset by job gains.[18] However, these research findings about the effect of foreign direct investment on U. S. foreign trade and employment yield only limited and partial answers.

Two additional research findings should be considered in providing a general assessment about what available knowledge tells us concerning the overall effects from foreign direct investment. One observation is that income from foreign direct investment and licensing contributes importantly to U. S. international earnings on current account. Receipts from these two sources account for over ten percent of U. S. foreign exchange earnings from the sale of goods and services. Over the past two decades earnings from these sources have grown more rapidly than export sales. The second finding is that foreign technologies have contributed importantly to U. S. industries, especially to industries where U. S. has a strong international competitive position. As illustrations, polyester fiber and commercial jet aircraft technology were acquired partially from the United Kingdom. Even for the computer (the highly acclaimed American innovation) a good deal of the early technology came from Germany and France. Large scale restriction of U. S. foreign licensing and direct investment would probably result in foreign retaliations, which would cut off U. S. firms from economically important technology.

Major Gaps

We lack knowledge about the contribution of foreign licensing and direct investment to the technological capability of the buyer and, by the way, to the seller as well. Also, little is known about the contribution of such transactions to earnings and sales of firms buying and selling technology through foreign licensing and direct investment. Finally, we do not have the information and analysis to assess the net effects of technology transfers on national employment, production, foreign trade or consumer benefits.

Two types of research are needed. One is the improvement of the concepts and methods for assessing the questions. The other is obtaining information about experience over a range of conditions. For example, we know pretty well that on average, the U. S. economy does not appear to be hurt from foreign licensing and direct investment by U. S. firms; but there are numerous claims of economic loss because of government policies limiting exploitation of technology through the optimum channels.

1. Technological Flows from Foreign Licensing and Direct Investment

Before government can effectively consider options to improve U. S. economic welfare from foreign licensing and direct investment greater understanding will be necessary about the gross and net technology flows from these transactions. Among the major gaps is absence of information and analysis about the magnitude and characteristics of technology transfers among different industries and for various technologies. We lack understanding about the influence on technology transferred on such things as the prices of productive resources, firm size and competitive conditions, and technological capabilities of suppliers and sellers.

There is little knowledge about the effectiveness and selection of alternative channels for transferring technology between and within firms. After all, the effectiveness of any government effort to regulate technology flows by placing constraints on a particular channel (e.g., direct investment) must consider the ability of buyers and sellers to use other channels (e.g., licensing). Along these lines little information exists about the two-way traffic of technology among industries and firms. We know that within industries there is large scale foreign direct investment and licensing. Within individual firms technology is exchanged among international subsidiaries, and used to enhance the technological innovativeness of the firm. A few industries, e.g., chemicals, have been studied, but the available information is sparse.[19]

2. Returns to Firms from Licensing and Direct Investment

The net value of technology transfers to nations from foreign licensing and direct investment depends importantly on the gains to the firms (both sellers and buyers) participating in these transactions. Unfortunately, little is known about the magnitude and character of these returns under various circumstances, e.g., characteristics of technology, market conditions, government regulations. As illustrations, despite data about rates of return on foreign direct investment and licensing fees, there is no information about the size, distribution and nature of earnings for firms from selling technology among these two channels. Little information and analysis exists about the decision criteria and processes whereby different firms set prices and conditions for foreign licensing and direct investment. Little is known about the influence of these transactions on the rate and direction of technological innovation within or among firms. Finally, despite all kinds of claims, there is little understanding about the extent to which government restrictions and regulations influence the earnings from foreign direct investment or licensing, or about the extent to which these restrictions inhibit international technology transfers.

On the buying side, little is known about the contribution of foreign licensing and joint ventures to the earnings of the firm. For example, we lack information and analysis about the distribution over various conditions of the costs of adopting technology acquired through licenses or joint ventures as opposed to internal R&D. Analogously, understanding is lacking with regard to the contribution of licensing or joint ventures to the earnings capabilities of the firm relative to other options.

3. Effect on U. S. National Economic Welfare

Despite the centrality of this question to public policy there exist only gross macro judgments. A major part of the problem is the analytical and empirical difficulties. Effects to the United States as a nation from international transactions involving technology transfers reflect the net outcome of the interaction of numerous variables and relationships. Many of these relationships are not well understood; some variables are not measured. For example, to estimate the effects of a technology transfer from foreign direct investment on U. S. employment requires, among other variables, estimates of the influence of this action on the exports of the host nation, other nations, and the United States including the product directly involved, components produced by suppliers, and competing products. Other information needed includes effects on incomes, exchange rates, etc.

Recognizing these difficulties more information and analysis are needed than has been produced thus far. For example, there exist no estimates about the effects of technology transfers from foreign licensing and direct investment on U. S. consumers from the increased competition. Little is known about the effects of foreign licensing or direct investment on sales and employment among producers of components, capital equipment, or auxiliary services. We also lack understanding about the adaptation of U. S. firms to increased competition. Finally, analyses and estimates for all these types of questions should consider the influences of various conditions (e.g., market structure, government policies) on the responses to be expected.

RDA Research on International Technology Transfer

The discussion now turns to a description of the Office of National R&D Assessment (RDA) research program on international technology transfer. The economic conditions and claims outlined earlier represent the policy context; and, the information needs and gaps just sketched form the foundation of this research effort. In addition, a brief description of the total RDA research objectives would also serve as a useful prerequisite to understanding the research effort of the Office with regard to international technology transfer. I will then just briefly outline the projects funded and conducted during the past two years. This list is intended to provide some idea about the kind of research products to be expected over the next year or two. Since there exist some preliminary research findings, a brief summary of these results also represents an appropriate conclusion.

Office of National R&D Assessment

The Office of National R&D Assessment was established in the summer of 1972 to provide an analytical capability, to supply objective analysis, and to define options for enhancing the contribution of science and technology to the United States. The research program is designed to achieve a fuller understanding of the relationships between government policy options and technological innovation, socioeconomic effects of technological innovations, and processes of technological innovation. The term technological innovation, as used in the official research program documents, is defined to include the processes from conception or generation of an idea to its widescale utilization by society including activities involved in the creation, research, development, and diffusion of new and improved products. processes, and services for private and public use.

The research relating to policy options examines the effects of government activities on the amount, rate, and direction of technological innovation. The purposes are to provide a basis for analyzing government involvement in technological innovation and to identify government policy options and practices which might increase the contribution of science and technology to the United States. Aspects of government activities include expenditures, taxes, patents, antitrust, and regulation.

The research on socioeconomic effects of technological innovation seeks to improve the conceptual frameworks and techniques available to identify and measure the socioeconomic variables needed to assess policy problems and options involving technological innovation. The research stresses increasing the empirical information about private and public returns from technological innovation including profits, productivity, household welfare, quality of work. This research element contains the topic of the effects of international technology transfer on the U. S. economy. International technology transfer involves two aspects of the process of technological innovation. It represents the diffusion of technology to production facilities located in another soverign territory; and it represents a source of technology for the United States in addition to R&D.

The research on innovation processes examines similarities and differences in the way R&D and innovation occurs in civilian sectors of the economy. The purpose is to improve understanding of the variables that influence those processes, including the effects of private and public involvement.

Research Strategy and Objectives

The objectives of the research about the effects of international technology transfer on the U. S. economy are to improve toos and to contribute information for assessing options for government action (including the "do nothing" option).

The strategy of the research has been to emphasize in the early efforts questions on the magnitude of technology transfer. After getting projects started on this question, the intention has been to give greater attention to examining the net benefits to the transacting firms and then moving on to assessment of the effects on industries and the nation. This research plan results largely from the judgment that the technology content of foreign licensing and foreign direct investment is fundamental to understanding technological innovation and to assessing benefits and costs from international technology flows. But, little research has been conducted on this topic.

Aside from the early effort to assess the state of the art, nine extramural research projects have been funded beginning with the Spring of 1973. Two projects were initiated in-house beginning early in 1974. Total funding has been about $550,000 for the nine extramural projects. Two projects have been completed and tentative results have been obtained for a couple of others. Preliminary results have also been obtained from the in-house research. Of the nine projects, eight emphasize the assessment of the magnitude or character of technology transfer in foreign licensing and direct investment. Three of these studies also examine net benefits to the firms or nations. The remaining study focuses on net benefits to the firm.

Research Projects

A descriptive listing should provide a rough idea of the RDA research on international technology transfer. More complete description of these projects is available in the RDA annual reports.

A National Bureau of Economic Research project, with Professor Robert Lipsey as principal investigator, has concentrated on assessing the character and rate of international technology diffusion from U. S. foreign direct investment in semi-conductors, pharmaceuticals, and synthetic materials. In addition, Professor Lipsey is testing to see the extent to which Department of Commerce data on overseas operations of U. S. firms can be used to assess the influence of their technological capability on foreign direct investment and exports.

A Forecasting International project is examining questions about the effect of various conditions (e.g., technological capabilities of buyers and sellers, competitive conditions, government policies) on the magnitude, character and pricing of technology transferred by U. S. firms in licensing to foreign firms.

Professor Stobaugh of Harvard is principal investigator of a team looking at a number of questions relating to technology and foreign licensing and direct investment. He already has completed (under a small separate study award) a preliminary assessment of the availability of information from public sources about technology transferred under various types of international transactions.[20] Currently, he has underway a project consisting of three studies. One study is examining the influence of relative prices of capital and labor on the technology transferred in foreign direct investment. He also is conducting a study to assess the influence of various conditions, including the character of technology and the level of R&D expenditures, on the extent to which a firm selects foreign licensing over foreign direct investment as a vehicle for exploiting a technology through foreign production. A third study in this project involves an attempt to design a simulation model to improve the capability of assessing the influence of various conditions on the country of location for production of a particular technology, and the consequences of this action on the output and exports of the United States and the other countries involved.

Dr. Robert Wilson, at Yale University, has just completed a study which assesses the influence of market and technology conditions on the rate of licensing by industries and firms. In another part of the study Dr. Wilson examines the influence of different variables (e.g., uncertainty, possibilities of technological exchange) on the fees and payments from licensing arrangements.[21]

At Battelle Memorial Institute, Dr. W. Halder Fisher has just begun a study to assess the extent to which foreign direct investment in U. S. advanced technology industries by foreign firms involves inflows and outflows of technology.

Professor Edwin Mansfield, at the University of Pennsylvania, is heading a team to examine the influence of foreign licensing and direct investment of U. S. firms on the rate, direction, and possibly location of their R&D.

At Stanford Research Institute, Donald Greene and Melvin Krauss prepared a conceptual framework and empirical procedure for obtaining information about the selection by firms of exports, foreign licensing, or foreign direct investment as vehicles for marketing technology in a foreign country.[22]

In addition to these extramural projects, RDA has two small internal studies. These analytical exercises are examining the macroeconomic data on U. S. foreign direct investment and foreign trade provided by the Commerce Department to look for evide ce of large scale U. S. technology transfer to other nations. One study, conducted by Dr. Sumiye Okubo, is analyzing foreign investment activities and the magnitude of foreign sales, production and earnings by U. S. firms in the various industry categories. The other study, conducted by Dr. Rolf Piekarz and Ms. Susan Morris, is examining in terms of technology content the behavior of U. S. foreign trade between 1963 and 1972.

Some Preliminary Results

There are few results to report at this time for two reasons. First, most of the research efforts described are in an incomplete, even preliminary, working status. Second, the research program involves a modest expenditure of research resources, say on the order of about three to four professional man years annually. Given this context, three preliminary results seem to be emerging from the research projects.

First, U. S. foreign direct investment does not appear to accelerate greatly the diffusion of technology to other industrial nations or to less developed countries. The small internal study shows that the major portion of investment expenditures by U. S. firms abroad occurs in other industrial countries and for industries or activities not noted for rapid technological advance. In addition, studies of foreign direct investment for selected product groups subject to rapid technological change (e.g., semiconductors, chemicals and pharmaceuticals), the location of production facilities of U. S. firms on other industrial countries does not markedly accelerate the diffusion of the advanced U. S. technology to these countries. In addition, examination of production subsidiaries in less developed countries for selected advanced technology products suggests these subsidiaries do not appear to enhance the technological capabilities of these countries.

Second, on a related topic, the preliminary findings from examining U. S. foreign trade data suggest the marked deterioration of the U. S. foreign trade position during the past decade cannot be readily traced to technology transferred by foreign licensing and direct investment by U. S. firms. The major portion of the deterioration occurs because of a sharp acceleration of U. S. imports of consumer durables, especially automobiles and radios, televisions, and phonographic equipment. Examination of the data show growing surpluses in advanced technology items largely aircraft, electronics equipment and components, chemicals and pharmaceuticals, and various kinds of non-electrical capital equipment.

Third, licensing tends to represent a substantially larger fraction of the patents of firms than is indicated by the value of the receipts from licensing obtained by firms. This outcome reflects two conditions. First, the fees for licensing reflect a heavy discounting of the value of the license predominantly because of uncertainty about the value of the patent to the licensee and much less as a result of the bargaining power of the parties. Second, a large fraction of licensing involves bartering either through cross-licensing arrangements or tie-in sales. In terms of relative frequency, firms tend to prefer licensing to foreign firms rather than domestic competitors. Also, licensing is more likely to occur in industries with high rates of technological innovation.

REFERENCES

1. The OECD study program is described in "OECD Work on Multinational Enterprises," The OECD Observer, April 1974, p. 4. I am not aware of any final publicly available reports from these efforts. UNCTAD has issued a number of reports from its program. A notable example is Guidelines for the Study of the Transfer of Technology to Developing Countries, a study by the UNTAD Secretariat (New York: United Nations, 1972). Along these lines UNITAR (United Nations Institute for Training and Research) has issued a number of reports assessing specific cases of technology transfers. Examples are Robert B. Stobaugh, "The International Transfer of Technology in the Establishment of the Petrochemical Industry in Developing Countries," 1971; and Lawrence H. Wortzel, "Technology Transfer in the Pharmaceutical Industry," 1971. Finally, two examples of the efforts of the UN Secretariat are Transfer of Operative Technology at the Enterprise Level (New York: United Nations, 1972) and The Impact of Multinational Corporations on Development and International Relations (New York: United Nations, 1974).

2. The contents and public policy issues involved in the Burke-Hartke bill are described briefly by Charles Culhand, "Economic Report/Labor and industry gear for major battle over bill to curb imports, multinationals," National Journal, Vol. 4 (January 15, 1972), pp. 108-119.

3. An example of legislation proposing to increase the tax burden on income of foreign direct investment by U. S. firms is HR 5086, "A bill to amend the tariff and trade laws of the United States to promote full employment and restore a diversified production base; to amend the Internal Revenue Code of 1954 to stem the outflow of United States capital, jobs, technology and production and for other purposes." This bill was introduced March 1, 1973. Proposals and issues involved in efforts to raise this tax burden are discussed by Richard S. Frank, "Washington Pressures/Multinationals Mobilize to Preserve Favorable Tax Status on Overseas Income," National Journal, Vol. 5, July 14, 1973, pp. 1019-1028.

4. The proposed IRS changes are amendments to regulations paragraph 1.861-8 under section 861 of U. S. Internal Revenue Code. These amendments were published under "Proposed Rules," Federal Register, Vol. 38, No. 116, Monday, June 18, 1973, pp. 15840-51. These changes were assessed by Robert B. Stobaugh, "The Probable Effects on the U. S. Economy of Adopting Amendments to Regulations, paragraph 1.861-8 under Section 861 of U. S. Internal Revenue Code," December 1973, mimeo.

5. In the 94th session of Congress, Senator William Roth proposed a bill (S.995) to authorize the government to regulate or bar investment by foreign governments on government enterprises. Senator Harrison Williams proposed a bill (S.425) which authorizes the President to prohibit in the name of national security, foreign policy or protection of the economy acquisition of five percent or more of the equity of any U. S. company. Hearings on these bills were conducted by the Senate Banking, Housing and Urban Affairs Committee in April 1975.

6. A report of the initial attempts of the Commerce Department to collect detailed data on foreign direct investment in the United States is reported by James L. Pate, "U. S. Attracts More Foreign Enterprises; Commerce to Gather Detailed Information," Commerce Today, March 31, 1975, pp. 2-3.

7. For a more comprehensive comparison of the growth of output per employed person for the United States with other industrial nations since the 1950's see OECD, The Growth of Output 1960-1980, (D cember 1970), pp. 24-44.

8. A discussion of the state-of-the-art in assessing productivity trends is presented by Rolf Piekarz and Eleanor Thomas, "U. S. Productivity Growth: An assessment of Perceptions and Prescriptions," October 1974, mimeo.

9. J. J. Servan-Schreiber, The American Challenge (New York: Avon Books, 1969); Christopher Layton, European Advanced Technology: A Program of Integration (London: Allen and Unwin, 1969).

10. A recent example is Richard J. Barnet and Ronald E. Miller, Global Reach, The Power of Multinational Corporations (New York: Simon and Schuster, 1974), especially Chapter 7, "Engines of Development?", pp. 148-184.

11. For a more detailed discussion of the views of labor unions, see Charles Culhane, "Trade Report/Labor shifts tactics on Administration bill, seeks concessions on imports, multinationals," National Journal, Vol. 5, July 28, 1973, pp. 1091-98; or the testimony and materials presented by Andrew Biemiller, Nat Goldfinger and Ray Denison during hearings before the Subcommittee on International Trade of the U. S. Senate Committee on Finance on March 6, 1973 as published in Multinational Corporations (Washington, DC: GPO 1973, pp. 299-367).

12. For a more complete presentation of this position see Michael Boretsky, "Concerns about the Present American Position in International Trade," in National Academy of Engineering, Technology and International Trade, Proceedings of the Symposium of October 14 and 15, 1970, as published in 1971, pp. 18-66.

13. For a comprehensive discussion on the state of knowledge of this topic see National Science Foundation, Research and Development and Economic Growth/Productivity, Papers and Proceedings of a Colloquium (Washington, DC: GPO, 1971).

14. For a discussion of the state-of-knowledge of this topic see M. Ishaq Nadiri, "Some Approaches to the Theory and Measurement of Total Factor Productivity: A Survey," Journal of Economic Literature, Vol. 8 (December 1970).

15. Most of the information about the current state of knowledge presented in this paper comes from National Science Foundation, The Effects of International Technology Transfers on U. S. Economy, (Washington, DC: GPO, July 1974).

16. The information about the statements concerning the loose relation between direct investment and R&D intensity are abstracted from Robert G. Hawkins, "Technology Transfer and Multinational Firms: The Home Country Perspective," March 1975 (mimeo).

17. The analysis for this statement appears in U. S. Tariff Commission, *Implications of Multinational Firms for World Trade and Investment and for U. S. Trade and Labor*, Report to the Committee on Finance of the United States Senate, (Washington, DC: GPO, 1973).

18. For studies in addition to the Tariff Commission analysis see Robert G. Hawkins, "*Job Displacement and the Multinational Firm: A Methodological Review*," Occasional Paper No. 3, Center for Multinational Studies, New York University (June 1972) and R. Stobaugh, J. Telesio, and J. Torre, "*Employment and Balance of Payments Effects of U. S. Foreign Direct Investment*," Center for Multinational Studies, Occasional Paper No. 2, November 1972.

19. Three examples of studies include: Gary C. Hufbauer, *Synthetic Materials and the Theory of International Trade* (Cambridge, Mass.: Harvard U. Press, 1966); John E. Tilton, *International Diffusion of Technology - The Case of Semiconductors* (Washington, DC: Brookings, 1971); Alvin J. Harman, *The International Computer Industry* (Cambridge, Mass.: Harvard U. Press, 1971).

20. Joan P. Curhan and Robert B. Stobaugh, "*Data on Multinational/Multiproduct U. S. Enterprises*," December 1974, available from NTIS.

21. Robert W. Wilson, *The Sale of Technology Through Licensing*, mimeo. Copy will probably be available from NTIS sometime during Summer 1975.

22. Donald S. Green and Melvin B. Krauss, "*A Research Approach to the International Transfer of Technology*," available from NTIS.

PART V: MULTINATIONAL TECHNOLOGY TRANSFER

The first three papers in this part are "Technology Transfer in a Multinational Firm" by P. D. Wilmot, "The Role of Technology in Development" by D. L. Guertin, and "How To Obtain Foreign Technology at Minimum Cost or Free" by W. Straube. The last paper by the late S. Thebaud is an exhaustive treatment of the plusses, minuses and sins of multinational corporations in their technology transfer activities.

In the paper by P. Wilmot, the various aspects and problems of the technology transfer in an international company are discussed. The author notes that the world is a large laboratory to the multinational firms and mistakes made and opportunities missed in one region can be avoided in another. The question is raised as to the extent to which the multinationals should cooperate with the lesser developed nations.

"The Role of Technology in Development" by D. L. Guertin acknowledges that while the international transfer of technology has had positive development benefits worldwide, both developing and developed countries are now raising questions about problems associated with this transfer process. Multinational corporations have been a major agent for international technology transfers and, therefore, many questions raised concern these corporations.

This paper has been prepared to:

> Review the conditions necessary for technological contributions to development.
>
> Highlight the contributions of multinational corporations to development through the technology transfer process.
>
> Discuss the concern and actions of developed and developing countries on the technology transfer process.

W. Straube's notes on "How To Obtain Foreign Technology at Minimum Cost, Or Free" asks if it is possible to get something for nothing and promptly replies "Yes." With that answer, the paper proceeds to discuss what is available, the fact that many technological discoveries go unused and unnoticed and suggests researching such diverse sources as the local library, the U.S. Patent Office, the United Nations, OECD, the U.S. Agency for International Development, General Electric Company and so on.

Advice is also given on how to obtain technology when the source of technology does not cooperate.

The last article in this part is a very thorough contribution by the late S. Thebaud.

Thebaud notes that the majority of research performed in the under-developed countries is generally of a theoretical nature and does not lead to the perfection of new technologies which could contribute to the development of these nations. Such being the case much of the technologies used come from industrial countries, and the lesser developed nations in many cases are thus subject to fiscal manipulation and profiteering.

The author discusses the concepts of technology and technology transfer, traces the origin of technologies imported by the lesser developed countries and cites figures of direct foreign investment in manufacturing activities in these nations. The role of patents and licenses, the means of importing technologies, methods of direct foreign investment and costs of technology transfer are explored as are problems of overpricing in the pharmaceutical arena.

The author cautions that in evaluating the desirability of importation of technologies by under-developed countries a distinction must be made between international commerce of technologies and international transfers of technologies between parent companies and their subsidiaries located in the Third World due to the greater susceptibility of the latter methodology to overpricing.

TECHNOLOGY TRANSFER IN A MULTINATIONAL FIRM

P. D. Wilmot

CIBA-GEIGY
Basel, Switzerland

Although there is much criticism in certain quarters of the multinational concern, it has played a vital role in the expansion of economies since the last world war. M.N.C.'s fulfil many functions for society and although, in the future, certain roles may no longer be played by them, they have shown a unique effectiveness in the past in one activity, which will be increasingly needed in the future and which should remain with them - technology transfer.

In this paper the various aspects of technology transfer in an international company will be discussed. The problems arising in this respect, with possible solutions also will be reviewed.

Current theories of strategic planning revolve around the question, "What business are we in". To answer this question is by no means as simple as it sounds and there is often no unique solution to this problem. The many options which face a large company in this soul-searching mission can only be decided in the context of environmental forecasts. The task is to look at a long range future and superimpose upon it the outlines of the business as it can then be at that future time. As the environment evolves so must the company and this implies a dynamic process of adding to and changing the skills of the company. If the company is in high technology, this implies a process of technology transfer. For such companies, which probably have a greater influence on changing society than all others, technology transfer is the vital activity.

A methodology of performing the long range analysis is first to analyze the company's place inside its industries. This is best done by a systems analysis in which the system which supplies the companies raw materials and technology is analysed, the system of transformation inside the company is examined and then the system in which its product and services are incorporated into the business of the customer is determined. (Fig. 1). The process must go even further. An understanding of the factors influencing the company's future can only be made if the immediate systems are placed into the systems chain which links primary product to the consumer. (Fig. 2).

What will influence the future of the company will be changes in relationships between critical parameters in the systems chains, particularly where competitive chains interact with the original series. In other words, markets may be lost. A determination of the value of the variables, usually in terms of cost or price is then required.

The process as outlined is so very complex that a rigorous treatment is out of the question. A largely intuitive choice of the key variables is what must be done and the future options determined against them. A reiterative process can then refine the solutions found so as to reduce the risk of error.

As threats to the business are revealed by this process, the reactions to them may be explored by examining alternative systems which will also meet the needs revealed. It is not likely that the technologies already mastered by the company will provide all the answers, although the possibility of transfer of technology from one sector to another inside must not be overlooked. The answer must usually be found in acquiring technology from outside (Fig. 3).

However, no technology is an entirely discreet quantity, for the spin-off from one skill will affect a neighboring skill. Therefore it is important to determine to what extent newly acquired skills will interact with existing skills. The object is to build up a synergistic combination of expertise. Such a policy has the advantage that if a skill has been acquired to meet a particular future and that future does not emerge, the ability thus gained is not wasted (Fig. 4).

A similar reasoning applies to research and development projects. In the past there was too great a tendency to introduce programmes aimed at particular individual opportunities. Today the relevance of a project to several potential applications must be assessed, with chances of success in each field quantified in order to spread the risks of the failure of a particular market to develop.

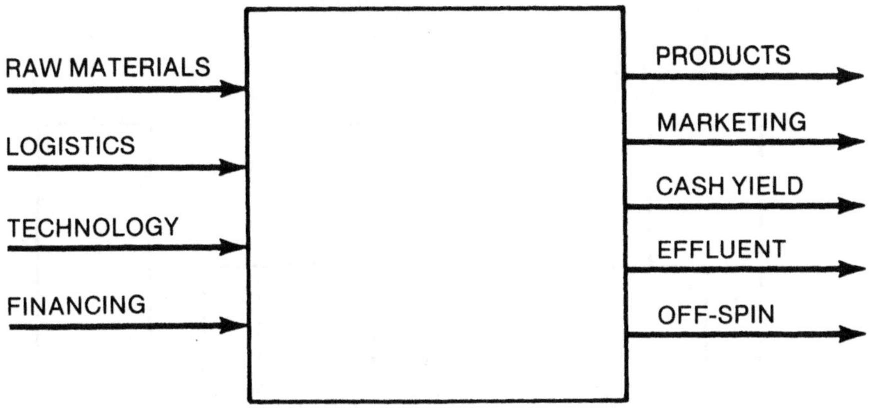

Figure 1. System Analysis of a Process

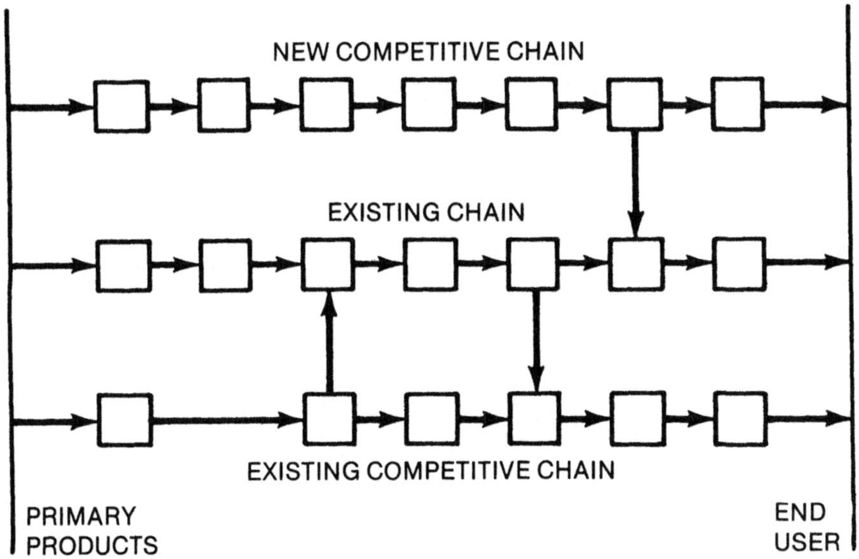

Figure 2. Systems Chain

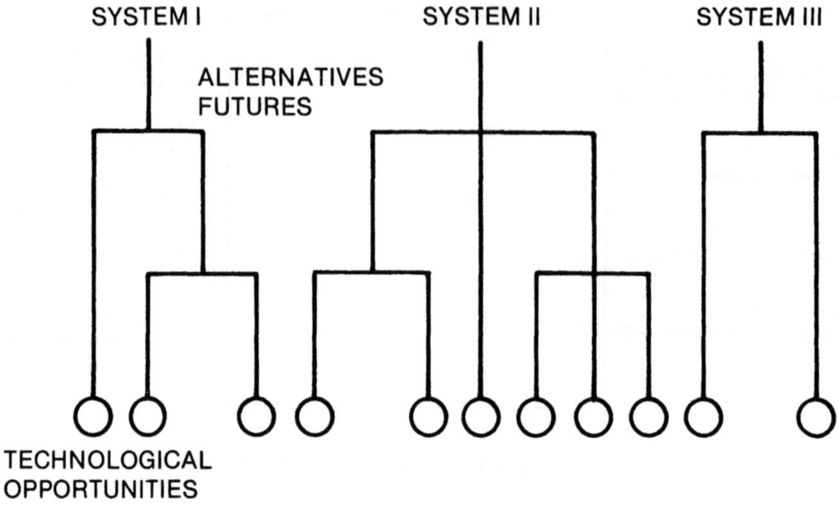

Figure 3. Forecasting

TECHNOLOGICAL OPPORTUNITIES	WITHIN CURRENT TECHNOLOGIES	COULD POSSIBLY BE ACQUIRED	OUTSIDE CURRENT TECHNOLOGIES

Figure 4. Technology Match with Futures

Conversely, old specialisms can become an impediment to organizational development and are better divested.

It is this process of technology transfer which gradually changes the shape of the company as the years go on and it is the vital stuff of strategic planning.

Now an M.N.C. is in a particularly favorable position to mold its future in this way since the number of environments it can react with are so many. One can then make mistakes on purpose in order to learn, to grow wiser and to grow. For these reasons it is particularly interesting to explore the ways in which an M.N.C. can undertake technology transfer and to discuss the problems that are met.

Since the world is the laboratory for the M.N.C., the mistakes made and opportunities missed in one region can be avoided in another. Furthermore, where new ideas are involved one can carry out a test in a less important area before attacking the main opportunity. It is often particularly useful to try new techniques in less sophisticated areas, because the business economy in these areas are less sophisticated and one can have much more freedom of action.

However, errors can be committed in this process, for if one is not fully alert as to the state of technology in the industry involved, there may have developed alternative technologies which are firmly entrenched. Other aspects of a socio-economic nature may make the technology less acceptable. So a full appreciation of the environment is necessary. Another temptation is to increase risks by using some new advance in technology in another environment where the infra structure may not be able to support it.

Taking account of such factors can be highly advantageous, for entirely new and distinct opportunities in OPEC and other less developed countries is a particularly interesting case.

The methods of undertaking such work involves a combination of actions. Well directed intelligence into these environments can often be the mainspring of action. However, employment of nationals from the countries concerned is a vital factor to success. These should be thoroughly informed of the skills and the longer range intentions of the company in order that they may be full partners in the transfer process. Their presence should not however inhibit visits to the area from the centre. Furthermore, there is no cheap alternative to bringing the local people to the centre for training and up-dating. Wherever possible the local unit should have the right to develop its own products and techniques, consistent with a cohesive world policy.

The biggest difficulty in this activity is management. It is therefore necessary to delegate line management away from the centre in order to avoid congestion in decision making. However, the strategic planning must remain at the centre for only at one point can the difficult options where to concentrate resources can be made. The decisions on technology transfer are thus a joint responsibility of the local line management and the central strategic control.

A further problem is management mismatch when new businesses are acquired. This difficulty must not deter the step from being taken, but it should always be recognized and catered to.

A final question is cooperation with outside bodies. When it is another company, the results appear to be most fruitful when they contribute in equal degree to the technology involved, each making quite different contributions. However, the big question facing M.N.C.'s today is to what extent they should cooperate with L.D.C. Governments. While such cooperation is necessary in many areas, M.N.C.'s are particularly aware of the fact that it is only their technology and their staff who are its ambassadors that keep them in business. To lock up their technology and their people in unfavorable deals with foreign governments, can only be a wasting disease, unless the training process and their research can produce results at a rate fast enough to meet the loss rate of these precious commodities. Faced with new pressures and demands from L.D.C.'s this is also the problem facing our entire Western society.

THE ROLE OF TECHNOLOGY IN DEVELOPMENT

Dr. Donald L. Guertin

Exxon Corporation
New York, NY

While generally acknowledging that the international transfer of technology has had positive development benefits worldwide, both developing and developed countries are now raising questions about problems associated with this transfer process. Multinational corporations (MNCs) have been a major agent for international technology transfers and, therefore, many questions raised concern these corporations.

Developing countries are concerned over their technological dependence, including the limited research and development sponsored by MNCs in their areas; the levels of fees charged for technology; the appropriativeness of technology provided by the MNCs with particular emphasis on its impact on employment; and, restrictions which may be imposed on the use of licensed technology.

Developed countries are also concerned about technological dependence, particularly in industrial sectors, such as computers and aerospace. Questions have also been raised in the United States, primarily by labor groups, on the possible competitive advantages given to other nations in world trade through the export of U.S. technology.

This paper has been prepared to:

Review the conditions necessary for technological contributions to development.

Highlight the contributions of multinational corporations to development through the technology transfer process.

Discuss the concern and actions of developed and developing countries on the technology transfer process.

Conditions for Technological Contributions to Development

As noted, both developed and developing countries are increasingly concerned about their dependence on others to meet their needs for technology. At times, in discussing these concerns, the fact that no nation is technologically independent is forgotten and the conditions necessary to support a strong national technological effort are not kept in mind.

As the developed countries invested about $42 billion in R&D in 1971[1] and the developing countries had only modest investments in R&D, it would be expected that developing countries would be dependent in this area. Even the developed countries, which individually make substantial investments in R&D, are dependent on the technology of others. An Organization for Economic Cooperation and Development study[2] has shown that of 110 major technological innovations, 43 occurred in Europe and 4 in Japan. The U.S. which has the highest dollar investment in R&D of any country had 74 of these innovations.

In reviewing the role of technology in development it is also necessary to review the conditions, other than R&D expenditures, necessary to support national technological efforts.

These conditions include: a market for the goods or services produced by the technology (either domestic or export); organizations and technical personnel, either national or expatriate, to successfully utilize the technology; suitable institutions to develop and update nationals engaged in technological activities and help identify the potential benefits of new technology; and, management systems which understand the application of technology in business enterprises. The capital necessary for plants or other facilities must of course be available.

The U.S., Japan, and other developed countries have generally been successful in importing technology because they satisfy these conditions. Developing countries often cannot.

Multinational corporations are often key agents in introducing technology developed in one country to other developed countries and to developing countries. These organizations can act on an international basis to introduce the technology developed by the more than $40 billion expenditures on R&D in developed countries, to each other, and, to developing countries.

They also provide international markets, which are needed because national markets are sometimes not large enough to support the investments necessary. They can initially provide technical staff to a new venture and train nationals to take over technological positions, assuming that the national educational systems produce enough scientists and engineers. Multinationals can also provide the management and capital needed to begin new business ventures and expand existing ventures.

The major role that multinationals play in providing technology for the development process makes them a national target, therefore, when concerns arise about technological dependence.

Because of their concern, developing countries in particular are searching for new ways to utilize technology to meet their national goals. Their objectives are to become more self-reliant, exert more control over the impact of technology on development (employment in particular), and lessen the costs of technology. Only limited resources are available for investment in technology and the training of technical personnel in most developing countries. Developing countries are, therefore, placing great emphasis on controlling the technological activities of multinationals to assure that they help meet national objectives.

Longer term, developing countries are beginning to develop national and regional strategies to improve their technological effectiveness and decrease their dependence on technology originating in developed countries and on multinational corporations in particular.

The Multinational Corporations Contributions to Development Through Technology Transfer

Before discussing the concern of governments in more detail, it is useful to review some of the contributions which multinational corporations have made to both developed and developing countries through the process of technology.

Developed Countries

Behrman in National Interests and the Multinational Enterprise,[3] has reviewed technological contributions of multinational enterprises in developed host countries. Examples of the benefits of technology transfer include:

> Accelerating mechanization of farming between 1938 and 1955 by raising tractor utilization by a factor of 8 in Britain (U.S. and Canadian agricultural machinery companies investments).
>
> Exploration of French oil reserves by seismic exploration techniques developed by a U.S. company (Exxon).
>
> Television advances in many countries by investments by Philips, a Dutch company
>
> Increases in productivity in British precision instruments and advanced instrumentation by U.S. investments.

Dunning's study[4] on the benefits of technology transfer into Europe indicated Europe's per capita real income had grown more rapidly than would have been the case without the transfer, and faster than that of the U.S. This occurred partly because: (1) New types of capital goods were introduced embodying technological improvements; (2) In 1950 Europe had limited capital equipment relative to the U.S.; and (3) Europe had increased capital per capita at a faster rate than the U.S. since 1950.

In a review article[5] on Japan's economic future, Henry Rosovsky emphasizes that a key element in Japan's unprecedented growth since 1950 has been foreign technology. Between 1950 and 1968, about 10,000 contracts were involved in this transfer and payments for technology exceeded $1.4 billion. Introduction of the technology permitted the modernization of old industries and the establishment of new industries under very favorable conditions. The purchase of cheap foreign technology avoided the need for Japan to duplicate at a higher cost technology already available from other nations.

In addition, the Japanese concentrated their expenditures on "winners", as the experience of others had demonstrated the most appropriate technology to meet their needs.

The Japanese were successful in using this approach not only because they had technologists to efficiently utilize the purchased technology but even more because of their high level and growth of investment, which was encouraged by high rates of return and a high savings rate.

Japan is less dependent on foreign technology today. According to Abegglen in Business Strategies for Japan[6] the proportion of agreements representing technology new to Japan and previously unlicensed dropped steadily from 70% in 1961 to only 33% in 1966.

Rosovsky believes that as Japan reaches technological parity in the 1970's continued high speed growth will become more difficult.

The United States has benefited significantly from the international flow of technology, to a large extent because of the effort devoted to matching advances in R&D, regardless of country of origin, to market needs. Examples of significance include:

Wankel engines: West German development.

Turbojet and purejet engines, which are essential to success of U.S. aircraft industry: cross licensing with British companies.

Memory cores for computers based on basic research in several European countries, Japan, and the United States.

Developing Countries

The benefits of technology supplied by multinational corporations to a number of developing countries are reviewed in an International Chamber of Commerce publication.[7] Examples are drawn from the petroleum industry, agriculture, pharmaceuticals, automobiles, farm machinery and other manufacturing concerns. Particular stress has been placed on the development and training of nationals in technical skills which has occurred.

Among the specific cases of significant technology transfers noted are:

The establishment of tobacco as a cash crop in developing countries.

Establishment of automobile factories in India.

Establishment of farm machinery plants in developing countries.

The history of technology transfer by General Electric into Brazil is reviewed in the National Planning Association (NPA) Case Study of the General Electric Company in Brazil.[8] This history demonstrates the longevity of the relationship between Brazil and GE and the variety of technology flows which have occurred. Highlights of these activities are noted below to illustrate the impact of a MNC on a developing country:

1883 - Brazil's first power plant for public street lighting.

1921 - First incandescent lamp plant. GE locomotives introduced.

1922 - Commercial refrigeration.

1930 - Transformer plant.

1936 - R&D lab.

1947 - Aluminum reduction mill.

1951 - Refrigerator plant.

Throughout this period GE supplied a wide variety of generators ranging up to 100,000 KW to meet general power needs.

Other NPA studies on Aluminum Limited in India, Firestone in Liberia, Creole in Venezuela, and Stan Vac in Indonesia demonstrate the wide variety of technological benefits, which have been introduced by MNCs.

Some additional contributions of technology to developing countries were discussed in the presentations by both Murphy of General Motors and Maisonrouge of IBM before the Group of Eminent Persons (UN), which studied the impact of multinational corporations on development and international relations. General Motors has developed a Basic Transportation Vehicle (BTV), which is a low-cost product requiring a minimum of sheet metal fabrication and designed with emphasis on ease of assembly, repair and low operating cost. The vehicle is now being produced in Malaysia, Portugal, Ecuador and the Philippines and will be made in other countries in the future. In Malaysia, the BTV sells for 30% less than an imported small pick-up truck. Maisonrouge noted the use of computers in Nigeria, Indonesia and Chile in areas such as economic analyses, oil exploration and census studies.

In a recent book, Private Foreign Investment in Development, G. L. Reuber[9] has reported on a number of aspects of the transfer of technology to developing countries. He reviews the number of product lines introduced by foreign manufacturing subsidiaries of 187 U.S. enterprises in the period 1901 to 1967. In the period between 1951 and 1967 more than 4,000 product lines were introduced. While information is limited, he believes that royalty fees generally represent a less expensive arrangement for obtaining technology than licensing fees.

Based on an extensive survey of sample projects, Reuber also notes that firms do adapt production, processing and quality control systems to local circumstances. In the case of production and processing methods, for example, out of a total of 78 projects studied adaptations occurred in 19 cases.

Concerns and Actions - Developed Countries

While the deepest concerns about dependence on multinational corporations for technology have been expressed by developing countries, developed countries are also sensitive on this issue.

In the U.S., multinational companies have been accused of weakening the country's international competitive position by exporting advanced American technology through foreign investment and licensing. The Hartke-Burke bill, was introduced with the aim of limiting the activities of multinationals abroad by restricting foreign investments and imports as well as unfavorable tax treatment of foreign income. It also had a provision to control the transfer of technology abroad. The bill would have authorized the President to prevent technology transfer through either foreign production or licensing if preventing the transfer would increase employment in the U.S. As noted in the introductory material, the U. S. is not the only nation which has demonstrated innovations in the technology area. Examples of the benefits of foreign technology in the automotive and computer fields have already been mentioned.

If the U.S. restricted technology flow, there would undoubtedly be restrictions by other countries. In areas such as environmental conservation research this might be especially damaging.

In addition, the results of basic research are conveyed largely by individual scientists and through scientific publications so that formal controls would not be as effective as might be anticipated.

As other nations can often provide technology packages, blocks on the transfer of U.S. technology would probably result in opportunities for other developed nations to sell their technology, capturing foreign markets and, on a secondary level, exports now associated with U.S. investment.

Moreover, a U.S. company which failed to produce a patented product abroad would face compulsory licensing or lapse of its patent rights in nearly all countries outside the United States. If its patent rights related to production processes, it would not even be protected by U.S. patent law for sales of that product in the U.S. market from unlicensed foreign production. Thus, preventing a U.S. company from transferring technology abroad through foreign production or licensing would only serve to harm the competitive position of that company, which has research costs built into its product (or licensing arrangements).

While some restrictions on U.S. foreign investment may be proposed, it seems that changes in tax treatment of foreign income will be emphasized and that technology movements will not be prevented.

The concern of Europeans about technological dependence was exemplified in The American Challenge.[10] The response of European nations has been directed primarily to strengthening R&D efforts by national companies and support has been directed in particular to the electronics and computer industries.

The European Economic Community has also urged concerted action to strengthen overall European capabilities in sectors such as data processing, telecommunications, transport, oceanography, metallurgy and environmental conservation. Euratom is a significant illustration of an organization approach to strengthening R&D. The French and British project on the supersonic Concorde illustrates that R&D is finally tested in the marketplace.

At present, it does not appear that any unusual action should occur in Europe which would block international transfer of technology.

Canada has passed tax legislation to encourage R&D in the past, but concerns have been expressed that affiliates of foreign companies have been most aggressive in responding to these incentives.

Canadian efforts now are aimed primarily at the general encouragement of R&D through the overall strengthening of Canadian-based corporations.

The Canadian government has also expressed concern about dependence on foreign R&D and the need for innovative activities to be strengthened in Canada. A new body, the Foreign Investment Review Agency has been formed headed by a commissioner of deputy minister's rank to study business proposals from non-Canadians, using the following criteria: the effect the new investment would have on competition and on economic activity including employment; the degree and significance of participation in the venture by Canadians, and the effect it would have in such areas as industrial efficiency and technological development for Canada. The last point is aimed at dispelling what Canadians call "the branch-plant mentality" that has accompanied much of foreign investment in Canada. Significantly, a government paper describing how the law will work noted that a potential investor's willingness "to locate new research and development" in this country could improve his chances.

Concerns of Less-Developed Countries (LDCs)

Developing countries are heavily dependent on developed countries for technology and, apart from general concern on this dependence, are, as noted earlier, specifically concerned about:

The level of payments for technology.

Conditions for licensing which are believed restrictive by less-developed countries.

The level of R&D conducted in their countries by MNCs based in developing countries.

The appropriateness of technology supplied, taking into account national goals and resources.

Because of these concerns, a number of developing countries have passed or are discussing laws or regulations which may seriously limit the international flow of technology. Questions on the appropriateness of technology supplied by developed countries, in particular with regard to impact on employment, were discussed at length at the UN meeting on MNCs, particular stress being placed on the appropriateness of technology to meet the needs of LDCs.

Payment for Technology

In most cases payments for technology from developing countries are made by affiliates of MNCs to the parent company in a developed country. Governments in reviewing these payments look at them in conjunction with dividends and other fees, which may be remitted and have raised questions on the overall payments being received by MNCs.

When considering alternatives, developing country governments raise the possibilities of obtaining technology on a licensing basis and apart from direct investment, to clearly isolate payments.

In discussions at the UN on MNCs, witnesses from developing countries suggested that LDCs might benefit from technical assistance from a central agency in negotiating fees.

The experience of Exxon, IBM and other companies generally shows that there is competition in meeting the technical needs of developing countries and that the negotiators of developing countries are well informed and skillful.

Restrictions on Licenses

A study by UNCTAD[11] presents an extensive list of restrictive business practices in the licensing field. There is, however, no commentary on the extent to which these practices currently pose problems for developing countries. Particular concerns are expressed on restrictions on exports, which make it impossible for the licensee to export products covered by the license to some countries.

When these agreements are between an affiliate and a parent company, there may be management reasons why unrestricted use of licensing is impractical. For example, Maisonrouge of IBM in discussing this subject at the UN hearings, pointed out the problems for IBM if salesmen representing several affiliates based in different countries called on a given customer. Other witnesses (Pfizer and GM) said that there were no restrictions on exports associated with these licensing arrangements with their national affiliates.

In cases where a company is licensing to a third party rather than an affiliate, there seem to be few cases where restrictions are imposed by licensors. Fees may, however, be higher if an unrestricted license is desired. In addition, a company may wish to limit licensing to the extent possible in areas where it is itself just developing markets.

A more detailed commentary on the UNCTAD study is presented in a Business and Industry Advisory Committee statement of May 1973.[12] This commentary draws extensively on a 1971 Memorandum of the International Chamber of Commerce. The BIAC report notes that:

> Very little concrete information is presented in the UNCTAD study.
>
> "So-called restrictive business practices can indeed sometimes be unwarranted. However in other cases they are a necessary condition for the making of investments on the starting of commercial or industrial activities."
>
> Each case must be carefully analyzed to determine impact on a developing country.

<u>R&D in Less-Developed Countries</u>

As discussed in the beginning of this paper, the overall level of R&D in developing countries is low and it is true that MNCs conduct only limited amounts of research in developing countries. It is unlikely that MNCs will sponsor significantly higher levels in the near future for economic and other reasons noted below.

In the petroleum process research area for example, technical programs are very expensive often involving operating expenditures of millions of dollars and large pilot plants which may cost $5 to $10 million. In Exxon, most pilot plant work is centralized in a location in the U.S.

In addition, major R&D efforts can generally only be undertaken in areas where: technical experts in a variety of fields are available for employment; universities provide opportunities for the staff of business organizations to be exposed to new technical developments; and, support services are available in areas such as instrumentation.

<u>Equity of the Patent System</u>

Some questions have even been raised on the equity of the patent system for LDCs. While there may be individual instances in which problems have occurred, it is difficult to imagine risk of the high expenditures now required for R&D if the potential rewards now available to the innovator were removed.

Appropriateness of Technologies

Developing countries have also raised questions on the appropriateness of technology considering their stage of development. The question also arises on whether less advanced technology utilizing a heavy labor component would be more appropriate than advanced technology requiring significant amounts of capital and less labor.

While accepting that some types of technologies may be inappropriate at a given stage in a country's development (i.e., motorcycles or motorbikes may be more appropriate than autos), generally investments which increase gross national products should benefit all members of a society if governmental policies in the area of taxation and infrastructure development are directed to meeting social needs. It is, of course, vital that new technology be introduced in an orderly manner, taking into consideration economic and social displacements which may occur.

In determining the type of technology which is most appropriate, governments should consider their long-term goals and broad economic policies and not only immediate impact on employment. For example, if export markets are important or programs are underway to determine the resources potential of a country, the most modern technology available will probably be needed. Governments should then outline their goals to corporations in negotiations to determine if there are common interests to establish a mutually profitable arrangement. In the UN discussion on multinationals, spokesmen of IBM stated that in their experience governments of developing countries wanted the best technology available.

Concerns and Actions - Intergovernmental Organizations

Both the Organization for Economic Cooperation and Development and the United Nations have studies underway on international investment and multinational enterprises. The UN has recently formed a Commission on Transnational Corporations, and the OECD has recently formed a new Committee to coordinate its existing efforts in this field. In addition to broad overview responsibilities, both of these groups have noted in their work agendas the need for codes of conduct or guidelines for behavior to guide the relations between multinational corporations and governments. Because of the concerns expressed by governments on technology transfer this is an area which probably would be treated in a code or set of guidelines.

In earlier studies on transnational corporations the UN (ECOSOC) had formed a Group of Eminent Persons to study the impact of multinational corporations on development and on international relations. The report of the Group[13] included a chapter on technology, which presented several recommendations of particular concerns to multinational corporations. They included host country:

> Evaluation of suitability of products to meet local needs.
>
> Screening of technology to be introduced.
>
> Requirements that MNCs make reasonable contributions to product and process technology needed in the nation or region.

In addition:

> Revisions of patent systems, in particular to reduce licensing costs.
>
> Exploration of ways of obtaining technology - separate from foreign investment.

Detailed comments by the USA-Business and Industry Advisory Committee to the OECD[14] on these recommendations are presented in Table I. More detailed comments are presented in the ICC Paper on the UN Report.[15]

The United Nations Conference on Trade and Development (UNCTAD) has done work in the area of transfer of technology and is now considering development of a code to guide technology transfer.[16] Adaptation of the code as now proposed would pose serious problems to multinational corporations now engaged in technology transfer. A number of governments of developed countries, including the U.S., have developed rather extensive commentaries on the problems raised by this code.

The pressure for change in the technology transfer process have also been expressed more recently in the UN Charter of Economic Rights and Duties of States endorsed by the UN General Assembly in December 1974 and by a statement of sovereigns and heads of states of the members of the Organization of Petroleum Exporting Countries at a meeting in Algiers on March 4-5, 1975. Article 13 of the UN Charter states in part:

TABLE I

USA-BIAC Comments on Recommendations in Report of Group of Eminent Persons on Technology Area

Recommendations	Comments
Host countries should evaluate suitability of products to meet local needs.	Raises the question of determination of suitability by free market forces versus state planning. This suggests that state planning is preferable to market mechanism in determining product needs of a country. While recognizing key role of governments in overall economic planning, experience indicates many problems in detailed product decision through state planning. Market mechanism has demonstrated flexibility and relatively rapid response to meet expressed needs. Depending on size of economies this could be major administrative problem.
Host countries should screen technology to be introduced. Appropriateness UN assistance.	Require very careful definition of LDC plans and goals. Replaces market mechanism by government planning. Assumes very strong administrative capabilities. Restriction of technology could lower the level of efficiency of MNC operations as well as decrease investment itself. This should be a matter to be decided by each host country, not an international issue; already some countries (e.g. in Latin America) are adopting a restrictive stance vis-a-vis technology transfers which could well inhibit this essential flow.

Recommendations	Comments
Host countries should require MNCs to make reasonable contribution to product and process technology needed by nation or region. Some R&D in affiliate allows export of affiliate technology.	In discussing this point it is necessary to carefully define what is meant by R&D. MNCs do provide product and process technology to host countries through transfer of know-how, training of local personnel. Generally not practical to do R&D in affiliates. High costs associated with R&D make it necessary to centralize.
International organizations should work to revise patent system and develop system where cost of technology to LDCs can be reduced.	This recommendation addressed to international organizations, not MNCs. DCs spend more than $40 billion a year on R&D, LDCs less than $2 billion. Costs must be judged in this perspective. Present patent system is basic element to product and process development.
World Patent Bank should be established.	Patents only one factor in use of technology. Know-how often more critical. Patents are basic to the free enterprise system and are held by private citizens who in most countries could not be legally compelled to share them.

Recommendations	Comments
Host countries should explore alternate ways of importing technology--separate from foreign investment.	This is already being done. Must be recognized that alternative methods of importing technology may prove more costly ultimately to host country. Effectiveness of approach will not be judged in the marketplace. In many cases believe MNCs may not sell technology at low price which may be expected by LDCs. Senator Jacob Javits, in his comments on the report, says, "It is certainly worth examining alternative means of acquiring technology, although it should be pointed out that what is actually reinforcing the position of the multinational corporation is two facts. First, technology becomes obsolete fairly rapidly and a constant supply of fresh technology is essential. Second, know-how concerning the capability of producing efficiently is much more than the technology which patents protect."
International agencies should assist.	Usually various technologies are available, but always there is one that is the best; it cannot be had on dictated terms.

"All States should cooperate in exploring with a view to evolving further internationally accepted guidelines or regulations for the transfer of technology taking fully into account the interests of developing countries."

The OPEC declaration emphasizes the need for acceleration of the development process through adequate and timely transfer of modern technology and removal of the obstacles which slowed the utilization and integrating of technology

As indicated above, the OECD has extensive studies underway on a number of issues under the general heading of international investment and multinational enterprises. In an effort to better understand technology transfer the OECD is now sponsoring studies of the transfer of technology process in the computer industry, the pharmaceutical industry, and the food processing industry.

The major objective of the OECD work is to develop a better understanding of technology transfer in anticipation of the possible development of guidelines for technology transfer. Because of recent OECD interest in developing overall guidelines for international investment and multinational enterprise, it may be necessary for the OECD to prepare some guidelines on technology transfer before their basic studies are completed.

The Business and Industry Advisory Committee to the OECD has therefore recently formed a Working Party to provide assistance to the OECD in this work. It is chaired by Duncan Davies, General Manager, Research & Development of Imperial Chemical Industries.

Professors C. A. Michalet, J. Dunning, and M. Castagne now plan on approaching MNCs through a questionnaire mechanism. The Working Party stresses the need for personal contact to better understand technology transfer, and representatives of the three industries to be studied stressed their willingness to cooperate in the OECD work.

In addition, the Business and Industry Advisory Committee (BIAC) Working Party will undertake the following:

Preparation of a paper on the conditions necessary for technology transfer.

Some case studies of actual specific technology transfer. These would be conducted by Professor F. R. Bradbury, University of Stirling, Stirling, Scotland.

Some suggested guidelines for technology transfer, possibly based on the Technology Section of the ICC Guidelines.

This is considered important by BIAC because, as noted earlier, the OECD has begun work on guidelines for MNCs which would include a section on technology. The OECD recognizes the difficulty of the exercise and would welcome any guidance on realistic guidelines, which we could supply.

Conclusion

Because of the increased interest of governments in the technology transfer process, it is going to be extremely important for MNCs to work with governments and intergovernmental groups in developing a clear understanding of the nature of the technology transfer process, the conditions necessary for technology transfer, and the constructive actions by either MNCs or governments which can improve the technology transfer process while protecting the legitimate interest of corporations involved and host and home governments. Because of the complex nature of the process, it will be necessary in the coming years for all parties involved to contribute to meaningful dialogues to set a firm foundation for action.

REFERENCES

1. Science Indicators 1972 - Report of the National Science Board 1973 - National Science Board - National Science Foundation. Free World: $42 billion; U.S.: $27.3 billion; European Economic Community: more than $10 billion; and, U.S.S.R.: about $14 billion.

2. Gaps in Technology - Organization for Economic Co-Operation and Development - 1970. More than one country has received credit for some innovations.

3. National Interests and the Multinational Enterprise - Tensions Among the North Atlantic Countries by Jack N. Behrman - 1969.

4. "Technology, U.S. Investment & European Economic Growth" by J. Dunning in The International Corporation, Edited by C. P. Kindleberger - 1970.

5. July/August 1973 CHALLENGE article by Henry Rosovsky on "Japan's Economic Future", page 6.

6. Business Strategies for Japan by James Abegglen - 1970.

7. The International Corporation and the Transfer of Technology By the International Chamber of Commerce - April 1972.

8. The General Electric Company in Brazil by Theodore Geiger - Ninth Case Study in an NPA Series on United States Business Performance Abroad - 1961.

9. Private Foreign Investment in Development, G. L. Reuber, Clarendon Press, Oxford, 1973.

10. The American Challenge by Jean-Jacques Servan-Schreiber, 1968.

11. Restrictive Business Practices in Relation to the Trade and Development of Developing Countries - Report by the ad hoc Group of Experts United Nations Conference on Trade and Development 26 April 1973.

12. Private Investment and Restrictive Business Practices in Developing Countries - Statement to Development Assistance Countries by Business and Industry Advisory Committee, May 1973.

13. Report of the Group of Eminent Persons to Study the Impact of Multinational Corporations on the Development Process and on International Relations (United Nations publication, Sales No. E.74.II.A.5).

14. A Review of the Report of the Group of Eminent Persons to Study the Role of Multinational Corporations on Development and on International Relations by the USA-BIAC Committee on International Investment and Multinational Enterprise, November, 1974. See Table I.

15. International Chamber of Commerce Comments on Part 1 of the Report to the United Nations Economic and Social Council of the Group of Eminent Persons on Multinational Enterprises, Document No. 191/79, June 10, 1974; ICC Committee on Part 2 of the Report of the UN ECOSOC of the Group of Eminent Persons on Multinational Enterprises, Document No. 191/81, June 24, 1974.

16. The Pugwash Code is a major input into this discussion.

HOW TO OBTAIN FOREIGN TECHNOLOGY AT MINIMUM COST, OR FREE

Win Straube

Pegasus International Corporation
New York, N.Y.

Is it possible to get something for nothing?

Yes, when the fish snaps at the lure and bites into the hook instead ... Today's lures for fish often are marvelous technological contraptions.

Which raises my first question: What is "technology?" That means the technology we are talking about? Is it applied science, industrial science? A systematic knowledge of the industrial arts? I think that we should define this, for otherwise you and I might be thinking of different things and attaching different values.

Someone defined "technology" as the science of getting things done easier. I would say that it is the human attempt of overcoming natural obstacles by the use of natural forces, such as in mechanical, electrical, aerodynamic and other sciences developed by man.

Successful attempts of harnessing or improving on nature are often visible in the form of patents or know-how. Industrialized countries seem to have amassed this type of technology, while the less developed nations would like to. Which shows, if we examine the words we use daily, that "development" is often equated with the "possession" of technology. In turn, "development" is equated with "progress". And who wouldn't want to make progress?

"Technology" nowadays is often used as a glamor word, something which is desirable, which makes those who have it look successful and strong. But are they really?

Which brings me to question number two, or a whole bunch of questions: Is this what we are after, i.e., technology? Or: What is it we are after? And why? Is it desirable?

No recent war has been won by a superiority in technology. Otherwise Nazi Germany would have won World War II with its flying bombs. The Americans would have been victorious in Vietnam.

Professor George M. Foster of the University of California at Berkley writes in "Traditional Cultures; and the Impact of Technological Change" (Harper & Row, Publishers, New York)

> "Americans wear cultural blinders, of which we usually are ignorant, which prevent us from fully understanding the needs and desires of the people we wish to help, and which make us insensitive to the full range of economic, social, and cultural consequences resulting from narrowly conceived development programs."

He also writes:

> "There can be no such thing as technological development in isolation. Perhaps the use of the term sociotechnological development would clarify our thinking, for development is much more than the overt acceptance of material and technical improvements. It is a cultural, social, and psychological process as well. Associated with every technical and material change there is a corresponding change in the attitudes, the thoughts, the values, the beliefs, and the behaviour of the people who are affected by the material change."

Before giving you some answers to where you can find technology for little cost or at no cost at all, I'd like you to ask yourself a very basic question - regardless of how marvelous the technology you are after may be - :

<u>Is there a need for it?</u>

Where is the possession or mastery of this technology going to lead you? Is this really where you want to go?

Obviously, technology is no cure-all. Applied with common sense it may be of great help. No doubt it brings about change. It is up to you and me as the change agents to make it a desirable change.

This question of value, however, human value, ought to be asked much more often, at least in my opinion, and if you wish you may want to read some books on this like the following:

Richard Buckminster Fuller: Operating Manual for Spaceship Earth. or

The Limits of Growth - by the Club of Rome. or

"The Future of the Future" by John McHale

and other books such as by Marshall McLuhan and others.

Which brings me back to the message of my medium:

In 1964 already the U.S. Patent Office alone, since its inception, had issued more than 3 million patents. The Scientific Library of the Patent Office contains over 100,000 volumes of scientific and technical books in various languages, about 70,000 bound volumes of periodicals devoted to science and technology, the official jounals of foreign patent offices, and over 7 million copies of foreign patents. Well over 2 million U.S. patents expired already 15 years ago.

From this you can conclude - and experience confirms - :

Many technological discoveries are never used and go unnoticed or are carefully hidden as corporate or national secrets.

Which could lead us to a condemnation of the patent system. And I for one am not convinced that the international patent system as it exists today is really benefiting humanity. In my opinion the patent laws of today are based on the thinking of the middle ages. Then monopolies were granted as a favor by royal consent or otherwise, and later by governments, in return for original knowledge made public. Today invention is no longer the sole privilege of some fortunate few who by their genius came up with new ideas such as a lightbulb, the telephone, or the like. Whole armies of well trained scientists and engineers work on the discovery or production of a new invention or "technology", i.e., intricate space equipment and instruments, and their parts and processes. No longer are simple mechanical and chemical secrets being discovered, but rather, systematic efforts are being made to come up with better products to serve predetermined purposes. And when you do come up with a product, there can seldom be a patent for it in the old sense of our patent laws. Nor would there be or should there be. Patents, in most instances, are no longer necessary. Maybe no longer desirable. But I don't think, that we need this justification in our efforts to obtain technology at little cost or absolutely free of charge.

What we <u>do</u> need, is a plan of where to look and how to go about it.

Statistics show that most technology comes from and goes to industrialized nations. In other words: Most technology is being generated by countries like the United States, Germany, Japan and others. At the same time countries of this type are most active in acquiring technology from each other. This means that if you are looking for technology, don't try in Nepal or Pakistan. Go to the most industrialized nations.

To tie in with the plan we are developing here, you may want to pinpoint the country or countries of your search instead of running all over the world. Some nations have longstanding expertise in specific areas, like the U.S.S.R. and the U.S. in oil field equipment, Japan and Germany in steelmaking equipment, Australia and Switzerland in windpowered generators etc. This way you are able to limit your search geographically, which may save a little cost right there.

Finding the specific sources will be the next step.

Your local library may be a good start.

The United Nations publish the so called UNITAR NEWS. Their Volume 6, No. 4 of 1974, for instance, is an exclusive issue on Technology and Development. The United Nations have depository libraries all over the world where United Nations documentation is available for consultation. In the U.S., as an example, all U.N. publications are available in many libraries across the country, including in my home town of Princeton, New Jersey at the Princeton University Library. Chances are that it is equally accessible to you in or near your home or place of work.

The United Nations publishes a lot of technological information which is often free or available at very nominal charges. Here are just a few recent examples:

A book by Walter A. Chudson on "The International Transfer of Commercial Technology to Developing Countries."

"Transfer of Technology from Japan to Developing Countries" by Terutomo Ozawa

"International Transfer of Automotive Technology to Developing Countries" by Jack Baranson

Also available are specific case studies, like on:

The Semiconductor Industry - Economics of Offshore Assembly.

Technology Transfer in the Pharmaceutical Industry by Lawrence H. Wortzel

Communications, Computers and Automation for Development by Ithiel de Sola Pool, Philip Stone, Alexander Szalai

The U.N. has other books also, like:

"The Search for New Methods of Technical Cooperation" by Harold Caustin.

A "Manual on International Procurement" (This is being published in English, French, and Spanish.) The author is Gösta Westring.

On another related subject:

"Emigration of Highly Skilled Manpower from Developing Countries" by Gregory Henderson. This book is already in its third printing. No wonder. Apparently many people want to find out where the brain drain is flowing to. No doubt it discloses the destination of these pilgrims on their way to the source of technology.

One more example of what is available from the United Nations:

A technical paper on "The Acquisition of Technology from Multinational Corporations." And you'll be amazed how much can be obtained from them.

To summarize source #1: The United Nations are a wealthy, readily available and inexpensive source of technology information. You can find most of the U.N. information in libraries in your home countries or wherever you travel. Here are just a few more super-national or international organizations which can help you in locating and supplying technology:

The Food and Agriculture Organization of the U.N. with its own Documentation Center.

And another one:

The Organization for Economic Cooperation and Development in Paris.

From these super-national sources of technology information let us go to the national sources. There are of course many more, and they come in all types and sizes.

Obviously, they vary according to the type of society we are dealing with. Most countries have Patent Offices which are open to anyone. Most Patent Offices not only store inventions and technology information regarding their own country, but also those of other industrially advanced nations. So, for instance, are U.S. patents available to Russian scientists through the U.S.S.R. Committee for Inventions and Discoveries attached to the Council of Ministers of the U.S.S.R.

Many nations, like Canada to pick only one, maintain a National Research Council, whose purpose it is to help domestic industries develop today's technology. In the U.S. a similar organization is called the Federal Council for Science and Technology. In other countries this type of government sponsored research organizations has other names. To use the United States as an example, however, other organizations such as the U.S. Bureau of Standards would be a good source also. So would other agencies of the U.S. Government itself. Actually, in America, the Government owns a wealth of patents and technology know-how which it is anxious to have used. Often, this technology is available free or at a nominal charge only.

In this category might be patents and know-how data, for instance, coming from NASA, the National Aeronautics and Space Administration. The American space flight program produced a lot of technological fall-out usable for down to earth applications.

Staying with the U.S. for a moment, the U.S. Office of Economic Opportunity maintains Community Action Programs which, again, make technology available for suitable projects.

Everybody may have heard of A.I.D., i.e., the U.S. Agency for International Development, located in Washington, D.C.

Also well known are the Technical Assistance Programs coming out of Washington.

Not only do national bodies such as Patent Offices, Research Councils, Ministries dealing with inventions and the like maintain extensive libraries on technology but they may also be able to help you with technology projects. Your local library may have some useful material, like Adrian Hope's book under the title "Why didn't I think of it first?" or Kenneth O. Kessler's "The successful inventor's guide".

Here is another national source in the U.S., which is similar to a library: The Technical Assistance Information Clearing House which publishes a Directory of American voluntary and non-profit agencies interested in technical assistance.

Other countries have similar organizations. Often these type of efforts are backed up by International Development Banks to make the money available for the exploitation of a technology, most often on favorable long terms at low interest rates. Instead of giving you a list of these financial institutions, which would take me into another subject, here is only one example:

> Die Kreditanstalt für Wiederaufbau in Frankfurt/Main, Germany which makes loans to developing countries.

Similar organizations as mentioned here are available under different names in most highly industrialized countries.

The third group of sources after super- or international and national, are sources which are mostly national, yet not necessarily supported by governments, but by specific interest groups or individuals.

Sources of this type are: newspapers, periodicals, trade and manufacturers associations, universities, research institutions, foundations, and individual companies. A detailed list of those would be too long here. Therefore merely a few typical examples:

As regards Universities I would suggest that you read a book by Archie M. Palmer: "University Patent Policies".

As an example from industry let me tell you about the so called "General Electric Programs for Productivity and Growth" which are a service in which General Electric makes its expertise available - at a price - to anybody interested. At a fraction of the original investment you can take advantage of major expenditures in research and development. For more information, under no obligation, about how you can gain from one or all of these programs, write to:

> Technology Marketing Operation
> General Electric Company
> Building 5-323
> 1 River Road
> Schenectady, N.Y. 12345

General Electric also has a subsidiary called:

> Business Development Services, Inc.
> at 570 Lexington Avenue in New
> York City.

That company supplies funding for the development and exploitation of inventions which General Electric considers useful. In other words: The company helps new inventors to get on their feet, provided the invention promises success. It helps in establishing new ventures and provides financial and managerial help, if necessary.

Well, I could give you a whole list of companies which BDS helped to put into business. Here are only two of them:

Solid State Scientific, Inc. in Montgomerville, Pennsylvania, which manufactures solid state CMOS integrated circuits and high frequency - high power transistors. At present SSSI circuits are used primarily in solid state watches, displays and other electronically controlled features of various types of equipment, including automobiles.

Spectrotherm Corporation of Santa Clara, California. The initial product of that company was a medical thermograph which is used by radiologists for the early detection of breast cancer.

So much to that.

To classify all sources of technology I would like to group them into two categories:

(1) Those that supply technology free or at minimal cost. I will call these the "open gallery" type. This means that you are free to come and look and negotiate for what you want to have.

(2) The sources which do <u>not</u> supply technology free or at minimal cost. They either ask outrageous amounts for their technology or flatly refuse to supply anything, nor wish to cooperate in one form or another. I will call them the "closed gallery" type, for they are not admitting you to their show or do so only after you have paid an excessive fee.

I gave you a sampling of the "open gallery" sources. Now let us deal with the "closed galleries", for also here are methods and means available of obtaining technology free or at a minimal cost or even to change a "closed gallery" into an "open" source.

Let us assume that a closed gallery type company or individual does not want to part with any technology - at least as far as you have heard. What do you do?

Well, never exclude the simplest approach: Just ask for it. After all, the owner may be flattered, he may have changed his mind or for whatever the reason, there always is a chance in change of attitude and circumstances.

Assuming the answer is NO, and assuming the information is patented, you can ask youself: What is the hurry? Why not wait 17 years and then get it for free?

Well, you may be in a hurry after all. It is often said that patents are only invitations to a lawsuit. In fact, patents are honored without suit by others in far greater number than they are ignored and infringed. Nevertheless, one important product of the patent system is the causing of others to design around inventions.

This opens a few avenues:

(a) The economics of a patent may not warrant defending it. This could be your opening.

(b) You may be able to improve on the improvement or otherwise design around it, thus completely avoiding the patent.

In that case make sure, however, that you really move forward. Consider that especially in North America manufacturers often follow a theory of "planned obsolescence". I've seen many times that would-be competitors copied old models of an industry leader all the way with mistakes and shortcomings in the product which could have been avoided with a little forethought, yet made the model unsaleable or too expensive the minute the original manufacturer came out with his improved version.

As an example: A major American pharmaceutical manufacturer developed a new product and obtained patents on it. It was a combination of vitamins and antibiotics which, as an additive to chicken feed, made chicken stay healthy and grow bigger. The product soon became an excellent seller around the world. It didn't take long and a foreign manufacturer copied the formula, even put a similar name on his product, and started competing with the American company. In the meantime, however, the American pharmaceutical manufacturer had readied step number two: which was a far higher concentrate of the same product, and this time in liquid form. While the original invention had been in granular form and rather bulky, a few drops of the new high power version would replace a bag full of the "old" product. And "old" is what it suddenly was. Especially in international markets where freight costs greatly add to overall costs, the liquid highly condensed version was easy to ship at a fraction of the cost of the original product. The manufacturer who had merely copied that old product now found himself with an outdated manufacturing plant and was forced to sell his suddenly insufficient copy at below cost in order to stay competitive. Eventually he went out of this line at a considerable loss in money, effort and prestige.

Let us continue looking for other open avenues.

Do not overlook that many patents have been abandoned, not necessarily by design, but because maintenance fees were not paid or for other reasons.

A little legal research may pay off: Look for mistakes which make the patent invalid like: publication before the patent was granted or the transmission of patentable information for the manufacture, sale, lease or use of the invention before actual granting of the patent.

Many companies do not obtain patents in all countries because they are expensive to maintain, restricting themselves to a few major countries only. This can open up a number of markets for you - cost free.

In analyzing the avenues open to you when the source of technology does <u>not</u> cooperate, there are three approaches:

(1) Economic considerations, like cost factors: Can you produce at the same rate or cheaper? If so, a joint venture with the owner of the technology might even make sense to him, or you may become his subcontractor. Kodak, for instance, made the Polaroid film for Polaroid for many years - at a healthy profit.

(2) Improved design or new art. One way I have seen this accomplished in a classic shortcut was when the research assistant was hired away from the professor who won the Nobel prize, and then improved on his master. The same or similar end results, of course, can be achieved without raising questions of ethics by separate, parallel or completely independent own efforts on your part.

(3) Legal efforts.

I am not trying to give you legal advice here. For that you should consult your patent attorney. I also suggest that you avoid litigation. It is expensive and gets you nowhere. The Professor who coined the word LASER (Light Amplification by Simulated Emission of Radiation) found this out the hard way. He holds various laser patents. With practically equal patent claims litigated in several major countries, about 50% were won and 50% lost.

Regardless of the logic and argument of your presentation, you are going to win some, lose some. In any case, you'll lose a lot of time.

Best of all will be a combined effort of businessman, engineer and attorney in designing the most effective approach for you.

Under certain circumstances you can safely ignore a patent, as Tom Arnold and Frank S. Vaden III point out in their book "Invention Protection for Practicing Engineers" published by Barnes & Noble Inc., in New York. Here are some more quotes from their book: (quotes abbreviated by me)

Ignoring a patent may be perfectly justified for a number of reasons. First, it may be determined that the patentholder is not by tradition aggessive in prosecuting patent infringement suits and therefore is not likely in your instance to proceed. Also, if the infringement is tenuous and only an arguable one, it is likely that the patent owner may never become aware of the infringement activity. Furthermore, even if the patent owner is aware, he may not evaluate chances of successfully enforcing the patent optimistically and therefore may never pursue the infringement issue. The best course may be to ignore the problem. However, the extent of exposure and the arguable defenses should be considered in combination with any overt decision to ignore.

A decision to ignore may also be made if the patent to be infringed is nearly expired. In such cases, the activity prior to the actual expiration of the troublesome patent might be so small that the patentee would not vigorously pursue the infringement issue.

Seeking a license, of course, may be one way of avoiding a patent. Obtaining an immunity from an infringement suit via a license may not be very expensive. Rather than push a patent-infringement issue to trial, it may well be the economic and sensible decision for both parties to enter into a license agreement based on a resonable royalty.

Sometimes the profit margin is very small, and practically makes the license route out of the question. However, some patent owners will grant a paid-up immunity from suit which is not based on sales and, if granted, would once and for all remove the patent as a danger. Also, perhaps a trade could be worked out, such as a cross-license.

Finally, if a patent is ever brought into court, the decision that the patent is or is not valid and infringed is going to be decided by a nontechnical judge. That is, the judge is very likely not to have engineering or technical competency and may completely miss in his judgment. There is no way to be absolutely certain, only the odds against infringement can be determined.

At this point let me mention a book by Victor C. Ferkiss "Technological Man: The Myth and the Reality". He says in there "The future will be like the present, only more so."

Or another book by D.G. Brennan, mathematician and expert on national security problems, and a member of the Hudson Institute, writing in "Toward the Year 2018": "Perhaps the most striking characteristic of modern civilization is not its technology, but the rate at which the technology is changing".

And this is, in my opinion, where your best opportunities lie: Change and the rate of change make possible advancement, shifts in technology. Yesterday's closed gallery becomes tomorrow's open gallery and vice versa.

Technology is available in abundance, and it can be shared in abundance. To get it for little cost or for free means to apply your own ingenuity instead of paying for somebody else's. The successful effort requires expertise from different schools as I have shown, possibly also from different geographic areas and cultural backgrounds. Pegasus International Corporation, the company which I head, is such a team of professionals, with offices around the world to help others in obtaining and transferring technology. I will be happy to go into more detail on this and related subjects regarding specific requirements if you wish to see me or write me separately on this.

I do hope that this brief presentation gives you an overview of the essentials to pursue in obtaining domestic and foreign technology at minimal cost or free.

You have to do your research ... of the market place, the potential for your product or technology you want to acquire, the economics, engineering and legal obstacles, then develop your approach and take your chances. If you are creative and resourceful you can form new markets, build new industries. But as my advice to inventors is to invent only what other people will want, my advice to you is to make sure that the technology you are going to obtain will provide the benefits which people will want and will be able and willing to pay for.

AN EVALUATION OF TECHNOLOGY TRANSFER IN UNDER-DEVELOPED COUNTRIES

Schiller Thebaud

National Center for Scientific Research
Grenoble, France

Studies made regarding scientific and technical research in under-developed countries show that these countries generally have less than 1.5 researchers for each 10,000 inhabitants, that is, 6.6 times less than a country like France. What's more, the majority of the research done in these countries is of a theoretical nature and does not generally lead to the perfection of new technologies which could contribute to their development. Consequently the "non-traditional" technologies they utilize come from industrialized countries. It might be useful to "evaluate" these technologies imported by under-developed countries. But beforehand, we must define the terminology to be used here.

The concept of technology

The concept of technology is traditionally used to designate the incorporation of scientific techniques into machines, tools, and more generally, manufactured products. In this context, the concept of technology designates a well-defined relationship between the activities of research - development and production of material goods.

In a larger context, technology is not limited to the incorporation of scientific knowledge into manufactured objects, but extends to the applications of this knowledge to non-productive domains such as health, education, etc. This is the definition Harvey Brooks uses when he defines technology as an ensemble of "codified and reproducible ways of doing things derived from national principles."[1] This definition of technology includes not only the applications of exact and natural sciences but also of social and human sciences. In addition, it includes the material (hardware) as well as the intellectual (software) applications of science.

For our purposes, we will define technology as a codified and programmed know-how, which depends on scientific knowledge. This know-how is the expression of a relationship between the system of research - development in which scientific knowledge is produced and other social systems to which this knowledge is applied. This is why we are justified in speaking not only about industrial and agricultural technology but also about medical technology or educational technology. It is advisable, however, to emphasize that technology which is "incorporated" into material goods plays an essential role in a society, because it is often a necessary condition for technological progress in spheres of non-productive activity.

The concept of transfer of technology

For several years there has been much discussion about "transfer of technology." The technological progress realized in certain domains such as, for example, the military in the United States, has suggested the idea of a transfer of this progress to other sectors of society. Thus, the definition proposed by Brooks for whom a transfer of technology is a "process by which science and technology are diffused throughout human activity."[2]

This author also distinguishes between two types of transfers of technology, vertical transfer and horizontal transfer. By vertical transfer Brooks means the process by which new scientific knowledge is incorporated into a technology and then into a product or process, or the process by which several existing technologies are combined to give birth to a new technology. By horizontal transfer, he means the adaptation of an existing technology to a new use such as, for example, the transformation of a military plane for civilian air transport. This topographical metaphor used by Brooks to describe the process of transfers of technology has been adopted by E. Jantch in his effort to define "the space of transfers of technology."[3]

The concept of transfer of technology is sometimes used in a much more narrow sense to designate the process by which technology is diffused among nations to give birth to new methods of production or to new products.[4] This definition of the term "transfer of technology" includes, in fact, very different phenomena. It can be a question of a sale of technology by one firm to another, in which case we must study the mechanisms by which prices for this technology are formed. It can also be a question of a true transfer of technology within a firm between, for example, the parent company and one of its subsidiaries. Regarding importation of technologies by under-developed companies, one should, therefore, make a distinction between international commerce of technologies and international transfers of technologies between parent companies and their subsidiaries located in the Third World.

The origin of technologies imported by under-developed countries

The technologies imported by under-developed countries originate in the practices of the firms of industrialized countries, practices which depend more and more on work done in their research laboratories. If one wishes to know the conditions in which the technologies imported by the under-developed countries are produced, one must analyze the principal characteristics of research in industrialized countries.

In most industrialized countries the research which is carried out by private enterprise absorbs more than half of the money set aside for research-development. The following table confirms this:

Table I

Percentage of Gross National Expenditure for R-D
Carried out by Private Enterprise

United States	66.4
Belgium	69.0
United Kingdom	67.3
Germany	65.9
Sweden	65.6
Japan	64.6
Austria	63.5
Italy	62.6
The Netherlands	55.5
Norway	51.7
France	49.5

Consequently it is a situation radically different from that of the under-developed countries where there is generally no research in industry. In addition, it must be pointed out that part of the research done outside of private enterprise also affects industry. This is the case, for example, with the costly research carried out in the laboratories of certain American federal agencies, such as the Atomic Energy Commission

(AEC) whose results are used by private industry. Indeed, the strategy of the USAEC consists of carrying out all research which will have medium and long-term effects, leaving for private enterprise the task of carrying out research which is profitable in the short-term.[5]

The enormous potential of private and public industrial research which presently exists in developed countries allows them to produce new technologies at a rate unprecedented in history, and to accumulate a know-how which places them in a monopolistic position vis-a-vis the under-developed countries on the international market of technologies.

This monopolistic position is all the stronger in that the research activities of developed countries are concentrated in the large enterprises. The following table shows that average expenditure for research and development per enterprise varies in direct proportion with the size of the enterprise:

Table 2

Average Expenditures for R-D per Enterprise According to the Size of the Enterprise (in Thousands of Dollars)

	USA 1964	France 1963	Belgium	Sweden 1964	Japan 1964
Enterprises employing less than 500 persons	54	142	85	3	14
500 - 900		397	122	98	72
1000 - 1999		620	187	505	
2000 - 4999	1,441	1,028	1,078	912	199
5000 - 9999		3,082	1,659	2,152	727
10,000 and more	27,700	9,896	3,195	7,419	3,833

In addition, studies regarding this problem done by the OECD have brought out the fact that in the United States, firms employing more than 5,000 workers represent 3% of the firms which have R-D activities and make 87% of the total expenditure for R-D. In France firms employing more than 5,000 workers represent 12% of the firms which have R-D activities and make 65% of the total expenditures for R-D. On the other hand firms employing less than 1,000 workers represent 58% of the firms which do R-D, and only make 12% of the expenditures for R-D.

This concentration of research efforts in the large firms is even more significant if one considers it in relationship to the absolute and relative total of the expenditures for the R-D carried out by the firms. In fact, in the United States, 28 firms have expenditures for R-D of more than 100 million dollars, thus covering 62.7% of the total expenditures for the R-D done by firms. And, 130 firms have R-D expenditures of more than 10 million dollars, representing a total of 83.5% of the total research-development expenditures of the firms. In France there is no firm which has research-development expenditures totaling more than 100 million dollars. It is estimated that only 16 firms carry out R-D programs valued at more than 10 million dollars, thus covering 43.4% of the total R-D expenditures of the firms.

These figures prove that industrial R-D is strongly concentrated in the large firms. They also show that because of their size and their financial standing large American firms do more research-development than their European competitors.

We are presently witnessing the growing internationalization of large corporations, the majority of which are of American origin. It is clearly evident from the study of direct American investments abroad from 1950 to 1970 that the amount of direct American investments abroad went from 11.7 to 67.7 billion dollars, that is, an increase of about 578% in 20 years. On manufacturing industries alone, the number of direct US investments abroad went from 3.8 to 29.4 billion dollars during the same period as shown in Table 3

Table 3
Direct Foreign Investment in Manufacturing Industries, Millions $[6]

	1950	%	1966	%	1970
All regions	3,831	100	22,050	100	29,450
By region:					
Canada	1,897	49.5	7,674	34.8	9,389
Mexico	133	3.5	797	3.6	1,108
Argentine	161	4.2	652	3.0	789
Brazil	285	7.4	846	3.8	1,112
Europe	932	24.3	8,879	40.3	12,225
South Africa	44	1.1	271	1.2	2,029 (1)
India	16	0.4	118	0.5	143
Japan	5	0.1	333	1.5	639
Philippines	23	0.6	180	0.8	...
Australia	98	2.6	999	4.5	
Miscellaneous	237	6.3	1,283	6.0	2,016

(1) Australia, New Zealand and South Africa.

This movement towards internationalization is all the more remarkable in that large American firms make an increasingly larger part of their investments outside of the United States. Thus, the amount of installation and equipment expenditures made by subsidiaries of American firms in relationship to the total of US investments in manufacturing industries went from 19.9% in 1963 to 22.6% in 1966.

Since more than half of the research-development done in developed countries takes place in private enterprise, and since this research-development is strongly concentrated in the very large firms, we are witnessing an increasing internationalization of these firms, as well as an increasing suspicion that the world market for technology may be becoming oligopolistic and in many cases monopolistic.

In a large firm which has significant expenditures for research-development, the resulting new technologies may be transferred among its various subsidiaries. As soon as a new process or product appears in a unit of the large firm, it is likely to be communicated to other relevant units.[7] It is not the same when the large firm negotiates with another firm. In this case the new technology is sold or exchanged for another technology (cross licences).

In order to clearly understand this difference one must point out the principal forms which the international division of labor may presently assume. In fact, one can distinguish:

> the division of labor among firms, co-ordinated by markets.
>
> the division of labor within the firm co-ordinated by the head of the firm.

A firm which perfects a technology legally gains control of it through a patent, which that firm alone may use or whose use it alone may authorize. In the first sort of division of labor, the firm owning the technology transfers it from one unit to another due to the uniqueness of the firms ownership rights.

This is why, with respect to the import of technologies by under-developed countries it is necessary to distinguish between: (1) the case where an enterprise in an under-developed country buys a technology from another firm; (2) and the case where a subsidiary of a firm benefits from a transfer of technology on the part of the parent firm or another subsidiary of this company. It is evident that in the second case prices do not reflect the laws of the market but obey the total strategy of the multinational firm.

The concentration of industrial research in large corporations and their internationalization result in the modification of certain structures of international trade. During the years 1963-65 one could notice that a large number of the exports of manufactured products came from industries with a high density of research. In the United States, for example, exports by industries with a high density of research represented at this date 51.5% of the total exports for products manufactured in that country. During the same period this percentage was 47.2% for Germany, 41.9% for the United Kingdom and 30.3% for France.

The correlation between the volume of industrial research and that of exports of manufactured goods has also been brought out by Keesing. The same result has also been established by other authors according to whom the industries which carry out the essential industrial research in the United States are those which ensure the majority of US exports of manufactured goods.[8]

Table 4
Distribution of Research Outlay, of Sales, and of Exports in US Industry in 1962 in %

	Total Expenditures for R-D	No. of scientists and engineers in R-D	Sales	Exports
For 19 industries	100.0	100.0	100.0	100.0
5 industries with a very high density of research	89.4	85.3	39.1	72.0
14 other industries	10.6	14.7	60.9	28.0

The above table shows that, in a sampling of 19 industries five of them accounted for 89.4% of the total expenditures for research-development and 72% of the total number of exports. If this is true, one might think that industries with a high density of research are more competitive on world markets than those which set aside relatively fewer funds for research. Thus, the concentration of R-D in large firms which are, in general, multinational gives them what one might call "technological monopolies" on world markets. In other words, the more research a firm does, the greater possibility it has to dominate the international market in its field.

As the majority of industrial research is concentrated in a small number of large firms, one might say that the international market for technologies assumes the characteristics of a monopolistic or oligopolistic market. Generally, the technologies produced by monopolies or oligopolies are the ones which are imported by under-developed countries.

The means of importing technologies by under-developed countries

Transfers of technology within a country can be made by the most varied means. Harvey Brooks has shown that they could be made when qualified people change their activities from one domain of science and technology to another. This is the case, for example, of a scientist who changes from fundamental research to work in experimental development. Transfers of technology may also occur when new missions or firms are launched by existing organizations. This is the situation with the civil application of military technical accomplishments. Transfers of technology may be complemented by the scientific and technical literature, educational programs, technical meetings, consultations with experts, personal contacts and, in particular contacts between supplier and client. These transfers also occur by means of licensing and know-how agreements or else by engineering and marketing agreements.[9]

If one refers specifically to the means of importing technologies used by Third World countries, one sees that the principal means are as follows: consultations with experts, licensing agreements, turn-key agreements, management agreements, engineering and construction agreements.[10]

Consulting and advisory activities

Under-developed countries often call on experts working for private companies or national or international organizations in order to get their advice on problems whose solution often demands much experience. The expertise can deal with the most varied subjects; thus it is difficult to evaluate its effect in a general way.

It has been noted that this method of "technological transfer" often had the disadvantage of being discontinous and did not contribute to the creation of a local scientific and technical infrastructure. One might also point out that the information given by these experts may be biased in favor of the interests of the institution or firm for which they work.

Some under-developed countries, in order to reduce this disadvantage habitually refer to several consultants belonging to rival firms or institutions. This procedure, although expensive, allows them to avoid choices which would be disastrous for these countries. Nonetheless, this amounts to a choice among several "competing scientific or technical informations."

Patents and licenses

Patents, according to Harvey Brooks, are a common means for transferring technology. The patent system grants the owner of an invention exclusive right to use it or to authorize someone else to use it. As it presently operates, this system establishes the legal appropriation of certain scientific and technical knowledge and makes it commercially exploitable by authorizing its use for a fee.

In under-developed countries, the patent system cannot be truly considered as a means for the transfer of technology. First of all, it has been established that the majority of patents granted in these countries belong to foreign firms. The following table shows that the percentage of patents granted to foreigners in under-developed countries most often exceeds 90% of the total number of patents granted in these countries:

Table 5[11]

Patents Granted to Foreigners in % of the Total Number of Patents Granted Between 1957 and 1961

Large Industrialized Countries		Small Industrialized Countries		Under-developed Countries	
U.S.A.	15.72	Italy	62.85	India	89.38
Japan	34.02	Switzerland	64.08	Turkey	91.73
West Germany	37.14	Sweden	69.30	United Arab Republic	93.01
United Kingdom	47.00	The Netherlands	69.83		
France	59.36	Luxembourg	80.48	Trinidad and Tobazo	94.18
		Belgium	85.55		
				Pakistan	95.75
				Ireland	96.51

More detailed studies done in certain under-developed countries such as Argentina, Chili and Peru show that the small percentage of patents granted to nationals in these countries belong not to firms but to isolated individuals and have almost no industrial and commercial importance. Therefore, we can say without exaggeration that patents in under-developed countries are granted to foreign companies.

The second characteristic of the patent system in the Third World is that patents belong to a small number of large firms, thus reflecting the concentration of industrial research on a world-wide scale. The third characteristic is that these patents belonging to large companies are not exploited in under-developed countries. Vaitsos[12] cites the case of Peru where, from 1960 to 1970, 4,872 patents were granted in the country's principal branches of industry. Of these 4,872 patents only 54 were used, that is, 1.1% of the total. The same is true in Colombia where, out of a sample of 3,513 patents, only 10 were used in that country.

Thus, when large corporations who have a monopoly over research-development are granted patents in under-developed countries, they have no intention of using them. Rather, it is to protect an export market against local and foreign competition. In fact, as soon as a patent is granted in a country, the firm holding this patent is the only one who can produce or import the patented process. In other words no other company, national or foreign, has the right to utilize this process without the authorization of the firm which has the patent for it. As the firm does not make use of the patent in the country, this means that it alone may import products manufactured using the patented process. This commercial monopoly permitted by the patent system in under-developed countries extends to non-patented products. Indeed, control over the importation of a patented product can limit the production of other goods if this product is an intermediate necessary for the manufacture of other goods.

Unlike patents granted in under-developed countries, licenses constitute a means for the transfer of technology since, by definition, they authorize the commercial exploitation of a patent. In fact, the authorizations for exploitation often have rather restrictive conditions which considerably limit the extent of their use.

Licensing agreements are often preferred to direct investment as a means of technological transfer when the foreign firm wants to avoid the risk of setting up subsidiaries in under-developed countries.

Direct foreign investment

The choice by international firms between licensing agreements and direct investment obviously depends on the firms strategy. Baranson has listed a number of reasons which can lead international companies to choose one or the other means of technological transfer.[13] According to him, large firms prefer direct investment to licensing agreements in branches of industry with a high density of research, in order to control the evolution of the market for their products, to avoid competition for "know-how", and to protect the standardization and brand name of their products.

Many other factors can explain the preference of firms in industrial countries for direct investment as a means of technological transfer. Direct investment can be a means of avoiding customs barriers in many countries, set-up to favor the creation of imports substitution industries. This "tariff jumping" seems to be a stronger motivation than that of trying to reduce production costs by direct investment.[14]

Another means for the transfer of technology is the formation of joint ventures, which can be a convenient solution when one wishes to avoid the risks of expropriation.

Engineering agreements

These agreements stipulate that one is contracted by another to plan, study and carry out a project. Specialized companies, called "engineering firms" take charge of this phase of the development of an industrial unit.

Management contracts

"Management" contracts are made by companies which ensure the management of the new industrial unit. By entrusting the management of their firms to a foreign company, under-developed countries practically give up the possibility of mastering the techniques they import.

"Turn-key" agreements

In these agreements it is stipulated that an enterprise will organize operations necessary for the installation of a firm and its normal functioning. Decision makers in under-developed countries often point out the disadvantages of these agreements which give them no access to the knowledge of the techniques necessary to develop and run the unit.

The principal methods of technological transfers cited above, must not cause us to lose sight of the fact that the interests of equipment suppliers, of the owners of the processes, of engineering and construction companies are often closely linked. As Cooper writes:

> "The supplier of proprietary technology nearly always has well-established links with engineering designers, construction companies and the like, who are better acquainted with the peculiarities of his process technologies than any other groups. Where the technology owner is a vertically-integrated company, many of these elements may actually be present in the company itself."

From what has just been said, it follows that the majority of the technologies imported through diverse means by under-developed countries come from large firms in industrialized countries and that the world market for technologies has all the characteristics of an oligopolistic market.

The technologies imported by Third-World countries result in payments in currency; efforts have been made to evaluate these payments. It is a matter of "direct" or rather "explicit" costs. There have also been attempts to evaluate the "indirect" or implicit costs of technologies imported by these countries. In fact, the impact of technologies imported by under-developed societies is not limited to direct or indirect costs, but extends to a certain number of effects which are not always measurable and which can be significant.

<u>The cost of technology transfer</u>

Before trying to evaluate the costs of imported technologies, one must know what he intends to estimate. In the majority of the studies done in Latin America, efforts have been made to calculate costs which have been the object of commercial transactions between firms established in these countries and firms located abroad:

Feasibility studies, that is, the study of the possibility of setting up a factory. A feasibility study is generally limited to the following points: market study, study of manufacturing techniques, investments, operation costs, factory location, transportation, study of the conditions of finances, including anticipated investments, and so on.

The preparation of and extension of feasibility studies to the analyses of production processes, industrial installations, and the product one wishes to manufacture.

Exploitation licenses and licenses for the use of commercial brand-names.

Technical assistance given by consulting firms whose head-offices are located abroad or by individual specialists living abroad.

Technical services rendered sporadically by consulting firms whose head offices are located abroad or by individual specialists living abroad who perform activities such as the supervision of the installation and operation of equipment, the purchase of equipment, manufacturing tests, training of national personnel, and so on.

In Brazil a study has been done which deals with 1,665 contracts relating to the importation of technologies. These contracts were made by 614 industrial firms located in Brazil with firms located abroad, during the period of January 1963 to December 1969. According to the results of this study the sums paid by Brazil during this period went from 42.5 million dollars to 90.8 million dollars, i.e., an increase of 114% in 6 years.

To appreciate the relative size of the cost of technology transfers for Brazil, one can compare it to the country's total imports or else to its gross domestic production.

Table 6
Importation of Technologies
Compared to Total Imports and to GDP[15]

Year	% of Expenditures for Importation of Technologies in Relation to Total Imports	% of Expenditures for Importation of Technologies in Relation to GDP
1959	2.8	0.18
1960	3.2	0.21
1961	4.6	0.22
1962	0.4	0.14
1966	3.3	0.38
1967	4.3	0.24
1968	3.8	0.25
1969	4.5	0.29
1970	5.0	0.31

According to this table, the expenditures for imported technologies varied from 0.14% to 0.38% of the GDP from 1959 to 1970. Compared to Brasilian imports of this period, they represented from 2.8% to 5% of the total. These expenditures, for imported technologies such as they were registered, are not therefore very high in relative value. One might also note that the percentage of expenditures for imported technologies in relation to GDP for Brasil, is slightly lower than that of Japan. In 1969 for example, this percentage was 0.29% for Brasil against 0.20% for Japan. If we take into account, however, the margin of error for such figures it is difficult to say exactly how significant these figures are. The volume of imported technologies seems to depend both on the level of industrial development and on the extent of industrial research in a given country. A country experiencing rapid industrialization must increase its importation of technology at least until it can produce a part of the technology which it needs. This is the case with Japan which in recent years has succeeded, in producing new techniques, thanks to the development of its industrial research. Brasil, on the contrary, satisfies nearly all of its technological needs by importation. Under these conditions, an identical percentage of expenditures for imported technologies in relation to the GDP would not have the same meaning for both Japan and Brasil: this illustrates Brazil's weaker industrial development and its very limited industrial research.

It would perhaps be worthwhile to analyze the expenditures for imported technologies in separate branches of industry and not simply for industry as a whole. According to the study already quoted, 46.3% of technology import expenditures in Brazil are made for transfer of technology dealing with vehicles. If we take into account technology transfer dealing with automobile parts this percentage rises to 55.3%.

This strong dominance of the automobile industry contrasts with the low total of payments for technological transfers intended for other industrial branches. The pharmaceutical industry, for example, accounts for only 4.1% of these payments. As for the machine-tools industry, so important for industrialization, it is not even mentioned in the study which only includes branches of industry which in 1969 received more than $500,000 worth of technologies.

Nevertheless, it is worth underlining that the above data deals only with the year 1969. It is obvious that the payments made for technological transfers depend on the existing industrial outlook. When an industrial branch experiences a fall in sales, its technological payments necessarily diminish; this was the case for the machine-tools industry of Brazil in 1969.

Beyond the influence of industrial outlook each branch uses technologies more or less complex and more or less expensive and this also influences the distribution of payments for imported technologies among the different branches of industry. One realizes this when we compare the average expenditure per contract for different industries of Brazil. The automobile industry, which accounts for more than half of the payments for imported technologies, also pays the highest average cost for technological acquisition contracts. A technological acquisition contract in the automobile industry cost on an average 9,636 cruceiros in 1969 against 391 cruceiros for the iron metallurgy industry.

The comparison of payments for technology transfers among different branches of industry provides us with useful ideas and information for elaborating technology policy in underdeveloped countries. The comparison allows us to see that these payments are concentrated in a very few sectors of industry and we can also see that these sectors have a very high cost of technology compared to the average cost of technology used in the other sectors.

Another interesting piece of information supplied by the Brazilian study concerns the distribution of technological payments according to the kind of company ownership. According to this study foreign firms located in Brazil realized 73.5% of the total of these payments during the period 1965-1969. On the basis of this data one could say that the essential flow of technologies between Brazil and foreign countries occurs among foreign firms. If we distinguish foreign firms which are subsidiaries or partners of companies located abroad and those which are independent, we can observe that the former import technologies worth 2.5 times more than technologies imported by the latter. In addition, it is important to point out that the foreign firms pay on the average 8 times more per contract than national firms.

Under these circumstances, one wonders if foreign companies overprice the cost of their technology or if they use more complex technologies than national companies. Although there is no data regarding this question the figures we have on the percentage of technology payments expended by foreign and national firms in each sector, do not seem to support the second assumption.

Some of the most interesting data of the Brazilian study concerns the percentages of technology impact payments among the different forms of technology acquisition for the period 1965-1969 The results obtained are as follows:

Technical assistance	68%
Manufacturing license	9%
Concession for usage of brand-names	6.1%
Technical services	12.2%
Project development	4.7%

The high percentage of payments for technical assistance is not surprising due to the fact that in Brazil foreign firms do not have the right to grant to their subsidiaries manufacturing licenses and licenses for the use of patents and commercial brand names. Therefore they generally use technical assistance for transferring technical information to these subsidiaries.[16]

From the study of the Brazilian situation we can see that this country sets aside 0.30% of its gross domestic product for technology importations, that the automobile industry accounts for more than half of these payments, that three-fourths of these payments are realized by foreign firms located in this country and that technical assistance is the means most often used by firms to import technology.

We would now like to compare the costs of imported technologies in several Latin American countries. We can see from the following table that the most industrialized countries of this region are those which pay the most for imported technologies. However, a close correlation does not exist between the cost of technologies imported by these countries and their level of industrial development. According to the figures in the table it seems that the cost of imported technologies tends to increase faster than the industrial development.

Table 7
Payments for Transfers of Foreign Technology in some Latin American Countries in 1969

Country	Total Payments (in $ million)	Gross domestic product (GDP) (in $ million)	P/GDP x 100	Industrial production ($ million) (IP)	Total payments/IP x 100
Argentina	127.70	23,843.	0.53	8,408	1.51
Brazil	90.79	30,862.	0.29	6,885	1.32
Mexico	67.20	32,287.	0.21	7,483	0.90
Chile	8.20	5,692.	0.14	1,490	0.55
Colombia	10.96	7,674.	0.14	1,405	0.78
Guatemala	1.81	1,725.	0.11	231	0.78
Honduras	.26	544.	0.05	77	0.34
Costa Rica	.64	887.	0.07	171	0.38

Source: International Seminar on Application and Adaption of Foreign Technology in Latin America, Santiago, Chile, May, June 1973.

In addition, we should note that for countries having had the same level of industrial development in 1969, the relationship between the cost of imported technologies and industrial production can be quite different. This is so, for example, in countries like Brazil and Mexico as well as Chile and Colombia. These differences are explained in large part by the method adopted by each country for calculating costs of technology transfers.[17] But they could also be due to the industrial structures of these countries to their power in negotiating the purchase of foreign technologies and to their legislation regarding this domain.

The division of payments for technological transfers among the different industrial sectors of Brazil, Mexico and Chile confirms what we have already observed for Brazil, that is the high concentration of these payments in a small number of sectors. The chemical and metal-mechanical sectors account for 77.9% of Brazilian and 63.1% of Mexican payments. As for Chile, the same two sectors cited above and the canned foods sector account for 80.9% of technological payments.

Other interesting data concerns the distribution of payments for technology transfer according to countries which sell them. Chile pays the United States 44.5% and Switzerland 30% of its technology payments. Brazil pays the United States 31.4% and West Germany 31.1% of its technology payments. From the preceding information we can try to outline a certain number of preliminary conclusions bearing on the direct cost of technology transfers.

The expenditures for importation of technologies compared to the Gross Domestic Product do not seem very high. In a country like Brazil, these expenditures represented 0.29% of the GDP and 5% of total imports in 1970. These percentages, with those of Argentina, are the highest for all of Latin America. If it were a matter, therefore, of the direct cost of imported technologies, the problem would not be critical.

The cost of imported technologies depends not only on the degree of industrial development but also on other factors such as industrial structures, legislation concerning the purchase of foreign technologies, the negotiating power of firms which import technologies and so on. These factors must be considered when one compares the technological costs of various countries.

One observes a very high concentration of payments for technological transfers in two or three industrial sectors of each country. This is due not only to the plan chosen for industrial development but also to the legal nature of firms in these sectors and to the fact that the average cost of technology in these sectors is higher than in other sectors, etc.

Technical assistance absorbs nearly half of the payments for technologies imported by Brazil and Colombia. This is so, at least for Brazil, because foreign companies, not having the right to grant manufacturing licenses and licenses for use of patents and commercial brand names to their local subsidiaries, generally use technical assistance for transfer of technical information to these subsidiaries. This contributes somewhat to the inflation of the technical assistance portion of all payments made for technology transfer.

The countries of Latin America receive the largest share of their technology from two or three industrialized countries; this reflects their heavy technological dependence vis-a-vis these countries.

The fact that in Brazil the unit cost of contracts is much greater for foreign firms than for national firms causes us to think that foreign firms overprice the cost of their technologies. This phenomenon should not be confused with the overpricing of imported products by the under-developed countries.

What has just been said about Latin America can be said for most under-developed countries. The following table shows the importance of technological costs in some African, Asian and Southern European countries.

Table 8
Payments made by some Asian, African and Southern European Countries under the title of Technological Transfer, in proportion of GDP and Exports

Countries	Year	Costs of transfer of technology in proportion of	
		GDP	Export
Nigeria	1965	0.78	4.2
Ceylan	1970	0.51	2.9
India	1969	0.12	2.7
Spain	1968	0.55	8.4
Turkey	1968	0.43	9.9

Source: Data taken from: Technology transfer report from the Secretariat of CNUCED November 10, 1971. The data concerning India probably does not reflect reality because it only covers the private sector. In this country, the public sector represents about 2/3 of industrial investments and is consequently responsible for the majority of payments for technology transfer in industry.

Overpricing in the industry of Latin America

Overpricing is the difference between the price paid for a given product by a company in an under-developed country and the price of this product on the "free", world market.[18] Overpricing is due to the fact that the independent firm of an under-developed country has weak negotiating power, compared to the suppliers from developed countries, whether for lack of information or because it has to deal with a monopoly.

The firm which has little information on the characteristics of the market for the product which it acquires, can agree to pay an "overcharge" which is in fact the cost of its ignorance. In this case, the market can be oligopolistic or competitive. But it is possible that even a well informed independent enterprise might agree to buy an "overpriced" product simply because the market for this product is monopolistic.

Overpricing does not occur uniquely between an independent company of an under-developed country and a company headquartered in an industrialized country. It can happen equally in exchanges between a parent company and its subsidiary located in an under-developed country. In this last case, overpricing assumes a completely different meaning. It is the means used to repatriate a part of the profits of the subsidiary company.

Overpricing is considered as an "indirect" cost of the transfer of technologies when it covers products which complement imported technologies. This is the case, for example, of materials used for production under license in under-developed countries.

Overpricing in the industry of Colombia

Colombia has produced a study on overpricing in a certain number of industrial sectors according to the type of ownership of the examined firm. The table reproduced below, shows that the average percentage of overpricing of intermediate goods is extremely variable according to the sectors of industry and the ownership of companies. In the pharmaceutical industry the average percentage of overpricing is 19% for the national companies and 155% for foreign owned companies. Likewise, in the rubber industry, we observe a large difference between national and foreign owned firms as to average percentage of overpricing for the intermediate products which they import. On the other hand, in the chemical and electronics industries the differences are less significant.

Table 9
Overpricing of Intermediate Goods according to the Branches of Industry and the Ownership of Firms in 1968

Sector	Ownership	Average % of Overpricing	Total Overpricing in US $ 1000
Pharmaceutical industry	National	19%	10,000
	Foreign	155%	
Rubber industry	National	0	
	Foreign	44%	
Chemical industry	National	22%	1,300
	Joint	20.2%	
	Foreign	25.5%	
Electronics industry	National	25.6%	
	Joint	6.5%	
	Foreign	16.6%	

Source: Vaitsos Constantino, Transfer of resources and preservation of monopoly rents - April 1970.

In addition, one can estimate the total overpricing for 1968 in the pharmaceutical industry alone at $10 million. This sum according to a study covering 70% of contracts of this type changes to $6 million in 1970 which represented approximately the total sum paid that year by the firms located in Colombia for fees, patents, brand-names and technical assistance. It follows that overpricing is a phenomenon which is financially much greater than the cost of technology transfer in the strictest sense of the term.

Overpricing in the pharmaceutical industry of Latin America

Peru

In 1970 the National Council of Scientific Research of Peru launched a study on the transfer of technology in Peruvian industry. The method followed was to choose 188 firms divided among the different sectors of industry, conforming to a certain number of criteria such as:

> The turnover of the firms chosen from a sector must represent 50% of the overall turnover of this sector.

The maximum number of companies retained must not exceed 30 per sector.

The sampling must include forms of national, foreign and joint capital.

The firms making up the sample must be different in size and use different types of industrial procedures.

We will set forth here the first results obtained concerning the pharmaceutical industry. In this sector, 28 firms make up the sample and had a volume of production representing 80.1% of the total for that sector. Moreover, the firms retained employed 55.4% of the total personnel employed in this sector.

The first significant fact which emerges from this study is that certain companies from the sample import products which are not overpriced and that only 10 firms among those forming the sample have overpriced prices.

One might note as well that the rate of overpricing varies enormously from one company to another, for both national as well as foreign firms.

Nevertheless taking into account the value of intermediate goods imported by the firms which are not subject to overpricing, the rate of overpricing for the group of firms studied reaches only 18.5% of the value of imported inputs.

The same inquiry tried to discover if foreign firms had a higher rate of overpricing than national firms. It was found that the foreign firms studied had an average rate of overpricing of 13.5% as opposed to 5.0% for the national firms.

This would seem to weaken the argument which states that national companies have a weaker power of negotiation than that of foreign firms.

From the study, one could also conclude that the national firms have an average rate of overpricing lower than that of foreign firms, and have greater negotiating power in the purchase of the intermediate goods which they use.

In reality the overpricing rate depends on the firms' negotiating power as well as their ability to inform themselves and it is probably this which explains why the rate can vary from 32 to 390% depending on the firm. But overpricing also depends on other factors and in particular on the foreign firms' ability to repatriate a part of their profits by overpricing the goods imported from the parent company.

The following table shows eight pharmaceutical companies profits, royalties and overpricing in relation to their capital:

Table 10
Profits, Royalties Overpricing in Percent of Capital in Eight Pharmaceutical Enterprises in Peru

National Firms	Profits/ Capital	Royalties/ Capital	Overpricing/ Capital
Enterprise No. 1	64%	0.7%	5.2%
Enterprise No. 2	10%	2.4%	0.0%
Enterprise No. 3	0%	1.2%	17.8%
Foreign Firms			
Enterprise No. 1	1.9%	37.4%	-
Enterprise No. 2	0.0%	17.0%	-
Enterprise No. 3	21.0%	6.3%	14.2%
Enterprise No. 4	0.0%	-	61.0%

In the case, for example, of the first national company the profit/capital ratio is 64% whereas the overpricing/capital ratio is only 5.2%. On the other hand, for foreign company No. 4 on the table, the profit/capital ratio is 0 whereas the overpricing/capital ratio rises to 61%. In the latter case, it is possible to hypothesize that the company repatriated a part of its profits by overpricing its imports of intermediary goods.

Argentina and Chile

One encounters the same phenomenon in the pharmaceutical industries of Argentina and Chile. The total overpricing on pharmaceutical products in Argentina alone has been estimated to be over 1.2 billion dollars (U.S.). For these products, the rate of overpricing varies from 0% to 7100%.[19]

As far as Chile is concerned, the study covered the importation prices of 50 pharmaceutical products. From this total, 9 products had included a rate of overpricing between 1% and 30%, 14 products showed a rate of overpricing varying between 31% and 100% and 14 products had rates of overpricing fluctuating between 100% and 770%.[20]

The analysis of cases of overpricing in Latin America permits us to make the following statements:

> Overpricing does not affect all enterprises. In the Peruvian pharmaceutical industry 10 firms out of 28 have "overpriced" prices.
>
> The rate of overpricing is extremely variable depending on the firms. In the Peruvian pharmaceutical industry it varies from 32 to 390% among the firms which have overpriced prices. As for the Argentinan pharmaceutical industry, it includes a product for which this rate reaches 7100%.
>
> The rate of overpricing is extremely variable depending on the industrial branches and ownership of companies. In Colombian industry this rate varies on the average from about 0% to 26% in the national sector and from 16% to 155% in the foreign sector.

Overpricing does not have the same significance in the case of a national enterprise or a branch of a foreign firm. In the first case, the overpricing is the cost of the ignorance of the enterprise which imports a product or, again, is the "excess price" paid to a supplier who holds an absolute monopoly on the sale of this product. On the second case, it seems that the overpricing is one of the means used by a subsidiary to repatriate a part of its profits.

The evaluation of imported technologies in the underdeveloped countries generally consisted in estimating the costs of these technologies and the overpricing of the products which support these technologies. In spite of the lack of precision of these estimates, it seems that overpricing is a much more important phenomenon than the direct cost of imported technologies. The Colombia example seems to show that the total overpricing is 8 to 10 times higher than the total of direct costs of the technology and that the sum of direct and indirect cost of the technology reaches about 1.3% of the GDP. In some countries like Brazil and Argentina, the sums paid for the purchase of technologies and under the title of overpricing reach a much higher percentage of GDP.

The evaluation of imported technologies in the Third World countries is not limited of itself to their direct cost and to overpricing of products used to support them. It must also take into consideration the restrictive commercial practices imposed on firms of underdeveloped countries by large foreign firms who hold "technological monopolies".

Clauses restricting export

These clauses are quite frequent in the contracts of technological acquisition between the firms located in developed countries and those located in under-developed countries. The technology is sold to a company of an under-developed country on the condition that the manufactured products resulting from this technology not be exported or be exported under certain conditions to other countries. The following table shows the degree of this phenomenon in some under-developed countries on which we were able to compile some data.

Table 11
Contracts Containing Clauses Restricting Exportation According to the Nature of the Restriction

Countries	Total No. of Contracts	Contracts with Restrictive Clauses		Total Prohibition or Previous Authorization	Nature of the Restriction	
		No.	%		Export Permitted only to certain Countries	Other Specific Restrictions
				in % of total no. of contracts including restrictions		
Peru	83	82	99	90	10	-
Mexico	109	106	97	62	4	34
Chile	175	162	93	38	-	-
Bolivia	35	29	83	93	7	-
Colombia	117	92	79	98	2	-
Equador	12	9	75	100	-	-
India	1051	455	43	40	53	7
Philippines	254	82	32	81	6	13
Argentina	60	17	28	53	47	-

Source: UNCTAD, Major Issues Arising from the Transfer of Technology to Developing Countries, 18 Dec 1972.

Many foreign subsidiaries in the under-developed countries verbally agree with the parent company not to export their products.[21] Since these subsidiaries have in general a greater exporting capacity than nonaffiliated companies, one can deduce that the exportation restrictions are much more important than the analysis of technologies commercialization contracts shows it to be. In support of what has just been said we can add that the exports of American subsidiaries in Latin America in several industrial sectors rarely exceed 10% of their total sales. In addition, it might be noted that even in the absence of restrictive exportation clauses, many local firms find it impossible to locate foreign markets for their products.

Revenue guarantee clauses

This clause concerns provisions stipulated in contracts for technological acquisitions whose purpose is to guarantee revenues to the supplier on the sale of technologies to underdeveloped countries. One of these clauses refers to the guarantee of fee payment at a fixed due date, independent of the degree of contract fulfillment.

Certain clauses guarantee the repatriation of profits in case of economic policy changes by governments. Such clauses concern the profit rate for firms of underdeveloped countries which import from abroad the technologies they need.

Tie-in clauses for sales linked to raw materials and intermediate products are frequent.

In the majority of contracts for commercialization of technologies we find clauses requiring the buyer of a technology to supply himself with raw materials and intermediate products from the seller. These clauses have the disadvantage of preventing all substitution of raw materials and intermediate products in the manufacturing of a product and thus any utilization of local raw materials. In addition, these raw materials and intermediate goods whose importation is required are sometimes, as we have seen, overpriced, which indirectly makes the costs of technology transfer higher.

Restrictions on access to local markets

The protection of the market where the purchased technology operates is obtained by means of certain intermediate clauses stipulated in the contracts of commercialization of technologies.

The supplier of the technology, under the guise of quality control and maintenance of standards, prevents the firm of the under-developed country from developing products competing with those which complement the purchased technology.

Likewise, the patent system such as it now functions in under-developed countries, blocks the entry of products competitive with those which can be manufactured according to registered but as yet unused patents. We have seen, in effect, that more than 90% of registered patents in under-developed countries belonged to foreign firms, and were not used in these countries. The sole purpose of the registration of these patents is to prevent competitive firms from gaining access to markets of under-developed countries.

There are of course other means used by firms which hold technological monopolies for controlling the markets of under-developed countries. Some for example, use their power of negotiation to obtain from governments of under-developed countries duties which protect against importation of products competitive with the products of their subsidiaries located in these countries.

Thus we can state that the evaluation of technologies imported by under-developed countries should not be limited to the estimation of direct costs of these technologies but must take into account the indirect costs connected with the acquisition of these technologies such as: overpricing, losses due to exportation restrictions and restrictions on access to local markets, and finally costs resulting from guarantee clauses and tie-in clauses on sales.

BIBLIOGRAPHY

ARAOZ, A. — Costos de la dependencia tecnologica in Ciencia nueva no. 28, 1973.

BARANSON, J. — Technology transfer through the international firm. American Economic Review, May 1970.

BOTERO G, HECTOR — Algunas cifras sobre el costo de la transferencia de tecnologia a Colombia. Bogota, Colciencias, Novembre 1971.

BROOKS, HARVEY — The Government of science. The MIT Press 1968.

CHESNAIS, G. et COOPER, C. — L'impact des progrès scientifigues et technologiques des pays avancés sur les pays sous-développés (roneo)

CNUCED — Directives pour l'étude des transferts des techniques aux pays en voie de développement. TD/B/AC-11/9,12 Septembre 1972, 123 p.

CNUCED — Transferts des techniques. Politiques relative aux transferts des techniques dans les pays du Pacte Andin: leurs fondements, 3ème session Santiago (Chili), 29 Dec 1972, 33 p. TD/107.

CNUCED — Major issues arising from the transfer of technology to developing countries. TD/B/AC - 11/10, 18 Dec 1972. 64 p.

CNUCED — Major issues in transfer of technology to developing countries. Addendum TD/B/AC - 11/10/Add/21 Dec 1971, 91 p.

COOPER, C. — Choix des techniques et modifications technologiques comme problème de politique economique. Revue internationale des Sciences Sociales no. 3, 1973.

COOPER, C. — Science Technology and production in the underdeveloped countries. An Introduction in the Journal of Development Studies, Vol. 9, October 1972.

DEMONTS — La recherche-developpement dans les firmes multinationales - Economic Appliquée 1967, no 4.

EDKAUS, R.S. — The factor proportions problem in underdeveloped areas, American Economic Review, September 1955.

GILLETTE, R. — Latin America: Is imported technology too expensive? Science Vol. 181, 6 July 1973.

GONOD, P. — Apercu theorique sur le transfert: technologique et les notions connexes Department des Affaires Scientifiques. UEA March 1972.

GRUBER, W., MEHTA, D., VERNON R. — The R-D factor in international trade and international investment of US industries. Journal of Political Economy, vol. 75 no 1, February 1967.

HAWTHORNE — The transfer of technology report prepared for a seminar on the transfer of technology to less industrialized countries. Istanbul 1970. OCDE.

HIGGINS — Economic Development. New York 1959.

HYMER, S. — The efficient (contradictions) of multinational corporations. American Economic Review, May 1970.

IBANEZ, Fernan — Economia chilena. Transferencia de tecnologia a la industria nacional in Panorama economico 27 p.

JANITCH, E. — La prévision technologique, OCDE.

JONES, GRAHAM — The role of science and technology in developing countries. London, Oxford University Press, 1971.

Junta National de Planificacion y coordination economica — Algunas caracteristicas de la transferencia de tecnologia, Quito Ecuador, sept. 1972, 39 pages plus annexes.

KATZ, JORGE — Patentes, corporaciones multinacionales y tecnologia. Un examen critico de la legislacion internacional in Desarrollo economico. Aoutjuin 1972 no 45, vol. 12.

LEWIS, A. — Le developpement économique avec les offres de travail illimitecs. Manchester School of Economic and Social Studies, mai 1954, traduction francaise BIRD, Paris 1953.

Ministerio de industria argentina — Analisis de la transferencia de la tecnologia externa a la industria argentina. Direccion National de Cooperacion industrial (ronco) juillet 1972, 42 p.

NORIEGA MORALES, Manuel — La transferencia de tecnologia externa hacia centro america in Boletin de la integracion, juin 1973, no 90.

PAUL, Arthur — Organizing the transfer of technology to developing countries in Industrialization and development, ed, by HE Hochcher and MC Hawk 1969.

SACHS, J. — Developpement, environnement et evaluation des techniques in Revue internationale des sciences sociales no 3, 1973.

SAGASTI. F, OXMAN — La transferencia de tecnologia hacia los paises del grupo Andino OEA marzo 1972.

SEABORG, GLENN T. — Science, technology and development: A new world outlook in Science, vol. 181, 6 July 1973, no 4094.

STRASSMANN W P — Technological change and economics development Ithaca, New York, 1968, 353 p.

THEBAUD, S — Problèmes de politique scientifique dans les pays sous-développés. IREP-IPEPS, Grenoble 1971, 125 p.

ULANOWSKI, A. W. — Estudio sobre transferencia de tecnologia, Consejo Nacional de Investigacion, déc. 1970.

UNITED NATIONS — Advisory Committee of the application of science and technology to development, 12c session Addis Abeba, Nov-Dec 1969.

VAITSOS, C. Patents revisited: Their function in developing countries. Lima, mars 1971. Secretariat du Marché Commun Andin, 62 p.

VAITSOS, C. The process of commercialization of technology in the Andean Pact: A synthesis. Lima, octobre 1971, 60 p.

WIONCZECK, M.S. et LEAL, L. Maria Vers une rationalisation du transfert de technologie au Mexique in Comercio Exterior du Mexico, juillet 1972.

REFERENCES

1. Harvey Brooks, The Government of Science (MIT Press, 1968), p. 255.

2. H. Brooks, Ibid, p. 255.

3. E. Jantch: La Prévision Technologique - OECD.

4. E. P. Hawthorne: The Transfer of Technology Report prepared for a seminar on the Transfer of Technology to Less Industrialized Countries, OECD. Instanbul 1970.

5. S. Thebaud, Technological Evaluation in the Domain of Nuclear Energy in the United States, (July 1974).

6. Survey of Current Business, (Sept 67, Oct 71) Department of Commerce. United States Business Investment in Foreign Countries, (Washington, DC, 1960).

7. Demonts, Research and Development of Multinational Firms Economic Appliquée.

8. W. Gruber, D. Meita, R. Vernon, "The R-D factor in international trade and international investment of US industries," The Journal of Political Economy, (Vol CXXV, No. 1, February 1967).

9. H. Brooks, The Government of Science, p. 269.

10. C. Cooper, The mechanisms for transfer of technology from advanced to developing countries, Science Policy Unit, University of Sussex, Nov 1970.

11. U.N. The role of patents in the transfer of technology to developing countries - New York, 1964.

12. C. Vaitsos, Patents revisited: Their function in developing countries. Lima, March 1971, p. 23.

13. J. Branson, Technology transfer through the international firm, May 1970

14. P. Gonod, The Problems of Technology Transfer in Latin America, General Secretariat OAS, (Washington, DC), p. 21.

15. Up to 1969, data of the Getulio Vargas Foundation and of the Central Bank. For 1970, non-official estimates.

16. The analysis of 146 technological acquisition contracts in the automobile industry of Argentina shows that:
    82.9% of this total include clauses of technical assistance and information.
    78.8% of this total bear on the purchase of manufacturing licenses.
    44.5% of this total have clauses concerning commercial brand names.
    27.4% of this total include clauses dealing with patents.
    18.5% of this total bears on the acquisition of know-how.

17. The data on the cost of technology transfers varies greatly depending on the sources.

18. Rate of overpricing - FOB-price for a country - international FOB price/international FOB price.

19. A. Araoz Costos de la dependencia tecnologica Ciencia neuva No. 28 - 1973.

20. Sagasti, Oxman - La transferencia de tecnologia hacia los paises del Grupo Andino - OEA marzo 1972.

21. A more recent inquiry including 80 contracts in Ecuador shows that 49 include clauses prohibiting export and 6 include clauses permitting export under conditions . . .

PART VI SUMMARY, SYNTHESIS AND REVIEW

Several characteristics of the NATO Advanced Study Institute on Industrial Technology Transfer at Les Arcs should be noted at the outset. First, the remarks which follow do not constitute a comprehensive survey of all that transpired during the two-week session. In selecting points for inclusion, Hahn and Doscher in the following chapter, have tried to reflect the major study findings reported and conclusions which participants reported from practical experience in working with various aspects of the transfer process. They also collected a set of particularly interesting observations and unanswered questions whose importance were ascertained by the frequency with which they appeared in discussion, or by the interest which they stirred when mentioned.

Secondly, Hahn and Doscher have worked with the assumption that it is unnecessary to go into great detail about definitions and models of technology transfer. They have attempted to reflect adequately the discussions of conceptual constructs and transfer models which transpired during the meeting. But, particularly in view of the published proceedings of the 1973 NATO Advanced Study Institute on Technology Transfer held at Evry, France[1]--which deal primarily with the basic concepts--definitions and models have not been emphasized.

Finally, the summary, to some degree, reflects the bias of its authors, characterized by a policy-orientation to the subject issues.

At the outset, a logical organizational approach for this summary and synthesis appeared to accord with sector interests: i.e., technology transfer in the public sector versus in the private sector; military to military and military to civilian technology transfer; international technology transfer among developed countries or to less developed countries and to east European nations; and so forth. However, upon sifting through and synthesizing the contents of the presentations and discussions, the findings largely ignored sector boundaries and suggested a different organizational format.

Accordingly, the organization chosen is as follows. The first part of the review comprises a synthesis of major points and questions raised during the session. These have been loosely grouped into four categories: (1) concepts, ideas and approaches to the technology transfer process; (2) mechanisms, flows, elements, and systems of technology transfer; (3) values, criteria, and decisions inherent in or associated with the transfer process; and (4) external factors indirectly affecting the transfer process.

The second part of the review constitutes a brief summary of the Stirling Conference [1975] which is reported to have generated a coherent set of ideas on the technology transfer process, developed subsequent to the 1973 NATO-Advanced Study Institute (Evry) on this same topic. The review of the conference (a written report of which will be published by the Stirling group in 1976) as it appears below, has been derived from the remarks of Allen Pearson presented during the final session at Les Arcs.

The third part of this review constitutes a compilation of the concluding plenary session comments and reactions of the participants. Following it is an alternative science policy perspective of technology transfer offered to the conference by Hahn and Doscher.

The final section attempts to make explicit four topics that pervaded the informal sessions and workshops but which were only dealt with obliquely in the full sessions. These are why transfer technology, and what are the criteria for a successful transfer? The topics of imbedded or systemic technology and intermediate/appropriate technology are also dealt with explicitly. The chapter closes with a review of technology transfer policy needs and prospects.

SUMMARY

Walter A. Hahn*
Susan L. Doscher

Library of Congress
Washington, D.C.

The ideas, findings, questions, arrayed in this part of the review suggest points of concensus, in some cases, points in conflict, and provide indications of areas in which our knowledge is flimsy, or at worst non-existent in the technology transfer field. When viewed collectively, these points are intended to give an overall picture of the content and tenor of the sessions and an indication of the state-of-the-art in the study and practice of technology transfer.

Concepts

Considering the first of the five identified categories--concepts, ideas and approaches to technology transfer--it is interesting to pose a question raised during the session by Eugene Kovach, "Is there a coherent body of knowledge of technology transfer?" With reference to the formal and informal sessions--as will be reflected in this review--this question could at once be answered in the affirmative and in the negative. There are concepts and principles which have won general acceptance, having withstood the test of time in the realms of theory

---

*This summary and synthesis does not reflect the position of the Congressional Research Service of the Library of Congress or of any other organization. In the first three sections of this chapter where the writers attempt accurately to report the sense of the meeting it does not necessarily represent their views. The authors are indebted to Ms. Wendy H. Schacht, Research Analyst, for assistance in preparing the written report.

and practice. On the other hand, there are many fuzzy areas in our understanding of the process, much of the literature has been identified as merely intuitive, and widespread attention has been called to the glaring lack of empirical research and sound data within the existing knowledge base.

As an example of concern over this last point, the report of a workshop chaired by William Fischer and Ian McNicoll on "Empirical Approaches to Understanding Transfer Processes in Technological Change" reflected a general feeling of dismay that in the face of empirical progress being made in other applied social science areas, so little has been done in technology transfer. The chairmen noted that participants in the workshop saw the lack of progress in empirical studies as retarding the ability to distill common elements from numerous case studies and stores of anecdotal evidence.

Ron Johnston, in his report of the proceedings of a workshop on mechanisms of technology transfer, affirmed that focused research can advance technology transfer from its present "art-form" to a more systematic practice. Johnston qualified this observation by noting that human judgement will always remain a critical element in technology transfer.

In considering the gray areas in the knowledge base, several participants, among them Frank Bradbury and Paul Jervis, specifically referred to the disparate concepts of technology transfer and technology innovation. As Jervis observed in his opening remarks, inevitably conferences on technology transfer end up talking about innovation. This observation was substantiated by presentations and discussions which tended to contribute to the ambiguity. At times the processes of technology transfer and innovation were spoken of almost synonymously, at other times sharp distinctions were drawn between them. Some spoke of the role of technology transfer in innovation, others, of the role of technological innovation in technology transfer. In many cases, semantic problems seemed to constitute, or compound the difficulty.

According to Babatunde Thomas, who was a spokesman for the interests of the less developed nations, technology transfer is a meaningless term. Thomas distinguished between technology transfer and technology acquisition, holding that the latter is important to the less developed countries both in concept and as a practical objective.

Assigning a different meaning to technology transfer, Admiral Ekas stated that to transfer technology is to spin-off technical information from research and development activities. Ekas identified the motivation behind technology transfer as one of problem-solving for customers. With reference to this last point, A.J. Wilson, representing public sector interests, agreed that technology transfer should be a problem-solving process, and that it should be specifically directed at public sector needs. Wilson noted, however, that public sector problem-solving was not as yet being realized to a significant degree through technology transfer.

Introducing another point of view, William Carey cautioned against belief in the unfounded assumption that there exists a reservoir of "technological applications held back by a dam", and that if we could find some way of opening the dam, large numbers of our problems would be solved. Carey stressed the need to understand the limitations of technology in itself, to appreciate that technology cannot be viewed as a sole solution, but instead as "one partner in a large company of solutions".

One concept that won general concensus among speakers and participants is that effective technology transfer, or technology acquisition, requires an appropriate scientific and technical infrastructure at the user end. This requirement was stressed particularly with reference to transfer to the less developed countries. Shiller Thebaud stated that the less developed countries must have the capabilities to identify needs, to formulate criteria by which to select appropriate technologies, and ultimately to be able to utilize the technologies selected.

Georgio Boggio spoke of the importance of an organizational infrastructure among members of the European Economic Community (EEC). The EEC has embarked upon the formulation of a common policy for science and technology, requiring the coordination of national policies and the implementation of joint actions of common interest. It is anticipated that this shared policy base will help to harmonize R&D priorities, improve efficiency in R&D, and reduce duplication of effort. Boggio pointed to the common policy base and coordinated interests as fertile ground for technology transfer whether it involves education programs, industrial cooperation, information systems, or the search for the solution to a common problem.

In his discussion of the quantification of technology transfer and its implications, Norman Nisenoff upheld the need for a "substructure" to support technology. The substructure affords the necessary receptivity to transferred technology and, according to Nisenoff, could provide a means for assessing the effectiveness of technology transfer efforts.

Although many other concepts and approaches to the study and implementation of technology transfer emerged, the above sampling is reflective of some of the major points.

Mechanisms

Perhaps one of the most often repeated and popularly recognized mechanisms for technology transfer is people. As previously stated there was concensus on the point that technology transfer occurs through people. According to Bradbury, technology transfer is by agents not agencies, and people both make barriers to the transfer of technology and make them permeable. As observed by Bernard Udis, people are important to the process because they bring to it experiences of both success and failure. Udis noted the importance of the latter, particularly in light of the fact that most of the accounts in the literature reports success stories only. Widespread recognition was accorded to the important of a technology broker, an individual or group of individuals who are capable of serving as a dynamic link between the source and user of the transferred technology. According to Philip Youle, technology transfer is a process involving real people at both the source and user ends, working towards socially desirable purposes. Philip Wilmot said that technology transfer is a systematic procedure but at the same time a highly intuitive process. In so saying, Wilmot implied the influence of people as a determinant of effectiveness. Johnston stated that people interfacing is important to technology transfer, but that personal interaction must have the backup of a formal written commitment to assure the effectiveness of transfer.

Diverging from the people aspects, Richard Trainor stated that new institutional concepts for conducting technology transfer are necessary. According to Samuel Bar-Zakay, in order to be effective, technology transfer mechanisms must provide a balance between the source and the user; there must be some type of mutuality of interests and a "partnership" between the source and user. In addition to mutuality of interest, Bar-Zakay pointed to the importance of a formal defined relationship i.e., a contract (as purported by Johnston) as an element in effective technology transfer.

Bradbury noted that technology transfer focuses on the process, not on the substantive technology per se. Similarly, Wilmot stressed the importance of management in the context of industrial high technology transfer. As an example, Wilmot spoke of a high technology industry becoming increasingly involved in technology transfer and innovation. As the technologies in question grow more complex, Wilmot said, the load on management grows decidedly heavier. With this increased management responsibility, there is a need to delegate and decentralize responsibilities, and yet simultaneously, there is a strong requirement for centralized strategic planning. Wilmot concluded that the decisions on technology transfer thus become a joint responsibility of the local line management and of central strategic control.

Turning from the management factor, another key element highlighted by a number of participants is that of information. Reporting on a workshop on the technology transfer process, Nisenoff stated that information transfer is essential, but not sufficient by itself, for successful technology transfer to take place. Information transfer per se, is not technology transfer. Addressing a different, but related point, George Tressel conveyed the importance of exploiting existing communication channels when attempting to implement technology transfer. Reporting on some recent research findings, Tressel stated that reliance on existing communications mechanisms can prove more efficient and productive, than can the formulation of new communications capabilities.

As a final observation included in this category, Joseph Carlson discussed the transfer mechanism of "capacity building." Relating closely to what was earlier termed the infrastructure concept, Carlson described opportunities for technology transfer to the public sector afforded by capacity building within the State and local governments. Carlson described the Urban U.S. Technology Systems Project as an example of an ongoing empirical experiment in State and local capacity building. This project, in essence, provides for technology agents in selected cities to serve as conduits and links between technology sources and public sector needs.

Values and Motivations

Technology transfer is not a value-free process. It is initiated, operated, accelerated, hindered, or curtailed by many diverse situational factors. The complexity of the technology transfer process -- which varies with the technology involved and the context in which it is being transferred -- was underscored in the proceedings, as some of the following highlights will indicate.

Several speakers asserted that effective transfer requires that the source or supplier of the technology consider the values of the intended user. Focusing on the apparent mismatch between technology suppliers and public sector needs, Wilson said a major obstacle to technology transfer is the lack of appreciation and understanding by the technological community of the real needs and objectives of the public sector. Conflicts in values must be overcome or accommodated for the transfer to be effective. As reported from a workshop session on the transfer process, the utility of a technology must be coupled with acceptability in order to effect a transfer. If values clash, a transfer is unlikely to occur. Nisenhoff asserted that the source and user must recognize each other's goals and that these goals change over time. Youle stated that problems associated with the transfer process cannot be solved from within the technology "box" but must instead be subject to outside value judgements and handled accordingly. As Win Straube pointed out, technology cannot develop in isolation, but instead it is both influenced by the impacts upon and environment in which it is developed. Human values must be factored into the development and transfer of technology, in terms of both planning and implementation of the process.

William Raney, in a discussion of the transfer of military technology to civilian users, pointed to several obstacles affecting it. Among them are requirements for proof of the value of the technology and cultural acceptance of the technology intended for transfer. In a similar vein, Denys Griffiths, among others, stressed the need for the source to have, or develop, credibility with the user. According to Robert Havlick the user must be present throughout the transfer process. User participation during the process was emphasized, particularly with reference to the public sector, as a means of assuring appropriateness of the technology and user acceptance. Eugene Stark countered this point to some degree by stating that user overdominance, or resistance, could limit the creativity of the supplier, thus restricting the potential benefits of the technology transfer process. According to Stark, the user should not be called upon for specifics at the early stages of the transfer process; instead, general user requirements should be ascertained initially, with the opportunity provided for more direct user participation in later stages.

There was general consensus on the point that technology must be appropriate to the culture and the science/technology infrastructure of the user if a successful transfer is to be effected. Again, the role of an infrastructure was viewed from various perspectives. Johnston stated that initial technology transfer can occur without a developed infrastructure, but one must be established to make the transfer actually take hold. According to Trainor, a complex and mature infrastructure can tend to limit effective transfer. On the other hand, McNicoll observed that a simple and immature (despite its age) infrastucture can limit effective technology transfer. Lindsay Anderson, in conjunction with spokesmen for public sector interests, stated that user fragmentation and/or disaggregated user needs, are causes of sluggish technological advance. Voicing a separate, but related point, Udis purported that in cases of international technology transfer, the process is more readily implemented between countries having the same level of technological sophistication.

Addressing another aspect, Raney noted that in almost all cases, technologies must undergo modifications, i.e., adaptive engineering, for use in different contexts. Bradbury claimed that in cases of successful technology transfer, decided change must occur in the user community as a consequence of the newly acquired technology.

The value of the transfer process per se became subject to question during the session. Ekas and Theodore Schlie posed the basic question of how much technology transfer is enough? Several of the participants challenged an implied assumption of the "technological imperative" and questioned the pervasive, underlying theme that technology transfer is inherently good. Carey cautioned against an overemphasis of the importance of the technology transfer process as a separate function. Carey stated that a more realistic grasp of its role could be gained only by placing it in a much broader contextual perspective.

Nisenoff warned that technology should not be transferred indiscriminately. With each transfer is a hidden cost; whimsical transfer can have a destructive effect. Similarly, Bradbury observed that barriers to transfer are not necessarily bad. Barriers can constitute positive checks on intended transfers, helping to preclude those which may be undesirable or of little utility to the prospective users. Griffiths pointed out that the technology transfer process is particularly useful when applied in a preemptive (future-oriented) problem solving mode. Crisis-response technology transfer is generally less desirable.

Several speakers, among them James Colvard and Pearson, hypothesized that there are "natural" technology transfer time cycles, and that no matter what mechanisms are instituted or barriers removed, it is difficult to accelerate the rate of transfer to any significant degree.

In conjunction with inherent values, built-in criteria, and other factors impacting directly upon the shape and operation of technology transfer, a wide range of environmental conditions also have a significant, if less direct or immediate, influence on the process.

External Factors

The following observations, relate to stimulants, impediments, and other influences on the transfer process, which derive from the situations in which the process is operating, or is prevented from operating.

From a world view, technology transfer functions in a large, uncontrolled environment. According to Marvin Cetron, technology transfer operates in the world environment in a crisis-response mode, i.e., in the context of such disasters as food, energy, and materials shortages and environmental degradation. Extant forecasting capabilities and early warning systems Cetron argued, could be employed to allow the transfer of technology to operate in an anticipatory mode. Technology transfer could help preclude the development of world crisis situations.

Viewing the world political environment vis-a-vis technology transfer, Donald Guertin pointed to several examples of national effort to promote self-sufficiency in technological development and thus, to simultaneously decrease international dependence for technological resources. Guertin indicated the now defunct Hartke-Burke bill--in part, proposing restrictions on foreign investments and imports--as an example of the U.S. initiative to limit the export of technology. Other actions on the part of the European Economic Community and Canada were raised to illustrate extant concerns over dependence on foreign R&D and other technological resources. Guertin identified this world political environment as one which would impose significant restrictions on the opportunities for useful and profitable technology transfer activities. Complementing Guertin's position, several speakers, notably Ekas and Youle affirmed that legislative policy can have a definite influence on the process of technology transfer. Guertin observed that despite the decided impact which legislative policy can have on technological development, non-technologists, particularly lawyers, dominate the shaping of policy codes vis-a-vis technology transfer. Stephen Feinman reported on the results of a study involving a survey and analysis of the literature pertaining to relationships between economic regulation and technological innovation. On the basis of the surveyable literature (which Feinman noted is in limited quantity) economic regulation on the whole has proved a hindrance to technological innovation. Along a similar theme, Rolf Pickarz stated that little is known about the impact of licensing, import/export and direct foreign investment policies on technological development and transfer. Pickarz said that this lack of understanding in large part results from the extremely weak data base available on the topic.

According to Leo Packer, industrial participation in technology transfer activities as technology suppliers is decidedly encouraged by a favorable political and economic user environment. In speaking of economic and political postures, Packer questioned the nature of the Federal Government role in international and domestic technology transfer activities. Although noting that there is still much to be learned about the impact of various types of governmental intervention in the transfer process, Packer stated that one cannot overestimate or underestimate the importance of government roles.

Speaking from a different perspective, Boggio said that efforts to coordinate R&D priorities and programs, and to develop cooperative institutions for science and technology, serve to enhance opportunities for effective technology transfer within the European Economic Community. Such cooperation, Boggio observed, helps remove financial, technical and regulatory barriers to technology transfer among the member countries.

Joseph Baker described an environmental motivation for technology transfer when he related the story behind the Burbank, California, City Council's action authorizing the city's entry into geothermal power production. Baker described a situation in which, despite risks and uncertainties associated with the technology, the need was of sufficient urgency to create a total receptivity to the new technology. Carey pointed out that crises, not rationality, drive the urban system. It seems, according to Baker's account, that rationality can, at times, be effectively combined with a crisis situation to lead to promising remedies through technology transfer efforts.

Environmental factors serve not only as stimulants to technology transfer, but can also serve to deter or prevent transfers from taking place. Considerations which tend to counter intentions for technology transfer were raised by Robert Rinne and Nick Montanarelli in noting that technology transfer may be appropriately restricted for reasons of security, safety, and proprietary advantage.

REPORT OF THE STIRLING CONFERENCE [1]

Held subsequent to the 1973 NATO Advanced Study Institute [1a] (Evry) on technology transfer, the Stirling Conference was convened with the intention of assessing and furthering the state-of-the-art in technology transfer theory. Since the proceedings of that conference were in preparation at the time of this meeting, Allen Pearson was requested to summarize the results for those attending the Les Arcs meeting. Pearson's remarks have been rearranged to follow the same four part format followed in the preceeding synthesis.

Concepts

One development deriving from the session was a new definitional construct for technology transfer. As explained by Pearson, technology transfer was placed in a different light by considering it in a broader frame of reference which he termed Transfer Processes in Technological Change (TPTC). This concept significantly widens the scope in which technology transfer is viewed, and according to Pearson, allows a more accurate view of the functions of the process. The conceptual construct of TPTC emphasizes process, allows for the examination of technology transfer vis-a-vis technological innovation and technology dissemination, and provides a base for the assessment of various innovation and diffusion models.

A central thrust of the conference centered on the examination of conceptual models, specifically the TPTC model. Participants in the Stirling Conference placed emphasis on the dynamic processes or "arrows" which link the "boxes" i.e., idea generation, problem solving, manufacturing and sales, consumer adoption, of technology transfer together. Pearson acknowledged weaknesses inherent in any type of conceptual model, indicating that a model which may make perfect sense to one individual could appear useless in the mind of another. The recognized shortage of empirical data, coupled with the low-level utility of the data which do exist, form an inadequate base for discussion of models that "really work". Confessing that Stirling did not produce any revolutionary or unique models that are likely to solve real world problems, Pearson did affirm the importance of model development for conceptualizing and for structured ordering and synthesizing of available data.

With reference to model development, data analysis and the like, Pearson highlighted the Conference discussion on the value of technology transfer research. Pearson reported that the character and products of technology transfer research were scrutinized and their merit upheld. Even if the majority of the reported information and published literature is anecdotal, much can be gained from a review of collected experiences. This type of information Pearson contended, allows for examination of causes for success and failure in transfer, and builds a necessary base against which to test and evaluate different models and mechanisms. Research has, and will continue to allow more accurate identification of problems with the opportunities for technology transfer.

Mechanisms

Pearson said that much of the Stirling discussion centered on mechanisms for technology transfer, a focus naturally emerging from the examination of conceptual models. Participants looked at examples of how universities attempt to transfer information. Considerable time was given to discussion of market situations vis-a-vis technology transfer, and to the importance of market surveys, and other marketing techniques to help to determine the viability of particular technology transfer activities. Attention also focused on the role of people in transfer and on the mechanism of licensing agreements.

Having broadly sketched the character of the discussion on mechanisms, Pearson observed that this tack led them to question the objectives and motivations for transfer.

Values and Motivations

In Stirling, as in Les Arcs, the question arose of why transfer technology? Stirling participants approached the question through an attempt to identify the objectives which motivated organizations to participate in technology transfer activities. In an effort to understand the motivations involved, discussion was conducted among representatives from government research establishments, research associations, universities and industry. As an abbreviated overview of this exchange, Pearson said that one fundamental reply to "Why transfer technology?" is that the process promises profit, greater efficiency, productivity, or the like, when posited against the long-term and short-term objectives of participating organizations.

External Factors

As a final point from the summary remarks of the Stirling Conference, the role of external or environmental factors must be considered. In the context of external influences on the transfer process, Pearson said that "contextual fit" was purported a significant determinant of the viability of transfer efforts. Paralleling contextual fit to the concept of infrastructure - the latter having been repeated often during the session at Les Arcs - Pearson noted that the technology being transferred must be acceptable to the cultural, social, political, etc., environment of the intended user, and that the user must be capable of absorbing and utilizing the technology, if a transfer is to be successful.

Posing a rhetorical question about how one goes about measuring contextual fit, Pearson offered a partial answer. It must basically come down to an ability to identify characteristics of the technology and characteristics of the environment into which it is being transferred to allow for an appropriate match to assure compatibility between the technology and the intended user.

Overview

In summing-up, Pearson made the interesting observation that at Stirling, the discussion of models led to an examination of mechanisms, which in turn led to an examination of motivations, and thus to an exploration of organizational goals and objectives. In other words, Pearson said, the discussion became somewhat circular, and thus gave an indication as to the dynamics and interrelationships of process and elements which combine to form the technology transfer system.

PLENARY DISCUSSION

Following the Hahn-Doscher Les Arcs synthesis and Pearson's summary of the Stirling Conference, the participants engaged in a brief but intense plenary discussion of the findings of both meetings and of technology transfer in general. When viewed collectively, the presentations, workshops and discussions at the meeting point to several specific areas of concensus and disagreement, and gave rise to a variety of unanswered questions. Some of these points are also considered below, again rearranged into the same four-part sequence.

Concepts

The meetings clearly pointed to areas of general agreement as to a conceptual view of the technology transfer process. Among some broad concensus points are: technology transfer is a dynamic process involving, at the least, a source from which the technology derives and a user by which the technology is newly applied; technology transfer brings about change in either the technology being transferred, or the user environment, or both; a "pull" approach to technology transfer is generally favored over the "push" technique, although the latter should, by no means, be abandoned; technology transfer procedes through a series of phases whether described after Bar-Zakay as research, adaptation, implementation and maintenance, or after Bradbury as idea-generation, problem-solving, manufacture and sales, and adoption and use, or according to other classification.

Contrasting the points of general agreement were a wide range of unsettled issues and questions which surfaced during the course of the meeting. One source of friction was semantics. It appeared that often it was not the principle or theory or practice that was in question, but instead, the words used to describe it. An illustration may be the distinction made by Thomas between technology transfer and technology acquisition. According to Thomas, technology transfer is a meaningless concept to the less developed countries, but technology acquisition is not. Yet, from other viewpoints, technology transfer is not considered a completed process unless the technology in question is effectively acquired and utilized by the user community.

In terms of concept and theory a problem which persisted throughout stemmed from the widely differing views as to what is technology transfer versus technological innovation? As indicated previously, a number of participants clearly distinguish the two processes, others interrelate them, and others speak of transfer and innovation as nearly synonymous. Unfortunately such differences were not resolved, although through the exchange of conceptual constructs and models, perhaps some new insights were gained and not a few prejudices reenforced.

Mechanisms

Reviewing the discussions of mechanisms by which the technology transfer process operates, Fischer observed that, in large part, they tended to overemphasize unique aspects of individual technology transfer experiences, and to skim over the commonalities among them. According to Fischer, this emphasis was misplaced. The study of technology transfer could be better advanced by focused concentration on the similarities among transfer experiences. He hoped that in this way a common data base could be generated from such information resources. Fischer stressed the importance of empirical research as a means to produce and synthesize appropriate data.

Values and Motivations

Dieter Altenpohl suggested that perhaps all those involved in the study, theory, analysis, assessment, classification, etc. of technology transfer were engaging in unnecessary activities. Technology transfer has occured without the benefit of research and literature before, and will probably continue to do so in the future Altenpohl contended. So perhaps all the study and discussion is superfluous to the functioning of the transfer process. Pearson sharply disagreed. Substantiating this position, Pearson highlighted the many references to the impact of international technology transfer on a nation's balance of payments, on a nation's internal technological growth, on foreign policy and international relations. Alternatively, Pearson noted references to the factors impacting upon the transfer process, i.e., government regulatory policies, import/export controls, standards, corporate growth policies, etc. Technology transfer does not occur as an isolated event or process. It is affected by, and in turn it affects, many things around it; adaptive engineering requirements, user receptivity, etc. With the world situation as it exists today, with the pervasiveness of technology and the growing interdependence among nations for natural and manufactured resources, Pearson contended that technology transfer cannot be permitted to operate unattended with no appreciation for possible short-term and long-term effects.

External Factors

With reference to the impact of various policies and operational guidelines on technology transfer, Bradbury corroborated concerns earlier expressed by Youle, saying that he was troubled by the small number of industrial representatives in attendance at Les Arcs and by the consequent inattention given to realistic versus idealistic policy and operational codes for industrial technology transfer. The meeting did little to advance an understanding or to develop workable guidelines for industries interested in entering into or expanding existing technology transfer activities. Speaking from a government perspective, E.W. Sapp said that he would have welcomed more thoughts and reactions from the industrial community. Although it is both important and interesting to obtain information from the academic communities and from various government representatives, Sapp said we must receive more feedback from the industrial communities, where technology transfer actually takes place in order to increase understanding and effectiveness of technology transfer activities.

Observations and Questions

Jervis, at the outset of the meeting, made a statement that was repeated both implicitly and explicitly throughout; that technology transfer is an immature field of study, a field largely supported by literature of an anecdotal, intuitive, or promotional nature. The existing literature is characterized by a limited quantity of empirical data. Several speakers, Nisenoff and Youle among them, observed that technology transfer is not a technology problem, but a complex, sophisticated process involving many situational and value-laden factors not directly related to the technology per se. The sessions bore out the complex quality of technology transfer, manifesting a general difficulty in trying to focus on the fundamental workings of it.

Bar-Zakay held that in planning for technology transfer, operational policy must appreciate and accommodate the needs of both source and user. Two representatives of the public sector, Edmond Rovner and Wilson, commented that technology transfer is not a clean process without conflict. Wilson elaborated, expressing his opinion that a characteristically "elitist" view held by the technology transfer "types" is in itself a barrier to technology transfer, as it impedes understanding of user objectives. Edward Helminski posed the difficult question, How can the sources or suppliers of technology, the researchers and practitioners of transfer, handle the conflicting values and/or goals of the user communities? Focusing on the other end of the spectrum, Helminski asked how the user is capable of discriminating among advocacy science and technology positions?

Questioning the overall utility of the technology transfer process, Carey asked if our rational expectations for transfer are excessive or realistic. Packer questioned the degree of awareness and use of the extant body of technology transfer knowledge by practitioners and policy makers. Packer purported that a clear understanding of the process is essential for responsible direction and management of technology transfer. Posing a rhetorical question, Packer asked, can technology transfer research provide decision-makers, both policy and operations oriented, with risk/benefit factor estimates, ranges and forecasts of alternative consequences?

Several overall observations pertained to the historical time frame in which we now examine technology transfer and its importance in international relations and foreign trade countries. Bruce Reiss commented that in the immediate post World War II period a "push" on the part of the user during the process was required in the 1960's. But now Reiss said, more balanced partnerships between users and suppliers are required for effective transfer. Packer observed that in modern times technology transfer has become more important in foreign affairs and trade as indicated by the recent signing of various international agreements for cooperation in science and technology. Thebaud focused on the relative merits of technology transfer to the less developed countries. He questioned whether it is more desirable for these countries to import technology or to develop internal capabilities to generate needed technological resources. Jack Baranson, on the basis of his research on technology transfer to the Peoples Republic of China, implicitly questioned whether or not the PRC user posture, i.e., characterized by reverse engineering activities and firm bargaining with suppliers, could be a model for less developed countries as users in the transfer process.

Other conceptual and practical questions arose as a consequence of individual perspectives on the technology transfer process -- perspectives characterized by a particular focus on the process i.e., user, supplier, entrepreneur, engineer, etc. and perspectives relating to different sectors in which the process is viewed, i.e., industrial, government, military, public sector, academia. In the overview, however, instances of agreement and disagreement generally pointed to a need to step back from situational peculiarities, semantic differences, contextual references, and to draw similarities from experiences, from anecdotal information, and from intuitive considerations, in an effort to build a common base of knowledge. It does not appear that we have yet established a sufficient knowledge base to support sound policy making and the formulation of program guidelines for technology transfer.

Picot Floyd's paper was a U.S. example of the transfer of a growing social technology -- technology assessment (TA) -- from its academic and federal government (Office of Technology Assessment) settings to use in the City of Clearwater, Florida.

No cases were offered of applying technology assessment to the potential or actual transfer of some technology from one setting or application to another. Maybe it is too soon in the development of TA to expect it to be applied to second uses of technology when there are so few examples of its assessment of first order applications. But implicitly, many speakers expressed concern for the indirect and long-range social, environment, economic, other technological and political impacts of transferring technology. Packer asked about "alternative consequences." Youle stated, "Technology without cultural values is a man who dies never to return." Guertin worried over a growing political climate that may restrict technology and its transfer. Both Wilson and Carey emphasized that the source must consider the values of the users. Pickarz said that little is known about the impact of both licensing and investment. Wilmot asked, in the context for both source and users, "Are there technologies that we should not transfer?" Rovner asked about the long range impact of present technology. Thomas charged that the transfer of "inappropriate technology is culturally wrong."

With reference to cultural values, Straube stated that from experiences in international technology transfer, value perceptions have been inordinately important to the potential effectiveness of transfer efforts. Discussions of technology transfer from developed to developing countries focused, in part, on the cultural challenges posed by the introduction of new technologies, and by the need to identify technologies "appropriate" to the situation in the less developed nations.

It was pointed out that specific technologies may be shown to have implicit values in themselves which are apart from those associated with the utility of the technologies. Such values must be appreciated and considered in conjunction with those characteristic of the supplier and potential user communities. Although appreciation for the importance of values in the technology transfer process is explicit, it seems that in practice they are not always accorded the importance owed to them. At times, they may form obstacles to what could be useful and beneficial transfers.

Hahn pointed out that of the many models of the transfer process few, if any, call for explicit analysis of the second order impacts, those beyond whether the technology transferred does the job it was transferred to perform. But it is the writer's impression that the tone of this meeting is that such a step should, and may be, included in revisions of the models and future actual processes. This raises many questions. Who has the responsibility to initiate the TA step in the TT process?

Who is the client? Who pays? Who performs the assessment and who are the participants in the process? Who has responsibility for implementing the findings?

TECHNOLOGY TRANSFER - A SCIENCE POLICY PERSPECTIVE

The foregoing material has been presented, first in the context imposed by the meeting as it unfolded, and secondly, as free of the biases of the synthesizers as possible. Up to this point the authors resisted intentionally injecting their opinions and comments into the proceedings. In this next section, their personal views were offered the plenary session. They reflect a viewpoint of technology transfer by professional staff to the national legislature and thus, predispositions are clear and explicit: the authors' are client-oriented and their clients' interests are at the highest levels of national public policy, program, and resource allocation decision making.

Federal legislators only occasionally deal with the explicit problem/opportunity labeled "technology transfer" (TT). Indeed, many will (and have) wondered what these jargon words mean and of what relevance they are to Congress. But participants in this conference will recognize that implicitly many legislative issues involve aspects of TT. International trade and commerce, mutual defense and economic arrangements, creation of new agencies and reorganizations, research and development, intergovernmental relations and public/private interfaces are but a few examples.

Regardless of the particular labels of the moment, technology transfer is viewed by the authors (in a Science Policy Research Division) as a key element of science (and technology) policy. Several speakers have placed technology transfer in a context of one element of the total R and D or innovation process. Others have seen it as both an explicit and an implicit step in the entrepreneurial process. Still others see technology transfer as a tool of diplomacy, an element of the bargaining process between nations. Technology transfer is additionally seen within nations, as a class of interactions among levels of governments and between the public and private sectors. Offered here is a slightly different science policy context to add to the variety of concepts and models characterizing this area of technology transfer.

Science Policy Dimensions

Patterned after the OECD definition, science policy is "in a deliberate and coherent basis for national decisions influencing the investment, institutional structure, creativity, and utilization of scientific research." It refers to both science <u>and</u>

technology (S and T). Note that S and T includes both the natural and social sciences. The role players on the science policy scene include analysts, scholars, philosophers, historians and practitioners of many learned disciplines. Also included are both the de jure and de facto decision makers at the technical, managerial, entrepreneurial and legislative policy levels. Two additional groups are often neglected in elitist discussions of science policy. First are the implementors: the creators, communicators, transmittors, facilitators, receivers and others actually involved in the intellectual and physical processes of science and technology. A second group, even more frequently neglected in science policy circles, are the affected parties. These are the consumers, environmentalists and "just plain folks" who are directly impacted by the primary, secondary or additional consequences of scientific and technological initiatives. They include, but go beyond, the users or receivers of the technology transferred as discussed in this meeting.

As defined above, science policy includes both science and technology, a point that is both generally understood and accepted. Science policy can, even must, be considered from two other and quite different dimensions. There is policy <u>for</u> governance of the scientific and technological sector of society. There is also the role of science and technology <u>in</u> overall or segments of public policy. The dual dimensions of science policy of course suggest the simple 2 x 2 matrix below:

	SCIENCE	TECHNOLOGY
POLICY <u>for</u> S and T	(1.1)	(1.2)
S and T <u>in</u> PUBLIC POLICY	(2.1)	(2.2)

Row one, Policy <u>for</u> S and T, is essentially a post World War II function. Scientists, engineers and technologists dominate the scene, establish the rules of entry and procedure, cartesian-reductionist paradigms reign perhaps to the exclusion of other forms of thought except for the usual jockeying for position and competition for resources. Its institutional forms include for example, the now defunct President's Science Advisory Committee - Office of Science and Technology in the U.S., the OECD Directorate of Scientific Affairs, the Japan Science and Technology Agency, national academies of science and engineering, and a plethora of scientific and engineering societies. In short, what is considered in row one are the ideas, style and activities of the scientific establishment.

But there is more to science (and technology) than attention to its own affairs and well-being. Row two, therefore, concerns the role of science and technology in public policy and in societal, environmental, economic and political affairs. Society's elected and appointed representatives, the market place, a variety of institutions, and that amorphous concept "the public" dominate the scene. Non-scientists set the rules and values and, as has often been cited, see scientists and engineers as being "on top, not on tap."

In the public sector the institutional forms are executive agencies, legislatures, and the courts. In the private sector there are industrial, academic, union, citizen and many other forms of organizations and groups. In contrast to the dominance and legitimate advocacy enjoyed by S and T in the row one context, in row two, S and T is but one of the actors responding to initiatives and forces beyond its control. More positively, it is here that S and T explicitly makes its contribution to the rest of society and to the maintenance of spaceship earth.

Before filling in the cells of the matrix some of the characteristics of the columns should be highlighted. Science (in this abbreviated and over simplified characterization) is an innerdirected activity, usually individually pursued. Its goals are to understand nature and to create new knowledge. To the performer, and to many sponsors, basic scientific research is performed for its own sake as a cultural activity similar to much art and music. It is ostensibly value-free i.e., the knowledge gained is objective and truthful. Science is intellectually a rather orderly affair but it is institutionally quite disorderly. Scientific research faces great uncertainty as to outcome but, relative to applied research and particularly to development, the costs are low.

Column two, technology, is a goal centered activity directed toward solving problems, sizing some opportunity, or otherwise achieving an explicit though not always clearly defined end. Technological endeavors are usually team efforts and are often interdisciplinary. They are managed, usually by or for a client. While new knowledge may often be a by-product, technological activities apply, synthesize and otherwise use existing information, knowledge, and skills.

Elements of the Matrix

The elements of each cell in the matrix will be only briefly described leading to a more intensive view of technology transfer in this alternative in perspective.

Basic research is in cell 1.1. Both individualistic and big science efforts are included. Cell 2.1 contains applied and exploratory research, a deliberate search of knowledge in specific areas, for filling gaps, or to be used for pre-determined purposes. To the performer of the research the distinction between basic and applied/exploratory may be meaningless but in the former, the sponsor leaves the choices to the research while in the latter, the sponsor gives varying degres of direction.

Development, Test and Evaluation is in cell 1.2. This is the application of scientific and technical knowledge to create new or modified capabilities, substances or products. Specific first-order results are planned for or sought from the D, T and E process: e.g., a bridge, a missile, a drug, an analysis, a policy or organizational concept.

A second element in cell 1.2 is Standards, both voluntary and mandatory. In this context, standards may be viewed mainly as a procedural convenience for the efficient and effective operation of S and T affairs. Outsiders to the process care little whether the thread size standard is 10-32 or 10-33 or whether their ice cubes freeze at 32 F or 0 C. There are major economic and national custom considerations concerning standards but the point here emphasizes their key role in S and T operations per se.

Technology Assessment (TA) is included in cell 2.2. TA concerns analysis of the unintended and second-order impacts of the conduct or results of any of the S and T activities discussed in the other three cells. TA looks at the consequences of technological initiatives on society, the economy, the ecosystem, other technologies, and politics. As such, the codes, conventions and values of society dominate those of the S and T establishment in contrast to the above situations for D, T and E and for Standards where the reverse is true.

Also included in cell 2.2, are those technological activities that are not the immediate result of research and development activities. In this meeting these have been in part, referred to as "the technological infra-structure." Included are tools, energy sources and conversion systems, a technologically educated and skilled work force, markets and social uses of technological things and processes. What is involved specifically are literally thousands to millions of small incremental changes, improvements, alternative uses, and combinations of these factors by nonprofessionally oriented, non-R and D laboratory types. Some writers argue that the largest percentage of technological activity and advancement in emerging and industrial society is in this "Technological diffusion" area. It is also labeled "imbedded technology" or "systemic technology."

Here again, the driving forces of markets, education, financial incentives, social acceptability, life style, etc., are more influential than the technological aspects per se. Imbedded technology is everywhere and thus we are often unconscious of its existence. It is deliberate but not always a managed innovation activity.

At last, this contextual discussion turns to the principal topic, technology transfer which is the third element of cell 2.2. The original matrix, now filled in, appears as below:

	SCIENCE	TECHNOLOGY
POLICY <u>for</u> S and T	Basic Research -individual -big science	Development, Test & Evaluation Standards -mandatory -voluntary
S and T <u>in</u> PUBLIC POLICY	Applied & Exploratory Research	Technology Assessment Imbedded/Systemic Technology Technology Transfer

<u>Technology Transfer</u>

As in the Development, Test, and Engineering case, technology transfer aims at first order results from the application of existing knowledge, capability or physical things. But it does so in a new setting or for another purpose. Note that information, know-how and skill, and physical things are individually and in combination parts of what we see as TT. The technology transferred may be for the same purpose but in another economic or social sector, e.g., from the steel to glass industry or from defense to civil use.

A transfer may also be effected from a technology's original use to a different purpose within the same sector. The electronics and medical industries provide sufficient examples of this phenomenon. Semiconductors were originally employed as components of calculators and later applied to digital watches. Similarly, the technology which produces light-emitting diodes used to yield the red numbering display in calculators has subsequently been transferred to the manufacture of digital watches. Transistors which were generated for application in transmission systems are also used in computers, calculators, and television and radio equipment. And as a final example, radioactive isotopes which have been developed within the field of medicine as a treatment for certain diseases have been used as tracer chemicals and as components of nuclear powered pacemakers.

Seldom is a technology transferred in pure or unchanged form. Among the terms applied to altering the device or process to fit the new use or setting is "application engineering." Whether more formal and deliberate as implied by the foregoing term or more casual, this alteration function is a key but often overlooked step in the TT process.

Hopefully, the purpose of this discourse on putting TT in its place (or at least in another place) will now become clear. Up to this point many Les Arcs speakers, both explicitly and implicitly, have classed technology transfer as one step in one or more invention-innovation models. Some speakers have emphasized bi-polar notions of push-pull or donor-recipient. Others have stressed the role of various types of in-the-middle transfer agents and agencies. There is a growing consensus that successful transfers intimately and actively involve people in addition to documents, drawings and tangible objects. These people-transferees may be third parties, recipient-pullers, donor-pushers or a combination of all three. All of these approaches are from the viewpoint of either one of the actors in the TT process or from that of the objective, external (usually academic) investigator whose subject of research is TT.

The science policy context offered above is from the standpoint of the public policy maker. This view understandably emphasizes the utility of the concept and practice of technology transfer in contributing to society, the economy, the ecosystem, other technology and of course to politics. The public policy maker starts with desired results in these areas and then considers the need for incentives, penalties, policies and procedures, institutions, resources and other elements of the climate for effective technology transfer necessary to achieve them.

HIGHLIGHTING SOME ADDITIONAL CONSIDERATIONS

In the workshops, and particularly in the almost continuous informal sessions, several topics came up in a variety of forms but were never focused or directly discussed in the plenary session. Two of these were questions: Why transfer technology? What constitutes a successful transfer of technology? The term technological infrastructure was used in several contexts but was never elaborated upon. The topic of intermediate or appropriate technology similarly was only lightly explored. Since these subjects were on the minds of the participants it seems appropriate to include them explicitly here in this final section.

Why Transfer Technology?

This question was omnipresent during the meeting, but little time was spent answering it explicitly. Understandably, all participants at this international meeting on technology transfer know why technology developed for one purpose should be or is transferred to another setting or put to another use. But some of the reasons are subtle and implicit. Others are in conflict. Below are listed what is undoubtedly a partial set of the reasons for technology transfer. Following each statement is a short commentary designed to highlight various aspects of the transfer motivation, but which is in no way meant to be complete. The point of this listing is to deal with the questions that, if technology transfer is a means, toward what ends is it directed? What are the motives? What forces are at play?

1. The Technological Imperative. Slightly overstated, this says that if a technological capability exists, we will (or should) use it. Some writers suggest this compulsion to spread technology is some sort of technological determination in which technology permeates society with a force and direction beyond control. For those who do not accept this depersonalized technological invisible hand, others ascribe similar attributes to techocrats, technologists and other symbols ranging from Dr. Frankenstein to Louis Pasteur. In the technology transfer community, the technological imperative is associated with push-type technology transfer and is exemplified by the "product champion" process.

2. Increased Efficiency and Image in R and D. This is the spin-off phenomenon, probably most clearly seen in the NASA technology utilization efforts. The idea embodied in the Space Act and its implementation was deliberately to search for and to facilitate secondary (to the space missions) uses of the technology developed with public funds. The existence of the National Technical Information Service and similar activities are another expression of the desire to get more than first-order utility from the public expenditures for R and D. And spin-off is good public relations. If the gun designers can also spin-off some butter, the pressure for the choice between them is reduced and the taxpayer may more easily both understand and condone what was done with his money. This motivation is also push in character but is accompanied by an access motion. At the least, the R and D agency must make available the technology (or its partial surrogate, technological information) in a

form easily and cheaply accessible to the public or to other organizations.

3. Meeting a Market or Public Sector Demand. This is pull technology transfer and starts with a perceived problem or opportunity to which some technological solution appears amenable. The transfer process may involve a conscious search for something to fill an existing process or product need. Many businessmen do not consciously think of their profit motivated response to a market opportunity as "technology transfer" although it may be a part of their product planning, development and production. In the public section this need identification often takes the form, "If we can land a man on the moon, why can't we _________?"

4. A Tool of Diplomacy. National possession of both specific and classes of novel technological capabilities create status and advantage in international relations. This advantage can be and is used both cooperatively and competitively through the transfer or withholding of the technology. It may be stretching the term "diplomacy" but included here is the role of TT in balance of trade and balance of payment matters.

5. Standardization and Efficiency of Use. The transfer of technology within multinational corporations and between national military forces are examples of transfer to permit more efficient and perhaps more economical operation across institutional and political boundaries.

6. Blocking other Technology. Moving extant technological processes and products into new markets to inhibit their penetration by competitors may be a reason over and above any immediate economic gains and may even be done with direct losses. Similar defensive transfer may be made for political or bureaucratic purposes.

7. Lower Risk and Cost. Adopting a technology that already exists offers fewer risks of unknowns as to performance characteristics and as to time of availability. Often product or process adaptation is cheaper than R and D and while the result may be less desirable performance characteristics, the bird-in-hand approach is very appealing.

8. Stealth and Expropriation. Industrial espionage and military spying, by whatever names, are forces to induce inadvertent technology transfer. National expropriation is more often for political or economic reasons but almost always results in unplanned technology transfer. Equally often, this technological transfer is incomplete to unsuccessful.

In typical transfer situations several of these motives may be simultaneously present. One party to the event may want to meet public or private need and the other to make a profit. The NASA engineer may feel the imperative to see his space innovation used in community health programs whereas the NASA administrator is pushing that same innovation in fulfillment of its Congressional "spin-off" expression in the Space Act, motivated by a desire to achieve efficient use and multiple results from the expenditure of public funds.

Some of the discussions at this meeting were unnecessarily heated and/or confused because the motives of the respective parties to the transfer process were not clearly understood. In other cases, these motives were understood but were unacceptable to one of the parties and it was this, not some defect in the transfer mechanism which hindered the transfer. This point will not be belabored further beyond saying that there appears to be considerable room for more explicitness and perhaps even more honesty in identifying motivational aspects of the transfer process.

What Constitutes a Successful Transfer of Technology?

Neither the plethora of literature on technology transfer nor the proceedings of this meeting have produced a satisfactory answer to this question. There is no agreement as to whether the question is directed solely toward the process of technology transfer or toward the substantive results achieved as a consequence of the transfer. For example, in his presentation, Udis pointed to the F-104 fighter plan as an excellent example of a successful transfer, but for the wrong requirement. Wilmot indicated that transfers were successful to the degree that they jointly met the donor corporations objectives and the receiver host country and user objectives. Maybe the clue to answering the question lies in being more explicit as to who benefits: the source, transfer agent, user, research/observer, some general and/or cumulative notion like "national good," or combinations of several of these?

Another aspect of success in transfer is what has often been mentioned as the "value" of the technology being transferred. The Nisenoff-Foster paper seems to offer attractive features here. Additional numerical indicators have been suggested by others including area of impact, numbers of individuals impacted, number of transfers, and duration of effect or repetition. Qualitative evaluations abound, usually in the form of, "The ______________ industry is now using the __________ process or product developed originally for the __________ (e.g., space) program." Each reader is invited to fill in his own favorite example.

The point here is not to suggest ultimate criteria for evaluating the degree of success in technology transfer. Rather it is to note that at this meeting there was little discussion of the question. But two things were implicitly clear: this is an important question to the technology transfer community and little appears to be going on that promises useful answers.

Imbedded or Systemic Technology

The term used often in this meeting -- technological infrastructure -- was used in parallel with the term in the science policy matrix presented earlier, imbedded or systematic technology. Herbert Holloman and Hahn at various times, have used the label "technological diffusion". Albert Rubenstein is the source of the word "imbedded" but Harvey Brooks also used that term in 1966 in the phrase "...the state of the art becomes imbedded in the system." Whether invented or unconsciously picked up somewhere, the writers also find themselves using the terms "systemic" and "micro TT" in connection with this fuzzy but somehow meaningful concept. Someone else suggested that it should be called "evolving technology". Regrettably, we find ourselves in one of those uncomfortable areas characterized by more words than meaning.

Summarizing from the earlier discussion, the characteristics of this evolving technology are: incremental, systematic, cumulative; pervasive; has not resulted directly from R and D; exists in many forms including a skilled work force, technical information and patents, tools and processes, new products and services; not a managed or programmed process per se; and is not described in the familiar literature of the science and technology establishment.

Although they will not be discussed here, many other elements of the "imbedded technology total system" should be mentioned. A broad set of training and educational personnel, facilities and materials are required to generate and sustain a viable technological infrastructure. Similarly, there must be appropriate standards, parts, supplies, and tools. And all of these require transportation, communication and energy support.

One can see literally thousands of examples of evolving technology in the trade and craft publications like: Purchasing, Railway Age, Machine Tool Review, RSI (Roofing/Siding/Insulation), Prairie Farmer, Construction Plant and Equipment, Popular Mechanics, Agricultural Engineering, Ocean Industry, and Pulp and Paper. Some examples include: Using long rivets to replace tube assemblies, galvanized wire staples to replace conventional roofing nails, patented angle adjustors for disk harrow blades, a non-welded locking link for tire chains, a notched belt for seed planting, a nickel/aluminum non-skid spray coating that is corrosion resistant, and a "cross-hair" pneumatic blade positioning device for paper coating machines.

Little quantitative information as to the number and frequency of these incremental advances (or at least changes) can be gleaned from this literature. Few, if any warrant the time and cost of patenting. There are of course no clues to how many items are even recorded, let along offered for publication. Then there is the editorial screening process both as to reader appeal and to fit publication space limitations. There is some evidence that those of very high potential for the market or in savings of time, labor, energy, etc., are never proposed for publication but held as proprietary. There is also some evidence that some ideas are described as if they existed physically or were in use to test potential customer interest. If a response is obtained from "floating" the idea, then a crash effort to make it is initiated.

The point of all this is to recognize that by whatever name, a very large factor in the level and effectiveness of an organization's or a nation's technological capabilities lies in these thousands of interrelated and cumulative technological bits. Without this technological infrastructure, little of the larger-size more sophisticated technology transfer that is the object of this meeting can occur. It must be included, as an element of the overall TT process. Additionally, can we learn anything useful about desired macro-TT from all this spontaneous and constantly occurring micro-TT?

Intermediate/Appropriate Technology

Intermediate technology is "intermediate" because it is more efficient and more expensive than primitive traditional methods yet cheaper by far than sophisticated technologies used and exported by rich countries according to a publications house by that name whose journal is entitled, Appropriate Technology. IT or AT (more initials.) is invariably more labor intensive, less capital intensive and usually requires less power and produces less pollution than advanced technology. Ernest Schumacher, author of Small is Beautiful, is a prime mover in promoting IT/AT in the developing countries. Robin Clarke and Lewis Mumford use the term "biotechnology" for almost the same concept and Murray Bookchin uses "ecotechnology". The Bolton Institute prefers "careful technology", i.e., technology applied in a thoughtful manner. Terms similar to these have been mentioned at this meeting such as Thomas' "inappropriate technology," Baranson's "reverse engineering" and "designing down", and Wilmot's "lower technology". Altenphol and Hahn used the terms intermediate technology.

A number of the papers at this meeting dealt with the transfer of older, lower, less sophisticated technology from a highly developed to a less developed setting. When the context was economic and/or use oriented, the tone of the descriptions was positive. Youle's presentation offered several examples. The source was making a profit or participating in a humanitarian venture and the receiver was benefiting in terms of increased production, power, transportation or some other enhanced capability. But when the context was technological, the overtones often sounded negative. Lower, old, obsolete, simple and other terms suggest a value system inherent in the technology itself. This is particularly strong from the source viewpoint but sometimes appear in the recipient view, as capsuled in a hypothetical quotationlike, "Don't send us your old steam plants, we want nuclear".

Much of the talk at this meeting about the technological infrastructure suggests that there is a growing awareness of the appropriateness of technology to various settings. In addition, many speakers also were explicit in discussing values and in recognizing the variations in values that may exist at the two ends of the transfer process. Some speakers appear willing to incorporate them as a key element of their transfer models and to recognize them in actual transfer operations.

Most of the IT/AT focus has been on developing nations. Also, the analogy was made by one speaker to the "undeveloped" technological situation in State and local Governments relative to Federal or private industry technology. In this frame of reference, the characteristics of IT/AT are as described in the opening paragraph of the section.

To some degree, this same concept can be applied in developed settings, particularly the highly developed ones. Added to the goals of labor intensity and reductions in capital investment, energy consumption and pollution are a variety of other forces. One motivation reflects fear of, and aversion to, high technology, big business, big government, standardization and the aura of anomie and insignificance associated with the mindless tasks of some manufacturing processes. The IT/AT approach is attractive to others who would choose a different image of the post-industrial society than that offered by the "more" and extrapolation forecasters. They want increased decentralization and diversity with shorter transportation to work and to markets.

Others wish to return pride and craftsmanship to the products and services rendered. Many want to create a production (and service) environment of fellowship and to be more directly involved or to relate production (and service) functions to the whole community and life style. These movements now go beyond the earlier scattered communes and individuals or small groups either preparing for selfsufficiency during the dark days preceeding doomsday or just "opting out". It is reflected in a significant growth of medium technology-aided hand crafts, cooperatives and increased neighborhood identification in large cities. Ernest Schumacher's T.V. film shows the revival of an economically viable "old style" brickyard in the U.K. Baranson's paper at this meeting described the decentralized, relatively small power generation systems in the People's Republic of China based on simpler and long-used technologies from other nations. Energy shortages, inflation and capital shortages are forcing "backward" changes in many industrial plans and do-it-yourselfers are expanding in almost all areas of the service industries.

All of these may be early signs of a possible shift in the major thrust of thinking on technology transfer. Perhaps they are a suitable subject for later meetings and more intensive investigation. Clearly such efforts will involve many types of people not present at this meeting and to whom some of the paradigms and algorithms of TT will seem very strange and maybe irrelevant.

TECHNOLOGY TRANSFER POLICY: NEEDS AND PROSPECTS

It seems safe to predict that with the continued penetration of science and technology into all aspects of society, and into national and international policy and program development, interest in technology transfer will persist. The question has repeatedly been raised as to the need for, or appropriateness of creating a national technology transfer policy. This question has effectively been answered in the negative to date, as no such policies have been formulated. It is a moot question as to whether or not the present level of understanding about technology transfer could be an adequate foundation for such a policy.

During the meeting, several participants spoke of international organizations currently working to generate policies which would encourage the transfer of technology. Perhaps in light of these movements national governments should devote serious attention to developing policy guidelines and initiatives which would encourage more widespread utilization of technological resources to achieve social and economic purposes.

When raising questions about technology transfer policy, institutional mechanisms for transfer are inextricably involved. During this meeting a variety of institutional forms were discussed e.g., multinational corporations; industrial efforts stimulated by market incentives; Public Technology Incorporated, serving as a broker between user and supplier; mutual defense arrangements; and government programs, both domestic and international. While little indepth or formal discussion transpired as to optimal or recommended organizational functional structures, these subjects were the frequent focus of sometimes heated informal debate. Some of the Federal agency programs in the United States are illustrative of problems ensuing from the institutionalization of technology transfer functions. These programs exhibit some success, but not nearly as much as might be expected from the extent of the expended efforts.

It seems appropriate, therefore, to end this summary and synthesis, with a brief presentation of some of the major policy institutional options. They may be loosely categorized as: 1) provision of an explicit Federal or National policy base for technology transfer; 2) establishment of a new Federal or intergovernmental institutional mechanism(s) for technology transfer; 3) establishment of a new independent organization--outside of government--to activate and manage technology transfer; 4) enhancement and/or creation of capabilities in the Provinces or States to effect technology transfer in both the public and private sectors; 5) international agreements, treaties and/or organizations; 6) preservation of the status quo.

These several policy and institutional directions are not mutually exclusive. Consideration of various alternatives may lead to decisions to combine several approaches for a workable legislative or executive positions. Obviously the alternatives displayed are not the only ones available, but reflect prominent approaches, some of which were mentioned at this meeting, stipulated in proposed legislation or executive announcements, or which have been implied by study and practice reported in the literature. Most of the examples given are from the United States, both for ease of communication and because of their familiarity to the authors.

National Policy

One alternative is the creation of an explicit policy base which would provide statutory authority for Federal and/or intergovernmental technology transfer programs. Declaration of a national technology transfer policy would provide legal justification for mission agency expenditures for pertinent program activities. Such a policy would alleviate some of the constraints to the development of effective agency transfer programs by providing a proper legal mandate. Among other benefits which could derive from a technology transfer policy are:

- Legal base for the development of appropriate personnel slots and job descriptions which are currently lacking in the Civil Service job profile;

- Clarification of agency thinking on transfer or research utilization issues, which may gradually influence the shape of R&D decisions -- particularly those concerning applied R&D;

- Underpinning for the development of explicit transfer activities through the provision of general program charters and guidelines;

- Legal justification for budget expenditures in technology transfer activities;

- Provision of authority for transfer of Federal technologies out of the Federal establishment into both the public and private sectors, as well as a mandate for interagency transfer at the Federal level to extend Federal utility of R&D results and to avoid duplication of effort where possible.

Provisions of a national technology transfer policy may encompass various objectives (related to the policy areas just mentioned) and may vary in the degree of specificity. With reference to the latter factor, a declaration of policy could be made to be extremely general, providing a basic statement of the importance of technological advance to the nation, the importance of optimal utilization of our scientific and technological resources for national growth, and the advantages of supporting and implementing technology transfer as a means to promote and extend the use of such resources. Alternatively, the policy could be made more specific by providing policy directives i.e., stipulating budget levels for technology transfer program activities, providing for the creation of new personnel slots, stipulating operational guidelines and program requirements. Technology transfer policy could also be directed at the alteration of decision making criteria for R&D programs, and of procurement policy in order to provide incentives for technology transfer, it could introduce tax incentives for transfer, impact upon Federal patent policy, or perhaps focus on technology transfer through people transfer by enhancing the opportunities for job mobility.

National Government Institutional Mechanisms

Another central policy thrust rests with the creation of a new organization, or the addition of responsibilities to an existing organization, for the purpose of directing, supporting, managing, etc. technology transfer. For example, various proposals for the establishment of new organizations for the explicit or implicit purpose of technology transfer have appeared in recent bills introduced into the U.S. Congress. One example is the National Science and Technology Policy and Organization Act of 1975 (H.R. 10230). This bill establishes a national science policy, and creates an Office of Science and Technology Policy in the Executive Office of the President. Among the provisions of the bill are that, "It is a responsibility of the Federal Government to promote prompt, effective, reliable, and systematic transfer of science and technology information..." and, "Federal patent policies should be developed, based on uniform principles, which have as their objective the preservation of incentives for technological innovation and the application of procedures which will continue to assure the full use of beneficial technology to serve the public." Another institutional approach to technology transfer is proposed in the National Policy and Priorities for Science and Technology Act of 1974 (S. 32). This act provides for a Council of Advisors on Science and Technology with responsibility for providing a coherent approach to the application of science and technology to critical and emerging national problems, and to coordinate the science and technology responsibilities of Federal agencies in the resolution of civilian problems. This same bill contains provisions which would encourage public sector technology transfer through an Intergovernmental Science and Technology Advisory Committee. Among its responsibilities, the Committee is to identify problems at the State, regional and local levels, to identify problems of highest priority for study and assessment, and to identify and foster ways to facilitate the transfer of the results of civilian R&D so as to maximize its application to public sector needs. A recent, though not current, legislative proposal, the Federal Technology Transfer Act (H.R. 1676) was introduced in 1972. This Act proposes the establishment of an Office for Technology Transfer, the Director of which is responsible for the establishment and administration of a program to facilitate technology transfer. The program would involve research on the transfer process and the creation of regional science and technology centers to obtain information on the needs and requirements of potential users of Federally developed technology, and to assist in the effective dissemination of such technology.

Organizational approaches to the institutionalization of technology transfer, other than those stipulated in the above proposals, have been considered as feasible. A technology transfer institution could be either directly or indirectly involved with the actual process of technology transfer. That is, an organization could be given the responsibility to directly promote technology transfer, i.e., through conducting assessments of potential user needs, directing available Federal technologies to these needs, coordinating Federal mission agency transfer activities, providing funds for transfer activities, encouraging transfer among Federal agencies, etc. Alternatively, an organization could function more in a regulatory capacity, like the U.S. Federal Trade Commission, or the Federal Communications Commission and have more of an indirect impact on technology transfer. Such an organization could have the legal mandate to influence, or to advise on policy that could impact upon the transfer process i.e., procurement policy, patent policy, regulatory standards promoting those which would require more widespread development of new technologies, R&D program formulation and priority setting. Such an organization could conceivably have the responsibility to review technology transfer activities, evaluate program effectiveness, advise on possible program changes, and by nature of its "central" location, that is representing the interests, it would be in a position to lend continuity, coordination, and cohesiveness to Federal activities.

In terms of budgetary provisions, a variety of alternatives also exists. Among them, the established office could be provided with a limited operational budget, or with contract and/or grant authority and provided with a suitably larger budget, or with a financial base to extend immediate operational capabilities, i.e., liaison activities, systems development information processing and disseminating.

Private Sector Institutional Mechanisms

Separate from the option of creating a Federal council, committee, etc., is the possibility of providing for the establishment of a private organization, which could function in the open market to promote technology transfer. Such an organization, which could perhaps receive startup funding, or some sort of Government subsidy or policy support, could function to link existing technologies with identified needs -- such services would be paid for in part by the user of the transferred technology, and in part by the supplier who would be provided with new market areas.

Advantages to a non-government institution stem from its ability to operate outside of the government system, thus in an environment less constrained by organizational barriers which have often been identified as obstacles to the effective transfer and utilization of existing Federally owned resources. Additionally, because an independent organization would not have to rely solely on public funds, it would be more able to assume some of the risks involved in promoting the transfer of technologies.

One possible form that such an organization could take has been advanced by a U.S. State of Washington group called Technology for the Public Interest. In essence, the group proposes the establishment of a federal-public corporation -- that is a corporation establishment of a federal-public corporation -- that is a corporation established by legislative mandate, but carried out by private enterprise with maximum encouragement and assistance from Federal agencies. A major thrust of this organizational proposal is to obtain a commitment of Federal focus on the barriers that preclude those goals from being achieved. The goals of the proposed corporation involve the effective transfer and utilization of existing scientific and technological resources to meet civilian problems and needs. The proposal for the Federal-Private Corporation is founded in the conviction that the Federal Government can serve as a catalyst to public interest technologies through such functions as: national priority setting; Federal planning and procurement policy; regulatory standard setting; instituting new incentives for technological innovation and transfer; and others.

Provincial and State Government Mechanisms and Capabilities

A fourth basic alternative is the establishment of new, and/ or the enhancement of existing, capabilities within provincial, state or government structures to effect the transfer of technology in both the public and private sectors. For example, in the United States, several States, California, Pennsylvania, New York, among others, have already provided for and effectively implemented technology transfer programs. Similarly, public interest groups representing State needs have shown increasing interest in the process of technology transfer as a way to utilize technological resources in meeting civilian needs. Among the more active of the public interest groups in this area are the Council of State Governments, through its Technical Assistance Program, Interstate Counsulting Clearinghouse, and Research Department; and the National Conference of State Legislatures, through its Science and Technology Committee. By way of alternating, the Federal Government could be mandated to provide financial, technical, and managerial assistance to the States in the initial phases of design and development of appropriate capabilities for technology transfer. In terms of financial support, the Federal Government might provide full funding, or a major portion of the required funds, for start-up activities within the States, with a provision for decreasing Federal funds over a specified time period, with the ultimate intent of state assumption of the financial responsibility to maintain their transfer capabilities.

The Federal Government could also perform a coordination function, to operate an intergovernmental "network", which would allow for information, research and demonstration coordination and cooperation. Additionally, legislation could provide authority for States to utilize Federal information and facilities in building, operating and maintaining transfer programs.

An illustration of an approach to the central involvement of States in technology transfer is the report Action Now of the National Action Conference on Intergovernmental Science and Technology Policy.[2] Specific resolutions and policy directives focusing on State science and technology activities and on partnerships with the Federal Government to enhance such activities are put forward.

International Policy and Organizations

Without reference to international technology transfer policy, a discussion of alternatives would be incomplete. The growing interdependence of nations in the modern world makes it impractical to speak only of domestic technology transfer policy. An example derives from Boggio's remarks on the European Economic Community, where member nations have come to the realization that inconsistent policies between nations constitute serious deterrents to economic and technological development. EEC member nations are beginning to develop common policy and program bases to facilitate the transfer and utilization of technology, to the benefit of the entire community. The requirement for coherent policies and programs is beginning to be recognized by the world community as well.

A key proposal was introduced in the United Nations by U.S. Secretary of State Kissinger in September 1975.[3] Postulated on the principal that development goals can be achieved only by cooperation, not by the politics of confrontation, the Kissinger proposal constitutes an operable response to the growing interdependence of all nations for economic stability and technological advance.

Signal provisions of the proposal include the creation of a new development security facility within the International Monetary Fund, to stabilize overall export earnings; and the creation of an International Investment Trust to augment the availability of capital for investment in local enterprises.

These provisions essentially form the institutional backbone of the broad-based proposal, which manifests particular concern and attention to the importance of technology transfer and utilization to industrial growth. Paraphrasing the Kissinger address, careful thought must be applied to the effective extension of extant practical devices for technology transfer, and the United States is prepared to join with other nations in examining appropriate new initiatives. Among the mechanisms suggested for extending transfer capabilities was support for the creation of an International Industrialization Institute -- to sponsor and conduct cooperative research on industrial technology; and support the establishment of an International Center for the Exchange of Technological Information -- to serve as a clearinghouse for the sharing of ongoing research and new findings relevant to development. These proposals represent potentially workable alternatives by which the international transfer of technology could be enhanced.

Preserving the Status Quo

This policy alternatives review to this point has excluded discussion of a logical and workable policy alternative, specifically, a decision to take no action and to thus opt for continuation of the status quo. At the present time, activities relating to technology transfer, whether they be concerned with study or practice, are largely independent, disconnected and uncoordinated. Governments are involved in technology transfer, with expectations that the process may afford a means by which public needs can be met, by which the return of the public investment in R&D can be increased or through which foreign policy and trade objectives can be realized. Business and industry are actively pursuing opportunities for technology transfer and are implementing the process, with entrepreneurial objectives and profit motives as primary stimulants. To the academic community, technology transfer is a subject for continued study and one focus in the basic pursuit of knowledge.

To date, decisive efforts have not been undertaken to organize or coordinate the diversity of technology transfer interests and activities. Any sample of the variety of ongoing studies, projects, and arrangements would undoubtedly show some which are ineffective, or at worst, total failures. On the other hand, there are numerous examples of effective efforts. In other words, technology transfer can, and is, operating effectively without the benefit of a cohesive policy and/or institutional base. The option of maintaining the status quo is a real one, and one which must be given as considered and careful attention as those proposing the establishment of a more focused technology transfer policy base and operational structure.

In summary, it may justifably be said that we, at once, know a great deal and very little about technology transfer. Discussions of mechanisms, concepts, motivation, manifest areas of understanding as to some of the elements, processes, policy requirements, operational capabilities, etc. inherent or related to the technology transfer process. At the same time, however, the discussions point to many gaps in our understanding, evidence problems in communicating both within and outside the technology transfer community, and demonstrate difficulties associated with the translation of existing knowledge into effective, operational technology transfer capabilities. Some say more research, analysis, data gathering and synthesis, are required, while others suggest that perhaps all the study and discussion is superfluous, that technology transfer can, and is, occurring without it.

The writers have no intention to summarize further or to reiterate the points highlighted in the preceding text. Drawing from the perspective we have gained as reviewers of the meeting, however, it seems reasonable to inject a note of optimism as the commentary concludes. Although, at times, it appears that sessions on technology transfer are experiences of deja vu, with many of the same thoughts and findings repeated over and over again, this meeting gave rise to a number of fresh ideas and approaches, raised a series of new, and important questions, and set some general guidelines as to future directions for research and implementation.

In the world of today, with science and technology so intricately woven into the fabric of our lives, technology transfer, whether it be specifically labeled as such or not, is a real and important process, and one which demands clearer understanding, policy support, and operational capabilities for implementation. The meeting at Les Arcs clearly shows that many steps towards meeting this demand are being taken in public and private institutions around the world.

REFERENCES

1. Conference on Technology Transfer: Research and Implementation, University of Stirling, Scotland, UK, July 1974.
   The substance of the material is published in textbook format in: F.R. Bradbury, P. Jervis, R. Johnston and A.W. Pearson (eds.), Transfer Processes in Technical Change, Leyden- The Netherlands: Noordhoff International Publishing, 1977.

1a. The proceedings have been published in: H.F. Davidson, M. Cetron and J.D. Goldhar (eds.), Technology Transfer, Leyden-The Netherlands: Noordhoff International Publishing, 1974.

2. Action Now - Resolutions of the National Action Conference on Intergovernmental Science and Technology Policy, Pennsylvania: Pennsylvania Office of Science and Technology, 1972.

3. US Secretary of State Kissinger, Address to the UN General Assembly's Special Session, New York, N.Y.: United Nations, September 1, 1975.

GPSR Compliance

The European Union's (EU) General Product Safety Regulation (GPSR) is a set of rules that requires consumer products to be safe and our obligations to ensure this.

If you have any concerns about our products, you can contact us on ProductSafety@springernature.com

In case Publisher is established outside the EU, the EU authorized representative is:

Springer Nature Customer Service Center GmbH
Europaplatz 3
69115 Heidelberg, Germany

Batch number: 10830943

Printed by Printforce, the Netherlands